International Human Resource Management

Globalization, National Systems and Multinational Companies

**Tony Edwards and
Chris Rees**

FT Prentice Hall
FINANCIAL TIMES

An imprint of **Pearson Education**
Harlow, England • London • New York • Boston • San Francisco • Toronto
Sydney • Tokyo • Singapore • Hong Kong • Seoul • Taipei • New Delhi
Cape Town • Madrid • Mexico City • Amsterdam • Munich • Paris • Milan

Pearson Education Limited

Edinburgh Gate
Harlow
Essex CM20 2JE
England

and Associated Companies throughout the world

Visit us on the World Wide Web at:
www.pearsoned.co.uk

First published 2006

ISBN-13: 978-0-273-65177-2
ISBN-10: 0-273-65177-3

British Library Cataloguing-in-Publication Data
A catalogue record for this book is available from the British Library

Library of Congress Cataloging-in-Publication Data
A catalog record for this book is available from the Library of Congress

10 9 8 7 6 5 4 3 2 1
10 09 08 07 06

Typeset in 9/12.5pt Stone Serif by 30
Printed and bound by Henry Ling Ltd, at the Dorset Press, Dorchester, Dorset

The publisher's policy is to use paper manufactured from sustainable forests.

Contents

Part One
The context for international human resource management

Part Two
The diffusion of international human resource management in multinational companies

Part Three
The management of international human resource practices in multinational companies

Contents

Contents

Preface

This book is about the management of international human resources (HR) and employment relations within multinational companies (MNCs). It aims to take a distinctive approach to the subject in terms of both its structure and its content.

There are a growing number of introductory texts in the fields of international human resource management (IHRM) and international/comparative employment relations. These texts can broadly be broken down into three types. First are those which are structured along country lines, with individual chapters on different countries and comparisons between them being implicit in the main and explicit in the introduction and conclusion. Examples of this are the collections edited by Kamoche et al. (2004) on HRM in Africa and Budhwar (2004) on HRM in Asia-Pacific and those by Bamber et al. (2004) and Ferner and Hyman (1998) that focus on national systems of industrial relations. These provide very detailed explanations of distinctive national patterns but are not designed to suit most IHRM courses and consequently do not tackle many of the issues on such courses. Second are those with a predominantly international business strategy focus that consider aspects of HR strategy in certain chapters. Good examples here are John et al. (1997) and Parker (1998). These books provide a lot of useful material on such issues as the strategies and structures of MNCs and the economic context in which such firms operate but, like the first category, they are not designed primarily for IHRM courses. Third are those that take a more thematic approach, with chapters on particular areas of HR policy, commonly pay and reward, training and development, recruitment and selection, and so on. Well-known recent examples include Harzing and Van Ruysseveldt (2004), Tayeb (2005), Dowling and Welch (2004) and Brewster and Harris (1999).

It is this third approach that is the most relevant to discuss. There are three further distinctions we make within this category. First, some of these books are mainly about the management of those managers and other senior staff who travel frequently between countries. A good example of this is the book by Dowling and Welch (2004). We see this as being one part of IHRM, an important one undoubtedly, but not the only one. Thus our focus is wider, incorporating the study of both managerial and non-managerial employees.

A second distinction that we make is between approaches to understanding IHRM that focus on national cultures on the one hand and those that focus on the wider institutional context on the other. The first of these is the one that is most widely used in international HR research more generally and features very strongly in some of the textbooks, such as that by Tayeb (2005). While not disregarding culture, we stress the benefits of seeing economic and social activity as being shaped by institutions at the national and international level. Consequently, we seek to adopt an approach that is primarily institutional but which incorporates analysis of how values and attitudes differ across borders.

A third issue is whether the whole book is written by one or two people or is an edited collection. The first of these, of which the books by Dowling and Welch (2004) and Tayeb (2005) are both examples, has the advantage of being more coherent in terms of style and approach. However, it requires the author(s) to write about all areas of IHRM, even those where they do not have particular expertise. In contrast, an edited collection, exemplified in the books by Brewster and Harris (1999) and Harzing and Van Ruysseveldt (2004), involves a large number of authors contributing one chapter each. This has the advantage of drawing on expertise from a range of specialists, but it runs the risk of the chapters having relatively little in common with one another and of there being relatively little in the way of themes running throughout the book. We have chosen a mid-way approach in this respect, writing Parts 1 and 2 of the book ourselves and then drawing on input from experts in particular areas in Part 3. In order to provide coherence throughout the book, we have established five clear themes.

Five main themes

The first theme is *globalization*, one of the most topical issues in IHRM. There are hotly contested debates concerning both whether the effects of globalization are broadly positive or negative and whether it is really novel or has historical precedents. We review these debates at the outset and proceed to examine the implications of the globalization process.

The second theme is the *challenges* that changes in the international economy have presented. Some of these challenges pertain to the ability of governments to regulate economic and social activity within their borders. Other challenges are felt at the level of the firm and comprise the opportunities and constraints that the process of globalization presents to managers within firms.

The third theme is the *embeddedness* of firms, and the structures and practices operating within them, in distinct national contexts. Despite the process of globalization, we know that 'national business systems' continue to differ from one another, and the persistence of these differences means that firms manage their workforces in nationally distinct ways. This is explored in a number of ways throughout the book.

Fourth, we demonstrate that many of the processes within the field of IHRM are subject to *contestation*. That is, the preferences and strategies of various groups within firms differ from one another and they use whatever sources of power that are at their disposal to advance and defend their interests. This is true for the globalization process in general and for the way that MNCs manage their international workforces in particular; while all organizations are characterized by political struggles between different groups of actors, this is especially the case for large, complex MNCs that cross national divides.

The fifth theme is of *change*. Few observers dispute that the field of IHRM is changing, but we critically examine the issue of whether developments in the international economic system are causing firms and countries that used to be organized along differing lines to be moving in the same direction, constituting a process of convergence.

Structure and content

The book is arranged in four parts. Part 1 (Chapters 1–4) attempts to address in a coherent way a wide range of the issues and debates that set the context for an understanding of IHRM practice.

In Chapter 1 we critically examine the concept of globalization, outlining the main arguments on either side of the so-called 'globalization debate'. We stress how IHRM activity needs to be understood not only in terms of globalization, but also as subject to a variety of pressures from other levels of analysis – namely the regional, the national and the organizational. We are interested here in the ways in which factors at all four of these levels combine in differing ways to influence IHRM strategy and practice in MNCs. Chapter 2 examines the role of national differences in IHRM more closely, contrasting cultural and institutional approaches to this issue, and considering attempts that have been made to synthesize the two into a more all-embracing view of 'national effects'. It also outlines recent ideas about how to more adequately explain the interaction between what managers do within organizations and the other three 'external' levels of analysis – the national, the regional and the global.

Whilst these first two chapters tend to be rather theoretical in their tone, Chapters 3 and 4 study two dimensions of MNCs that impact more directly upon IHRM activity, namely the variety of explanations concerning why firms internationalize and the alternative strategies and structures that MNCs can pursue. Chapter 3 considers how we understand and define the MNC, and the role of MNCs in globalization, in particular looking at processes of expansion. It is clear that MNC managements operate with only a partial knowledge of different business systems and national environments, and so the alignment of appropriate strategies and structures is crucial, as is the question of how to transfer knowledge across borders and between business units. Hence Chapter 4 looks in more detail at strategy making, and stresses the importance of micro-politics and organizational power relations as key drivers and shapers of the actual practice of strategy. We note here that despite the often strong arguments that competitive advantage comes through operationalizing a truly 'transnational' strategy, in practice this is often extremely difficult as companies remain embedded in distinct national contexts, something we highlight with a discussion of the so-called 'country-of-origin effect'.

In Part 2 (Chapters 5–7) the book picks up many of the issues raised in Part 1 and considers the diffusion of IHRM strategy and practice in more depth.

Chapter 5 outlines a number of aspects of the diffusion of HR practices across borders within MNCs. We see that national systems provide both opportunities for, and constraints upon, this process, and we again stress the political dynamics involved in diffusion, and how these informal processes are as important an explanatory factor as more formal structures. Chapter 6 considers diffusion in the particular case of cross-border mergers and acquisitions (M&As), highlighting again the distinct influence of 'national effects', both the nationality of the parent firm and the ways that HR issues are handled differently in different 'host' environments. We also see here the highly political and contested nature of change, illustrated by key questions at various stages of the merger process (e.g. how to populate senior management positions, where to locate head offices and where cost cutting should have the biggest impact). In Chapter 7 we note how in recent years flows of foreign direct investment (FDI) and trade have become less concentrated in particular areas and consider the HR implications of internationalization into so-called 'developing nations'. We debate the impact of foreign MNCs in China, and again show how actual outcomes are contingent upon particular national characteristics as well as upon the relationship between politics and structure. Particular barriers to the transfer or diffusion of knowledge can be a feature of such national contexts, and we explore the implications of these for MNCs.

The focus of the book then moves in Part 3 (Chapters 8–13) to examine substantive HR issues in an international context.

We begin in Chapter 8 by examining the challenges facing MNCs in the increasingly important area of knowledge management and knowledge transfer, picking up on the issues raised in Part 2. It is often argued that companies should operate in a 'transnational' way that allows for flexibility and the facilitation of learning, and here we set the issue of knowledge transfer within the context of debates on the nature of knowledge and knowledge management. We discuss the importance of organizational learning in international partnerships (mergers, international joint ventures, etc.) as well as in the deployment of expatriate staff, and highlight how difficult it can be to transfer knowledge on an international scale given that it is often situated in particular national contexts.

The next two chapters consider two aspects of the management of international staff: how they are developed for international assignments (Chapter 9) and how they are recruited and selected (Chapter 10). Chapter 9 again stresses the importance of understanding the context of management assignments and the role of the individual manager in organizational learning. We discuss the particular attributes necessary for success in this area and outline some of the initiatives that MNCs can profitably take, such as cross-cultural awareness training and multicultural team building. The impact of both global and local pressures is also apparent in Chapter 10 in terms of their influence upon recruitment and selection processes. We pay particular attention here to the argument that the rise of international managers is creating a distinct group, a 'global elite', from which MNCs can recruit. We conclude that this is something of a myth, as managers are never truly 'rootless', and those on assignments often stay in countries where they have been successful, such that processes of globalization again encourage divergence as much as they encourage convergence. The key lesson for practitioners is the need to keep in mind the specific set of circumstances surrounding each assignment.

The issue of pay and reward is addressed in Chapter 11, that of employee representation in Chapter 12 and that of corporate social responsibility in Chapter 13. Chapter 11 outlines the variety of different national contexts that companies face when developing international reward strategies, considers the factors that explain this cross-national variation and looks at how these factors impact upon the degree of genuine 'strategic choice' that managers have. National settings are again seen to put constraints upon, as well as provide opportunities for, innovation in management strategy, and while no easy 'one best way' prescriptions are available in this area, HR nevertheless has a crucial role to play in the assessment of national patterns and the development of considered pay arrangements. The area of employee representation is one where managers in MNCs increasingly need to take strategic decisions regarding their approach, especially those within Europe. Chapter 12 again considers national variety in terms of forms of employee representation, and explains some of the approaches that companies are taking. We see that although there is an increasing significance to international developments, implementation still remains largely the responsibility of managers at a local national level. Finally, Chapter 13 considers another topic rapidly moving up the hierarchy of issues that MNCs seek to address, namely that of corporate social responsibility (CSR). Here we take a critical look at what companies actually do in the name of CSR, and assess the debate over regulation versus voluntarism. We stress the important role that HR professionals can play in this area of policy, one which is often seen as no more than a 'corporate gloss' and yet has the potential to have a significant impact.

We return to summarize the five key themes of the book in Part 4, Chapter 14. Of particular significance is the stress on the interdependence between nationally distinct business systems and the internal politics of multinationals. This relationship is interdependent in the sense that groups of actors within MNCs derive some of their power and influence from their familiarity with their local context, while at the same time the actions of large MNCs have the potential to shape the evolution of local systems. This argument is an integral thread in the book, and it is illustrated throughout by reference to the themes of globalization, challenge, embeddedness, contestation and change.

Throughout the book the approach is to establish relevant theoretical and conceptual material and to supplement this by reviewing the empirical evidence. In order to allow students to relate this to organizational contexts, we illustrate the issues with case studies in every chapter. We also provide review questions and suggestions for further reading. The idea for the book came from our experience of teaching final-year undergraduate and masters students over a number of years at Kingston University, and all of the contibutors have either worked at, or have some other connection with, the university. We were constantly telling students that there was no one best book in the area of IHRM, but rather a number of useful books that they would need to look at. We intended to produce a book that, while we would certainly not claim is 'the best', we hope takes a more integrated approach than many others in the field.

References

Bamber, G., Lansbury, R. and Wailes, N. (eds) (2004) *International and Comparative Employment Relations*, London: Sage.

Brewster, C. and Harris, H. (1999) *International HRM: Contemporary Issues in Europe*, London: Routledge.

Budhwar, P. (ed.) (2004) *Managing Human Resources in Asia-Pacific*, London: Routledge.

Dowling, P. and Welch, D. (2004) *International Human Resource Management: Managing People in a Multinational Context*, London: Thompson.

Ferner, A. and Hyman, R. (eds) (1998) *Changing Industrial Relations in Europe*, Oxford: Blackwell.

Harzing, A-W. and Van Ruysseveldt, J. (eds) (2004) *International Human Resource Management*, London: Sage.

John, R., Ietto-Gillies, G., Cox, H. and Grimwade, N. (1997) *Global Business Strategy*, London: Thompson.

Kamoche, K., Debrah, Y., Horwitz, F. and Muuka, G.N. (eds) (2004) *Managing Human Resources in Africa*, London: Routledge.

Parker, B. (1998) *Globalization and Business Practice: Managing Across Boundaries*, London: Sage.

Tayeb, M. (2005) *International Human Resource Management: A Multinational Company Perspective*, Oxford: Oxford University Press.

Contributors

Authors

Tony Edwards is a Senior Lecturer in International Human Resource Management at King's College London. His research focuses on the management of labour in multinational companies. His doctorate, completed in 1997, examined the ways in which multinationals identify innovative practices in their foreign operations and subsequently diffuse these to the domestic operations, termed 'reverse diffusion'. Subsequent research has investigated the influence of the US business system on employment relations in US multinational companies and the management of labour during and after international mergers and acquisitions. He has published extensively in journals such as the *Journal of Management Studies*, *British Journal of Industrial Relations*, *International Journal of Human Resource Management* and *European Journal of Industrial Relations*. Tony is currently engaged in a large-scale survey of employment practice in multinationals in the UK.

Chris Rees is a Reader in Organisation Studies in the School of Human Resource Management at Kingston University. His research interests are (i) international and comparative employment relations, and (ii) the sociology of workplace change. He is currently studying the employment relations and human resource implications of cross-border multinational mergers (with Tony Edwards). He has published in a number of journals, including the *European Journal of Industrial Relations*, *Organization Studies*, *Work Employment & Society*, *Personnel Review* and *Employee Relations*. He has published reports for the Chartered Institute of Personnel and Development (CIPD), the Department of Trade and Industry (DTI), the European Foundation and the European Commission. He is Module Leader for 'International HRM' on Kingston's MA Human Resource Management degree programme.

Contributors

Christine Edwards is Professor and Head of the School of Human Resource Management at Kingston University. Her earlier work investigated the management of industrial relations in coal mining and the railways and in several private sector companies, including Cadbury-Schweppes, Black&Decker and British Airways. Her current research concerns the transfer of human resource management across national boundaries, the issues surrounding the management of work–life balance policies and the role of public-sector first line managers. Articles published on this work can be found in the *British Journal of Industrial Relations*, the *Journal of Human Resource Management, Employee Relations* and the *British Journal of Management*.

Stephen Gourlay is a Reader in Knowledge Management in the School of Human Resource Management at Kingston University and Course Director of the MSc in Management and Business Studies Research. His primary research interests are in the areas of knowledge management and organizational learning. There are four overlapping themes in this work: communities of practice, knowledge creation, tacit knowledge and knowledge transfer. His teaching responsibilities are in research methods, knowledge management, organizational learning and strategic human resource management. He has published a number of conference papers, book chapters and articles in these fields, most recently a paper presented at the *Organizational Knowledge, Learning and Capabilities* conference and in the *British Journal of Management* and the *Journal of Management Studies*.

Fiona Moore is a Senior Lecturer in the School of Human Resource Management at Kingston University. She is an industrial anthropologist who received her doctorate from the University of Oxford, in 2002, on strategic self-presentation among local and expatriate employees in a German multinational company. She teaches international human resource management. Since 2003, she has been conducting research at an Anglo-German automobile plant, exploring issues of globalization, diversity and work–life balance. Her recent papers can be found in *Global Networks, Management International Review* and the *International Journal of Human Resource Management*; her monograph *Transnational Business Cultures: Life and Work in a Multinational Corporation* is available from Ashgate.

Sanjiv Sachdev is a Principal Lecturer in the School of Human Resource Management at Kingston University. A key part of his teaching is on labour aspects of corporate social responsibility. More recently, his research has focused on employment relations aspects of public service reform, currently examining the UK prison service and preparing a comparative study of UK and US prison privatization. He has published a book with H. Morris and B.H. Willey, *Managing in a Business Context* (Financial Times Prentice Hall, 2002), written for the *Guardian* and various practitioner publications and had work published by the think-tank Catalyst and the Institute of Employment Rights. He has also published work in several journals, including the *British Journal of Industrial Relations, Employee Relations* and *Renewal*.

Keith Sisson is Emeritus Professor of Industrial Relations in Warwick Business School's Industrial Relations Research Unit (IRRU), having previously been its Director for many years. He has published widely on the role of management in industrial relations, including *The Reality of Human Resource Management* published by the Open University Press in 2000. He has been extensively involved in cross-national comparative research funded by the Economic and Social Research Council (ESRC) and the European Foundation, being co-ordinator of the latter's investigation into the role of direct participation in organizational change, known as the EPOC (Employee Participation in Organizational Change) project. As well as writing and editing a string of publications based on this output, he is co-author with Paul Marginson of *European Integration and Industrial Relations: Multi-governance in the Making* published by Palgrave in 2004. He has just stepped down after two-and-a-half years as Head of Strategy Development at ACAS and plans to work on a book on employment relations matters.

Guy Vernon is a Temporary Lecturer in the Management Centre at King's College London. His research centres on the character of the social regulation of work and its implications for work organization and outcomes/performance. One element of Guy's research has been a collaborative study of the management of reward in multi-national companies, conducted with a group from across Europe. His research is published or forthcoming in several journals, including the *European Journal of Industrial Relations* and *Employee Relations*.

Jean Woodall is Professor of Human Resource Development and Associate Dean of the Business School at Oxford Brookes University. She is also the current Editor-in-Chief of *Human Resource Development International*. She has co-edited *New Frontiers in HRD* with Monica Lee and Jim Stewart (published by Routledge 2004), and *Ethical Issues in Contemporary Human Resource Development* (published by Palgrave 2000) with Diana Winstanley, with whom she also co-authored *Management Development: Strategy and Practice* (published by Blackwell 1998). She has published on a wide range of topics including career management for women, work-related management development, international management development, ethics and human resource development, human resource outsourcing, and professional learning.

Miao Zhang is a Senior Lecturer in the School of Human Resource Management at Kingston University. Her teaching and research interests centre around the nature of human resource management strategy in multinational companies: in particular, localization strategies, the transfer of human resource management policies in multi-national companies, and human resource management issues in multinationals operating in/from developing countries. She has a number of publications in this area, including the journal article 'Transferring Human Resource Management Across National Boundaries: the Case of Chinese MNCs in the UK' (*Employee Relations* 2003). She is currently conducting follow-up research on human resource management issues in Chinese multinationals and working on a project examining US and UK companies operating in China.

Acknowledgements

We are grateful to the following for permission to reproduce copyright material:

Figure 2.1 from *Culture's Consequences: International Differences in Work-related.Values,* Sage (Hofstede, G. 1980), reprinted by permission of Geert Hofstede, © Geert Hofstede; Tables 3.1, 7.1 and 7.2 from *World Investment Report: The Shift Towards Services,* United Nations Publications (2004). The United Nations is the author of the original material; Figure 4.1 from *What is Strategy – and Does it Matter?,* Thomson Learning (Whittington, R. 2001), p. 3; Table 5.1 from *Varieties of Capitalism: The Institutional Foundations of Comparative Advantage,* Oxford University Press (Hall, P. and Soskice, D. 2001), p. 20, by permission of Oxford University Press www.oup.com; Table 9.1 from 3Ms Leadership Competency Model: An Internally Developed Solution in *Human Resource Management,* Vol. 39, 2 and 3, John Wiley and Sons, Inc (Alldredge, M. E. and Nilan, K. J. 2000) © John Wiley and Sons, Inc. Reprinted with permission of John Wiley & Sons, Inc; Table 10.1 from the Myth of the 'International Manager' in *International Journal of Human Resource Management,* 11, 1, Taylor and Francis (Forster, N. 2000) http://www.tandf.co.uk/journals.

In some instances we have been unable to trace the owners of copyright material, and we would appreciate any information that would enable us to do so.

Part One

The context for international human resource management

Chapter 1

Globalization and international management

Chris Rees and Tony Edwards

Key aims

This chapter has the following key aims:

- to discuss the concept of globalization, and to locate economic globalization within the context of cultural, social, political and technological change;
- to outline the main aspects of the 'globalization thesis' and its implications for international management;
- to describe and assess the various criticisms that have been made of the globalization theorists;
- to introduce different levels of analysis for understanding management action in multinational companies – the global, the regional, the national and the organizational.

Introduction

Senior managers are commonly urged to develop a global strategy, but to balance this with the need to adapt to local circumstances, the so-called 'global-local' issue. The rhetoric of globalization is widespread in political circles, with many politicians anxious to stress the demands of the global economy in narrowing policy options concerned with the handling of the economy. It is a concept that has been embraced by academics, with the number of articles and books featuring globalization in the title now running into the thousands, and it is part of the vocabulary of journalists and management gurus. While the issues discussed in this book are generally couched in terms of the *international* and the *comparative*, we feel it is necessary to locate these themes against the backdrop of the notion of *globalization*, which has come to dominate the popular discourse in the field of international management. It is the nature of globalization and its implications that we address in this chapter.

What is globalization?

Most existing formulations of the term globalization are ambiguous or inconsistent, and debate is often mired in polarized exchanges. On one side of these exchanges are those who exuberantly proclaim that the greater part of social life is determined by global processes in which national cultures, national economies and national borders are dissolving. This group are known as the 'strong globalists' of whom Korten (1995) and Ohmae (1990) are members. Another set of observers deny there has been much significant change in the international economy, arguing that many aspects of the globalization argument are either exaggerated or not unprecedented. Writers such as Doremus et al. (1998), Hirst and Thompson (1999) and Zysman (1996) are firmly in this camp. Commenting on this polarization, Scholte observes that 'much discussion of globalization is steeped in oversimplification, exaggeration and wishful thinking. In spite of a deluge of publications on the subject, our analyses of globalization tend to remain conceptually inexact, empirically thin, historically and culturally illiterate, normatively shallow and politically naïve' (2000: 1). One reason for these problems is to do with the common failure to clearly define what globalization means. It is essential that we unpick this very slippery concept if we are to make meaningful statements about its implications for international human resource management (IHRM).

Part of the confusion surrounding the term globalization is the way it is often used interchangeably with a range of other concepts, such as internationalization, liberalization, universalization, westernization and modernization. Other sets of terms that are often used in conjunction with globalization are particularly concerned with its implications for social structure: old capitalism, new capitalism or post-capitalism? cultural homogeneity or heterogeneity? an extension of modernity or the dawn of postmodernity? While we cannot encompass all of these debates in this book, we will be highlighting certain aspects of them, most notably the implications of the development of capitalism for nation states and multinational companies (MNCs).

A further element in the ambiguity surrounding globalization is to do with the number of areas in which the term is used. Again drawing upon Scholte (2000), a range of activities and themes can be summarized, all of which highlight important aspects of the concept:

- global communications – air transport, telecommunications, electronic mass media;
- global markets – products, sales strategies;
- global production – production chains, sourcing of inputs;
- global money – currencies, bank cards, digital cash, credit cards;
- global finance – foreign exchange markets, banking, bonds, insurance business;
- global organizations – governance agencies, companies, corporate strategic alliances;
- global social ecology – atmosphere, biosphere, hydrosphere, geosphere;
- global consciousness – world as a single place, symbols, events, solidarities.

In this book we will be highlighting certain relevant aspects of these developments. Our focus is primarily upon global production and global organizations (with contextual issues around global markets and global finance). Within this sphere our primary focus is on the *economic* arguments about globalization and their political consequences in terms of their implications for organizations and management. We would also argue that *economic processes* drive and constrain most of the *cultural* and *social* phenomena that are included in the more extensive and all-encompassing versions of the concept.

When defining globalization we can distinguish between those definitions that focus on the quantitative linkages between countries and the growth of these linkages on the one hand, and the qualitative nature of these linkages on the other. In relation to the former, an implicit view which is commonly adopted is that the last quarter of the twentieth century witnessed *a step change in the pace of growth in the linkages between countries*: trade and foreign direct investment increased sharply; financial markets were deregulated and subsequently became highly internationalized; information exchange across borders became dramatically quicker and cheaper; and so on. It is this definition which underpins much of the work that is commonly characterized as the 'strong globalization thesis'.

In relation to the latter, globalization has been defined as a process in which there is *a growth in the functional integration of national economies*. Those who define globalization in this way commonly argue that the ties between countries are becoming stronger. For instance, whereas simple trading linkages often unravel in the event of a war or trade dispute and hence can be seen as shallow linkages, the growth of foreign direct investment and international subcontracting has produced global production 'chains' that are deeply embedded in the workings of the international economy. Peter Dicken, one of the foremost writers on globalization, sees this as an important distinction in identifying what is novel in the contemporary period:

> 'Although in quantitative terms, the world economy was perhaps at least as open before 1914 as it is today – in some aspects, such as labour migration, even more so – the nature of its integration was qualitatively very different. International economic integration before 1914 – and, in fact, until only about four decades ago – was essentially *shallow integration*, manifested largely through arm's length trade in goods and services between independent firms and through international movement of portfolio capital. Today, we live in a world in which *deep integration*, organized primarily within the production networks of transnational corporations (TNCs), is becoming increasingly pervasive.' (2003: 10–12)

This quotation highlights the role of, and interaction between, so-called 'transnational corporations' and nation states, a key theme that runs throughout the book.

The globalization thesis

At the heart of the 'strong' globalization thesis is the notion of a rapid and recent process of economic globalization. A truly global economy is claimed to have emerged, or to be in the process of emerging, in which distinct national economies, and therefore strategies of national economic management, are increasingly irrelevant. The world economy has internationalized in its basic dynamics, is dominated by uncontrollable market forces, and has as its principal economic actors and major agents of change truly 'transnational' corporations that owe allegiance to no nation state and locate wherever on the globe market advantage dictates.

A number of different strands to this approach can be identified. As Child (2002) outlines, what they have in common is a lack of sensitivity to particular nations or regions as special contexts, referring instead to 'universal rationales'. This *universalism* is seen to arise from ubiquitous economic and technological forces, and predicts an increasing *convergence* between modes of organization as countries develop similar economic and political systems, accelerated by the process of globalization. Child thus describes these perspectives as *low-context* in that they 'do not grant national context any analytical significance over and above the characteristics that happen to characterize a country at any point in its development' (2002: 28). They minimize the impact of national distinctiveness and contain a strong presumption of eventual convergence.

Technological, psychological, political and economic universalism

Technological change is often seen as one of the most important contributory factors underlying globalization. Information and communications technologies are seen to offer ground-breaking new ways of handling information which have implications for the design of effective organizations. Child (2002) again neatly summarizes the key debates. Some argue that whatever the national setting, the adoption of a given technology will have the same influential consequences for the design of a viable organization and for the way that social relations at work are consequently structured. In this view, different production technologies are seen as *determining* particular structures and behaviours independently of the local context. Coming from a more sociological perspective, critics of these ideas have concluded, by contrast, that decisions reflect managerial preferences for control over the work process rather than any technological imperative. For example, Scarborough (1996) has argued that the possibilities presented by IT for organizational redesign are worked through the social construction of different classificatory systems.

While the argument that the cross-national spread of very similar technologies across organizations brings similar consequences almost certainly oversimplifies the picture, it is undeniable that technological developments have brought about important changes in transport and communications. The transformation of electronic and telephonic communications means that the speed and cost of transmitting information across borders have fallen sharply, something that is immediately apparent from the growth of the Internet (see Figure 1.1). The fall in real terms in the cost of international travel has meant that people travel more frequently for the purposes of tourism (see Figure 1.2). The reduction in the cost of international travel coupled with the reduction of barriers to migration in areas like the EU have led to a growth in international migration (see Figure 1.3).

Allied to the technological argument is psychological universalism, in which there is an implicit assumption that all human beings share common needs and motivational structures. It is also assumed that the design of work organization as well as managerial

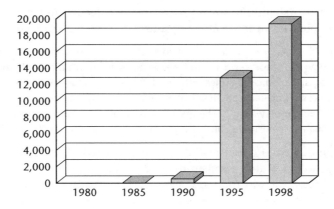

Figure 1.1 Internet hosts

Source: data from Guillen (2001)

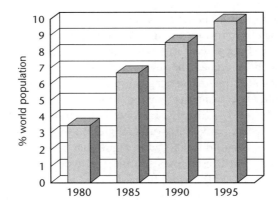

Figure 1.2 International tourist arrivals

Source: data from Guillen (2001)

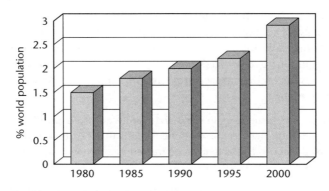

Figure 1.3 Stock of international migrants

Source: data from Guillen (2001) and Wolf (2004)

control and reward systems must treat this as a major exigency. As Child observes, these ideas are well established in the study of organizations and management:

'For the past 100 years, from scientific management through to contemporary industrial and social psychology, there has been a search for a generally applicable theory of motivation at work ... While these psychological theories differ in detail, they take individuals or groups as their focus, more or less in isolation from their cultural and social context. Thus people are regarded as essentially the same everywhere ... The assumption of universal human needs has importantly informed the analysis of utility that underlies much economic theory.' (2002: 31–32)

Once again, fundamental criticisms have been advanced of these arguments (Child 2002: 32). Psychological universalism may be a plausible notion when considering basic human needs, such as food and security, but it is highly questionable when addressing so-called 'higher-order' needs that are of a cognitive rather than material nature, such as esteem and self-actualization, since these are expressed primarily through social norms and are thus subject to cultural definition.

A related argument is to do with political universalism. The fall of the Berlin Wall and Iron Curtain led many to believe that more and more countries were converging on the model of society found in much of Western Europe and North America. This view was most famously expressed in Fukuyama's (1993) book *The End of History and the Last Man* in which he argued that ever larger parts of the world were converging on liberal democracy and free-market capitalism, and that there was no other form of society that we could expect to emerge as superior. Hence, for Fukuyama this convergence represented the 'end of history'. However, the implication that social, political and economic systems are converging on a single model has been severely criticized by others, such as Huntingdon (2002), who argue that several major societal systems can still be discerned, that these constitute major divides across the globe, and that any pattern of convergence is therefore limited.

Despite the evident weaknesses in the arguments concerning technological, psychological and political universalism, the prevalence of these arguments has set a context in which economic explanations of globalization have taken place. Much of the globalization thesis draws from economic theory, which centres on the allocation of scarce resources through the pursuit of utility via the market mechanism. By extension it purports to explain the formal organization of economic activities by firms as an economically rational response to market conditions. The 'convergence' aspect to the argument is that 'free-market' economics will eventually prevail in all societies and present a common context for management. As Child notes, mainstream economic theory

'endeavours to apply principles in ways that rarely accord a positive value to national specifics ... regard[ing] them as market imperfections that constrain economically optimum behaviour ... National conditions tend to be treated as constraints on the effective operation of the market system.' (2002: 30)

There are many powerful advocates of the benefits to governments of encouraging economic globalization through programmes of deregulation and privatization. The most prominent newspapers and magazines that focus on economics, such as *The Economist* and *The Wall Street Journal*, extol the virtues of such an approach. Many influential think tanks and policy institutes, such as the Organization for Economic Co-operation and Development (OECD), praise non-intervention by governments, liberalization, transparency and freedom of capital movements. Moreover, the dominant philosophy in the international economic institutions such as the World Trade Organization (WTO) and the International Monetary Fund (IMF) is similarly pro-market forces and anti-government intervention. Globalization, in this view, will produce most benefits if companies and consumers are left to their own devices.

The controversial role of the IMF

In the last few years, the so-called 'anti-globalization' movement has strongly criticized the way that globalization has affected the world's poor, and has targeted not only MNCs as the causes of the problems but also international institutions like the IMF. Criticisms from the collection of groups that comprise this movement are not surprising, but recently the IMF has been heavily criticised by a source much closer to home, namely Joseph Stiglitz, who from 1997 to 2000 was the chief economist and senior vice-president of the IMF's sister organization, the World Bank.

The formal role that was accorded to the IMF when it was established after the Second World War was to facilitate the growth of international trade, to promote international monetary co-operation and to contribute to stability in levels of exchange rates and in balance of payments. A principal way in which it has sought to do this is by lending money to countries experiencing financial difficulties, by making 'the general resources of the Fund temporarily available to members' as the IMF puts it. National governments are often reluctant to use this option, partly because of the stigma associated with it – for years the Labour Party in Britain was ridiculed by its opponents for going 'cap in hand' to the IMF in 1976 – but also because of the strings that were attached to the loans.

Indeed, it is the nature of the strings that has been the focus of much of the Stiglitz critique of the IMF. Stiglitz argues that the economists at the IMF have been locked into a narrow focus on free markets and minimal government intervention in the economy as the solution to economic crises. The root of this view, according to Stiglitz, is the IMF's diagnosis of the currency crises affecting many Latin American countries in the 1970s and 1980s, in which expansionist and interventionist policies by irresponsible governments were seen as the cause of high and rising inflation. The prescriptions for this scenario – reductions in government spending, freeing up competition in hitherto regulated sectors and privatizing state-owned firms – became the knee-jerk response of the IMF to all economic crises.

Consequently, Stiglitz argues, those countries that encountered crises in the late 1990s, particularly Russia and many in South-East Asia, were subjected to the IMF's standard solutions, regardless of whether the source of the problems was the same as those diagnosed by the Fund in Latin America. This had a number of adverse consequences: some countries were forced to rapidly liberalize banking systems even where there was little chance of genuine competition in the medium term, leading to the establishment of privately-owned, unregulated monopolies; countries such as Korea were cajoled into privatizing their state-owned firms, despite the relatively favourable performance of these firms and the fact that the country's problems were clearly in the private sector; the medicine of abolishing exchange controls merely exacerbated the problems in many Asian countries in 1997 by allowing massive outflows of capital; and the austerity measures of cuts in government spending and increases in interest rates were spectacularly ill-suited for countries entering a recession.

For Stiglitz, these problems stem from the influence of the 'Washington consensus', by which he means a set of economic policies geared towards allowing markets to operate with minimal government intervention. Moreover, he argues that the IMF's policies have been closely tied to the interests of the US Treasury and the financial institutions in Wall Street. The IMF has defended itself from this critique, arguing that it is developing more flexible policy prescriptions and is learning from its mistakes (see Rogoff 2002). Nonetheless, most observers agree that a consequence of the IMF's actions has been that it has contributed to a globalization process in which the role of sovereign governments has reduced and the role of MNCs and international speculators has increased.

For further details and contrasting perspectives on the IMF, see:
Stiglitz, J. (2002) *Globalization and its Discontents*, New York: Norton and Co.
IMF website at http://www.imf.org
Rogoff, K. (2002) An Open Letter, available at http://www.imf.org/external/np/vc/2002/070202.htm

Case study question: *Why do you think that the IMF pursues policies that have the impact that Stiglitz identifies?*

Developments in economic globalization

The developments described above set a context within which the international economy operates, and many observers have claimed that this has facilitated a number of trends that are unprecedented and deserve to be described with a term that is distinct from internationalization, namely globalization. A number of basic tenets make up this 'strong' globalization thesis:

- national and regional economies are becoming dominated by a new global system of economic co-ordination and control in which competition and strategic choices are organized at the global level;
- national and international firms are becoming subordinated to transnational firms that differ significantly from them and are accountable only to global capital markets;
- the ability of nation states to regulate economic activities is rapidly declining, and global markets increasingly dominate national economic policies;
- national economic policies, forms of economic organization, and managerial practices are converging to the most efficient ones as a result of global competition.

One of the key developments here is the internationalization of financial markets. Over the last 20 years the barriers to transferring money from one country to another have greatly reduced. Exchange controls – the mechanisms that governments use to restrict flows of money into and out of their countries – have fallen out of fashion, frowned upon by bodies like the IMF as we noted above. Accompanying these shifts in government policy have been technological developments that have greatly reduced the cost and time involved in transferring money across borders. The result has been an explosion in the movements of 'hot' money across the globe, with the pattern of movement being driven by the available returns. The *daily* exchange of foreign currencies is now $1.2 trillion, more than 100 times the amount traded 30 years ago and, for example, more than the *annual* gross domestic product (GDP) of France (Gray 1998; Legrain 2002; see also Figure 1.4). Moreover, the stock of financial assets held by foreigners grew in the last part of the twentieth century to unprecedented levels (see Figure 1.5).

International trade has also increased sharply. During the post-war period trade has grown consistently faster than national output in the developed economies, the

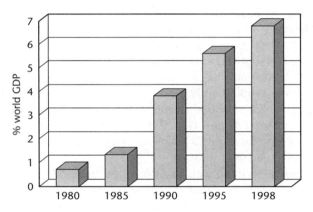

Figure 1.4 Daily currency exchange turnover

Source: data from Guillen (2001)

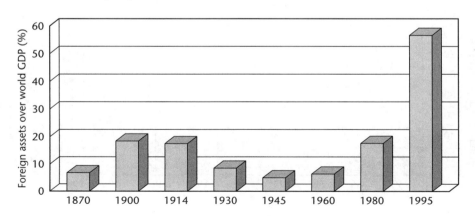

Figure 1.5 Growth in foreign assets over world GDP

Source: data from Wolf (2004)

result of which is that a higher proportion of the goods and services that are bought and sold are produced in one country and sold in another (see Figure 1.6). In fact, many goods and services are produced through integrated global 'chains' of firms across a number of different countries (Gereffi 1999). Perhaps most notable of all is the increasing domination of the international economy by MNCs. These firms are commonly portrayed as 'stateless' economic actors that behave qualitatively differently from more nationally-based competitors (Bartlett and Ghoshal 1998; Doz and Prahalad 1993; Hedlund 1993). Together with the expansion of international trade and growth of international capital markets, the increasing power of MNCs has been linked to the emergence of a 'borderless world' in which national boundaries and the states controlling them have less economic significance than the decisions of transnational business elites and financial markets. In general this process is seen as diminishing the significance of different kinds of national and regional forms of economic organization in favour of a new cross-national form of capitalism that is in the process of replacing them through superior efficiency.

It is beyond question that the scale of economic activity controlled by MNCs has grown sharply in the last 20 years or so. The United Nations Centre on Transnational Corporations estimates that there are around 61,000 multinationals in the world controlling around 900,000 subsidiaries. These firms make annual sales of $19 trillion and directly employ around 54 million people. The stock of foreign direct investment (FDI) controlled by MNCs increased steeply, from $560 billion in 1980 to $7,123 billion in 2002 (UN 2004; see Figure 1.7). This was driven mainly by the sharp growth in cross-border mergers and acquisitions, which rapidly increased the extent to which many MNCs are spread across countries.

However, it is not simply the scale of MNCs and the resources they control that is significant. There are also important developments in the way these firms structure themselves and the strategies that they pursue. This issue is considered in depth in

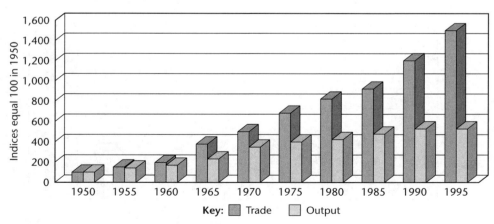

Figure 1.6 Trends in world trade and output

Source: data from Hirst and Thompson (1999)

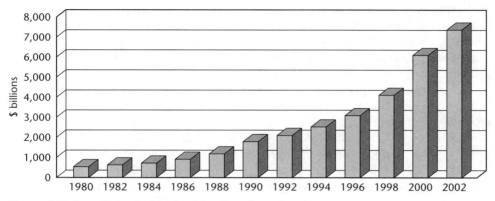

Figure 1.7 Growth in the stock of foreign direct investment
Source: data from UN (2004)

Chapter 4, but it is worth noting here the argument that the pressures of globalization are forcing companies to move towards new structures and strategies. For instance, according to Bartlett and Ghoshal (1998), the new economic environment is creating the need for a new type of organization – the *transnational* organization – which recognizes new resources and capabilities, captures them and then leverages the advantages on a worldwide scale. Although the extent to which many MNCs can be characterized as truly transnational can be disputed, as we will see, there are many examples of MNCs moving towards a greater geographic dispersion of business activities.

One of the implications of this trend for human resource management (HRM) is the emergence of a highly flexible international cadre of transnational managers, capable of implementing the very complex strategies involved. The strong globalization thesis predicts that instead of having careers that are driven by vertical moves up the organizational hierarchy, the focus will shift to managing lateral moves aimed at broadening and sharpening experience. The way in which managers are allocated to assignments and temporary projects will become more cross-functional, cross-business and cross-geography. We deal with the development of international managers in more detail in Chapter 9, looking specifically at career management and internationalization, and at how they are recruited and selected in Chapter 10.

Responses to the globalization theorists

This strong globalization thesis has attracted a range of critics. The principal objection is that close examination of the relevant data undermines many of the central claims about the extent and novelty of what is occurring in the name of globalization. Authors such as Hirst and Thompson (1999), Ruigrok and van Tulder (1995), Doremus et al. (1998) and Wolf (2004) have made a series of points which throw a quite different light on the nature of the international economy, and these can be summarized as follows:

● *The present highly internationalized economy is not unprecedented.* In some respects, the current international economy is less open and integrated than the regime that prevailed from 1870 to 1914. This shows up most starkly when we examine patterns of migration. The nineteenth century witnessed the biggest migration in history as 60 million Europeans moved to the Americas, 60 per cent going to the USA. In the latter quarter of the twentieth century the overall numbers of people migrating (on a legal basis at least) were lower than they had been 100 years earlier. One estimate suggests that only 2.5 per cent of the world's population reside in a country that is not their original one (Legrain 2002: 113). This is largely because of clampdowns on immigration by the developed economies in general and the USA in particular (Hirst and Thompson 1999). Even in the European Union, where freedom of movement across borders has removed formal obstacles to migration, levels of migration as a percentage of the population are actually very low. In other respects, the international economy is more open and integrated, but the change looks less than dramatic when viewed in historical perspective. A good illustration of this is trade. Trade volumes increased remarkably quickly in the nineteenth century, so much so that in 1914 they stood at 45 times their value in 1780, but the two world wars and the Great Depression of the early 1930s markedly reduced international trade. The growth since 1945 should be seen to some extent as a recovery from these effects. If the contemporary period is compared with the period before the First World War, then trade volume has clearly risen but its growth looks less spectacular: whereas cross-border trade was 18 per cent of global GDP in 1914, it was 25 per cent in 2000 (Legrain 2002: 108; see also Figure 1.8).

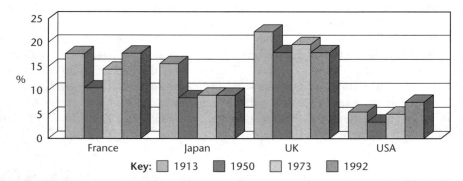

Figure 1.8 Exports as a proportion of GDP
Source: data from Hirst and Thompson (1999)

● *FDI remains heavily concentrated in the advanced industrial nations.* Capital mobility is not producing a massive shift of investment and employment from the advanced to the developing countries. Thus, the world economy is far from being truly 'global'. Rather, trade, investment and financial flows are concentrated in the so-called 'Triad' of Europe, Japan and North America, and this dominance seems set to continue. Moreover, companies are not becoming 'footloose' or 'global' players but in large part remain rooted in one of the three regions of the Triad. For example, German MNCs are overwhelmingly concentrated in Europe, with some minor operations in North America and Asia (see Figure 1.9). The developed economies account for around 85 per cent of outward FDI and also receive just over 65 per cent of inward FDI (UN 2004). When one considers the greater population of the developing countries, this concentration appears even more remarkable. Africa, with a population of around one billion, receives just 2.3 per cent of total FDI, and India, with a population of nearly one billion, receives just 0.3 per cent. Even China, which has witnessed a massive increase in FDI, receives only around 6 per cent of the total but accounts for over 20 per cent of the world's population. In other words, most of the people in the world are virtually written off the map as far as any benefit from this form of investment is concerned, and therefore there is severe inequality in terms of who receives and benefits from FDI.

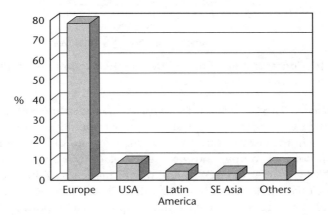

Figure 1.9 Distribution of the subsidiaries of German MNCs
Source: data from Hirst and Thompson (1999)

● *Transnational firms are relatively rare*. Genuinely *transnational* companies appear to be relatively rare. Most companies are based nationally and trade *multi*nationally on the strength of major national location of assets, production and sales, and there seems to be no strong tendency towards the growth of truly international companies. Even among the largest 100 MNCs in the world, which are those that we might expect to be the most globally oriented, the evidence points to the strong roots that these firms have in their original national base (see Figure 1.10). The UN conducts an analysis of this group of firms looking at the proportion of their assets, sales and employment that is located abroad; the 'Transnationality Index', which is an average of these three ratios, shows that most of these firms are concentrated in their original home country. We know from other sources that most MNCs retain very strong linkages with the financial system in their country of origin and fill most senior managerial positions from the home base. The weak development of globally-oriented firms is consistent with a continuing *internation-alizing* economy, but much less so with a rapidly *globalizing* economy. MNCs still rely on their home base as the centre for their economic activities, despite all the speculation about globalization.

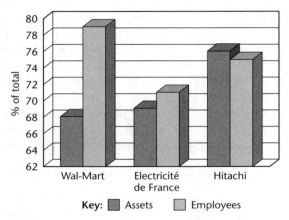

Figure 1.10 Concentration of three MNCs in their country of origin
Source: data from UN (2004)

● *Global economic flows are minor when compared to domestic flows.* While it is unquestionably the case that trade and FDI have grown rapidly in the last 50 years, and especially so in the last 25 years, their overall levels are still quite small when compared with domestic output and income. In relation to international trade, while there is a debate about the most useful way of measuring how important levels of trade are to national economies (Hirst and Thompson 1999: 62–65), even the higher estimates suggest that merchandise exports as a proportion of GDP are only around 20 per cent in countries such as France and the UK and as low as 10 per cent in others such as the USA and Japan. Moreover, many sectors are dominated by purely national or sub-national level organizations and, hence, are relatively free from the pressures of globalization. Those activities conducted by the state in most countries, such as education and health provision, are examples, as are many private services such as hairdressing and cleaning.

A key implication of these qualifications to the 'globalization thesis' is that the forces for convergence in national forms of economic organization in general, and the organization of firms in particular, are not as great as is commonly implied. A key consequence is that national differences in these respects remain significant. Moreover, societies with different institutional arrangements will continue to develop and reproduce varied systems of economic organization with different economic and social capabilities in particular industries and sectors. In this sense, economic mechanisms do not operate in isolation from their *societal context*, as some versions of economic theory suggest. As Whitley (2000) puts it, 'there is no systematic rationality governing economic activities that lies beyond, and separate from, any specific set of social arrangements'.

Indeed, while some of the actions of MNCs may lead to common processes across countries, in other respects they take advantage of national differences and, therefore, are actively reproducing nationally distinct practices. There remain important national differences in the attractiveness of locations for investment and other business activity. MNCs try to reap benefits from the specific advantages associated with each system in which they operate; these advantages are not just those associated with the cost of labour, but extend to capturing a body of knowledge and skills within a local workforce, access to markets and the ability to tap into a cluster of successful firms in a particular industry and region. In Chapter 2 we consider in more detail the literature on national systems of innovation, production regimes and national business systems. This literature points to real differences in the way countries have traditionally gone about their innovative activity and established their typical business environment, and how business is conducted therein. Moreover, companies need national legal and commercial policy provisions to protect their investments and their products from being copied, and are therefore dependent upon these national regulations. These constraints prevent them being entirely 'stateless'.

Even in those aspects of economic activity where globalization is most prevalent, it should not be assumed that globalization only leads to greater homogeneity and uniformity across countries. Globalization does not have a consistent social impact, but rather causes greater change in some national systems than others depending on the nature of the phenomena in question. Moreover, idealized procedures and practices are usually transformed considerably when they are introduced in the domestic economy (Boyer and Hollingsworth 1997; Hollingsworth and Streeck 1994). There is no particular reason, then, to expect that growing international competition, per se, will lead to radical business-system change, let alone that it will do so in a single direction. Child sums this up well:

> 'Paradoxically, at the same time as transactional boundaries weaken, there is an increased awareness of cultural differences and a growing celebration of cultural diversity ... Globalization may therefore be stimulating divergent as well as convergent developments in organization. On the one hand it facilitates a centralized standardization of organizational practices and products; on the other it promotes local identities which encourage decentralized organizational responses.' (2002: 46–47)

Globalization and change in national business systems

To what extent, then, does the growing internationalization of economic activity really threaten the basis on which 'national capitalisms' have been founded and thus lend support to the globalization thesis? Whitley (2000) provides a thorough assessment of the issue, considering the conditions under which globalization is likely to result in the qualitative transformation of distinctive national forms of economic organization. Have these conditions been met? Are they likely to be met? We consider these issues in more detail in this section, and in so doing we draw heavily upon Whitley's work and paraphrase much of his argument. For Whitley, the increasing globalization of economic activities is thought to result in major changes to existing forms of capitalism in three ways. We summarize his views on each in turn.

1 Globalization may change the nature and behaviour of firms that engage in large-scale international co-ordination and control, which in turn could transform the characteristics of their *home* business system.

Whitley considers the factors that affect whether MNCs become transformed into qualitatively different kinds of companies from their domestically based national competitors as a result of their cross-border operations, as well as the processes through which changes in the nature of MNCs could impinge upon their domestic business system. The way in which MNCs transfer practices developed in their foreign subsidiaries to their domestic operations has been referred to as 'reverse diffusion', and is something we address in more depth in Chapter 5.

Whitley concludes that for MNCs to change their fundamental characteristics as they internationalize depends on stringent conditions being met. The size of their foreign investments and operations must be significant relative to their domestic ones if they are to form a significant centre of gravity within MNCs. More significant than the relative amount of foreign assets is the type of business system in which they are located. Other things being equal, the more a company's key assets and activities are located in a distinctive and different environment from its domestic one, the more potential there is for the structures and strategies operating in that location to create a significant impact on the wider firm. However, the evidence is that large firms investing abroad tend to be more committed to countries that *share* key institutions with their home society than those that are strongly contrasting (Pauly and Reich 1997), and even where they do sharply contrast, one course MNCs can take is to *adapt* to this prevailing pattern rather than seek to remodel the parent firm along these lines.

Even where MNCs do see clear benefits in changing their domestic operations in order to incorporate structures and practices from their foreign subsidiaries, they may face barriers arising from the central characteristics of the domestic business system. This is particularly the case where the domestic business system lacks the necessary institutional supports for firm-level practices. For instance, Whitley notes that British MNCs operating in Germany would find it difficult to implement the German training and work-system practices in their domestic operations given the very different institutional environment they face at home. The institutional environment in the home system may not only lack the necessary supports but may also present a number of barriers to such 'reverse diffusion', as the following case study on US MNCs illustrates.

Reverse diffusion in US multinationals: the case of Imco

There are several reasons why we might expect reverse diffusion to be particularly prevalent in US MNCs. First, we might expect the deregulated nature of the labour market in the USA to present few barriers to firms introducing practices that originated in other countries; union membership at around 12 per cent is very low by international standards and unions are more or less absent from large swathes of the economy. Second, US firms are the leading outward investors, spreading their operations across Latin America, Europe and, more recently, Asia. Third, Whitley (2001) argues that US MNCs have tended to maintain tight financial controls over their foreign subsidiaries but allow them to develop what he terms 'distinctive organisational capabilities'. All of these factors make reverse diffusion more likely.

The issue has been considered by Edwards et al. (2005) in a study of five US firms. One of these, Imco, is a manufacturer of chemical-related products and is a large multinational spread over approximately 40 countries. The case study provided evidence of the company's UK subsidiary making innovations in HR practices. The most obvious example of this is the introduction of a system of teamwork in production, involving the reorganization of the shop floor with team leaders replacing supervisors. A further key aspect of this system was a reduction in the number of pay bands for production workers, with a fall from twenty to ten (two of which are hardly ever used, meaning in effect there are only eight bands) under the team-based system. Managers at the UK plant were delighted with the new system, and tried to push it to the US parent as a practice that could beneficially be deployed in the US operations.

However, the US managers did not implement this practice. The principal reason appeared to be that they were concerned that it would upset the carefully constructed climate of employment relations in the domestic plants. Imco is one of a number of large US firms that Jacoby (1997) describes as 'welfare capitalist', a key characteristic of which is a fierce ideological commitment to keeping unions out of the plant. One way in which they do this is by ensuring that their own pay system compares favourably with unionized sites belonging to other firms. In this context, reorganizing the pay scales by reducing the number of bands would run the risk of creating discontent among some workers who perceive themselves to be worse off, relatively or absolutely, and this would create fertile conditions for unions to recruit members.

Thus one barrier to reverse diffusion in the USA is the anti-union stance of many big firms and the delicate nature of employment relations in many of their sites. The wider study of five companies also revealed other barriers. For example, the handling of operational issues such as HR appears not to be as decentralized as Whitley portrays, and in fact many US firms have influential and large corporate HR departments that exert considerable influence over international operations. The evidence indicated that these departments see attempts by subsidiaries to carve a role for themselves in the formation of international policies as a threat, reducing the corporate HR department's claim on resources and its prestige.

In conclusion, reverse diffusion in US MNCs does have the potential to cause significant change in the nature of employment practice in firms' domestic operations, and by implication be a force for change in the US business system more generally. However, the extent to which this occurs in practice is constrained both by the way that US MNCs are structured and organized and by the dominant features of the US business system.

For further details, see:

Edwards, T., Almond, P., Clark, I., Colling, T. and Ferner, A. (2005) 'Reverse Diffusion in US Multinationals: Barriers from the American Business System', *Journal of Management Studies*, 42, 6.

Case study question: *How might reverse diffusion affect managers and employees in the domestic operations of MNCs?*

In summary, significant change in the dominant system of economic organization in a particular region or country as a result of firms' *outward* FDI depends on a number of quite demanding conditions being met, conditions which are not likely to be realized together very often, and the extent of likely change in a business system as a result of outward FDI is dependent on these conditions.

2 Globalization implies *inward* FDI and capital-market internationalization which may alter the rules of the competitive game in *host* business systems.

Whitley also considers how the growing internationalization of trade, investment and capital might affect *host* business-system norms and characteristics. The likelihood that inward foreign investment and control of economic activities, and the internationalization of financial flows, will significantly change business-system characteristics is similarly structured by the strength and cohesion of host economy institutions and their closeness to particular characteristics of the economic co-ordination and control system.

The overall weight and relative significance of FDI is obviously a critical factor. Where foreign firms dominate an economy, it is likely to be subject to the influences of other business systems. The influence of US FDI over the Irish economy is an obvious example of this. In most economies, however, no single source of inward FDI has had such an effect, and a number of different nationalities of MNCs combine with substantial domestic ownership and control of economic activities. Where this is the case, qualitative changes to host business-system characteristics are more varied.

In addition, the more dependent foreign firms are on the expertise of actors in the host business system, the less likely they are to change prevailing patterns of behaviour. Moreover, the impact of any change introduced by outside enterprises depends on the centrality of the sector concerned to the economy, as well as on the strength of the particular institutions connected to different spheres of activity. Whitley gives the example of Japanese manufacturing firms, which have probably been able to have more influence on UK companies than their Japanese counterparts in financial services because of the dominant role of the latter sector in the UK economy and its closer ties to political and bureaucratic elites.

In summary, significant shifts in national business-system characteristics as a result of foreign firms controlling economic resources and activities in an economy depend once again on a range of contingent factors.

3 **Globalization may generate a new *supranational* level of economic organization and competition that in time will come to dominate national and regional systems.**

The final issue that Whitley considers is the likelihood of a separate and distinct international system of economic organization becoming established and dominating national systems. The growth both of cross-border co-ordination and control of economic activities by managerial hierarchies and of competition between firms on a worldwide scale has led to suggestions that a new kind of international system of economic organization is becoming established. As we have already noted, this system is said to be dominated by distinctive 'transnational' firms that have considerable autonomy from national institutions and agencies and are able to pursue competitive strategies on a *global* rather than a national or regional basis. Such firms develop characteristics that are more similar to each other than those of their domestic competitors, and their strategies are more focused on each others' resources and actions than those of domestic firms.

For this new kind of international business system to be genuinely different and to dominate domestic systems, its ownership relations, inter-firm connections and employment relations would need to be organized in distinctive ways across national boundaries, and such patterns would need to be fairly well established and stable. This would require the emergence of distinctive and powerful international agencies, institutions and interest groups to support and reinforce them.

We have already outlined some of the weaknesses in these arguments and others can be identified. One such weakness is that the internationalization of regulatory agencies and institutions typically involves considerable competition for control over their form, remit and resources between national groups and interests. As Whitley points out, the nature and behaviour of the EU, for example, reflects the dominant groups involved in its establishment and subsequent development. The single European market has by no means resulted in standardized norms and rules governing economic activities across Europe, due to the tenacity of national institutional arrangements and national business systems. Moreover, the number of industries where global dominance by a small number of firms has developed is still quite small, and competitive strategies remain national and regional in many sectors.

However, there are other sources of evidence which do point towards the emergence of a genuinely global economic order. The regulation of some product markets is moving away from the national level, a case in point being the pharmaceuticals sector. In Europe, the EU has taken on the role of approving new drugs for sale in any country within the Union, gradually superseding the role of national regulators which maintain jurisdiction over drugs licensed before 1997. In labour markets, too, there is evidence of international regulations complementing, and in some cases superseding, national ones. Haworth and Hughes (2003), for instance, have argued that the International Labour Organization (ILO) has managed to establish a fledgling system of international labour standards despite fierce opposition, and both the EU and the North Atlantic Free Trade Area (NAFTA) have incorporated an element of employment regulation into their processes of integration. Perhaps most significantly, Sklair (2001) argues that a 'transnational capitalist class' emerged in the latter part of the twentieth century that is closely linked to the activities of MNCs. This new elite is comprised of senior executives in MNCs (the corporate fraction), globalizing bureaucrats and politicians (the state fraction), globalizing professionals (the technical fraction) and merchants and the media (the consumerist fraction) (2001: 17). Sklair argues that this new transnational capitalist class is not only removed from any one particular business system but is also 'more or less in control of the processes of globalization' (2001: 5).

There is clearly disagreement about the extent to which a new global economic order that is distinct from national business systems has emerged, or is likely to emerge in the future. Our interpretation of the evidence is that such a new system is only in its very early stages of development; it has presented some challenges to the character of some national business systems, but has not brought about fundamental convergence between them. Indeed, we would stress the tenacity of national characteristics and the enduring significance of *national* institutions.

We have reproduced Whitley's arguments in some detail here, as his analysis in effect constitutes a rigorous 'test' of many aspects of the globalization thesis, and in each case the evidence he gathers suggests that more cautious conclusions need to be drawn. His research demonstrates the incremental and 'path-dependent' nature of change in industrial societies. Significant change in national 'business systems' implies substantial shifts in ownership relations, the division of organizational labour, the level and/or type of non-ownership co-ordination processes, and/or employment and labour relations. As Whitley concludes, such changes are large scale and far reaching, requiring considerable institutional restructuring and realignment of major societal interests, and – crucially – they are unlikely to develop simply as a consequence of economic globalization.

Our discussion of the globalization thesis and consideration of its weaknesses highlights the importance of the national dimension. In the next chapter we consider this aspect in more detail, outlining the various ways in which the 'national effect' can be conceptualized and understood in terms of its impact upon management action. We can see already that the 'global' and the 'national' constitute two distinct contexts for interpreting IHRM, but they are not the only two. In the remainder of this chapter we briefly sketch out four different 'levels of analysis' within the field. This is important as these form a backdrop for much of the discussion in subsequent chapters.

Conclusion: understanding international management action

If we are interested in the complex relationship between globalization, national systems and companies, then this already provides us with three distinct 'levels of analysis' for interpreting and understanding human resource management strategies and practices. Considering the impact or implications of global economic trends first, we might in broad terms call this the *globalization effect*. We have outlined a number of the aspects of the globalization effect earlier in the chapter. While some strands of this argument are difficult to substantiate, there remains enough of substance to argue that genuinely global influences on management action are significant: unquestionably, developments in IT mean that ideas and technologies are spread around the globe more quickly than ever before; large chunks of the world that were until recently closed off from the international economy are rapidly becoming integrated into it; and many sectors that have hitherto been subject to close regulation and ownership restrictions have been liberalized and, subsequently, internationalized. Moreover, a key feature of globalization has been the growth of MNCs and the chains of production and service provision that they control, while a set of international regulations and a developing 'transnational elite' is emerging partly as a consequence of the activities of MNCs.

While some of the growing connections and linkages between national economies warrant the term global, others should more accurately be described as regionally focused. Thus the second level of analysis we can distinguish is a *regional effect*. As noted above, the dominant patterns of trade and FDI are within three key regions of the world, namely North America, Western Europe and East Asia. The major flows of international economic activity are either between these three 'Triad' regions or within one of them. Marginson (2000) has developed this point in arguing that MNCs operate principally at the 'sub-global' level, rather than either a purely global or local level. In particular, he describes Europe as a 'distinct economic, political and regulatory space' and argues that MNCs are increasingly organizing themselves at a European level, both in terms of their formal structure and their orientation.

Although these global and regional trends are important, they have not fully eroded nationally distinct influences on management actions. In terms of the influence of states or national systems in different countries, we can call this third level of analysis the *national effect*. This refers to the distinctive differences between business systems and the role of national institutions (financial, educational and governmental). We know that despite pressures for change, financial systems continue to differ markedly across countries. Some national financial systems, such as those in operation in the USA and the UK, are characterized by arms-length and fluid relations between senior managers in firms and shareholders and by an active 'market for corporate control' in the form of takeovers. In contrast, the dominant features of other financial systems, such as those in Germany and Sweden, are of close and stable relations between managers and owners and considerable continuity in ownership patterns (see, for example, Hall and Soskice 2001). A further example of the national effect stems from the work of the 'societal effects' school (Maurice et al. 1986) which in a series of studies demonstrated fundamental differences in forms of work organization between Britain, France and Germany, reflecting deep-rooted differences in systems of education, training and industrial relations. The interrelationships between the institutional and cultural aspects of countries' economies combine to form nationally distinct 'business systems'. While the global and regional effects may challenge some aspects of national distinctiveness, and lead to changes in important respects, the national level remains a highly significant one.

Fourth, in addition to the global, regional and national, we can distinguish the *organization effect*. The nature of the three effects already discussed certainly sets parameters within which organizations operate, but it does not completely determine the strategies and practices at company level. There are a range of contingent factors at company level that allow managers to devise courses of action that may differ from those of their competitors, and some of these relate to the way that MNCs are structured. For instance, MNCs that are organised around highly standardized or integrated production systems across borders are those that are most likely to be influenced by the pressures of globalization and regionalization into engaging in the transfer of practices across borders; in contrast, those that are a collection of disparate operations with little in common across countries are much less likely to do so. However, the contingent factors at company level are not simply to do with formal structures but also include power relations between actors at different levels within MNCs. That is, strategies within MNCs are in part the result of political activity within them. Therefore, the organization effect is crucial in mediating the influences that arise from the global, regional and national levels.

In this book we are interested in the complex interaction between these four sets of effects. We do not privilege one set of issues above the others. As we have seen in this chapter, much recent literature overplays the extent of the impact of *global* economic forces. At the same time, much of the business strategy and HRM literature overplays the *organization* effect in terms of exaggerating the degree of 'strategic choice' and scope for action that individual managers have to successfully introduce their chosen strategies. We do not share this populist view of managers as all-powerful strategic 'change agents', but rather we argue that management actions and policies need to be considered in light of the constraints imposed and opportunities provided by operating in particular contexts. Since much of the literature addressing these contexts is concerned with the implications of *national* differences, it is to a consideration of this issue that we now turn in Chapter 2 .

Review questions

1 What is meant by economic globalization, and what evidence exists to show that it is taking place?

2 What are the major arguments advanced by those who question the so-called 'strong globalization thesis'?

3 Consider the relationship between 'globalization effects' and national business systems. Do you think that distinctive national patterns are likely to survive during the first half of the twenty-first century?

4 To what extent do you feel it is useful to distinguish between different 'levels of analysis' (i.e. global, regional, national and organizational) in understanding IHRM? How might these distinctions be considered ultimately misleading?

Further Reading

Dicken, P. (2003) *Global Shift: Reshaping the Global Economic Map in the 21st Century*, London: Sage.

Summarizes the various theories informing the globalization debate, and provides a comprehensive discussion of the complex interrelationships between national level factors, multinational companies and changing technologies.

Hirst, P. and Thompson, P. (1999) *Globalization in Question: The International Economy and the Possibilities of Governance*, 2nd edn, Cambridge: Polity Press.

Discusses a wide range of issues concerning international political economy, and presents a vast range of data and evidence to undermine the arguments of those who see globalization as new and pervasive.

Stiglitz, J. (2002) *Globalization and its Discontents*, New York: Norton and Co.

Also provides a powerful critique of certain aspects of the 'strong globalization thesis', but focuses more on the controversial role of the International Monetary Fund and the World Bank in recent economic crises.

Whitley, R. (2000) *Divergent Capitalisms: The Social Structuring and Change of Business Systems*, Oxford: Oxford University Press.

A comprehensive and scholarly attempt to describe and explain the major differences in economic organization between market economies in the late twentieth century, based on the notion of distinctive 'national business systems'.

References

Bartlett, C. and Ghoshal, S. (1998) *Managing Across Borders: The Transnational Solution*, Boston: Harvard Business School Press.

Boyer, R. and Hollingsworth, J.R. (1997) 'From National Embeddedness to Spatial and Institutional Nestedness', in J.R. Hollingsworth and R. Boyer (eds) *Contemporary Capitalism: The Embeddedness of Institutions*, Cambridge: Cambridge University Press.

Child, J. (2002) 'Theorizing About Organization Cross-Nationally: Part 1 – An Introduction', in M. Warner and P. Joynt (eds) *Managing Across Cultures: Issues and Perspectives*, London: Thompson.

Dicken, P. (2003) *Global Shift: Reshaping the Global Economic Map in the 21st Century*, London: Sage.

Doremus, P., Keller, W., Pauly, L. and Reich, S. (1998) *The Myth of the Global Corporation*, Princeton: Princeton University Press.

Doz, Y. and Prahalad, C.K. (1993) 'Managing MNCs: A Search for a New Paradigm', in S. Ghoshal and E. Westney (eds) *Organization Theory and the Multinational Corporation*, London: Macmillan.

Edwards, T., Almond, P., Clark, I., Colling, T. and Ferner, A. (2005) 'Reverse Diffusion in US Multinationals: Barriers from the American Business System', *Journal of Management Studies*, 42, 6.

Fukuyama, F. (1993) *The End of History and the Last Man*, New York: Penguin.

Gereffi, G. (1999) 'International Trade and Industrial Upgrading in the Apparel Commodity Chain', *Journal of International Economics*, 48, 37–70.

Gray, J. (1998) *False Dawn: The Delusions of Global Capitalism*, London: Granta.

Guillen, M. (2001) 'Is Globalization Civilizing, Destructive or Feeble? A Critique of Five Key Debates in the Social Science Literature', *Annual Review of Sociology*, 27, 235–60.

Hall, P. and Soskice, D. (2001) *Varieties of Capitalism: The Institutional Foundations of Comparative Advantage*, Oxford: Oxford University Press.

Haworth, N. and Hughes, S. (2003) 'International Political Economy and Industrial Relations', *British Journal of Industrial Relations*, 41(4), 665–82.

Hedlund, G. (1993) 'Assumptions of Hierarchy and Heterarchy, with Applications to the Management of the Multinational Corporation', in S. Ghoshal and E. Westney (eds) *Organization Theory and the Multinational Corporation*, London: Macmillan.

Hirst, P. and Thompson, P. (1999) *Globalization in Question: The International Economy and the Possibilities of Governance*, 2nd edn, Cambridge: Polity Press.

Hollingsworth, J.R. and Streeck, W. (1994) 'Countries and Sectors: Concluding Remarks on Performance, Convergence and Competitiveness', in J.R. Hollingsworth, P. Schmitter and W. Streeck (eds) *Governing Capitalist Economies*, Oxford: Oxford University Press.

Huntingdon, S. (2002) *The Clash of Civilizations: And the Remaking of World Order*, New York: Free Press.

Jacoby, S. (1997) *Modern Manors: Welfare Capitalism in the Twentieth Century*, Princeton: Princeton University Press.

Korten, D.C. (1995) *When Corporations Rules the World*, West Hartford, CT: Kumarian Press.

Legrain, P. (2002) *Open World: The Truth About Globalisation*, London: Abacus.

Marginson, P. (2000) 'The Eurocompany and Euro Industrial Relations', *European Journal of Industrial Relations*, 6, 1, 9–34.

Maurice, M., Sellier, F. and Silvestre, J.J. (1986) *The Social Foundations of Industrial Power*, Cambridge, MA: MIT Press.

Ohmae, K. (1990) *The Borderless World: Power and Strategy in the Interlinked Economy*, New York: Harper.

Pauly, L.W. and Reich, S. (1997) 'National Structures and Multinational Corporate Behavior', *International Organization*, 51, 1–30.

Rogoff, K. (2002) 'An Open Letter', available at http://www.imf.org/external/np/vc/2002/070202.htm

Ruigrok, W. and van Tulder, R. (1995) *The Logic of International Restructuring*, London: Routledge.

Scarborough, H. (1996) 'Strategic Change in Financial Services: The Social Construction of Strategic IS', in W.J. Orlikowski, G. Walsham, M.R. Jones and J.I. DeGross (eds) *Information Technology and Changes in Organizational Work*, London: Chapman and Hall.

Scholte, J.A. (2000) *Globalization: A Critical Introduction*, London: Macmillan.

Sklair, L. (2001) *The Transnational Capitalist Class*, Oxford: Blackwell.

Stiglitz, J. (2002) *Globalization and its Discontents*, New York: Norton and Co.

United Nations (UN) (2004) *World Investment Report: The Shift Towards Services*, New York: UN.

Whitley, R. (2000) *Divergent Capitalisms: The Social Structuring and Change of Business Systems*, Oxford: Oxford University Press.

Whitley, R. (2001) 'How and Why are International Firms Different? The Consequences of Cross-Border Managerial Coordination for Firm Characteristics and Behaviour' in G. Morgan, P. Kristensen and R. Whitley (eds) *The Multinational Firm: Organizing Across Institutional Divides*, Oxford: Oxford University Press.

Wolf, M. (2004) *Why Globalization Works: The Case for the Global Market Economy*, New Haven: Yale University Press.

Zysman, J. (1996) 'The Myth of a "Global" Economy: Enduring National Foundations and Emerging Regional Realities', *New Political Economy*, 1(2), 157–84.

Chapter 2

National systems and management action

Chris Rees and Tony Edwards

Key aims

This chapter has the following key aims:

- to examine the implications of national cultural differences for management action;
- to consider in depth the institutional aspects of national business systems;
- to outline theoretical approaches which attempt to combine or synthesize these different approaches.

Introduction

We concluded from the review of the 'globalization thesis' in Chapter 1 that increasing managerial control of economic activities in multinational companies (MNCs) has not led to a 'borderless world' in which the decisions of transnational business elites are detached from the influence of nation states. Recent patterns of internationalization have generated important changes in the characteristics of the international economy and in the strategies of leading firms in most economies, but this has not meant that national systems have lost their influence. The internationalization strategies of MNCs can bring about significant changes in the *domestic* business system, but they only tend to do so under a set of particular circumstances. They can also impact upon *host* business systems, although here their influence is mediated by local institutions and agencies, and the more cohesive and resilient these are (as in Sweden, for example) the less the system is likely to change as a result of foreign firms developing a significant presence.

Globalization is, then, less significant in its scale and consequences than some enthusiasts claim. Further, the ways in which the international management co-ordination of economic activities is developing reflect established patterns of economic organization and competition at national level, such that these structure any emergent properties of a new transnational business system. This chapter attempts to specify more clearly the dimensions of these established patterns through an examination of the nature of national differences in business systems in general and patterns of human resource management (HRM) more particularly.

We structure this chapter in terms of the two major analytical categories which are most often utilized to explain the importance of the national dimension. These are, first *cultural* theories and, second, *institutional* theories. Both of these can be classed as *high-context* approaches, in that they both focus on national level factors, as opposed to global factors, when accounting for differences between organizations, and further they expect these national differences to persist over time regardless of economic globalization.

Cultural perspectives

Cultural perspectives place the 'low-context' theories that we outlined in the previous chapter into what are considered to be their appropriate cultural context. Economic utilities, personal motivations and the ways information is interpreted and used are seen to be strongly influenced by national cultures. The two best-known cultural perspectives that have been applied to management are those of Hofstede (2001) and Trompenaars and Hampden-Turner (1997). Both see cultural values as deep-seated and enduring, as varying systematically between societies, and as conditioning what is acceptable organizational practice. These arguments have a pervasive influence in current management thinking and discourse. As Child observes:

> 'The cultural perspective has for some time provided the dominant paradigm in comparative studies of organization ... Attention to culture has an intuitive appeal to practising managers, for whom it serves as a convenient reference for the many frustrating difficulties they can experience when working with people from other countries, the source of which they do not fully comprehend.' (2002a: 33)

National culture is said to impact organizations by selecting and framing the particular sets of organizational values and norms that managers perceive as being consistent with the basic assumptions that are developed within their countries (as a product of national patterns of early childhood, formative experiences and education, language, religion and geography). Differences in national culture affect organizations in many ways and are widely seen as central to international human resource management. They influence attitudes in international negotiations, which themselves may determine the outcome of investments, trade and ownership within organizations. They also create assumptions about: appropriate pay systems and the importance of distributive justice; the importance of centralization and hierarchies within organizational structures; the extent to which the manager-subordinate relationship facilitates effective performance management; and attitudes towards job and career mobility.

The problem of adequately defining and measuring national culture is one of the key challenges confronting cross-cultural research. Unfortunately, a great variety of different instruments have been used to measure culture, and there is little agreement regarding any definitive value scale suitable for measuring cultural differences among nations. However, there is fairly convincing evidence that values do differ, and a popular method for defining and comparing national cultures focuses on the concept of a *value system*. This is what Hofstede attempted.

In a landmark study of national cultures, Hofstede – who defines culture as the 'collective programming of the mind' which distinguishes the members of one group or category of people from another – analysed survey data from 116,000 employees of IBM in more than 40 different countries. He initially identified four, later five, basic dimensions to express differences between national cultures. His empirical research examined the distribution of work-related attitudes among national sales and service subsidiaries in IBM. The nature of the data and the methods employed to analyse them have been the subject of considerable controversy. McSweeney (2002), for instance, argues that Hofstede's study suffers from a number of important weaknesses, such as the assumption of cultural homogeneity within a country and the difficulty of generalizing for a national culture on the basis of sometimes quite small samples of one occupational group in one company.

Despite these problems, the findings are widely used in IHRM research. Statistical analyses of the data showed that the dominant values of the employees in these national subsidiaries varied on the following five primary dimensions of national culture:

- *Power distance* – this refers to the extent to which people in a particular culture accept and expect that power in institutions and organizations is and should be distributed unequally.
- *Uncertainty avoidance* – this indicates the extent to which people in a culture feel nervous or threatened by uncertainty and ambiguity and create institutions and rules to try to avoid them.
- *Individualism/collectivism* – in an individualistic culture people tend to look after their own interests and those of their immediate family. In contrast, in a collectivist culture there is a tighter social framework in which each person respects the group to which he or she belongs.
- *Masculinity/femininity* – in a masculine culture the dominant values are said to be advancement (promotion), ambition, assertiveness, performance, and the acquisition of money and material objects. In a so-called 'feminine' culture values such as the quality of life, maintaining personal relationships, and care for the weak and the environment are emphasized.
- *Time orientation* – originally termed 'Confucian dynamism', this relates to the time horizons that people in different cultures are oriented towards, with some looking several years ahead in deciding upon particular courses of action and others geared to the shorter term.

The model that Hofstede developed categorizes 40 of the nations studied into distinct clusters according to their rank scores on each of the five dimensions (for a summary, see Tayeb, 2000: 320–22). He also attempted to identify clusters of countries according to their cultural attributes (see Figure 2.1). While this research has been heavily criticized for a number of reasons, it does have one immediate and important

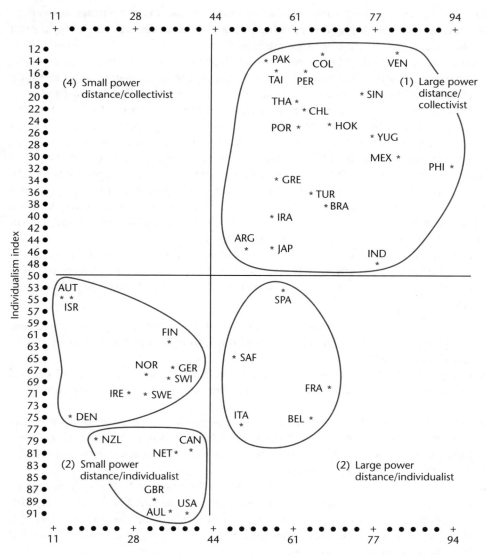

Figure 2.1 Hofstede's cultural clusters: power distance versus individualism

Source: Hofstede (1980, see Gooderham and Nordhaug 2003: 137) Copyright © Geert Hofstede

implication for IHRM. That is, if national cultures vary across a number of important dimensions, then those differences in national culture suggest that models and theories of management and organizations may have a limited applicability to countries outside of the culture cluster within which they were originally developed.

As Sparrow and Hiltrop (1994) have observed, MNCs vary in the extent to which they recognize cultural diversity. If managers believe the impact of national culture to be minimal, as in the case of the *parochial* organization, the policy will be to ignore differences in employee values, norms and preferences. On the other hand, if managers view all other ways of doing things as inferior, as in the *ethnocentric* organization, then their policy will be to minimize the impact of cultural diversity by, for example, recruiting a homogenous workforce. The tendency to hold one's own way as being the best is, of course, often reinforced by stereotypes of other cultures and nationalities. Finally, if managers recognize both cultural diversity and its potentially positive impacts, as in the case of the *synergistic* organization, the human resource policy will be to create a truly international workforce and to use the similarities and differences among the nationalities to create new forms of management and organization.

Differences in *national culture* are also important in terms of IHRM because of their potential impact on *organizational culture*. Both managers and researchers frequently point to the importance of organizational culture as a source of competitive advantage and the important role of HRM practices in creating and maintaining this culture. But, as Sparrow and Hiltrop remark, it is often assumed that

> 'the creation of a strong organizational culture erases or moderates the influence of national culture ... [and] that the values of employees working for the same organization – even if they come from different countries – are more similar than different. However, the evidence suggests that our national culture is so deeply ingrained in us that ... it cannot easily be erased by any external force [such as a company culture].' (1994:77)

Thus, it is unlikely that even truly *transnational* organizations will find it easy to move 'beyond nationality' in terms of employee attitudes and values.

The culturalist approach has become very popular in IHRM research, representing the mainstream of the subject. Writers have used national culture as a way of explaining why MNCs of various national origins adopt different HRM practices. For example, Ngo et al. (1998) examined the effect of the country of origin of US, UK and Japanese MNCs in Hong Kong. On the basis of marked differences between the MNCs according to their nationality and further marked differences with a sample of local firms, they argue that a number of aspects of the home country culture influence the nature of HR practices in the foreign MNCs. The culturalist approach has also been used extensively to explain the way in which MNCs adapt to host country cultures. An illustration of this is Tayeb's (1998) study of a US multinational in Scotland, in which she argues that the parent company's global approach had to be adapted to several aspects of the local culture.

Despite this evidence on the importance of national cultures, some fundamental problems remain with the way the term is conceptualized and applied. There are, for instance, concerns over the theoretical status of culture. Is culture all pervasive, as Hofstede has argued, taking primacy over other factors in terms of predictive power? If so, then the comparative study of organization across cultural boundaries employing concepts and equivalent operational measures derived from only *one* culture becomes hazardous in terms of validity criteria. As Child points out, if meanings vary in different societies then 'this questions the equivalence between cultures of any comparative concept and its operational measurement. Universalistic concepts and their standardized measurement of the kind that cross-cultural scholars like Hofstede have employed become suspect on the basis of this argument.' (2002a:33)

Child notes, moreover, that we still do not have an adequate theory of the relevance of culture for organization, and he asks: which organizational features are shaped by culture; how are they so influenced; and what is the significance of culture vis-à-vis economic, technological and political factors? Furthermore, to what extent are cultures themselves shaped by national economic, technological and political factors through the mediation of lifestyle, mass media, government ideology, and so on?

In addition, it is a common assumption in much of the business strategy literature that national differences can simply be expressed in cultural terms, and that the 'nation' can be used as the unit of analysis for culture. This is highly questionable for two reasons. First, almost all countries, but particularly large ones, are characterized by considerable heterogeneity. That is, there are considerable variations within countries according to regions, social classes, ethnic groups, and so on. Second, as Ferner (2000) puts it, a key problem with these cultural approaches is that they *explain* relatively little, and simply raise further questions. How, for example, did particular values and attitudes come to characterize a particular country? And how can we account for change over time in these values and attitudes? A useful way forward in cross-national research, therefore, is to address the societal origins of cultural differences, bringing us on to the arguably more fruitful area of institutional theories.

Institutional perspectives

These perspectives emphasize that management and business have different *institutional* foundations across countries. Key institutions are the state, the legal system, the financial system and the family. Taken together, such institutions constitute the distinctive social organization of a country and its economy. The forms these institutions take and their economic role are seen to shape different 'national business systems' or 'varieties of capitalism' (Hall and Soskice 2001; Orru, Biggart and Hamilton 1997; Whitley 1999, 2002). In the context of the ideas about globalization raised in the last chapter, Whitley sums up the importance of national institutions as follows:

'Cross-border economic flows and coordination processes depend overwhelmingly on national state legal systems, enforcement mechanisms, and institutional arrangements to manage risks and uncertainty sufficiently to enable strategic decisions to be made. Internationalization, then, remains highly interdependent with national agencies' and institutions' structures and actions. As a result, its effects on established systems of economic organization and firms are greatly guided and limited by variations in these national institutions.' (Whitley 1999:122)

Institutional theorists stress the historical 'embeddedness' of social structures and processes. This carries two particularly significant implications for the cross-national analysis of organizations. First, institutions are likely to be 'sticky' in the face of economic and technological change in the sense that they are relatively slow to change. Second, social organization influences a country's ability to efficiently undertake certain kinds of production or other economic activity. National institutions such as education systems and the structure of social relations can, through their impact on the degree of ascription or achievement in the society, impact on the ability of a country to base its economic wealth creation on innovation rather than, say, mass production. Institutionalists therefore argue that the conditions of economic survival through specialization around national strengths tend to preserve *nationally distinctive patterns* of organization, even within an open and globalized economy. One illustration of this is that levels of taxation continue to differ markedly between countries. As Figure 2.2 shows, despite periodic fluctuations, the differentials in taxation levels were still greater at the end of the 1990s than they were in the 1960s.

We can see immediately a number of obvious ways in which national contextual factors help shape and determine IHRM practices. As Sparrow and Hiltrop (1994: 52–59) explain, the role of the state, financial systems, national systems of education and training, and labour relations systems combine to form a dominant 'logic of action' in each country, and these will guide management practice. The social, legislative and welfare context influences many areas of IHRM, such as: recruitment and dismissal; the formalization of educational qualifications; aspects of industrial relations, pay, health and safety; the working environment; the nature of the employment contract; levels of co-determination and consultation; and so on. Moreover, a major difference between HRM in the USA and Europe, and indeed between European countries, is the degree to which HRM is influenced and determined by state regulations. Such differential national labour legislation reflects established political traditions concerning the extent to which employee rights should curtail the autonomy of managers to respond to pressures in a way that they see as appropriate. Generally speaking, legislation affording employees consultation

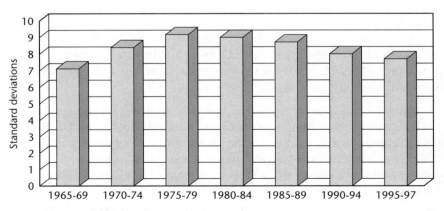

Figure 2.2 National differentials in tax regimes
Source: data from Hobson (2003)

and negotiation rights is stronger in Europe than in the USA, although there is considerable variation within Europe between, for example, the relatively deregulated UK and the more regulated countries such as Germany and Sweden.

As noted in the previous chapter, these national differences are not static characteristics that act only to constrain management action. Rather, MNCs will seek advantages from national differences. They will look for particular comparative and competitive strengths in locational advantages associated with national or regional production, innovation and business systems. Commonly, apparently minor advantages associated with a specific part of their overall production process are decisive in location decisions as MNCs create complex international divisions of labour based on locational specialization, forming what Gereffi (1999) has termed 'global commodity chains'. One illustration of a region that has attracted MNCs is the Jaeren district of Norway. This has developed a cluster of firms engaged in the production of advanced industrial robots. A leading local firm, Trallfa Robot, was taken over by the Swiss–Swedish MNC ABB in the late 1980s, creating ABB Flexible Automation. Prior to the acquisition, ABB produced most of its robots for the European car makers in Vasteras in Sweden, but instead of restructuring by closing down the Jaeren plant and moving production to Sweden, ABB increased capacity and employment in its Norwegian subsidiary in order to capture the externalities available in the local area, namely the pool of skilled labour and the existence of specialist suppliers. In this way the presence of ABB has *strengthened* the local innovative and business system, rather than undermined it. A quite different situation is that of the Bangalore region of India which has been the recipient of much investment by European and US companies in call centres and information processing centres. An example was the decision by British Telecom in 2003 to transfer many of its call centres from the UK to India. In this instance, the company was motivated primarily by the availability of computer-literate, English-speaking staff who could be employed at a fraction of the cost of their UK counterparts.

There is a wide variety of research that has lent support to the 'institutional approach'. A number of detailed studies have examined the processes by which particular systems of economic co-ordination and control developed their distinctive features in different countries, and how contextual – especially institutional – factors might account for these. In a wide-ranging and authoritative overview, Whitley (1999) suggests that there are two dominant approaches to understanding how societal institutions structure organizational forms:

● *The European 'societal effects' school* – the most well-known example here is the studies of work organization and control in German, French and UK manufacturing enterprises conducted by Maurice, Sorge and colleagues (e.g. Maurice et al. 1986). They identified considerable national variations in how firms in the same industry and using similar technologies structured and controlled work processes. These resulted, in large part, from differences in skill development and certification processes and in union structures which were – and remain – highly varied across these three societies, thus exerting 'societal effects' on work systems.

● *American 'new institutionalism'* – much of this focuses on how organizations reproduce particular templates and forms which are authorized by central agencies and
dominant ideologies as being legitimate, efficient, 'best practice', and so on.
Dominant conceptions of rationality and effectiveness are seen as generating distinctive templates for organizations that constrain their structures and strategies if
they are to be widely accepted as legitimate social actors. As a result, organizational forms tend to become remarkably uniform within societies dominated by
particular institutional conventions. This school has its roots in DiMaggio and
Powell's (1991) landmark study.

The 'national business system' approach

While Whitley (1999) notes the contribution of these research traditions in arguing
that societies with different institutional arrangements will continue to develop and
reproduce varied systems of economic organization with different economic and
social capabilities in particular industries and sectors, he nevertheless feels that they
do not go far enough. In his words,

> 'The "societal-effects" approach and many of the broadly defined institutionalist analyses ...
> showed that differences and changes in central institutional arrangements and agencies
> have had significant and quite long-standing consequences for the ways in which firms
> organize and control work, establish networks, and develop growth strategies. However, rel-
> atively few comparative studies have focused on how they have led to the development of
> distinctive systems of economic organization more generally.' (1999: 15)

Given the existence of varied forms of economic organization, important questions
arise to do with *why* they persist and *how* they change. To answer these questions
requires the specification of the interdependencies between particular characteristics
of these distinctive forms and the dominant institutional arrangements that govern
them. Whitley thus presents a framework for identifying the central differences
between established systems of economic organization and control in contemporary
market economies that explains these in terms of specific features of their institutional environments. As discussed in the last chapter, his 'comparative business
systems' approach represents one of the more sophisticated attempts to utilize institutionalist arguments. Economic activity, according to Whitley, is *socially constituted*
and *institutionally variable*, such that the way that economic actors relate to one
another can only be understood by examining the nature of the societal context, and
research into differences between countries must be sensitive to the ways that these
contexts differ across borders.

A key debate among institutionalists is the extent to which the dominant institutions across countries are converging on particular types. One area in which there has
been such a debate is the nature of collective bargaining structures, something that is
discussed in the following case study.

Convergences or divergences in national systems: the case of forms of collective bargaining

There have unquestionably been some common developments across countries in terms of the role and influence of trade unions. The most obvious of these is the fall in union membership. The vast majority of countries have experienced a significant fall in the proportion of the workforce that belongs to a trade union, although the declines have started from greatly different levels and the pace of change has also differed markedly. More controversially, it is sometimes argued that the nature of collective bargaining between employers and unions has also experienced a common pattern. The greater competition brought about by globalization has led employers to seek to move away from forms of bargaining that limit the flexibility they have to set pay and conditions in line with their own circumstances. Thus firms across countries have sought to move towards bargaining at the level of the firm rather than joining with other firms to set pay and conditions, or to move away from bargaining altogether. Is there evidence of convergence on this issue?

Kathleen Thelen (2001) has addressed this issue by making use of a distinction between two different types of business system. The first of these are 'co-ordinated market economies' (CMEs) in which there exist a number of forms of non-market co-ordination through networks and extra-firm institutions promoting associations between firms. CMEs generally are characterized by: stable and close relationships between shareholders and firms; a large state, particularly a welfare state; and relatively strong laws protecting workers' rights and the position of unions. In industrial relations terms, this type of business system, which is found in a number of variants across continental Europe, has tended to have relatively centralized collective bargaining arrangements, often at the level of the sector and sometimes at the level of the whole economy. In contrast, 'liberal market economies' (LMEs) rely primarily on markets to organize economic activity, and associations and co-operation between firms are relatively rare. In LMEs, the prime examples of which are the UK and the USA, relations between shareholders and firms tend to be fluid and distant, the state plays a relatively minor role in the economy, labour markets are deregulated and unions receive little formal support (legal or political) from government. Collective bargaining in LMEs is not only more restricted in its coverage when compared with CMEs but also differs in that it takes place at a more decentralized level, normally the firm or workplace (see Hall and Soskice 2001 for a fuller discussion).

To what extent, then, has the process of globalization led to convergence in the nature of collective bargaining across these two types of business system? Considering CMEs first, Thelen argues that in Germany, Sweden and Italy there continues to be a good deal of inter-firm co-ordination, particularly through sector-level agreements. In Germany, there have been only limited attempts on the part of employers to break away from sectoral collective bargaining, and some of these have been thwarted. In Sweden, the distinctive system of economy-wide bargaining that was a key feature of the 'Swedish model' of industrial relations for much of the post-war period collapsed in the mid-1980s, but inter-firm co-operation has not disappeared as it has been replaced with bargaining at the sector rather than firm level. In Italy there has in fact been a renewal of co-ordination across firms for the purposes of bargaining with unions, with the move to the sector level constituting growing *centralization*.

In contrast, in the USA and the UK the pressures of greater international competition have led most firms in a quite different direction. In the USA there has been a collapse in the presence of unions across large swathes of the economy, particularly in the southern states and in the growing service sector. Even where employers do bargain with unions, there is little inter-firm co-ordination. In the UK, the tradition of sector-level bargaining that existed for decades in industries such as metalworking and banking has almost disappeared as employers retreated from such arrangements, while there has been significant growth in the proportion of workplaces that do not deal with unions.

Thus what has occurred in the last 20 years or so is not simple convergence across countries. Rather, there are marked differences in the extent and form of collective bargaining across different types of business system. There may be convergence within these clusters but certainly not across them, and the trend towards decentralization of collective bargaining is not universal. This is an illustration of a wider point, namely that the pressures of globalization may bring about change in national business systems, but these changes do not take them all in the same direction.

For further details, see:
Thelen, K. (2001) 'Varieties of Labor Politics in the Developed Democracies' in P. Hall and D. Soskice (eds) *Varieties of Capitalism: The Institutional Foundations of Comparative Advantage*, Oxford: Oxford University Press.

Broader frameworks for interpreting international management action

So far in this chapter we have seen that despite claims of growing convergence and the 'globalization' of managerial structures and strategies, the ways in which economic activities are organized and controlled differ considerably between countries. We have outlined the two major theoretical approaches that seek to account for and explain these national differences, the first based around the notion of national cultures and the second giving more credence to institutional factors. While it is clear that much of the research into national differences is well developed and analytically rigorous, there remains something of a rigid division between the 'culturalists' on the one hand and the 'institutionalists' on the other. If both sets of factors have a bearing upon international management strategies and practices, how can we look to combine them?

As well as the cultural–institutional divide, there is also the problem that both of these perspectives might give undue primacy to *national* factors and consequently downplay the way these interact with *global*, *regional* and *organizational* factors. In terms of the different 'levels of analysis' that we discussed at the end of Chapter 1, how can we relate the national effect to these other three levels of analysis?

We briefly consider these questions in this final section by drawing on recent ideas that have sought not only to combine the global with the national, and the cultural with the institutional, but also to move away from rigid analytical categories and towards a more 'holistic' conception of the interaction between different levels of analysis.

Child (2002b) argues that the global (or 'low-context') theories tend to be mainly concerned with forces that are *material* in nature and take effect through socially structured activities such as markets and programmes of technological innovation, while the national (or 'high-context') perspectives identify influences on organizations that are mainly *ideational* in character. He also points out that the values and norms to which the ideational refer are expressed and reproduced through the medium of social institutions, some of which have their own highly structured forms, such as legal systems. Hence material and ideational forces – or the global and the local – are interrelated.

In trying to reconcile different approaches, Child draws heavily upon Max Weber's (1964, 1978) framework for the analysis of socio-economic development. Weber focused on the *material* and *ideational* forces driving social change, and used his framework to account for the emergence of the Western capitalist system, as well as bureaucracy as its characteristic organizational form. Child demonstrates how Weber's concepts of 'formal rationality/materialism' and 'substantive rationality/idealism' have a close correspondence with those of 'global/low context' and 'local/high context' within IHRM and comparative management studies. In Weber's analysis, materialistic and ideational forces have the potential to impact upon each other, and Child develops a framework which utilizes this notion and applies it to international management. According to Child, the Weberian framework

> 'qualifies the current dominance that economic universalism enjoys in policy discussions by stressing the need to allow room for the influence of ideas and values. Equally, it cautions against any tendency to ascribe over-riding explanatory power to national culture.' (2002b: 44)

Such a conception of the material and ideational forces on organizations can be located within the framework we developed at the end of Chapter 1. The material forces in Child's model represent the pressures arising from globalization and regionalization, and these effects can lead to changes in the nature of national systems. The ideational influences, on the other hand, are mainly linked to the national level, and throw light on the way in which cultures and institutions are interrelated and interdependent; as Child puts it,

> 'When institutions change, people may adapt their values quite rapidly.' (2002b: 44)

Sorge (2004) summarizes a number of arguments which similarly seek to integrate the cultural and institutional. If culture is indeed reflected in an individual's values and 'mental programming of the mind', as Hofstede (2001) argues, then these values and individual preferences will be adjusted according to a collective framework of norms, and vice versa, any collectively instituted traditions depend always on legitimacy – in other words, people complying because of ethical or utilitarian reasons. Thus Sorge concludes that institutions are 'created, modified or held in place through the mental programming of actors ... [which itself emerges] through the confrontation of actors with fairly stable and robust patterns.' (2004: 133)

Many of these arguments draw upon the action/structure dichotomy in social theory, as developed by sociologists such as Giddens (1986). As Sorge notes, the main point here is that individual behaviour and social structure should be seen as reciprocally constituted: on the one hand it is impossible to imagine a normative custom, instituted to be more or less binding, as not being kept in place by acting individuals, yet on the other hand these individuals do not make behavioural choices without regard for institutional norms. This is essentially what is meant by Giddens's notion of 'structuration'.

So, what role is there for the 'social actors' in MNCs, i.e. managers, and how do they and their organizations relate to, and interact with, the various layers of 'social structure' within which they are immersed?

There are various other ideas currently gaining ground which seek to grasp the complex interplay between the organizational, the national, the regional and the global and attempt to provide conceptual tools for understanding the dynamics of the relationship between them. Much of this work is inspired by a desire to move beyond some of the fairly sterile debates around national and global effects. Research emphasizing the importance of national and societal influences has certainly served as a necessary corrective to simplistic arguments about the pressures for universalism and convergence, as we have seen in both this and the previous chapter. However, a common approach to MNCs and 'host' business systems is to talk of the firm as engaging in either the transfer of home country practices to various host countries, adapting their approach to fit these or some form of hybridization of global and local forces. This view tends to both (a) assume that the nature of national business systems are 'givens' as far as MNCs are concerned, and (b) play down the scope for, and importance of, internal disputes and conflicts within MNCs. We consider each of these points here.

Countering the view of national business systems as 'givens', an emerging body of work stresses the way in which MNCs are able to exert considerable influence over their environment. A prime example of this concerns McDonald's. Royle (2000) argues that the fast-food chain has gone to great lengths to circumvent the employment regulations in place in the countries in which it controls operations through a range of 'avoidance strategies'. MNCs not only have the power to manipulate national level regulations but can also exert influence on the way that international and regional institutions function. For instance, the creation of, and amendments to, the trading arrangements established by the World Trade Organization and European Union are processes in which MNCs are powerful lobbyists. More generally, as we saw in the previous chapter, the corporate elites within MNCs are part of a 'transnational capitalist class' that Sklair (2001) argues is more or less in control of the process of globalization. When viewed in this light, MNCs are active participants in the creation of both the 'globalization effect' and, especially, the 'regional effect', given the way in which they are concentrated in the so-called Triad regions.

Viewing the MNC as operating within a 'transnational social space' (Morgan et al. 2001, 2003) is one way of emphasizing the connections between the organization and both regional and global effects. It can also be used to highlight the importance of internal disputes and conflicts within MNCs. The argument here is that multinational firms should be considered as distinct from national firms in so far as they create organizational boundaries that cross national and institutional contexts. In doing so, senior managers seek to impose order on what are distinctive institutional settings. Practices and procedures that work routinely in one national context can become problematic in different national contexts, each of which has distinctive 'rules of the game' as to how economic activities and firms are to be co-ordinated. One consequence of this is that the MNC constitutes an inherently disordered or, at the very least, segmented social space.

As Morgan et al. (2003) argue, corporate-level managers will attempt to order this 'transnational social space' in many ways. The creation of common policies and procedures and the application of formal means of monitoring and accounting for performance are bureaucratic ways through which order is instilled, while the creation of common organizational cultures is another way in which control is sustained. This influence from the centre may be challenged by other groups of actors within the company where they see their interests as being threatened by central control. Actors within subsidiaries control resources to which those at corporate level do not have access, such as knowledge of the local business context and other particular types of expertise. Thus *power relations* are central to the internal workings of MNCs.

While the concept of 'transnational social space' is sometimes presented as opening up the possibility of theorizing beyond the company/country and actor/structure dualisms (cf. Boussebaa and Morgan 2004), we prefer to see these as fundamental distinctions, while stressing the need to recognize the interdependence between them. As we also argue elsewhere (Edwards et al. 2005; Rees and Edwards 2003) *extra*-firm institutions at the macro level and *intra*-firm political processes at the micro level are strongly interconnected.

The nature of these political processes, and the responses of organizational actors at a variety of levels within MNCs, vary markedly across firms. As Ferner and Edwards (1995: 244) argue, various 'channels of influence' are likely to be found in different combinations across different types of MNC. For instance, the headquarters of MNCs that are highly integrated across borders are likely to rely heavily on formal authority relations to ensure that subsidiaries comply with their demands, whereas this type of influence is likely to be much weaker in MNCs with a more devolved or 'federal' structure. In sum, the internal workings of MNCs are a key part of the *organization effect*, and the relations between groups of actors are one source of variation between MNCs in their responses to global, regional and national influences.

Conclusion

In this chapter we have argued that the way that economies are organized and firms operate continues to differ across countries, and that the concept of 'national business systems' – being comprised of interlocking sets of institutions and structures in different spheres of economic activity – is a useful way of conceptualizing these differences. Variations across business systems give rise to markedly differing management styles and employment practices. Moreover, we have argued that these systems are dynamic and evolve in response to external pressures. Firms, particularly large international ones, are active agents in this process, responding to the pressures of globalization and regionalization, and exerting a degree of influence over the nature of national-level institutions and cultures. In other words, there are interdependencies between the global and the local, between cultures and institutions and between management actions and social structures.

We would argue that this conceptual framework provides a more helpful way of thinking about these issues than the standard management mantra of 'think global, act local'. The logic of this analysis is that a focus on MNCs is central to understanding the ways in which economies and companies internationalize in general, and the many implications for IHRM in particular. This is part of the rationale for this book's primary focus on MNCs, and it is to explanations for the growth of these organizations that we turn in the next chapter.

Review questions

1 Why are some of the perspectives that emphasize the importance of national-level factors often described as 'high context', while those emphasizing global factors are described as 'low context'?

2 What are some of the main ways in which national cultures are said to impact upon organizations and management?

3 Consider some of the criticisms that are often made of the culturalist approach. Do you think that the institutionalist emphasis on 'national business systems' offers a more fruitful approach to understanding national differences?

4 What contribution does the concept of 'transnational social space' seek to make to our understanding of international management action?

Further reading

Ferner, A., Almond, P., Clark, I., Colling, T., Edwards, T., Holden, L. and Muller-Camen, M. (2004) 'The Dynamics of Central Control and Subsidiary Autonomy in the Management of Human Resources: Case Study Evidence from US MNCs in the UK', *Organization Studies*, 25(3), 363–91.

> An interesting study of US companies that illustrates many of the arguments concerning the importance of channels of influence and control mechanisms in MNCs, as well as highlighting the significance of internal political processes.

Hofstede, G. (2001) *Culture's Consequences: Comparing Values, Behaviors, Institutions and Organisations Across Nations*, 2nd edn, Thousand Oaks, CA: Sage.

> Summarizes Hofstede's seminal study on culture and management, describing the way he constructed each of the cultural dimensions he refers to, and discussing subsequent studies that have drawn upon his ideas.

Morgan, G., Kristensen, P.H. and Whitley, R. (2001) *The Multinational Firm: Organizing Across Institutional and National Divides*, Oxford: Oxford University Press.

> A more scholarly and academic book, which begins with an outline of the 'transnational social space' argument before moving on to a series of essays exploring in some depth various aspects of the relationship between organizational, national, regional and global processes.

Sorge, A. (2004) 'Cross-National Differences in Human Resources and Organization', in A-W. Harzing and J. Van Ruysseveldt (eds) *International Human Resource Management*, 2nd edn, London: Sage.

> A highly accessible and readable overview of the major aspects of both the culturalist and institutionalist perspectives, which also considers practical and theoretical ways in which they might be combined.

References

Boussebaa, M. and Morgan, G. (2004) 'Organising Across Borders: Differences in British and French Conceptions of Management and Their Impact on a Management Development Programme', paper presented at the Conference on 'Multinationals and the International Diffusion of Organizational Forms and Practices', IESE Business School, Barcelona, 15–17 July.

Child, J. (2002a) 'Theorizing About Organization Cross-Nationally: Part 1 – An Introduction' in M. Warner and P. Joynt (eds) *Managing Across Cultures: Issues and Perspectives*, London: Thompson.

Child, J. (2002b) 'Theorizing About Organization Cross-Nationally: Part 2 – A Synthesis', in M. Warner and P. Joynt (eds) *Managing Across Cultures: Issues and Perspectives*, London: Thompson.

DiMaggio, P. and Powell, W.W. (eds) (1991) *The New Institutionalism in Organizational Analysis*, Chicago: University of Chicago Press.

Edwards, T., Coller, X., Ortiz, L., Rees, C. and Wortmann, M. (forthcoming, 2006) 'National Industrial Relations Systems and Restructuring in Multinational Companies: Evidence From a Cross-Border Merger in the Pharmaceutical Sector', *European Journal of Industrial Relations*.

Ferner, A. (2000) 'The Embeddedness of US Multinational Companies in the US Business System: Implications for HR/IR', DMU Business School Occasional Papers.

Ferner, A. and Edwards, P. (1995) 'Power and the Diffusion of Organizational Change in Multinational Enterprises', *European Journal of Industrial Relations*, 1(2), 229–57.

Gereffi, G. (1999) 'International Trade and Industrial Upgrading in the Apparel Commodity Chain', *Journal of International Economics*, 48, 37-70.

Giddens, A. (1986) *The Constitution of Society*, Berkeley: University of California Press.

Gooderham, P. and Nordhaug, O. (2003) *International Management: Cross-Boundary Challenges*, Oxford: Blackwell.

Hall, P. and Soskice, D. (2001) 'An Introduction to Varieties of Capitalism', in P. Hall and D. Soskice (eds) *Varieties of Capitalism: The Institutional Foundations of Comparative Advantage*, Oxford: Oxford University Press, 1–68.

Hobson, J. (2003) 'Disappearing Taxes or the "Race to the Middle"? Fiscal Policy in the OECD' in L. Weiss (ed.) *States in the Global Economy: Bringing Domestic Institutions Back In*, Cambridge: Cambridge University Press.

Hofstede, G. (2001) *Culture's Consequences: Comparing Values, Behaviors, Institutions and Organisations Across Nations*, 2nd edn, Thousand Oaks, CA: Sage.

Maurice, M., Sellier, F. and Silvestre, J.J. (1986) *The Social Foundations of Industrial Power*, Cambridge, MA: MIT Press.

McSweeney, B. (2002) 'Hofstede's Model of National Cultural Differences and Their Consequences: A Triumph of Faith – a Failure of Analysis', *Human Relations*, 55(1), 89–118.

Morgan, G., Kristensen, P.H. and Whitley, R. (2001) *The Multinational Firm: Organizing Across Institutional and National Divides*, Oxford: Oxford University Press.

Morgan, G., Kelly, B., Sharpe, D. and Whitley, R. (2003) 'Global Managers and Japanese Multinationals: Internationalization and Management in Japanese Financial Institutions', *International Journal of Human Resource Management*, 14(3), 398–408.

Ngo, H., Turban, D., Lau, C. and Lui, S. (1998) 'Human Resource Practices and Firm Performance of MNCs: Influence of Country of Origin', *International Journal of Human Resource Management*, 9(4), 632–52.

Orru, M., Biggart, N. and Hamilton, G. (eds) (1997) *The Economic Organization of East Asian Capitalism*, Thousand Oaks, CA: Sage.

Rees, C. and Edwards, T. (2003) 'HR's Contribution to International Mergers and Acquisitions', *CIPD Research Report*, London: Chartered Institute of Personnel and Development.

Royle, T. (2000) *Working for McDonald's in Europe*, London: Routledge.

Sklair, L. (2001) *The Transnational Capitalist Class*, Oxford: Blackwell.

Sorge, A. (2004) 'Cross-National Differences in Human Resources and Organization', in A-W. Harzing and J. Van Ruysseveldt (eds) *International Human Resource Management*, 2nd edn, London: Sage.

Sparrow, P. and Hiltrop, J.M. (1994) *European Human Resource Management in Transition*, Hemel Hempstead: Prentice Hall.

Tayeb, M. (1998) 'Transfer of HRM Practices Across Cultures: An American Company in Scotland', *International Journal of Human Resource Management*, 9(2), 332–58.

Tayeb, M. (2000) *International Business: Theories, Policies and Practices*, Harlow: Pearson Education.

Thelen, K. (2001) 'Varieties of Labor Politics in the Developed Democracies' in P. Hall and D. Soskice (eds) *Varieties of Capitalism: The Institutional Foundations of Comparative Advantage*, Oxford: Oxford University Press.

Trompenaars, F. and Hampden-Turner, C. (1997) *Riding The Waves of Culture: Understanding Cultural Diversity in Business*, 2nd edn, London: Nicholas Brealey.

Weber, M. (1964) *The Theory of Social and Economic Organization*, New York: Free Press.

Weber, M. (1978) *Economy and Society*, Berkeley: University of California Press.

Whitley, R. (1999) *Divergent Capitalisms: The Social Structuring and Change of Business Systems*, Oxford: Oxford University Press.

Whitley, R. (2002) 'Business Systems', in A. Sorge (ed.) *Organization*, London: Thomson Learning.

Chapter 3

The internationalization of the firm

Tony Edwards and Chris Rees

Key aims

This chapter has the following key aims:

- to consider alternative definitions of multinational companies;
- to familiarize the reader with the main explanations for why firms expand into other countries;
- to review the strengths and limitations of these explanations and their implications for international human resource management;
- to examine the extent to which firms have become globally dispersed.

Introduction

The growth of multinational companies (MNCs) is without doubt one of the driving forces of the process of internationalization. For Dicken (2003: 198), they are 'the primary shapers of the contemporary global economy'. MNCs dominate many industrial sectors, such as automotive, electronics and oil, while they are increasingly coming to dominate parts of the service sector as well, especially finance and telecommunications. The sheer scale of the operations of the largest multinationals gives them considerable influence over nation states. Comparisons of the gross domestic product (GDP) of countries on the one hand and the 'value-added' created by MNCs (a better measure than sales, which is more widely used) on the other show that 37 of the largest economic entities in the world are MNCs (Legrain 2002: 140). MNCs account for around two-thirds of international trade, and the stock of their foreign investments grew at an average annual rate of around 15 per cent between 1985 and 2000 (Dicken 2003).

This chapter considers the processes through which domestic firms become internationalized and the implications of this for international human resource management (IHRM). It begins by tackling the question of how to define an MNC. At first sight this may seem to be a straightforward task, and indeed it is one that is often taken for granted in much academic work. However, as we will see, there are alternative definitions that one can use, with varying implications for how we view the impact of MNCs. The principal part of the chapter explores the various factors that may motivate senior managers to expand the firm across national borders. Why would they seek to operate in more than one country? We will consider the strengths and weaknesses of various explanations that have been advanced to explain this phenomenon. We will see that most of these take as their starting point the idea that there are inherent disadvantages in operating across countries and that, consequently, managers of a firm contemplating setting up foreign subsidiaries need something to enable them to overcome these difficulties. We contrast this conventional view with an examination of an alternative way of looking at the issue: namely, that operating internationally has significant advantages stemming from the power relations between such firms and nationally organized governments, institutions and associations. Building on this, we go on to briefly consider the extent to which MNCs have become 'global' in nature. If there are power advantages to be gained from a high geographic spread of activities then might we expect MNCs to seek to become widely dispersed across countries, reducing their dependence on any one country? Competing perspectives on the globalization of the firm are reviewed and an assessment is made of the empirical underpinning of each.

Defining a multinational company

What is a multinational company? Answering this question requires a consideration of the definition of a firm. The pioneering work here is that of Coase (1937), later developed by Williamson (1975), who argues that firms exist in order to avoid the 'transactions costs' involved in market exchange. These costs have a number of sources: the uncertainty associated with market transactions; the costs of acquiring knowledge from other agents; and the difficulty in devising complex contracts that cover every eventuality. Where these costs are significant, there will be an incentive for an economic agent to avoid them through setting up a firm to co-ordinate production, thereby substituting the hierarchy of firms for the market. This line of analysis, therefore, defines a firm as 'the means of co-ordinating production without using market exchange'. In other words, firms are defined in terms of the ownership of productive operations.

From this definition of the firm flows the most widely used definition of a multinational firm. The significance of transactions costs is likely to be even greater at the international than at the national level since firms will be faced with more uncertainty and higher search costs in obtaining information. Thus many economists have adopted the Coasian approach in defining a multinational as a firm in which the co-ordination of production without using market exchange takes the firm across national boundaries through foreign direct investment (FDI). The focus here is on legal ownership of operations in at least two countries as the defining feature of what constitutes a multinational (e.g. Buckley and Casson 1976). We term this the 'narrow' definition of a multinational.

A key aspect of the approach taken by Coase, Williamson, and Buckley and Casson is the distinction between market and non-market transactions. However, some authors have questioned the significance of this distinction. For example, Cowling and Sugden (1987) argue that this approach pays insufficient attention to the power relationship between one unit and another within a production chain, whether they are part of the same organization or connected through a market relation. They contend that in most production chains there is a 'centre of strategic decision making' that is able to exert a significant degree of control throughout the chain, regardless of whether units are legally owned or formally independent. What the Coasian definition misses, therefore, is the way in which a multinational can exert control over operations outside its formal, legal boundaries. For this reason, Cowling and Sugden define a multinational as 'the means of co-ordinating production from one centre of strategic decision making where this co-ordination takes a firm across national boundaries' (1987: 12). The focus here is on the *control* of productive operations in at least two countries rather than the legal *ownership* of them. We call this the 'broad' definition.

The broad definition has the conceptual advantage over the narrow definition of capturing the wider impact a multinational has throughout the production chain. Some multinationals rely extensively on subcontracting and franchising to suppliers or retailers. Nike is an excellent example. In some ways, Nike is a very large firm, with enormous sales and large profits, yet it only employs around 20,000 people. This very low level of employment is due to the fact that Nike subcontracts all of its manufacturing to formally independent suppliers mainly in Asia, where it is estimated that around half a million people depend on Nike for their employment. These subcontractors are only nominally independent: they produce to Nike specifications; they sell at prices determined by Nike; and in many cases they produce only for Nike. In addition, some human resource (HR) practices within the subcontracted firms are determined by Nike, both directly through the firm's Code of Conduct (discussed in more detail in Chapter 13) that covers such issues as maximum working hours and conventions on overtime and indirectly through the cost constraints that Nike imposes on its subcontractors. Other firms in the textile sector use the practice of franchising to retail outlets, of which Benetton is a prime example. The company does not own any of its stores, but nonetheless exerts a high degree of control over them, determining the nature of the clothes they sell, the prices they charge and the layout of the stores. The narrow definition does not provide a conceptual tool for analysing the control that MNCs such as these exert throughout the production chain.

However, the broad definition is not so useful in assessing the legal obligations of MNCs. For instance, MNCs are not liable in law for environmental damage arising from the operations of subcontractors, nor are they responsible for cases of discrimination in employment that occur in their subcontractors. In analysing the responsibilities of firms in these respects, therefore, the narrow definition is the more appropriate. In addition, while MNCs exert some influence over HR matters in their subcontractors as we saw above, the degree of control is not as great as in the operations owned by multinationals. For instance, it is unheard of for MNCs to demand that their subcontractors establish performance management systems, but this is a common requirement that the headquarters (HQs) of MNCs impose on their own operations. A further reason to use the narrow definition in assessing the impact of MNCs is that it is much easier to operationalize. Generally, companies do not provide information on the numbers of people employed in subcontracted or franchised operations, nor is it easy to obtain information on their turnover or assets, making it difficult to use the broad definition to assess the scale of the operations that MNCs control. Consequently, most of the agencies that collect data on MNCs, such as the United Nations (UN), use the narrow definition. Therefore, while the broad definition usefully highlights the importance of control of processes of production and service provision, in this chapter and in the rest of the book we are normally constrained into using the narrow definition. This is what we do unless we state otherwise.

Motivations for internationalization

We now turn to consider the various explanations that have been advanced to account for why firms internationalize or, in other words, why MNCs exist. A number of these explanations, from a variety of theoretical starting points, are considered in this section. We start with explanations that have been advanced to explain the emergence of the first multinationals.

Origins of the first MNCs: the search for raw materials

For many writers, the emergence of MNCs is an entirely logical step in the development of international capitalism. The internationalization of capitalist economies is commonly seen as having progressed in three stages: from the circuit of commodity capital through trade; to the circuit of money capital through 'portfolio' investments; to the circuit of productive capital in the form of MNCs (see Dicken 2003: 200–02). While international trade has a long history dating back several centuries, the other two circuits began to internationalize in the nineteenth century. Much of the investment by foreigners in productive activities abroad in the 1800s took the form of portfolio investment. This involved financial investors holding a stake in an enterprise but not assuming any responsibility for the management or operation of the company. In the case of the UK, much of this portfolio-type foreign investment was in infrastructure projects in parts of the British Empire (John et al., 1997: 18–19). A growing tendency during the nineteenth century, however, was for firms to be owned directly by foreign investors. Many of these were what has been termed 'free-standing companies' in that they were owned by individuals or institutions in one country but operated solely in another. This type of firm was not multinational in the sense that their owners did not own or control productive activities in more then one country. Corley (1994, cited in John et al. 1997) estimates that at the beginning of the First World War, 55 per cent of Britain's outward investments were of the portfolio type and a further 35 per cent were in the form of free-standing companies. The remaining 10 per cent were accounted for by FDI by the fledging group of MNCs.

One motivation for these firms to internationalize was the desire to secure a stable source of raw materials. Some firms sought to take direct control over the production of these raw materials in order to absorb the profit margin that would otherwise accrue to an independent producer and, perhaps more importantly, to prevent a rival cornering the market. This explanation helps to account for the emergence of some of the earliest British multinationals, such as Cadbury and Dunlop. In some cases this type of FDI led to workers in the developing countries being highly dependent on MNCs, particularly where the foreign firm had control of a number of plantations, farms or mines. In this type of multinational there was relatively little central influence on employment practice in the subsidiaries; the firms tended to install an expatriate to run the subsidiary but the international HR department that is found in many MNCs today was almost entirely absent.

The lure of cheap labour

In the post-war period, many argued that the motivation for a firm to become multinational was not so much access to raw materials as access to a different factor of production: labour. In 1980 Frobel and his colleagues published a book entitled *The New International Division of Labour* that was concerned with developments in the manufacturing sector that were leading firms based in the 'core' economies of the advanced industrial states in Europe and North America to locate an increasing amount of production in the 'periphery' of the developing economies. In explaining the attractiveness to domestic firms of becoming multinationals, their focus was clearly on cost minimization. They argued that three developments in the post-war period were making it easier and more attractive for firms to shift production away from the core to the periphery. First, improvements in transportation and communication made it cheaper and quicker to transport manufactured goods across the world. Second, changes in technology made it possible to de-link the production process so that it took place in disparate sites and could be performed by largely unskilled workers. Third, the growing pool of cheap and unprotected labour in urban areas in the developing countries provided a cheap and disposable workforce.

Taken together, these developments provided a strong incentive for firms in the core to become multinational. Frobel et al. (1980) predicted that FDI would increasingly flow to the periphery as firms took advantage of the wide differences in wages across countries. They argued that this gave rise to a 'new international division of labour' (NIDL) in which the routinized, low-skill operations of a firm such as assembly were located in the developing countries, while the more specialized, high-skill operations such as design, administration and marketing were retained in developed nations. Frobel et al. (1980) argued that the development of the NIDL resulted in greater exploitation of labour. Manual workers in the core economies faced the threat of job loss as production was shifted abroad, leading to higher levels of unemployment and/or less favourable terms and conditions. Accordingly, Freeman (1995) argued that the pay and employment prospects of unskilled workers in the developed countries were adversely affected by this element of globalization. The prospects of workers in the developing countries were also bleak as the jobs brought to these areas were characterized by low pay and long hours. Moreover, the NIDL thesis predicted that the inflows of FDI would contribute little to the development of human capital in the developing countries since the jobs were largely low skilled in nature.

The NIDL concept has been severely criticized, however. In its simplest form, it does not take account of productivity differences between countries, which partially offset wage differentials. This is particularly important for MNCs in which the production process requires skilled workers. Moreover, in many industries labour costs are a small and declining proportion of total costs. Oman (1994, cited in Ferner 1997) estimates that only 3 per cent of the costs of firms manufacturing semiconductors are comprised of pay. The incentive to expand into areas of cheap labour is minimal for such firms. Perhaps the biggest failing of the NIDL concept is that it takes a one-dimensional approach to why firms invest abroad, focusing solely on cost minimization. Consequently, it pays no attention to factors besides cheap labour which are key determinants of MNCs' location decisions, such as access to markets. Because of these theoretical weaknesses, the NIDL concept could not explain the patterns of FDI in the post-war period; in contrast to the NIDL's prediction that FDI would be drawn to the developing nations exhibiting low wages, the dominant pattern is one of FDI being concentrated within the Triad of major developed economies, primarily those in Europe and North America.

More recently, a similar but more sophisticated explanation for how companies internationalize has centred on the notion of 'chains' of operating units across countries. From this perspective, Gereffi (1999) uses the term 'global commodity chains' to describe the way in which production processes are co-ordinated by one key player, which then structures the process that a product goes through from conception to consumption. For example, the production of Slazenger tennis balls is co-ordinated across nine different countries with firms in each country having a distinct role: the balls are designed by academics at Loughborough University in the UK; the clay is mined and transported from South Carolina in the USA; the tins that contain the balls are manufactured in Indonesia; the balls themselves are produced in Bataan, a special economic zone in the Philippines; and so on (*Guardian*, 2002). In this way, the various parts of the production process are 'delocated' from each other and, while these are carried out by nominally independent firms, they are actually closely controlled by the lead agent, Slazenger (see Kaplinsky 2000 for a discussion of the similar idea of 'value chains').

Where MNCs have grown in this way, HR matters tend to be seen as primarily local rather than global issues. For those operations that are subcontracted, this is primarily because the MNC tends to set only broad parameters for employment practice within which the suppliers must operate, as argued above. For those operations carried out within the confines of the multinational, HR matters are also decentralized because the operations carry out quite distinct functions, meaning that such issues as the skill and education levels of the workforce, the level of autonomy with which employees tend to work and the degree to which they are irreplaceable or substitutable all vary markedly. Thus the 'delocation' of the production process is accompanied by a decentralization of the HR function.

By focusing on the interaction between geographic dispersion of operations on the one hand and the relative incentives of retaining work in-house or outsourcing it on the other, the notion of international chains of production represents an advance on the NIDL thesis. In particular, it provides an explanation for why FDI remains concentrated in developed economies, with the growing international links with developing economies coming principally through arm's-length trading relations. Arguably, however, even this more sophisticated approach pays insufficient attention to factors other than the costs or quality of labour in particular and production more generally. This points to the need to turn to other explanations.

The product life cycle model

John et al. (1997) note that even in the late nineteenth century, many MNCs originated from a desire to expand or maintain sales rather than to secure a source of raw materials or cheap labour. Therefore, an analysis of factors of production needs to be complemented with explanations that focus on access to markets. This is particularly true for US manufacturing firms setting up foreign subsidiaries in Europe. One of the earliest attempts to explain the large flows of US FDI is the 'product life cycle (PLC)' model developed by Vernon (1966). Fundamental to this model is the idea that there is a locational element in the production process as products evolve.

Vernon's (1966) starting point was that US firms tended to develop new products in their home market, partly because of its sheer size and partly because of the high income level of most Americans. Production during the first phase of the life cycle, therefore, was located in the domestic economy and these production operations served not only the US market but also other markets through exporting. Vernon argued, however, that over time it would become more difficult to serve these other markets through exporting because local firms, which had greater expertise and contacts in the business environment in question, began to emulate the product. The second phase of the life cycle, therefore, involved the firm setting up production operations in the main overseas markets, mainly in Europe and Canada, with a limited amount of exporting continuing to the smaller markets elsewhere in the world. The lower production costs in Europe and Canada compared with the USA led to these production locations being used to serve the smaller markets, displacing the exports from the USA (the third phase). Subsequently, the lower-cost European and Canadian locations were used to serve the US market, leading to cutbacks in US production (the fourth phase). Eventually, as the product became mature and production became standardized, the attractiveness of lower-cost locations became greater and production shifted to developing nations.

In its original form, the PLC model of why US firms invest abroad was too mechanical; in practice, firms did not work through the stages in the cycle as predictably as the model suggested. In later work, Vernon (1974) developed his earlier ideas by linking the stages in the life cycle of a product to different forms of oligopoly. The first of these was the 'innovation-based' oligopoly in which firms competed through technological and organizational innovations. During this phase production remained concentrated in the firm's home base. Over time, the advantages to be gained from innovation were reduced as they became exhausted, and competition centred on the cost savings to be derived from the scale of operations. Generating economies of scale could be realized through setting up international operations, leading firms to emulate their competitors in building up a network of foreign subsidiaries. In this phase, the foreign plants were concentrated in major market economies, with the firms' international scale acting as a barrier to entry. As gains to be realized from economies of scale were exhausted, firms sought further cost reductions through shifting their operations to low-cost developing nations. This is the stage that Vernon termed the 'senescent' oligopoly.

Vernon's ideas were useful in showing how production shifted across different parts of the world as products evolved, and were developed to explain the location decisions of the largest group of outward investors: US firms. The thesis he advanced has the advantage over the NIDL thesis of recognizing that firms invest abroad not only to cut costs but also to compete more effectively in product markets. However, one problem with his PLC model is that many MNCs across a range of sectors have not shifted production to low-cost nations but rather have remained concentrated in the developed market economies. It is to a consideration of why this is so that we now turn.

'Market seeking' foreign direct investments

In many cases it may be very difficult, sometimes impossible, for a firm to serve a market in one country through locating its operations in a different country. Firms serving a national market through exports may be at a disadvantage compared with local producers in that they are seen as foreign by consumers. This is particularly likely to be the case where consumers are patriotic in their preferences, seeking to buy from firms that employ workers in their own country and that contribute to the national economy. Governments, too, may be keen to buy products and services from firms that operate in their country in order to promote employment and growth. Thus firms may expand into a country to overcome this disadvantage. As well as being advantageous to have a local presence for this reason, firms may also benefit from having a local presence because this gives them employees in the local environment who are well placed to understand the market concerned. Thus the local presence helps the firm generate expertise in the product market that would be difficult to obtain through exporting. Having a local presence can also help to avoid tariffs or quotas which firms relying on exports sometimes face. This has been a particular motivation for Japanese firms setting up in the EU. In some industries, moreover, it may be imperative that firms have a local presence. This is the case where the immediacy of consumption demands that firms locate their production or service provision operations in the market, as is the case in hotels and catering, for instance.

Where access to markets is the motivation for a firm to become a multinational, the implication for their role as employers is that the jobs they bring to a host nation will be less insecure than proponents of the NIDL (and to a lesser extent the PLC) predict. The ability of a multinational to relocate in search of cheaper labour will be constrained by the need to maintain an operating presence in the market. Indeed, such MNCs might seek to adapt to local employment practices and to 'be viewed as "good employers" locally, leading them to provide better pay and conditions than the local average' (Marginson 1994: 70). In this scenario, the HR function will have an active role in ensuring that the package of terms and conditions, and the quality of working life more generally, are seen as favourable, at least compared with local norms.

It is clear, therefore, that 'market seeking' investments will be a major motivation for firms to become multinationals. This factor helps generate a better understanding of the dominant pattern of FDI, which demonstrates that it is the major developed market economies that are the main recipients. While there are clear incentives for firms to internationalize for this reason, the question that remains is how they will be able to compete effectively alongside national firms in these markets. If firms start from a disadvantaged position, how will they be able to overcome this? We will now consider this question.

Efficiency advantages

The conventional answer to this question is that firms must have some source of competitive advantage which those in other countries do not have. The pioneering work on this issue was that of Stephen Hymer (1976) who argues that firms wishing to operate in foreign markets start at a disadvantage compared with domestic firms. This disadvantage stems from the greater expertise that domestic firms enjoy within the country in question: their familiarity with the language and business traditions; their expertise in the market; and their established links with key institutions such as government bodies. In order to undertake FDI, Hymer argues that firms must possess a 'firm-specific advantage' (also referred to as an ownership-specific advantage) that would enable them to overcome the disadvantages of being foreign-owned.

This advantage could take a number of forms. It some cases it will stem from features of the domestic business system in which the firm originated. One example is where the financial system affords firms a stable source of finance, as has historically been the case for Swedish firms. Another example is where the strength of the technological base of a country enables firms to secure a technological advantage over competitors in other countries, of which Japanese manufacturers are an example. Alternatively, the firm-specific advantage may be something that the firm has developed itself. The patents that pharmaceutical firms have over drugs they have developed are prime examples, as are the brand names possessed by soft-drink manufacturers and hotel chains. The firm-specific advantage may stem from economies of scale: arguably, the size to which many US firms had grown in their domestic market in the post-war period gave them an advantage over firms in other countries when it came to expanding abroad.

A further area in which firms may enjoy a firm-specific advantage is expertise in the management of people. Where this is the case, there are important implications for human resource management (HRM). As Japanese MNCs expanded into Europe and North America in the 1980s and 1990s, for instance, they brought with them many practices developed in their home base. Many of these firms made concerted attempts to minimize waste and inventory through techniques such as 'just-in-time' production. The adjunct to the 'hard' aspects of Japanese-style production is a set of employment practices designed to minimize disruption and secure a degree of commitment to product quality. Thus Japanese firms in the UK have exhibited a preference for a range of employee involvement practices and either for not recognizing a union at all or for dealing with a single union very much on their own terms (e.g. Oliver and Wilkinson 1992). A different example is in the fast-food sector. McDonald's has expanded internationally on the basis that it has developed a winning formula in the USA that it seeks to replicate in other countries. This involves very tight control over the operation of its restaurants, highly standardized supplies and a concerted attempt to avoid unions wherever it operates (Royle 2000). Marginson (1994: 70) argues that where this is the motivation for firms to become multinational, they are likely to be 'innovators' in labour practices; the transfer of the firm-specific advantage involves the adoption of practices that may be unusual in the host environment. In this context, a key role for the HR function is to aid in the transfer of these innovations, an issue we consider in more depth in Chapter 5.

While the existence of firm-specific advantages helps to explain why foreign firms may be able to compete effectively in the 'backyard' of their competitors, it does not explain why they need to set up wholly-owned subsidiaries in other countries. Given the complexities in co-ordinating production or service provision over great geographic distances and across a range of diverse business environments, why don't firms with a firm-specific advantage simply license or franchise to a different firm? As we saw earlier, many firms such as Nike and Benetton do just this, so why not all? We will consider this question next.

Internalization

Many have argued that the answer lies in market failure. Many mainstream economists assume that markets will always operate efficiently and will spring up where there are economic agents who are interested in exchanging something. However, there are not well-developed markets for many of the factors which constitute a firm-specific advantage and, therefore, they cannot easily be traded. While a firm may be able to license a tangible asset like its brand name, it will be much more difficult for it to license an intangible asset. How can a firm accurately value something like expertise in work organization, for instance? If a firm's advantage lies in the trust relations it has developed with a key financier, how can this be traded or licensed? How can a firm guarantee through complex and contingent contracts that a brand name will be used in ways that do not rebound on it?

Where the advantage that a firm enjoys cannot be traded in the market there is an incentive for the firm to use it itself in other business systems. This approach to why firms internationalize is known as 'internalization' because the firm is deploying the assets it has within the legal boundaries of the firm. In other words, the hierarchy of the firm is used in preference to market exchange. Theoretically, the approach draws on the work of Williamson (1975) and others on transactions costs that we encountered earlier in the chapter, and has been developed by a number of writers (e.g. Buckley and Casson 1976; Rugman 1981).

Where firms expand across borders in order to internalize an intangible asset, this requires the existence of structures which are capable of sharing knowledge and expertise across borders. There are a variety of structures that firms may use in order to facilitate such knowledge exchange, something that is discussed in more detail in Chapter 8. Perhaps the key way in which MNCs have achieved this is through deploying expatriate managers in key positions in their foreign subsidiaries. Recently, a number of MNCs have developed a cadre of managers and senior professional employees who roam across the organization, taking with them knowledge of organizational innovations developed in one part of the group. The ways in which MNCs develop such a group is discussed in Chapter 9. A parallel development is for MNCs to instigate other structures which bring together key employees from different parts of the organization, such as international committees and meetings.

So far, we have reviewed a number of competing explanations as to why firms internationalize, stressing a variety of factors as the key motivating factor. Some have focused on access to factors of production, while others have concentrated on securing a strong position in product markets through local production. A different starting point has been to examine the advantages that a firm gathers from its domestic environment and a related approach is to look at how the international firm can overcome deficiencies in market exchange. What is needed is a framework which integrates these and it is to this that we now turn.

Dunning's eclectic paradigm

While there is no universally accepted framework, the most widely accepted, and certainly the most widely cited, is Dunning's (1993) 'eclectic paradigm'. It is eclectic in that it draws on a range of theoretical approaches to establish a framework that can be used to analyse the decisions of senior managers in firms as to whether to expand internationally or not. As we will see, the framework summarizes many of the ideas that have been described above. Dunning argues that firms will engage in international production or service provision where three conditions are satisfied.

The starting point is that firms must possess an ownership-specific advantage that is not available to competing firms based in other countries. This point draws on the work of Hymer (1976), which we reviewed above, and can take the form of tangible assets, such as a brand name, or intangible assets, such as know-how and expertise. Firms must possess these in order to overcome the disadvantage of being a foreign producer. On their own these do not provide a strong enough motivation for a firm to become multinational since the firm could use them at home and rely on exporting. The second condition, then, is that it be advantageous to firms to 'internalize' their firm-specific advantage. As we have seen, it is often difficult to sell or license an intangible asset and, where this is the case, firms can best exploit it through deploying the asset themselves through international operations. Dunning argues that internalization is particularly attractive to firms that rely on specialist knowledge to give them a competitive advantage, such as pharmaceutical firms' reliance on intensive research and development (R&D). These two conditions on their own are not sufficient to convince a firm to internationalize, however, since it could still serve foreign markets through exporting. The third condition is that the firm stands to benefit from 'location-specific advantages'. As the term suggests, these are advantages that accrue to firms of any sort but which are fixed in a particular location and so have to be used in that location. Access to raw materials, cheap or highly skilled labour and proximity to product markets are all examples. Dunning argues that firms would internationalize where all three conditions are satisfied.

Dunning's paradigm has many strengths, notably the way it incorporates a wide range of work into one framework, but it also has some weaknesses. The first limitation is that the paradigm portrays firms as rational economic agents. In reality, managers have 'bounded rationality' (Cyert and March 1963) and make decisions on the basis of limited information. In the absence of perfect information, location decisions are inevitably influenced in part by ideology and prejudice. For example, where a firm does not have reliable and comparable data relating to the strength of trade unions in different countries, the decision as to which country to invest in is made in part on the basis of assumptions and preconceptions. Moreover, the key decisions that affect a firm's strategic direction are not always reached unanimously but rather are the result of compromises between actors who favour different courses of action (Mintzberg 1987). Thus the framework says little about the political process of decision making in firms.

The second problem that some authors have highlighted with Dunning's approach is that it starts with a questionable assumption. The rationale for the condition that firms must possess an ownership-specific advantage if they are to become a multinational is that there are inherent disadvantages from operating internationally, such as linguistic and cultural differences between countries. Hence, the starting point is: why internationalize? Yet there are also inherent *advantages*. The principal advantage stems from the geographic scope of a multinational's operations which accords it a powerful position in its dealings with nationally based institutions and associations. Thus in negotiating tax breaks and aid packages with governments, MNCs may be able to extract concessions on the basis of their (perceived) 'footlooseness'. Similarly, in negotiating with trade unions, MNCs may seek to use the threat of relocation to gain acceptance of new working practices or changes to terms and conditions. Thus for writers such as Dicken (2003), the correct question should be: why *not* internationalize?

If there are inherent advantages from a high geographic scope, then it is pertinent to examine the extent to which MNCs have become widely spread internationally. To what extent have MNCs transcended their dependence on their home base? Should we see MNCs as being 'global' in nature, detached from their country of origin?

The international growth of Unilever

Unilever is one of the biggest companies in the world – it employed 234,000 people and made annual sales amounting to €43 billion in 2003 and has an international history dating back more than a century. Its vast geographic scope and its evolution over time make it an interesting case in which to investigate the variety of factors that have motivated the firm to expand across the world.

The company was formed through a merger in 1930 of the UK firm Lever Brothers and the Dutch-owned Margerine Unie. The marriage created a unified company with a single board of directors but with two parent companies with joint ownership, one based in Rotterdam and one in London. The growth of both companies into other countries prior to the merger and the subsequent international growth of Unilever itself demonstrate the variety of motivations for firms to expand across borders.

The growth of Lever Brothers in the early years of the twentieth century was clearly motivated by a desire to access raw materials that were not available in many other locations. For example, in 1910 Lever acquired W.B. MacIver and Company, a Liverpool-based firm that had significant interests in the timber trade in Nigeria, and the following year it set up a large oil palm plantation in the Belgian Congo. The growth of Unilever into Africa continued in 1929 with the establishment of majority control over the United Africa Company (UAC), a subsidiary that had substantial interests in the primary sector in many countries inside and outside Africa. By the end of the 1970s it is estimated that this subsidiary alone employed 70,000 people. Where firms such as Unilever are large enough to establish a degree of monopsonistic control over local labour markets, and have the geographic scope to switch resources from one location to another (or at least can credibly threaten to do so), then they have the potential to use this power to downgrade terms and conditions of employment.

However, it was not only control over raw materials that led Unilever to grow internationally; access to markets has also been a key factor. For example, during the 1950s the UAC subsidiary greatly expanded its operations in Ghana, West Africa's richest state at the time, and in Nigeria, which had a population of around 40 million. Geoffrey Jones (2000) argues that these large potential markets provided important growth opportunities for the company. More recently, Unilever has expanded its food manufacturing operations in many developed nations. In this division, proximity to the large consumer markets was crucial given the perishability of products like ice cream. This motivation has different implications for how the firm behaves as an employer; where securing access to markets is central to explaining a firm's growth, employment is likely to be more secure and terms and conditions are likely to compare favourably with those of other firms in the target market.

The motivations for engaging in foreign investments has shifted over time in Unilever. In part, this has to do with the life cycle of products. For instance, the margins that could be earned on some products that Unilever was engaged in fell as alternative, substitute products became available. It also has to do with changes in the political and economic circumstances of the various countries in which the firm possessed operating units. The general instability and high inflation in particular in West Africa in the 1970s led Unilever to scale down, and eventually abandon, some of its operations in the region. The shifting

▶

motivation to engage in FDI was also shaped by changes in the financial system in London. During the 1980s, institutional shareholders began to put pressure on Unilever to improve the returns to shareholders, and in this context the UAC subsidiary, which had tended to prioritize growth in volume and market share, became subject to rationalization. In 1994, Unilever disposed of any remaining interests it still had in UAC. Though it retained some manufacturing interests in Africa, the region now represented a much smaller proportion of the firm's overall operations.

Today, the company is often cited as an example of a truly global firm. That is, it is organized to serve markets across the world and has no one country to which it shows any particular allegiance. While such claims are often made about international firms, it does seem as though it is justified in this case. Unilever's global reach shows up in a number of respects. As we saw above, its ownership and ultimate control does not reside in any one country, while it has operating units in almost 100 countries and sells its products in another 50. Perhaps most significantly, its sales are widely spread across the world: 42 per cent in Europe; 24 per cent in North America; 17 per cent in Asia Pacific; 12 per cent in Latin America; and 5 per cent in Africa and the Middle East.

For further details, see:
Jones, G. (2000) *Merchants to Multinationals: British Trading Companies in the Nineteenth and Twentieth Centuries*, Oxford: Oxford University Press.
Unilever website at http://www.unilever.com

Case study question: *In what ways has the shifting orientation of Unilever's operations had implications for the way it manages its international workforce?*

The arrival of the 'global' firm?

Over the last ten years it has become commonplace for senior managers of MNCs to describe their organizations as 'global' firms. For example, Philip Condit, who became Boeing's chairman in February 1997, outlined his vision for the future of the company on taking up his position. Boeing, he said, would become less US-focused and instead would be transformed into a 'global enterprise' by 2016, its centenary year:

> 'I believe we are moving towards an era of global markets and global companies. I think it is advantageous that your workforce, your executive corps, reflect that.' (Condit, quoted in *Financial Times* 1997).

Indeed, it has become commonplace for managers and observers to talk about the 'globalization' of the firm. It is often asserted that many large MNCs are no longer dependent on their original home base; rather, they are positioned to serve a global market, they respond to the pressures and demands of the global economy and they draw on knowledge and expertise from across the globe. In academic writing on this subject, too, the 'global' view of MNCs is also evident, as we saw in Chapter 1. Many MNCs, some argue, have become so internationalized that they have detached themselves from their home business system.

The best-known exponent of this line of argument has been Ohmae (1990, 1995) in his writing concerning the 'borderless world'; he argues that the ability of the nation state to regulate and control economic activity has been dramatically reduced by globalization. At the core of this process, according to Ohmae, are 'global' corporations that are 'nationalityless' and are able to shift to whichever part of the world promises the highest returns. Robert Reich has written in a similar vein. In a famous article in the *Harvard Business Review* (1991) Reich addressed debates about national competitiveness by posing the question: 'Who is Us?' He argues that a country's competitive position is not primarily determined by 'national' firms but rather by 'global' ones. The performance of the US economy, for instance, is shaped as much by foreign multinationals such as Thomson and Honda as by US firms like General Motors and IBM. In essence, Reich argues that nationality is no longer an important or meaningful concept in large MNCs. One interpretation of this apparent development is to see it as the logical consequence of the advantages that a firm accrues from becoming international. The more international the firm becomes, the more powerful it is in relation to domestically based actors such as governments and trade unions. Thus there are strong incentives for firms to become increasingly spread across countries and to sever their ties with their original home base.

However, these developments are by no means universal tendencies; many observers have questioned the extent to which MNCs are global in nature. Reacting to some of the claims reviewed above, a counter-literature emerges. Many writers argue that, far from being detached from their home base, MNCs remain firmly rooted in, and influenced by, their country of origin. Ruigrok and van Tulder (1995), for instance, challenge the 'myth' of the global firm. Based on an examination of the largest 100 MNCs in the world, they conclude that 'not one of these can be dubbed truly global, footloose or borderless. The argument of the globalization of the firm is unfounded and untenable' (1995: 168). Legrain (2002) argues that firms that are supposedly global or stateless are in fact firmly rooted in their home base. Doremus et al. (1998: 3) argue that MNCs 'are not converging toward global behavioral norms' but rather continue to be deeply influenced by their country of origin. Perhaps the best-known exponents of this view are Hirst and Thompson (1999: 95) who also refer to the myth of the global firm, arguing that the 'home oriented nature of multinational activity across all dimensions seems overwhelming'.

This counter-argument was made on a number of grounds. Principally, statistics concerning the geographic breakdown of the sales, assets and employment of MNCs demonstrate that most MNCs remain heavily concentrated in their home country and in the countries neighbouring it. The way in which MNCs are embedded in their home country shows up in a number of other ways: MNCs are owned largely by shareholders of the country of origin and raise finance predominantly at home; the key strategic functions in MNCs, such as the HQ and R&D facilities, are generally in the home country; and the senior managerial boards of MNCs are still dominated by home country nationals. See Table 3.1.

Table 3.1 The world's top 100 non-financial TNCs, ranked by foreign assets, 2002[a] (millions of dollars and number of employees)

Ranking in 2002 Foreign assets	TNI[b]	Ranking in 2001 Foreign assets	TNI[b]	Corporation	Home economy	Industry[c]	Assets Foreign	Assets Total	Sales Foreign[d]	Sales Total	Employment Foreign	Employment Total	TNI[b] (per cent)
1	84	2	83	General Electric	United States	Electrical & electronic equipment	229,001	575,244	45,403	131,698	150,000	315,000	40.6
2	12	1	13	Vodafone Group Plc[e]	United Kingdom	Telecommunications	207,622[f]	232,870	33,631	42,312	56,667	66,667	84.5
3	67	7	85	Ford Motor Company	United States	Motor vehicles	165,024[f]	295,222	54,472	163,420	188,453	350,321	47.7
4	16	3	15	British Petroleum Company Plc	United Kingdom	Petroleum expl./ref./distr.	126,109	159,125	145,982	180,186	97,400	116,300	81.3
5	95	8	87	General Motors	United States	Motor vehicles	107,926[f]	370,782	48,071	186,763	101,000	350,000	27.9
6	45	9	48	Royal Dutch/Shell Group[g]	United Kingdom/Netherlands	Petroleum expl./ref./distr.	94,402[f]	145,392	114,294	179,431	65,000	111,000	62.4
7	73	12	47	Toyota Motor Corporation	Japan	Motor vehicles	79,433[f]	167,270	72,820	127,113	85,057	264,096	45.7
8	22	10	21	Total Fina Elf	France	Petroleum expl./ref./distr.	79,032[f]	89,450	77,461	96,993	68,554	121,469	74.9
9	65	–	–	France Telecom	France	Telecommunications	73,454[h]	111,735	18,187	44,107	102,016	243,573	49.6
10	41	6	39	ExxonMobil Corporation	United States	Petroleum expl./ref./distr.	60,802	94,940	141,274	200,949	56,000[i]	92,000	65.1
11	53	15	51	Volkswagen Group	Germany	Motor vehicles	57,133[f]	114,156	59,662	82,244	157,887	324,892	57.1
12	86	20	86	E.On	Germany	Electricity, gas and water	52,294[f]	118,526	13,104	35,054	42,063	107,856	40.2
13	78	22	81	RWE Group	Germany	Electricity, gas and water	50,699	105,116	17,622	44,110	55,563	131,765	43.4
14	40	4	36	Vivendi Universal	France	Media	49,667[f]	72,682	30,041	55,004	45,772	61,815	65.7
15	50	16	57	ChevronTexaco Corp.	United States	Petroleum expl./ref./distr.	48,489	77,359	55,087	98,691	37,038	66,038	58.2
16	29	17	38	Hutchison Whampoa Limited	Hong Kong, China	Diversified	48,014	63,284	8,088	77,244	124,942	154,813	71.1
17	46	–	–	Siemens AG	Germany	Electrical & electronic equipment	47,511[f]	76,474	50,724	77,244	251,340	426,000	62.3
18	94	30	91	Electricité de France	France	Electricity, gas and water	47,385	151,835	12,552	45,743	50,437	171,995	29.3
19	66	13	63	Fiat Spa	Italy	Motor vehicles	46,150	96,990	24,560	52,638	98,703	186,492	49.1
20	31	19	44	Honda Motor Co. Ltd	Japan	Motor vehicles	43,641[f]	63,755	49,167	65,366	42,885	63,310	70.5
21	9	18	11	News Corporation	Australia	Media	40,331	45,214	16,028	17,421	31,220[i]	35,000	90.1
22	6	39	5	Roche Group	Switzerland	Pharmaceuticals	40,152	46,160	18,829[i]	19,173	61,090	69,659	91.0
23	19	11	18	Suez	France	Electricity, gas and water	38,739	44,805	34,165	43,596	138,200	198,750	78.1
24	58	27	60	BMW AG	Germany	Motor vehicles	37,604	58,192	30,211	39,995	20,120	96,263	53.7
25	64	26	75	Eni Group	Italy	Petroleum expl./ref./distr.	36,991[f]	68,987	22,820	45,329	36,973	80,655	49.9
26	48	21	20	Nestlé SA[g]	Switzerland	Food & beverages	36,145[f]	63,007	34,870	57,508	150,232	254,199	59.0
27	98	35	97	DaimlerChrysler AG[f]	Germany/United States	Motor vehicles	35,778[f]	196,375	46,137	141,491	72,560	365,571	23.6
28	63	14	52	Telefonica SA	Spain	Telecommunications	35,720	71,327	11,286	26,874	88,401	152,845	50.8
29	62	23	65	IBM	United States	Electrical & electronic equipment	34,951[f]	96,484	48,427	81,186	178,602[i]	315,889	50.8
30	92	–	–	ConocoPhillips	United States	Petroleum expl./ref./distr.	32,094[f]	76,836	10,074	56,748	23,934[i]	57,300	33.8
31	99	34	95	Wal-Mart Stores	United States	Retail	30,709	94,685	40,794	244,524	300,000	1,400,000	23.5
32	52	32	53	Sony Corporation	Japan	Electrical & electronic equipment	29,821[f]	69,476	42,858	61,284	94,000	161,100	57.1
33	44	29	45	Carrefour SA	France	Retail	28,594[f]	40,804	31,809	65,011	271,031[i]	386,762	63.0
34	70	60	61	Hewlett-Packard	United States	Electrical & electronic equipment	28,247[f]	70,710	33,286	56,588	56,326[i]	141,000	46.2
35	5	24	3	ABB	Switzerland	Machinery and equipment	28,155[f]	29,533	17,144[i]	18,295	131,321[i]	139,051	94.5
36	42	25	35	Unilever[g]	United Kingdom/Netherlands	Diversified	27,937[f]	46,752	27,614	46,122	193,000	258,000	64.8
37	10	28	7	Philips Electronics	Netherlands	Electrical & electronic equipment	27,880	33,849	28,673	30,099	140,827	170,087	86.8
38	34	–	–	Novartis	Switzerland	Pharmaceuticals	25,874[f]	45,588	20,588	20,906	40,282	72,877	70.2
39	39	33	40	Aventis SA	France	Pharmaceuticals	25,753[f]	32,574	14,767	19,506	37,802[g]	78,099	65.7
40	101	–	–	AOL Time Warner Inc	United States	Media	23,476[h]	115,450	8,329	40,961	18,555	91,250	20.0
41	72	31	69	Repsol YPF SA	Spain	Petroleum expl./ref./distr.	23,121	39,902	11,303	34,516	14,072	30,110	45.8
42	32	38	24	AES Corporation	United States	Electricity, gas and water	22,784[f]	33,776	6,542	8,632	24,284[i]	36,000	70.2
43	90	41	96	Deutsche Post World Net	Germany	Transport and storage	22,782[h]	170,503	21,820	37,131	108,609	327,676	35.1
44	57	40	54	BASF AG	Germany	Chemicals	22,694	36,781	17,878	30,473	39,078	89,398	54.7
45	83	–	–	Endesa	Spain	Electricity, gas and water	22,460	50,503	5,528	16,305	12,334	26,354	41.7
46	30	66	25	Anglo American[g]	United Kingdom	Mining & quarrying	22,450	33,581	12,821	20,497	147,000	177,000	70.8
47	33	45	27	Compagnie De Saint-Gobain SA	France	Construction materials	22,361	31,604	19,708	28,636	122,373	172,357	70.2
48	93	49	90	Philip Morris Companies Inc	United States	Diversified	21,513[f]	87,540	35,683	80,408	40,795[i]	166,000	31.2
49	68	52	68	Pfizer Inc	United States	Pharmaceuticals	21,161[f]	46,356	11,611	32,373	72,000[i]	120,000	47.2
50	85	72	94	Mitsui & Co Ltd	Japan	Wholesale trade	21,020[f]	54,286	46,979	108,541	14,611[i]	37,734	40.2
51	21	44	33	Royal Ahold NV[g]	Netherlands	Retail	20,598	25,933	46,343	59,293	236,698	341,909	75.6
52	59	58	73	Procter & Gamble	United States	Diversified	20,282	43,706	21,524	43,377	61,200[i]	98,000	52.8
53	97	77	98	Hitachi Ltd	Japan	Electrical & electronic equipment	20,189[h]	84,489	15,589	67,172	83,478[i]	339,572	23.9
54	36	43	29	GlaxoSmithKline Plc	United Kingdom	Pharmaceuticals	19,992[f]	35,821	29,320	31,899	58,471[g]	104,499	67.9
55	56	51	59	Pinault-Printemps Redoute SA	France	Retail	19,240[f]	31,474	13,936	25,894	53,871	108,423	54.9
56	104	5	82	Deutsche Telekom AG	Germany	Telecommunications	19,172[h]	120,589	309	24,397	78,146	255,969	15.9

Table 3.1 Continued

Ranking in 2002		Ranking in 2001		Corporation	Home economy	Industry[c]	Assets		Sales		Employment		TNI[b] (per cent)
Foreign assets	TNI[b]	Foreign assets	TNI[b]				Foreign	Total	Foreign[d]	Total	Foreign	Total	
57	24	47	10	Diageo Plc	United Kingdom	Beverages	18,526[f]	26,729	12,637	14,971	26,999[i]	38,955	74.3
58	2	55	2	Thomson Corporation	Canada	Media	18,125	18,542	7,735	7,915	41,300[i]	42,000	97.9
59	75	42	58	Bayer AG	Germany	Pharmaceuticals/chemicals	17,957	43,706	14,923	28,021	52,000	122,600	45.6
60	69	67	74	Matsushita Electric Industrial Co., Ltd	Japan	Electrical & electronic equipment	17,941[h]	65,028	32,373	60,694	166,873	288,324	46.3
61	3	71	4	Holcim AG	Switzerland	Construction materials	17,499	18,364	7,875	8,391	49,765	51,115	95.5
62	25	65	22	Volvo Group	Sweden	Motor vehicles	17,441	27,367	17,982[m]	19,234	45,740	71,160	73.8
63	87	70	76	Renault SA	France	Motor vehicles	17,441[f]	55,799	21,206	34,370	35,351[i]	132,351	39.9
64	61	73	66	Dow Chemical Company[l]	United States	Chemicals	17,386	39,562	16,350	27,609	24,725	49,959	50.9
65	27	59	32	Coca-Cola Company[n]	United States	Beverages	17,379[f]	24,501	13,089	19,353	45,100	56,000	73.0
66	100	64	88	Mitsubishi Corporation	Japan	Wholesale trade	17,285	67,213	15,613	109,296	12,182[i]	47,370	21.9
67	102	–	–	Telecom Italia	Italy	Telecommunications	17,251[h]	84,946	6,693	32,957	21,653[h]	106,620	20.3
68	80	50	28	National Grid Transco	United Kingdom	Energy	16,541	35,574	6,169	13,473	9,975	27,308	42.9
69	26	94	41	Lvmh Moët-Hennessy Louis Vuitton SA	France	Luxury goods	16,409[f]	22,451	9,965	12,006	33,996	53,812	73.1
70	47	68	37	Singtel Ltd.	Singapore	Telecommunications	15,775[f]	19,071	3,247	5,801	9,877	21,716	61.4
71	38	92	34	British American Tobacco Group	United Kingdom	Tobacco	15,592[f]	26,129	25,041[m]	37,117	60,107	85,819	65.7
72	15	78	14	Astrazeneca Plc	United Kingdom	Pharmaceuticals	14,796[f]	21,576	16,969	17,841	46,800	57,500	81.7
73	28	82	23	Nokia	Finland	Machinery and equipment	14,528[f]	24,454	28,058	28,392	30,099	52,714	71.8
74	105	95	100	Verizon Communications	United States	Telecommunications	14,239[f]	167,468	3,269	67,625	19,513	229,497	7.3
75	43	80	43	Bertelsmann	Germany	Media	14,108[i]	23,260	11,938	17,321	48,920	80,632	63.4
76	51	79	49	McDonald's Corporation	United States	Restaurant	13,771	23,971	8,951	15,406	237,269[i]	413,000	57.7
77	23	46	26	BHP Billiton Group	Australia	Mining & quarrying	13,753[f]	20,578	15,731	17,506	23,259[i]	34,801	74.5
78	14	56	12	Stora Enso Oyj	Finland	Paper	13,398	15,971	9,885	10,560	26,820	36,960	83.4
79	37	75	17	Du Pont (E.I.) De Nemours	United States	Chemicals	13,127	19,094	8,165	12,091	29,177	43,853	67.6
80	81	69	78	Scottish Power	United Kingdom	Electric utilities	13,040[h]	34,621	12,584[p]	24,006	29,755[i]	79,000	42.6
81	60	76	67	NTL Inc	United Kingdom	Telecommunications	12,971	19,903	3,992	7,559	6,268	15,490	52.8
82	1	61	1	Johnson & Johnson	United States	Pharmaceuticals	12,862[f]	13,041	3,265	3,265	14,922[i]	15,130	99.1
83	91	88	84	Thyssenkrupp AG	Germany	Metal and metal products	12,814[f]	40,556	13,843	36,298	34,218[i]	108,300	33.8
84	76	74	71	Alcatel	France	Machinery and equipment	12,783[f]	30,574	15,485	33,740	88,404	191,254	44.6
85	49	57	42	Duke Energy Corporation	United States	Electricity, gas and water	12,688	27,130	9,963	15,652	50,559	75,940	59.0
86	103	–	–	Cemex S.A.	Mexico	Construction materials	12,247	49,113	2,181	15,663	4,400	22,000	19.6
87	35	81	30	Canadian National Railway Company	Canada	Transportation	12,193[f]	21,738	4,366	7,036	17,568	26,752	67.9
88	82	–	–	Vattenfall	Sweden	Electricity, gas and water	12,050	24,030	2,384	6,110	6,879	22,114	41.9
89	71	83	19	Metro AG	Germany	Retail	11,821[f]	24,030	22,546	48,738	84,825	196,462	46.2
90	17	–	–	Reed Elsevier	United Kingdom/Netherlands	Publishing and printing	11,727	14,042	5,743	14,042	27,300	36,100	78.2
91	18	–	–	Alcan Inc	Canada	Metal and metal products	11,678[f]	17,538	11,541	12,540	38,000	50,000	76.8
92	96	90	92	Merck & Co	United States	Pharmaceuticals	11,388	47,561	8,300	51,800	28,600	77,300	25.7
93	88	86	16	Samsung Electronics Co., Ltd.	Republic of Korea	Electrical & electronic equipment	11,388	51,964	28,298	51,964	28,300[i]	82,400	38.5
94	20	–	–	Danone Groupe SA	France	Food & beverages	11,313	16,238	9,486	12,822	79,945	92,209	76.8
95	77	96	79	Alcoa	United States	Metal and metal products	11,109[f]	29,810	7,379	20,263	73,500	127,000	43.9
96	79	93	80	Abbott Laboratories	United States	Pharmaceuticals	11,073	24,259	6,687	17,685	33,000[i]	71,819	43.1
97	8	–	–	Publicis Groupe SA	France	Business services	11,021[f]	11,508	2,407	2,768	31,871	35,681	90.7
98	7	–	–	Interbrew SA[q]	Belgium	Beverages	10,665[f]	11,684	6,000	6,614	31,682[i]	35,044	90.8
99	4	–	–	CRH Plc	Ireland	Lumber and other building materials dealers	10,596[f]	11,066	9,535	10,210	47,335	49,889	94.7
100	74	53	62	Motorola Inc	United States	Machinery and equipment	10,433[f]	31,152	18,169	37,621	53,350	97,000	45.6

Source: UNCTAD/Erasmus University database (see UN 2004).

a All data are based on the companies' annual reports unless otherwise stated.
b TNI, or 'Transnationality Index', is calculated as the average of the following three ratios: foreign asset to total assets, foreign sales to total sales and foreign employment to total employment.
c Industry classification for companies follows the United States Standard Industrial Classification as used by the United States Securities and Exchange Commission (SEC).
d Foreign sales are based on the origin of the sales unless otherwise stated.
e Data for outside Northern Europe.
f In a number of cases companies reported only partial foreign assets. In these cases, the ratio of the partial foreign assets to the partial (total) assets was applied to total assets to calculate the total foreign assets. In all cases, the resulting figures have been sent for confirmation to the companies.
g Data for outside Europe.
h Foreign assets data are calculated by applying the share of both foreign sales in total sales and foreign employment in total employment to total assets.
i Data were obtained from the company as a response to an UNCTAD survey.
j Foreign employment data are calculated by applying the share of foreign assets in total assets and foreign sales in total sales to total employment.
k Foreign employment data are calculated by applying the share of foreign assets in total assets to total employment.
l Data for outside Germany and the United States.
m In a number of cases companies reported only partial region-specified sales. In these cases, the ratio of the partial foreign sales to the partial (total) sales was applied to total sales to calculate the total foreign sales. In all cases, the resulting figures have been sent for confirmation to the companies.
n Data for outside North America.
o Data for outside the Netherlands and the United Kingdom.
p Foreign sales are based on customer location.
q Data for outside Western Europe.

Note: The list includes non-financial TNCs only. In some companies, foreign investors may hold a minority share of more than 10 per cent.

This alternative view throws doubt on the extent to which firms will automatically realize benefits by spreading their wings further and further afield. Indeed, it suggests that MNCs tend to retain strong linkages with their country of origin and therefore continue to be influenced by the business system in this country to a greater extent than any other system. Moreover, it also suggests that in making foreign investments, multinationals favour locations which are near to their home country and only gradually reach out to countries further afield. One explanation for this is that offered by the 'Uppsala' model. Developed by academics at the University of Uppsala, the basic idea behind the model is that the internationalization of the firm is a gradual process that arises from a series of incremental decisions rather than a few grand leaps forward. This is because firms lack the knowledge and resources about operating in other business systems due to the 'psychic distance' between countries, which is defined as the 'factors preventing or disturbing the flows of information between firms and markets' (Johansson and Wiedersheim-Paul 1975). As firms gradually acquire knowledge about other systems they begin to enter new markets, initially through exporting via an independent representative, then through a sales subsidiary and finally through a full production facility. Crucially, psychic distance is highly correlated with geographic distance; while there are exceptions, generally speaking the business systems that are close to one another tend to have stronger commonalities in terms of the nature of the dominant institutions than those that are far apart. Thus this provides an explanation for why MNCs tend to hold the majority of their foreign investments in countries that neighbour their original base.

This picture of gradual internationalization fits the evidence. The UN has for many years published data on the extent to which the largest 100 MNCs in the world are internationalized. Combining the ratios of foreign sales to total sales, foreign assets to total assets and foreign employment to total employment, a 'Transnationality Index' (TNI) is constructed in an attempt to measure the degree to which these firms are concentrated in their home country. During the 1990s the TNI has risen slowly but steadily, from 51 in 1990 to 57 in 2002 (UN 2004). A different approach has been to measure the degree of financial internationalization. Hassel et al. (2003) have developed an index which captures three aspects of the ownership and control of firms: the extent of foreign shareholdings; the number of listings on foreign stock markets; and the adoption of international accounting standards. Applying this measure in Germany, they found great variability in the extent to which German MNCs have an internationalized ownership and accounting structure. While they do not produce time series data, it is highly likely that those MNCs that are the most internationalized in this respect, such as Bayer, Deutsche Telekom and Siemens, have become more internationalized in recent years.

Conclusion

This chapter has considered the process through which firms expand into different countries. It has contrasted various explanations for why firms internationalize, examining the role of access to, and control over, factors of production, the evolution of products, access to markets that would be difficult to serve through exporting, and the exploitation of a source of efficiency that is unique to the firm. The most widely used model that integrates various approaches – Dunning's eclectic paradigm – was then reviewed and a critique was provided. One key criticism of the paradigm is that it plays down the advantages from being multinational, suggesting that MNCs have a strong incentive to become genuinely globally spread. In fact, relatively few MNCs are global in orientation, partly because they have only partial knowledge about, and understanding of, business systems in different countries and consequently they tend to expand incrementally.

Some of the issues discussed here raise further questions. For instance, given the diversity of business systems in which MNCs operate, how do they organize themselves to manage units across these systems? Another important question relates to the transfer of expertise. As we have seen, deploying knowledge and expertise that is firm-specific can constitute one source of competitive advantage, so how is this transferred? Furthermore, in relation to the growing internationalization of the firm, the principal channel through which many MNCs increased their international spread in the late 1990s was through cross-border mergers and acquisitions. Such deals have very important HR implications. These issues are tackled in turn in the next three chapters.

Review questions

1 What are the relative strengths and weaknesses of the narrow and broad definitions of MNCs?

2 What are the limitations of the 'new international division of labour' as a device for explaining why companies internationalize?

3 Why do firms 'internalize' a competitive advantage and what are the implications of doing so for their role as employers?

4 Do you think that the next ten years will witness the emergence of genuinely 'global' firms?

Further reading

Dicken, P. (2003) *Global Shift: Reshaping the Global Economic Map in the 21st Century*, London: Sage, Chapter 7.

This chapter contains a concise summary of many theories of internationalization including a useful account of Dunning's eclectic paradigm.

Johansson, J. and Wiedersheim-Paul, F. (1975) 'The Internationalisation of the Firm: Four Swedish Cases', *Journal of Management Studies*, 12(3), 305–22.

This is the classic exposition of the Uppsala model that focuses on the way that firms expand into new countries in a series of incremental steps as they acquire new knowledge. It is also useful for Chapter 8 on knowledge management.

Marginson, P. (1994) 'Multinational Britain: Employment and Work in an Internationalised Economy', *Human Resource Management Journal*, 4(4), 63–80.

This article explores the various motivations for firms to expand overseas and links each of these to the implications of their approach as employers. The analysis is located in a discussion of the UK context.

UN (United Nations) (2004) *World Investment Report: The Shift Towards Services*, New York: UN.

The UN's *World Investment Report* is the most authoritative site for information on the scale of the operations controlled by MNCs. It is very useful for reference purposes.

References

Buckley, P. and Casson, M. (1976) *The Future of the Multinational Enterprise*, London: Macmillan.

Coase, R. (1937) 'The Nature of the Firm', *Economica*, 4, 386–405.

Corley, T. (1994) 'Britain's Overseas Investments in 1914 Revisited', *Business History*, 36(1), 71–88.

Cowling, K. and Sugden, R. (1987) *Transnational Monopoly Capitalism*, Brighton: Wheatsheaf.

Cyert, R. and March, J. (1963) *A Behavioural Theory of the Firm*, Englewood Cliffs, NJ: Prentice Hall.

Dicken, P. (2003) *Global Shift: Reshaping the Global Economic Map in the 21st Century*, London: Sage.

Doremus, P., Keller, W., Pauly, L. and Reich, S. (1998) *The Myth of the Global Corporation*, Princeton: Princeton University Press.

Dunning, J. (1993) *Multinational Enterprises and the Global Economy*, Reading, MA: Addison Wesley.

Ferner, A. (1997) 'Multinationals, "Relocation", and Employment in Europe' in J. Gual (ed.) *Job Creation: The Role of Labour Market Institutions*, London: Edward Elgar.

Financial Times (1997) 'Management: Flight Plan from Seattle: Philip Condit tells Michael Skapinker how he hopes to turn Boeing into a Global Company over 20 Years', 12 March.

Freeman, R. (1995) 'Does Globalization Threaten Low-Skilled Western Workers?' in J. Philpott (ed.) *Working for Full Employment*, London: Routledge.

Frobel, F., Heinrichs, J. and Kreye, O. (1980) *The New International Division of Labour*, Cambridge: Cambridge University Press.

Gereffi, G. (1999) 'International Trade and Industrial Upgrading in the Apparel Commodity Chain', *Journal of International Economics*, 48, 37–70.

Guardian (2002) 'New Balls Please', 24 June.

Hassel, A., Hopner, M., Kurdelbusch, A., Rehder, B. and Zugehor, R. (2003) 'Two Dimensions of the Internationalization of Firms', *Journal of Management Studies*, 40(3), 705–23.

Hirst, P. and Thompson, P. (1999) *Globalization in Question: The International Economy and the Possibilities of Governance*, 2nd edn, Cambridge: Polity Press.

Hymer, S. (1976) *The International Operations of National Firms: A Study of Foreign Direct Investment*, Cambridge, MA: MIT Press.

Johansson, J. and Wiedersheim-Paul, F. (1975) 'The Internationalisation of the Firm: Four Swedish Cases', *Journal of Management Studies*, 12(3), 305–22.

John, R., Ietto-Gillies, G., Cox, H. and Grimwade, N. (1997) *Global Business Strategy*, London: Thompson.

Jones, G. (2000) *Merchants to Multinationals: British Trading Companies in the Nineteenth and Twentieth Centuries*, Oxford: Oxford University Press.

Kaplinsky, R. (2000) 'Spreading the Gains from Globalisation: What Can Be Learned From Value Chain Analysis', IDS Working Paper No. 110, available at http://www.ids.ac.uk/ids/bookshop/wp/wp110.pdf

Legrain, P. (2002) *Open World: The Truth about Globalisation*, London: Abacus.

Marginson, P. (1994) 'Multinational Britain: Employment and Work in an Internationalised Economy', *Human Resource Management Journal*, 4(4) 63–80.

Mintzberg, H. (1987) 'Crafting Strategy', *Harvard Business Review*, July–August, 65–75.

Ohmae, K. (1990) *The Borderless World*, London: Collins.

Ohmae, K. (ed.) (1995) *The Evolving Global Economy: Making Sense of the New World Order*, Boston: Harvard Business Review Press.

Oliver, N. and Wilkinson, B. (1992) *The Japanization of British Industry: New Developments in the 1990s*, Oxford: Basil Blackwell.

Oman, C. (1994) *Globalisation and Regionalisation: the Challenge for Developing Countries*, Paris: OECD (Organization for Economic Cooperation and Development).

Reich, R. (1991) 'Who is Us?', *Harvard Business Review*, January–February, 53–64.

Royle, T. (2000) *Working for McDonald's in Europe*, London: Routledge.

Rugman, A. (1981) *Inside the Multinationals*, London: Croom Helm.

Ruigrok, W. and van Tulder, R. (1995) *The Logic of International Restructuring*, London: Routledge.

UN (United Nations) (2004) *World Investment Report: The Shift Towards Services*, New York: UN.

Vernon, R. (1966) 'International Investment and International Trade in the Product Cycle', *Quarterly Journal of Economics*, 80, 190–207.

Vernon, R. (1974) 'The Location of Economic Activity' in J. Dunning (ed) *Economic Analysis and the Multinational Enterprise*, London: Allen & Unwin.

Williamson, O. (1975) *Markets and Hierarchies*, New York: Free Press.

Chapter 4

International strategy and structure in multinational companies

Tony Edwards and Chris Rees

Key aims

This chapter has the following key aims:

- to consider the meanings of the term strategy and to understand the different 'schools' of strategy;
- to become familiar with the main influences on international strategy and some of the key work on various strategies that multinational companies follow;
- to understand the nature of the 'transnational' strategy and structure, and the problems in operationalizing it.

Introduction

This chapter examines the nature of strategy and structure in multinational companies (MNCs). It considers what is meant by 'strategy' in firms in general and then looks at its international dimension. We then consider the key aspects of strategy and structure in international as opposed to domestic firms. Having done this, the main part of the chapter reviews some of the best-known typologies in this field, spelling out the varying strategies that firms pursue, the strengths and weaknesses of these and their implications for international human resource management (IHRM). We go on to investigate power relations between different groups of organizational actors within MNCs and the implications of the embeddedness of MNCs in their country of origin for strategy.

What is strategy?

The term 'strategy' is one of the most widely used in business life: business schools run numerous courses in 'strategic management' or 'business strategy'; economists talk of the importance of a firm's 'strategic assets'; consultancy firms earn huge commissions from advising firms on the development of a 'strategy'; and managers routinely refer to their 'strategy' in all kinds of situations. In multinational firms it is commonplace to refer to international business strategy and, more specifically, a number of academics have written about the concept of 'strategic international human resource management' (SIHRM). Yet what does 'strategy' or 'strategic' actually mean?

The term originates from Greek where it referred to the role of a military commander. Hyman (1987) notes that in a military context, strategy relates to 'the planning and organization of an extended campaign: hence the contrast with tactics, meaning literally the arrangement of forces for a single battle'. The notion of long-term planning, Hyman argues, is a feature of many modern definitions of strategy; Chandler, for example, defines strategy as the 'determination of the basic long-term goals and objectives of an enterprise, and the adoption of courses of action and the allocation of the resources necessary for carrying out these goals' (Chandler 1962: 13).

While the emphasis on long-term planning is a feature of many definitions of strategy, there remains significant variation in the way the term is used. Whittington (2001) identifies four approaches to what strategy is that are fundamentally different from one another. In doing so, he identifies two 'dimensions' to strategy. The first of these relates to the 'outcomes' of strategy: is strategy solely about maximizing profits or is it pluralistic, about achieving a range of goals of which profit maximization is one? This dimension is depicted on the vertical axis of Figure 4.1. The second dimension, which appears on the horizontal axis, concerns the 'processes' of strategy, distinguishing between the view that it is the product of deliberate planning on the one hand and emergent, the result of accidents of history, compromises and inertia, on the other. These two dimensions give rise to four approaches, which are located in each of the quadrants in Figure 4.1 and are considered in turn.

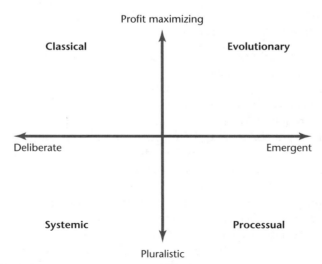

Figure 4.1 Whittington's generic perspectives on strategy
Source: based on Whittington (2001)

The classical approach

The conception of strategy used most widely in business textbooks is that which sees strategy making as a considered and rational process geared solely towards maximizing profits. From this perspective, it is assumed that senior managers systematically scour their environment, analyse the resulting information, design clear courses of action and implement these in a consistent way. Whittington (2001) cites Michael Porter's work as one of the best-known examples of this approach, while the work of Alfred Chandler (cited above) is also of the classical school. Chandler was concerned with the product diversification followed by many large firms in the early part of the twentieth century and argued that this 'strategy' demands a suitable structure. He saw the 'multidivisional' structure as the best suited to firms with multiple products since it allows senior management to concentrate on long-term planning and investments and devolve operational responsibility to managers in the divisions. Hence, the notion of 'structure follows strategy'.

The classical approach is surely too simplistic. It sees managers as omniscient, able to develop a clear understanding of their environment. In the international context there will be many aspects of social and economic life across countries about which even very senior managers are unaware or which they misunderstand. Moreover, the classical approach glosses over contradictions, tensions and conflicts within organizations, which are likely to be particularly acute in multinational firms given the diversity of the national business systems in which they operate. It is highly likely that organizational actors in different countries will have divergent priorities – not just to maximize profits – and will seek to advance these. Thus the classical approach has been criticized for envisaging too deliberate a conception of strategy and too narrow a range of possible outcomes.

The evolutionary approach

The second group of writers on strategy that Whittington identifies, the evolutionists, share with classicists the belief that maximizing profits will be the sole outcome of strategy. However, they differ in seeing the environment as too unpredictable for planning in the classical sense; senior managers have 'bounded rationality'. Rather than being the product of deliberate planning, strategies (and structures) emerge as much by accident and chance and the process of natural selection through competition in product and financial markets then delivers its judgement. Thus it is market forces rather than managerial planning that ensure that only the most profitable firms survive. The economist Oliver Williamson (1975) is cited as one of the key writers from this perspective: the strategy that firms should pursue is simply 'economy' – to keep costs under control and hope for the best!

The main criticism of this approach is that the process of natural selection through competition in markets is not always as strong as evolutionists assume. Many product markets are dominated by one or a small number of firms, and 'barriers to entry' ensure that this state of affairs can endure. Financial markets, too, will not always exert strong pressures for natural selection; in many countries there is not an active market for corporate control through takeovers, for example. The market power that many firms enjoy affords key organizational actors some scope to pursue goals other than solely maximizing profits. Arguably, this degree of freedom from market imperatives is particularly relevant for multinational firms since some of these have established dominant positions over international markets through branding, technological expertise or some other source of competitive advantage.

The processual approach

The way in which organizational actors seek to pursue their favoured goals is the key feature of the processual perspective. Processualists share with evolutionists a scepticism about the rational and objective model of strategy formation which underpins the classical school, but differ from them in that they have less faith that markets will ruthlessly weed out any firms with a 'sub-optimal' strategy. Organizations are viewed as being comprised of individuals and groups with a diverging range of interests, each of which seeks to advance their own aims. Thus processualists see strategy as emerging from a series of negotiations, compromises and bodges, the result of a political rather than a purely rational process. As a consequence, the outcomes of strategy can include goals other than just the maximization of profits. Cyert and March (1963) and, more recently, Henry Mintzberg (1987) are the most well-known authors from this school; the latter has written about the 'emergent' nature of strategy. For firms that straddle different business systems, the divergence of interests within organizations is likely to be of particular significance, creating fertile ground for political activity within MNCs.

The processual approach has been criticized less for what it says and more for what it ignores. A full understanding of how strategies are formed, so one critique goes, should focus on the 'embeddedness' of organizational actors in their social contexts. Thus the priorities and aims of individuals and groups are formed in the context of 'a network of social relations that may involve their families, the state, their professional and educational backgrounds, even their religion and ethnicity' (Whittington 2001). The importance of the social context is the starting point for the fourth approach.

The systemic approach

The systemic approach to strategy is less pessimistic than processualists about management's capacity to carry out plans and much more optimistic than evolutionists about the ability of firms to survive with a sub-optimal strategy. For this school, the structural context of the firm strongly shapes the nature of strategy; the objectives and practices of strategy are viewed as dependent on the particular social system in which strategy making takes place. An important contribution of the systemic perspective is to stress differences between countries in corporate strategies; if the social and economic systems differ from country to country, so too will the process and outcomes of strategies. As we saw in Chapter 2, Whitley (1999) has shown how national business systems vary and how firm behaviour varies accordingly, while Lane (1995) has used the similar concept of 'industrial order' to make the same point. Thus the structural context of a particular country will not automatically determine that firms must maximize profit, but rather there will be a range of possible outcomes.

One criticism of the systemic school, which is consistent with the processual perspective, is that divergences of interest within organizations do not receive enough weight. While the approach appears to be strong in its ability to account for national differences, it says less about conflicts of interest within organizations. As noted above, the extent to which organizational actors have divergent aims and priorities is likely to be greatest within multinational firms. As we will see later in the chapter, careful analysis of the conduct of employment relations in MNCs reveals the importance of political processes between layers of management in shaping the nature of employment practice.

Summary

Whittington's summary of the various perspectives concerning strategy is a helpful tool in helping us define and analyse the meaning of strategy in IHRM. The two dimensions of strategy – the outcomes and processes – are continuous; students of strategy can adopt intermediate positions along these. Consequently, the four perspectives should be seen as 'ideal types' with each containing a number of variants. We return to this typology later in the chapter in order to analyse some of the dominant writing on SIHRM. It is to a consideration of this literature that we now turn.

Key influences on strategy and structure in international firms

'The world's largest companies are in flux. New pressures have transformed the global competitive game, forcing these companies to rethink their traditional worldwide strategic approaches.' (Bartlett and Ghoshal 1998: 3)

So begins perhaps the best-known book on strategy in MNCs. Bartlett and Ghoshal (1998) identify three key forces on managers in international firms. First, by definition, multinationals operate in a variety of national cultures; the values, attitudes and tastes that people hold continue to differ across countries. This 'multiculturalism' that MNCs face can be seen as a force for *local differentiation*, defined as the need to be responsive to the local environment. Second, in many industries, firms have come under great pressure to achieve economies of scale at the international level. Ghoshal and Bartlett argue that technological developments in the production of consumer goods such as radios, televisions and watches have meant that scale is a key factor in shaping competitive success. Many firms have responded through developing internationally integrated production processes. Thus a second identifiable pressure on international strategy is the force of *global integration*. Third, international firms are under pressure to respond to rapidly evolving markets, with products and technologies having shorter life cycles. One way of responding to this is through seeking to link their international operations and transfer expertise across them. Consequently, a further pressure is for *worldwide innovation*.

These competing pressures on international strategy are evident in differing mixes from one sector to another and from one period to another. Bartlett and Ghoshal (1998) identify different organizational forms that are more or less suited to meeting these competing demands. Over the course of the twentieth century, the nature of these pressures has evolved, and the authors identify periods in which particular organizational forms were in evidence. (The issue of terminology can be confusing here; some use the term multinational or global firms in a generic sense while others attribute particular connotations to each. To avoid confusion, in this section we use terms in italics when there is a particular connotation.)

The *multinational* form

The period from 1920 to 1950 is what Bartlett and Ghoshal call the 'multi-domestic' era. In these decades the basis on which competition took place differed significantly from one country to another; consumer tastes varied and protectionism by governments was rife, resulting in pressures for local differentiation being dominant. The strategy and associated structure best suited to these conditions is what Bartlett and Ghoshal term the *multinational*, which they define as a collection of national companies that manage their local businesses with minimal direction from headquarters (HQ) – see Figure 4.2. This approach is very good at achieving national responsiveness and has much in common with Perlmutter's (1969) *polycentric* firm and Porter's (1986) *multi-domestic* approach.

What are the human resource (HR) implications of this organizational form? A key implication is that there is likely to be very little influence on personnel policy and practice in operating units from the corporate HQ; decision making on issues to do with employment practice are highly decentralized in this type of firm. Accordingly, there is unlikely to be a significant number of expatriate managers as decisions will

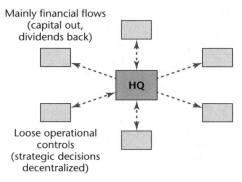

Figure 4.2 **The multinational firm: a decentralized federation**

be left to local managers. A further implication is that there will be little requirement for knowledge and expertise to be diffused across borders as all parts of the production or service provision process are carried out in one location.

The *global* form

The period from 1950 to 1980 was characterized by a number of developments: transport and communication costs began to fall in real terms; the minimum efficient scale fell, making economies of scale more important; and trade became less regulated. During these decades, US firms expanded their international operations, particularly into Europe. One important motivation for this growth in foreign direct investment (FDI) was to take advantage of the opportunity of realizing economies of scale through the creation of 'mini-replicas' of home country operations. Thus foreign units are closely modelled on domestic ones. Bartlett and Ghoshal (1998) identify this as the *global* approach, arguing that it produces standardized products in a highly cost-efficient way and is therefore good at achieving efficiency through global integration (see Figure 4.3). There are similarities here with Perlmutter's (1969) *ethnocentric* style in which home country values predominate and foreign subsidiaries are managed as a cultural extension of the parent.

In terms of HR, the replication of the home country approach means that there is some implementation of home country practices in foreign subsidiaries, particularly in relation to work organization. Thus there will be a distinctive parent company approach to human resource management (HRM). One way in which this occurs is through the use of expatriates as 'enforcers' of HQ policy and, consequently, firms with the global strategy use a number of people on international assignments. One concern that some observers in host countries have expressed about this sort of multinational is that the replication of home country operations means foreign plants tend towards being 'screwdriver' operations; that is, the high-tech operations such as research and development are retained in the country of origin and the subsidiaries are characterized by routine assembly work with a high proportion of jobs being low skill in nature.

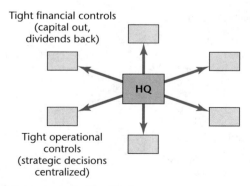

Tight financial controls (capital out, dividends back)

HQ

Tight operational controls (strategic decisions centralized)

Figure 4.3 The global firm: a centralized hub

The *international* form

The period from 1950 to 1980 was also characterized by a further pressure on MNCs, namely the importance of spreading innovations across the firm. Bartlett and Ghoshal describe the way in which many international organizations responded to this pressure: 'The strategy of a third group of companies is based primarily on transferring and adapting the parent company's knowledge or expertise to foreign markets' (1998: 17). These firms, termed *international*, are less centralized than the *global* firms since local management is able to vary the nature of the products or services to the national market, but are much more centralized than the *multinational* firms (see Figure 4.4). This type of firm does not correspond directly to any of Perlmutter's types of multinational, but can be seen as a hybrid of the *polycentric* and *ethnocentric* firms.

The implementation of centrally developed innovations has implications for HR in foreign subsidiaries. Managers at local level are responsible for implementing such innovations and, more generally, for ensuring that the expertise and knowledge transferred from the centre is harnessed and deployed. Thus while they are unlikely to be subject to the same degree of control that subsidiaries of *global* firms are subject to, there will certainly be requirements from the HQ with which they must comply. As a consequence, the role of managers on international assignments differs from the role of those in *global* firms: they are less likely to be 'enforcers' of corporate policy, and more likely to be key points of contact between HQ and subsidiaries and facilitators of the transfer of expertise and knowledge from the centre. Finally, concerns over the limited contribution of foreign-owned firms to the local economy are likely to be less acute in relation to *international* firms. Indeed, this group of firms may be seen as a mechanism through which new technologies and practices can be spread across borders, although some may harbour concerns that these innovations are developed abroad.

The *transnational* firm

Bartlett and Ghoshal argue that over the last two decades or so, developments in technology and markets have meant that more and more industries are characterized

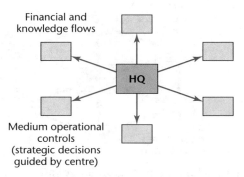

Figure 4.4 **The international firm: a co-ordinated federation**

by the simultaneous pressures to be locally responsive, achieve efficiency through global scale and to diffuse innovations across their sites. Thus while each of the three types of firm identified above may be adept at responding to one of these pressures, none of these types allow a firm to respond to all of them. The authors present a fourth type of firm, the *transnational*, as offering the 'solution' to these competing pressures (see Figure 4.5). There is a clear prescriptive element in this respect: they see the *transnational* form as 'necessary for every company that operates in an international environment' (Bartlett and Ghoshal 1998: 20).

The *transnational* form involves the creation of an integrated network of sites, each of which possesses a distinct role. The plants within the network have differentiated roles in that their brief is to specialize in a particular part of the production or service provision process. As a result of this differentiation, the plants have some freedom to respond to local factors and so meet the pressure for local differentiation. The integration of international operations through the network also provides for scale efficiencies to be realized at the global level, thereby achieving a degree of global integration. In addition, the diffusion of knowledge and expertise within the interdependent network affords scope for worldwide learning. Bartlett and Ghoshal argue that in this way the *transnational* can respond to all three of the key pressures on firms operating across borders. This organizational form has much in common with Perlmutter's *geocentric* firm, while the idea of an integrated network also features strongly in Hedlund's (1986) notion of the *heterarchical* firm.

The *transnational* form has a number of important implications for HR. The practices in place at plant level will in part reflect innovations in other parts of the network, not just those in the home country as in *global* and *international* firms. Moreover, a key part of the facilitation of the network is a cadre of managers roaming from site to site, serving as the 'glue' holding the firm together and bringing about the exchange of knowledge and expertise. What distinguishes a *transnational* in this respect is that the international assignees will not originate only from the parent company. For those concerned about the role of a subsidiary in contributing to the

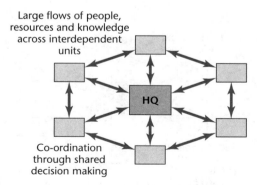

Large flows of people, resources and knowledge across interdependent units

HQ

Co-ordination through shared decision making

Figure 4.5 The transnational firm: an integrated network

development of a host country, the *transnational* promises much since each plant will be accorded a specialist role.

The idea of the *transnational* organizational form is very important for IHRM. Indeed, the concept of an integrated network is central to much recent writing in this field. Dowling et al. (1999) note that a number of authors advocate the network form and claim that a growing number of MNCs are moving towards it. The networked multinational, they argue, is characterized by five dimensions: 'delegation of decision making authority to appropriate units and levels; geographical dispersion of key functions across units in different countries; de-layering of organizational levels; de-bureaucratization of formal procedures; and differentiation of work, responsibility, and authority across the networked subsidiaries' (1999: 50).

The idea of a network features strongly, if implicitly, in the 'integrative framework of strategic international human resource management' proposed by Schuler et al. (1993). They assert that MNCs

> 'are realising that every possible source of competitive advantage must be identified and uti-lized. And as they are searching, particularly firms pursuing total quality management, they are realising that a systematic approach to developing human resource policies and practices may, in fact, give competitive advantage ... A major goal of MNEs is facilitating learning and the transfer of this learning across units.' (1993: 427)

Later in the article they argue that HR policies can assist in the integration of the business: 'In doing so they must be consistent with the needs of the business to achieve competitiveness, be flexible and facilitate the transfer of learning across units' (1993: 431).

The international network is a key feature of one of the organisational forms found by Bird et al. (1998) among Japanese MNCs. They distinguish four types of MNC: the 'exportive' in which there is a strong home country imprint; the 'adaptive' in which firms adapt to local practice; the 'closed hybrid' which consists of a grudg-ing acceptance by managers at the HQ that the parent company approach needs to be partially adapted to local conditions; and the 'open hybrid' which is based on an openness to adopting innovations from wherever they come. It is the last of these approaches that fits the networked or transnational firm since it is based on the shar-ing of innovations across the firm. The authors note that the open hybrid is the most expensive to operate, but they stress its advantages:

● It is the form in which affiliates have the 'highest organisational learning capabil-ity, particularly with regard to the diffusion of ideas' (1998: 167);
● It offers a high degree of integration and coordination through a 'high diffusion of HRM innovations in a multilateral fashion' (1998: 168);
● It is highly flexible because these firms are able to 'borrow ideas from three sources – local firms, parent company, or other affiliates' (1998: 169).

The clear implication is that this is an organizational form that MNCs can benefit from adopting.

How useful is the concept of an integrated network in general and Bartlett and Ghoshal's *transnational* solution in particular? Are MNCs all finding it a 'necessary' element to operating internationally, as the authors claim? And is it a key part of the 'solution' to managing across borders? One way of assessing these questions is to return to the various conceptions of strategy outlined in the first part of this chapter. Bartlett and Ghoshal's work, along with much of the IHRM writing, has a strong classical element. It is not wholly classical – they are sensitive to some of the complexities of strategy making – but it is undoubtedly influenced by the classical tradition. We consider in turn the two main objections to this tradition: first, that it sees strategy making as a deliberate, rational process; and, second, that it pays too little attention to the 'embeddedness' of strategy in its social context.

The importance of organizational politics in multinational companies

Many writers on strategy, as we saw above, stress the importance of the micro-politics of organizations in the development of strategies. Firms are comprised of a range of groups each with their own goals and priorities. Moreover, each of these groups, to a greater or lesser extent, possesses some resource of value to others in the organization that they can use to advance their own agenda. In this way, strategies emerge as a result of bargaining and compromise between groups of organizational actors and, consequently, strategies tend to evolve slowly. Bartlett and Ghoshal's approach plays down the role of organizational politics since there is relatively little attention devoted to how different groups may have different aims and seek to advance them. Yet, recent research into the internal workings of MNCs and the development of 'strategies' in IHRM has revealed the importance of micro-political processes.

One obvious source of tension within MNCs is between managers at the corporate HQ and those in a subsidiary in a different country. Those in the former group may seek to advance their own position by developing global policies, while those in the latter may strive to maximize their autonomy. As an example, Edwards et al. (1993) provide evidence that the French subsidiary of a UK multinational was able to resist orders from the centre concerning the timing of a redundancy programme. In doing so, managers at the profitable French plant knew that the French market was important to the wider company and that corporate managers were dependent on them to serve this market. They knew that the HQ could not sack them and send expatriates to take over: few of the UK senior managers spoke French and their understanding of the French legal and institutional context was poor. A related source of tension between groups of managers within MNCs is between expatriate and indigenous managers. The former may seek to establish themselves as key players in the operation to which they have been sent, while the latter may resent their presence. Broad's (1994) study of a Japanese MNC in the UK revealed the way in which UK managers formed informal networks from which Japanese expatriates were excluded. These networks served to share information from rumours and gossip in the plant and this information was kept from the Japanese, whose limitations in English meant they could not access the information directly.

While the managers of units within a multinational possess some sources of power, those at the HQ do so too, of course. The most obvious resource that the HQ controls is the funds for new investment. Research in the car industry has revealed the way in which corporate managers systematically compare the performance of their sites in different countries, and use these comparisons to exert pressure on actors at plant level to improve quality and costs. Commonly, these comparisons are tied to investment decisions so that, in effect, the plants compete against one another for the allocation of investment. In this way, the centre is able to exert growing influence over working practices at plant level (Mueller and Purcell 1992; Martinez and Weston 1994). Case study research has revealed similar processes to be in evidence in MNCs in the pharmaceutical and food sectors (Frenkel 1994; Coller 1996). Sisson et al. (2003) review evidence from a range of sources to show that such 'benchmarking' among MNCs is now widespread, particularly within regions such as Europe.

Managers at the corporate HQ also have the ability to use the promotion of unit managers to senior positions within the company as a source of power. The pay and promotion prospects of unit managers can be tied in part to their willingness to be active participants in the network, both through inputting practices into it and through adopting practices that originated elsewhere. Once again, case study evidence has revealed the importance of this source of power in facilitating the multilateral diffusion of practices across borders: those managers promoted or given international assignments take with them knowledge of practices that have operated successfully in one part of the organization and spread this to other operations (Coller and Marginson, 1998; Edwards 1998).

ABB: a test case of the transnational strategy

Perhaps the most widely cited example of a transnational company is ABB. This firm was formed through a merger between ASEA of Sweden and Brown Boveri of Switzerland and operates in a range of sectors, from industrial power to transport equipment. Since 1987 the firm has engaged in a string of acquisitions across the world so that it has a significant presence in the Americas and Asia as well as in Europe. Using the Transnationality Index that we came across in Chapter 3, the United Nations (UN) ranks ABB as the fifth most internationalized of the largest 100 MNCs in the world (UN 2004). The former CEO, Percy Barnevik, was renowned for supposedly creating a radically new approach to managing international operations. In his own words, ABB is simultaneously 'global and local, big and small, radically decentralised but with central control'.

Bartlett and Ghoshal describe ABB as a 'classic transnational organisation' (1998: 259). A key element of this orientation, they argue, is the devolution of responsibility for operating performance to the managers of the 1,300 business units; accompanying this was the creation of a very small corporate HQ employing just 150 people. This was a key part of

Barnevik's stated aim of putting 'individual initiative and personal responsibility … at the heart of the company's philosophy' (quoted in Bartlett and Ghoshal 1997: 30–31). When there was a problem in one of the units, senior management of the company would 'reach down to the front lines', but their objective was to 'help rather than interfere' (Bartlett and Ghoshal 1997: 189).

Coupled with devolution to operating units was an attempt to 'encourage global teamwork and co-operation between companies and countries' (Bartlett and Ghoshal 1998: 265) – the creation of the network that is central to the transnational form. Bartlett and Ghoshal ascribe the firm's success in doing so to two key aspects of its approach. The first was creating 'stretch', defined as the setting of ambitious goals that are to be achieved through a set of common values. In ABB a 'policy bible' containing the firm's key principles was distributed across the organization with the intention that this would appeal to individuals' own values and induce them to channel their creative capabilities for the good of the organization. The second was to establish trust, which the authors argue is 'vital to the development and nurturing of the collaborative behaviour that drives effective revitalisation' (1998: 268–69). Apparently, an emphasis on employee involvement in decision making, and a structure comprising numerous cross-national boards and teams, allowed a sense of 'organisational fairness and equity' to develop.

But is the process of managing international operations as straightforward as this? The interpretation that Bartlett and Ghoshal put on the workings of ABB has been challenged by Belanger et al. (1999). On the basis of a detailed case study of the firm across several countries, Belanger and his colleagues argue that Bartlett and Ghoshal too readily accept top managers' views of how ABB operates and, consequently, downplay the tensions and contradictions that are a key feature of organizational life in MNCs.

In particular, the way in which 'learning' takes place is highly politicized, resting on competitive relations between plants that create pressure on local actors to adopt practices from other plants. Senior managers possess a number of sources of power that enable them to pressurize local management into adopting practices from other parts of the group. Perhaps most obvious among these is the management of the career patterns of managers in the company: those that are seen as obstructive to the working of the network face the prospect of not progressing to more senior posts or, in some cases, being sacked. Further, business area management controls capital investment decisions, and in some divisions also allocates orders from customers. Those plants that have been good 'corporate citizens' can be rewarded with new investment and orders, while those seen as problematic can be punished. These resources, Belanger et al. argue, have enabled the centre to exert a growing influence over the plants.

Equally, however, local actors can draw on their embeddedness in local environments to shape the extent of corporate influence and the way it takes place. One instance is the performance of the plants. A system known as the 'ABB Olympics' seeks to assess and rank each plant in terms of a range of aspects of performance, such as costs, quality and throughput times. Those plants that perform well in these league tables are able to use this to increase their autonomy from business area and corporate management; the profits that their plant contributes to the group can be seen as a source of power. A further illustration of the political activity in which local actors can engage was the creation of an uneasy alliance between some local managers and the union in the Hull plant in Canada in response to the parent company's plans for restructuring (Belanger et al., 2003: 482–83).

The evidence presented by Belanger and his colleagues illustrates the importance of political activity within MNCs. The establishment of an integrated network of plants collaborating with one another as envisaged by Bartlett and Ghoshal is likely to be a contested, rather than a straightforward, process. Indeed, the resources controlled by actors at plant level may be used to block the operation of a network as local actors seek to preserve their autonomy. In sum, where a multinational seeks to integrate its operations into a network, the way this operates is likely to be governed more by power relations between different groups than by values and trust.

For further details on contrasting perspectives on ABB see:
Bartlett, C. and Ghoshal, S. (1998) *Managing Across Borders: The Transnational Solution*, London: Hutchinson, Chapter 12.
Belanger, J., Berggren, C., Bjorkman, T. and Kohler, C. (1999) *Being Local Worldwide: ABB and the Challenge of Global Management*, Ithaca, NY: Cornell University Press.

Case study question: *What does the case of ABB tell us about the ease with which MNCs can establish collaborative networking between their sites?*

The case of ABB together with wider research evidence, some of which was cited above, demonstrates the importance of micro-political processes in MNCs. This has implications for the 'integrated network' that appears to be favoured by many writers on IHRM. Such networks do not always operate in a harmonious, coherent way; rather they are political constellations of groups of organizational actors whose aims and priorities are often divergent. The extent to which organizational actors are able to achieve their aims when these aims diverge from those of other groups is determined in part by the resources they have at their disposal. As Kristensen and Zeitlin put it, the multinational is 'a battleground among subsidiaries representing and mobilizing their own regional capabilities and national institutional means against the rest' (2001: 192). Hence, divergences of interest within a multinational are worked out through the exercising of power relations.

The implications of recognizing the contested nature of international networks are significant. In particular, some groups of actors or units within a multinational may be able to block the diffusion of practices; they may seek to resist pressure to adopt a practice that originated elsewhere and may also be reluctant to input information on new practices into the network for fear of this undermining their competitive position. This is not to deny that multilateral sharing of information can and does occur through 'networking' within MNCs, but it should be emphasized that senior managers will often need to overcome resistance to this process and will need to use the resources at their disposal to bring this about. Edwards et al. (1999: 290) argue that in many MNCs diffusion occurs through networking between plants, with this underpinned by HQ control over investment decisions and the prospects of plant managers. They use the term 'networking within hierarchy' to describe this process.

As we have implied, the way that micro-political processes within international networks of managers operate is shaped in part by the linkages between organizational actors and their environment. The sources of power that actors possess is in many cases a product of their environment, as demonstrated by the example of the French subsidiary of the UK MNC described above. Thus these actors are not detached, calculating individuals but rather are embedded in their environment, which we now explore in more depth.

The embeddedness of strategy

A key aspect of the systemic perspective that we examined earlier in this chapter is the notion that a firm's strategy is firmly embedded in its particular economic and social context. This idea is something that Bartlett and Ghoshal discuss in identifying a firm's 'administrative heritage', which they define as a company's 'existing organizational capabilities as shaped by various historical and structural factors' (1998: 39). This administrative heritage, which the authors argue makes firms to some extent 'captives of their past', stems from some factors internal to the organization, such as the role of the founders and leaders and the influence of the history of the firm. It also stems from the impact of national culture which gives a firm 'a way of doing things' and shapes the values and behaviour of senior management.

However, the systemic perspective demands a much fuller appreciation of the way a multinational's 'country of origin' is important in shaping the way it operates at the international level; this approach is quite clear that there is much more to a national influence than simply 'culture'. The role of the family can be a crucial factor in creating variations between countries in the way firms operate. For instance, Whitley (1991) describes the importance of the family unit in Taiwan in creating a set of entrepreneurial small and medium-sized firms, many of which are linked together through wider family networks. The role of the state, too, varies significantly from country to country. In relation to France, Whittington and Meyer show how 'the state, elitist educational institutions, and the great financial and industrial enterprises have long been closely interlinked' (2000: 95). The nature of financial institutions also varies from country to country, with the bank-centred system of industrial finance in Germany, in which investment banks hold significant stakes in firms and have close relationships with their managements, contrasting with the market-centred system in the UK and the USA, where shareholdings are dispersed across a range of institutions and individuals and relationships between these and senior managers are distant. As we argued in Chapter 2, the notion of culture is clearly inadequate to capture these national differences as it neglects important institutional factors, leading many to prefer the term 'national business system'.

The distinctiveness of national business systems, despite current talk of globalization, matters because most MNCs remain firmly rooted in their original country. As we have seen in earlier chapters, most MNCs remain disproportionately focused on the home country across a number of dimensions. Even those MNCs that are highly internationalized in terms of sales are concentrated in their home country in other respects. Ericsson, for example, has over three-quarters of its voting shares held by Swedish financial institutions. This concentration of key activities in the home base means that the centre has a disproportionate influence on strategy formulation. Hence, international strategies continue to reflect a significant 'country of origin' effect. For instance, a considerable body of evidence concerned with employment practice in the foreign subsidiaries of US MNCs indicates that they have been particularly hostile to trade unions and systems of collective representation, and have sought to implement HRM practices such as performance-related pay and employee involvement programmes (Edwards and Ferner 2002). Japanese MNCs are also influenced by their domestic business system when they operate outside Japan, one aspect of which is the use of a high number of expatriates to oversee the adoption in their subsidiaries of some Japanese-style forms of work organization, such as team-based working and just-in-time production (Whitley et al. 2003). While there is less evidence for MNCs of other nationalities, the embeddedness of MNCs appears to create a detectable influence from the country of origin (see Ferner 1997 for a review).

Crucially, MNCs may not easily be able to shed this effect; whether they like it or not, they may find that they cannot leave their 'national baggage', as Ferner and Quintanilla (1998) put it, at home. In this respect, Bartlett and Ghoshal (1998), in arguing that MNCs will move towards a transnational orientation over time, appear to overestimate the ease with which MNCs can shed their 'administrative heritage'. For instance, recent research into US MNCs in Europe has revealed that the financial system in the USA is an important factor in shaping the way they manage their international workforces (Edwards and Ferner 2001). In particular, the active market for corporate control and the emphasis on quarterly financial reporting has subjected many US MNCs to 'short-term' pressures. Given their embeddedness in this financial system, it is not easy for them to free themselves from this influence.

AutoPower – shaking off its US origins?

The way in which MNCs are embedded in their country of origin, and the way that this continues to shape the way they operate, is clearly illustrated by the case of AutoPower. This firm originated in the Midwest of the USA in the early part of the last century and rapidly became the major employer in a relatively small town. The founding family of the company took an active part in the management process, playing a key role in setting the style and values that characterized the organization. AutoPower is now a multinational employing approximately 30,000 people in 12 different countries.

The influence of the founding family has been significant. Management style in the firm's original location in the Midwest was paternalistic: pay and conditions tended to be favourable compared with other firms; job security was high (until recently); and employees were provided with a range of fringe benefits. To some extent, this paternalism has been carried over into the firm's international operations, particularly those in UK. The influence of the founding family can also be discerned in relation to its dealings with trade unions. Unlike many US firms that grew in the first half of the twentieth century, AutoPower did not experience bitter disputes with trade unions. The attitude of the founding family was to allow employees to decide whether to join a union and, if sufficient numbers did so, management would recognize and negotiate with the union. This relatively relaxed, constructive approach to dealing with unions also shows up at the international level. A third area where the original owners were influential was in relation to 'diversity'. As long ago as the 1960s, senior managers were emphasizing the importance of having the composition of the workforce in all their locations reflect the ethnic composition of the community. Latterly, the firm has introduced a global policy stipulating that the benefits accruing to the wives and husbands of employees should also accrue to unmarried and same-sex partners.

As well as the style and values that were strongly influenced by the founding family, there have also been a number of global policies that have been devised in the company's HQ. One particular example is the system of teamworking. This was the product of a team of engineers and managers and involved the creation of teams of operators working flexibly within a cell. This model of organizing production was gradually diffused to all of the firm's international operations. All in all, it is clear that the nature of IHRM in AutoPower strongly reflects its US roots.

This 'ethnocentric' approach has been challenged recently by those in AutoPower's international operations. At a meeting of HR managers from across the company, the presentation of a new corporate initiative for a global policy on the repatriation of employees who have been on international assignments provoked a mini-rebellion from HR managers outside the USA. Many complained that the development of the firm's international policies did not reflect the diversity of the company's operations, and that if it claimed to be a genuinely internationalized firm with international markets as its main growth area then its policies should reflect this.

This protest was acted upon by senior HR managers who appeared to recognize the legitimacy of the concerns. One response was to commission the HR managers from India and the UK to devise a 'template' outlining the way in which international HR policies would be devised in the future, allowing substantial input from HR people in the subsidiaries. Another indication that the firm was striving to be less US-focused was the appointment of a Chinese-American, who had been head of HR in China, as head of international HR. In addition, and perhaps most significantly, responsibility for the development of a new performance management system was given to a UK HR manager who is on an assignment in the corporate HQ and is leading an international team of eight, only two of whom are American. This is seen by many in the company as a marked departure from the way HR policies had been developed in the past, and a pointer to how they will be developed in the future.

However, the legacy of the firm's embeddedness in the USA has not proven so easy to shake off. Over the last few years the company has become more subject to pressures from outside financial institutions. A consequence is that senior managers have begun to attach more importance to quarterly budgets and financial targets, since this is how they are assessed by the institutions. When a downturn hit the product market in 2000, the immediate response was to slash costs, an element of which was to greatly reduce the travel budget. This meant that convening meetings of the team members was impossible and the leader of the initiative has worked from the corporate HQ with just one other person also based there. Moreover, the interest in the experiment by senior HR people has waned as they have become focused on managing the redundancies that are accompanying the downturn.

The upshot has been that the much celebrated shift towards subsidiary input into decision making has had a great deal less impact than had been envisaged. Three years after their creation, the templates guiding the development of international HR policies are not in evidence, and policies appear to be created and rolled out from the HQ in the way that they had previously. International networking in AutoPower proved to be quite difficult to realize.

For more details, see:
Edwards, T., Almond, P., Clark, I., Colling, T. and Ferner, A. (2005) 'Reverse Diffusion in US Multinationals: Barriers from the American Business System', *Journal of Management Studies*, 42(6), 1261–86.

Case study question: *Is it inevitable that MNCs will encounter difficulties in trying to make their approach less ethnocentric?*

While the country of origin effect is an important influence on HRM in MNCs that is not always easy to shed, neither is it set in stone. As multinationals mature and become more internationalized, the influence of the country of origin may diminish. Indeed, evidence from studies of German, French and Swedish MNCs indicates that many have adopted structures and practices traditionally associated with Anglo-Saxon MNCs, such as international product divisions with devolved responsibilities, share options and performance-related pay (e.g. Ferner and Quintanilla 1998; Mtar 2001; Hayden and Edwards 2001). (This is considered in more depth in Chapter 5.) These developments have eroded the influence of the country of origin, but they have not eradicated it; the MNCs in these studies still reflect their national origins in significant ways.

Conclusion

The changing nature of the external environment within which MNCs operate has had important implications for the internal organization of multinationals: differences persist in the nature of the national systems in which MNCs are located; globalization has presented opportunities for firms to realize more fully economies of scale at the international level; and rapidly evolving technologies and shorter product life cycles have created pressures on firms to engage in innovation and learning across their operations. As we have seen, much writing on strategy in MNCs in general, and SIHRM in particular, urges firms to create a flexible network in which units have differentiated roles and share expertise with one another and in which responsibility and authority are diffused. Indeed, there is some evidence that many firms are clearly seeking to instigate networks that have the capability of transferring knowledge and expertise across the firm.

However, in two important respects the popular vision of networks appears to be flawed. First, as is the case for all organizations, MNCs are political animals in which there are multiple interest groups, each of which will seek to use the resources at their disposal to advance their own interests. This does not mean that networking will not occur, but it does imply that senior management merely establishing the formal architecture of a network will not be sufficient on its own. Rather, the precise nature of networking will depend on the exercising of power. Second, networks transcend a range of distinctive business systems and are disproportionately influenced by the original home base of the multinational. In this way, even MNCs that are characterized by a highly internationalized network of operations continue to exhibit a country of origin effect.

It is evident that one of the key consequences of the strategies and structures that MNCs adopt is the transfer of practices across their operations. The extent, process and substance of transfer will all be shaped by the nature of these strategies and structures. This is the subject of the following chapter.

Review questions

1 What are the relative strengths and weaknesses of the classical, evolutionary, processual and systemic perspectives on strategy?

2 Why do Bartlett and Ghoshal see the 'transnational' form as the solution to managing across borders?

3 What sources of power do managers in the operating units of MNCs commonly hold?

4 What are the sources of the country of origin effect in MNCs?

Further reading

Broad, G. (1994) 'The Managerial Limits to Japanisation: A Case Study', *Human Resource Management Journal*, 4(3), 52–69.

A fascinating case study on the way in which attempts by a Japanese multinational to transfer 'high involvement management' practices to its UK operations were thwarted by the concern of UK managers to preserve their traditional role.

Edwards, T. and Ferner, A. (2002) 'The Renewed "American Challenge": A Framework for Understanding Employment Practice in US MNCs', *Industrial Relations Journal*, 33(2), 94–111.

This article presents a framework of 'four key influences' that shape the way that MNCs manage their international workforces and then reviews the evidence concerned with US MNCs.

Ferner, A. (1997) 'MNCs and the Country of Origin Effect', *Human Resource Management Journal*, 7(1), 19–37.

This is the most widely cited paper that discusses the country of origin effect. It does so through a discussion of the variety of ways in which MNCs are embedded in their original home base.

Mueller, F. and Purcell, J. (1992) 'The Europeanisation of Manufacturing and the Decentralisation of Bargaining: Multinational Management Strategies in the European Automobile Industry', *International Journal of Human Resource Management*, 3(1), 15–34.

This article examines the way that the HQs of MNCs in the automotive sector routinely use 'reward and punish' tactics in their investment decisions so as to ensure that subsidiaries comply with their demands.

References

Bartlett, C. and Ghoshal, S. (1998) *Managing Across Borders: The Transnational Solution*, Boston: Harvard Business School Press.

Belanger, J., Berggren, C., Bjorkman, T. and Kohler, C. (1999) *Being Local Worldwide: ABB and the Challenge of Global Management*, Ithaca, NY: Cornell University Press.

Belanger, J., Giles, A. and Grenier, J. (2003) 'Patterns of Corporate Influence in the Host Country: A Study of ABB in Canada', *International Journal of Human Resource Management*, 14(3), 469–85.

Bird, A., Taylor, S. and Beechler, S. (1998) 'A Typology of International Human Resource Management in Japanese Multinational Corporations: Organizational Implications', *Human Resource Management*, 37(2), 159–72.

Broad, G. (1994) 'The Managerial Limits to Japanisation: A Case Study', *Human Resource Management Journal*, 4(3), 52–69.

Chandler, A. (1962) *Strategy and Structure: Chapters in the History of the American Industrial Enterprise*, Cambridge, MA: MIT Press.

Coller, X. (1996) 'Managing Flexibility in the Food Industry: A Cross-National Comparative Case Study of European Multinational Companies', *European Journal of Industrial Relations*, 2(2), 153–72.

Coller, X. and Marginson, P. (1998) 'Transnational Management Influence Over Changing Employment Practices: A Case Study', *Industrial Relations Journal*, 29(1), 4–17.

Cyert, R. and March, J. (1963) *A Behavioural Theory of the Firm*, Englewood Cliffs, NJ: Prentice Hall.

Dowling, P., Welch, D. and Schuler, R. (1999) *International Human Resource Management: Managing People in a Multinational Context*, Cincinnati: South Western.

Edwards, P., Ferner, A. and Sisson, K. (1993) 'People and the Process of Management in the Multinational Company', *Warwick Papers in Industrial Relations*, No. 43, Coventry: Industrial Relations Research Unit (IRRU).

Edwards, T. (1998) 'Multinationals and the Process of Reverse Diffusion', *International Journal of Human Resource Management*, 9(4), 696–709.

Edwards, T. and Ferner, A. (2001) 'Wall Street, Short-termism and the Management of Labour in US Multinationals', paper presented to conference 'Multinational Enterprises: Embedded Organisations, Transnational Federations or Global Learning Communities', Warwick, 6–8 September, 1–21.

Edwards, T. and Ferner, A. (2002) 'The Renewed "American Challenge": A Framework for Understanding Employment Practice in US MNCs', *Industrial Relations Journal*, 33(2), 94–111.

Edwards, T., Rees, C. and Coller, X. (1999) Structure, Politics and the Diffusion of Practices in Multinational Companies', *European Journal of Industrial Relations*, 5(3), 286–306.

Edwards, T., Almond, P., Clark, I., Colling, T. and Ferner, A. (2005) 'Reverse Diffusion in US Multinationals: Barriers from the American Business System', *Journal of Management Studies*, 42(6), 1261–86.

Ferner, A. (1997) 'MNCs and the Country of Origin Effect', *Human Resource Management Journal*, 7(1), 19–37.

Ferner, A. and Quintanilla, J. (1998) 'Multinationals, National Business Systems and HRM: The Enduring Influence of National Identity or a Process of "Anglo-Saxonisation"', *International Journal of Human Resource Management*, 9(4), 710–31.

Frenkel, S. (1994) 'Patterns of Workplace Relations in the Global Corporation: Towards Convergence?' in J. Belanger, P. Edwards, and L. Haiven (eds) *Workplace Industrial Relations and the Global Challenge*, Ithaca, NY: ILR Press.

Ghoshal, S. and Bartlett, C. (1997) *The Individualized Corporation: A Fundamentally New Approach to Management*, London: Heinemann.

Hayden, A. and Edwards, T. (2001) 'The Erosion of the Country of Origin Effect: A Case Study of a Swedish Multinational Company', *Relations Industrielles*, 56(1), 116–40.

Hedlund, G. (1986) 'The Hypermodern MNC', *Human Resource Management*, 25, Spring, 9–36.

Hyman, R. (1987) 'Strategy or Structure? Capital, Labour and Control', *Work, Employment and Society*, 1(1), 25–56.

Kristensen, P. and Zeitlin, J. (2001) 'The Making of a Global Firm: Local Pathways to Multinational Enterprise' in G. Morgan, P. Kristensen, and R. Whitley (eds) *The Multinational Firm: Organizing Across Institutional and National Divides*, Oxford: Oxford University Press.

Lane, C. (1995) *Industry and Society in Europe: Stability and Change in Britain, Germany and France*, Aldershot: Edward Elgar.

Martinez, M. and Weston, S. (1994) 'New Management Practices in a Multinational Corporation: the Restructuring of Worker Representation and Rights', *Industrial Relations Journal*, 25(2), 110–21.

Mintzberg, H. (1987) 'Crafting Strategy', *Harvard Business Review*, July–August, 65–75.

Mtar, M. (2001) 'French Multinationals' International Strategy', Ph.D. thesis, University of Warwick.

Mueller, F. and Purcell, J. (1992) 'The Europeanisation of Manufacturing and the Decentralisation of Bargaining: Multinational Management Strategies in the European Automobile Industry', *International Journal of Human Resource Management*, 3(1), 15–34.

Perlmutter, H. (1969) 'The Tortuous Evolution of the Multinational Company', *Columbia Journal of World Business*, January–February, 9–18.

Porter, M. (1986) *Competition in Global Industries*, Boston: Harvard Business School Press.

Schuler, R., Dowling, P. and De Cieri, H. (1993) 'An Integrative Framework of Strategic Human Resource Management', *Journal of Management*, 19(2), 419–59.

Sisson, K., Arrowsmith, J. and Marginson, P. (2003) 'All Benchmarkers Now? Benchmarking and the "Europeanisation" of Industrial Relations', *Industrial Relations Journal*, 34(1), 15–31.

UN (United Nations) (2004) *World Investment Report: The Shift Towards Service*, New York: UN.

Whitley, R. (1991) 'The Social Construction of Business Systems in East Asia', *Organization Studies*, 12(1), 1–28.

Whitley, R. (1999) *The Social Structuring of Business Systems*, Oxford: Oxford University Press.

Whitley, R., Morgan, G., Kelly, W. and Sharpe, D. (2003) 'The Changing Japanese Multinational: Application, Adaptation and Learning in Car Manufacturing and Financial Services', *Journal of Management Studies*, 40(3), 643–72.

Whittington, R. (2001) *What is Strategy – and Does it Matter?* London: Routledge.

Whittington, R. and Meyer, M. (2000) *The European Corporation: Strategy, Structure and Social Science*, Oxford: Oxford University Press.

Williamson, O. (1975) *Markets and Hierarchies*, New York: Free Press.

Part Two

The diffusion of international human resource management in multinational companies

Chapter 5

The transfer of human resource practices in multinational companies

Tony Edwards and Chris Rees

Key aims

This chapter has the following key aims:

- to examine the features of the host environment that inhibit diffusion or require that practices be altered to fit local conditions;

- to consider the possible directions in which practices flow across a multinational company;

- to investigate the organizational characteristics of multinational companies that promote or hinder diffusion;

- to examine the processes of diffusion, focusing on the relationships between actors at different levels of the organization.

Introduction

A central theme so far in this book has been the opportunities and challenges that differences between national business systems pose for multinational companies (MNCs). For instance, in Chapter 4 we saw how these differences have led to a number of organizational forms being adopted by MNCs, none of which provide a completely satisfactory structure with which to deal with the various pressures that they face. One key element of many of these organizational forms, particularly the much-vaunted 'transnational' structure, is the emphasis placed on the diffusion of practices across a firm's international operations.

In this chapter we consider four specific aspects of the diffusion of practices. First, are some employment practices more readily diffused than others? And in what ways are practices amended to fit a new environment? Second, from which national business systems are practices likely to emerge? And, relatedly, which units are likely to be the recipients of diffusion? Third, are some MNCs more likely to transfer practices across their operations than others? What are the characteristics of MNCs that predispose them towards engaging in the transfer of practices? Fourth, through what mechanisms and channels are practices transferred? How do various organizational groups persuade and cajole others into accepting the transfer of practices?

In addressing these questions, we view differences in national business systems as at the same time enabling and constraining the transfer of practices. These differences are a prerequisite for transfer since without the diversity of practices that result from distinct national systems there would be little incentive to look to diffuse practices across sites in different countries. There is a parallel here with Gray's (2002) argument that globalization is brought about by variations in national forms of organizing economic activity; if it were not for these variations, Gray argues, there would be little incentive for economic activity to cross borders. Differences between national systems also constrain the scope for diffusion, however, since they act as a force for MNCs to adapt to local conditions. In this way, 'varieties of capitalism' simultaneously create and close off scope for diffusion. Moreover, diffusion within MNCs can be one force for change in national business systems themselves since the introduction of new practices can be subsequently diffused throughout a host economy. These themes run throughout the chapter.

The diffusability of employment practices

Throughout this book we emphasize the 'embeddedness' of employment practices in particular national contexts. That is, practices originate and become established in a given legal, institutional, political and cultural context. To some extent, they are dependent on this context and cannot operate in a different environment. The extent of this dependence varies from one area of human resource management (HRM) to another; in other words, the 'diffusability' of some practices is higher than that of others.

The ease with which a practice can be diffused across a multinational is shaped partly by its dependence on 'supportive and distinctive extra-firm structures' (Hayden and Edwards 2001). These extra-firm structures can underpin the operation of a practice that would not function in their absence, and include such things as legal obligations on firms, institutions in the labour market and the values, expectations and assumptions that characterize employment relations in a particular country. All employment practices are, of course, to some extent dependent on these legal, institutional and cultural 'props'. The ease with which a practice can operate outside its original home environment – in other words, the extent to which a practice is 'diffusable' – is determined in part by its dependence on these props.

One area of human resource (HR) in which these props are central is training. Some aspects of a firm's approach to training are dependent on supportive institutions, an example of which is the 'dual' system of training in Germany. The role of the colleges, training bodies, employers' associations and trade unions in administering, monitoring and certifying the system provides crucial support for firm-level practices; without these supports, firms are unlikely to find it feasible to operate such practices. Consistent with this, Dickmann's (1999, 2003) study of German multinationals showed that they have been constrained in their attempts to introduce

German-style vocational training into their UK subsidiaries because the UK economy lacks the 'broader business institutions necessary to underpin particular practices' (Edwards and Ferner 2004). Of course, some training practices, particularly those that are employer-led, are more diffusable in that they are less dependent on a set of supportive institutions.

The distinctive characteristics of the national business systems in which MNCs operate can also limit the diffusion of practices in a further way. Managers at the headquarters (HQ) of a multinational may seek to operate a practice in a number of countries but might be prevented from doing so by the legal, institutional or cultural 'constraints' of the country to which the practice is directed. Organizational actors in the recipient unit may try to resist its introduction and may use their legal powers, rights provided by institutions or appeals to the importance of local 'custom and practice' in order to thwart the HQ's plans. In this sense, some practices may not be diffusable because of the constraints posed by the nature of the host business system.

One area where such constraints are notable is in relation to practices designed to secure greater numerical flexibility, which may have to be adapted to fit the prevailing labour market traditions in each country. For instance, the tendency to use part-time workers is dependent on there being a pool of workers willing to accept such jobs. Other forms of numerical flexibility, such as annualized hours, temporary contracts and changes in shift patterns, have to be negotiated with employee representatives and a multinational's ability to transfer them across its sites is clearly influenced by the attitudes and strength of organized labour in the countries in which it operates. However, these constraints clearly do not close off scope for diffusion altogether, particularly to those countries that are relatively deregulated and where unions are weak, and some evidence points towards MNCs being able to use their power to lever change in shift patterns (Martinez and Weston 1994).

In many instances, therefore, these constraints are partial rather than absolute: that is, managers at the HQ may be able to diffuse a practice, but it may need to be altered so that it can be implemented in the new business system. As Edwards and Ferner (2004) put it, a 'practice may not operate in the same fashion in the recipient as in the donor unit but, rather, may undergo *transmutation* as actors in the recipient seek to adapt it to pre-existing models of behaviour, assumptions and power relations'. Thus the formal substance of a practice may be diffused but the operation of this practice may differ between countries.

One illustration of this process is the adoption by many US-based automotive firms of Japanese forms of work organization over the last decade or so. Maccoby (1997) argues that in implementing these practices, US companies have tended to place less emphasis on the devolution of responsibility to teams of operators which characterizes the nature of teams in Japan, and instead have retained the distinctive supervisory relationships characteristic of their US-based operations. In a similar vein, Broad (1994) has shown how the UK managers in a UK transplant of a Japanese multinational resisted moves by the parent firm to shift responsibility for quality to teams of operators, preferring to retain the right to take decisions in this area themselves. Broad (1994: 58) argues that this reflects the 'traditional obsession of British managers with prerogative and secrecy'. In both cases, practices were diffused, but took on a different form in the new environment.

Differences between national business systems, therefore, limit the diffusability of employment practices, a theme we return to in more detail in Chapter 8 on knowledge management. This is partly because practices are dependent on the 'props' present in the system in which they originate, and partly because their introduction to other countries is subject to the 'constraints' posed by the recipient systems. We have also seen how practices can be modified, or 'transmuted', to fit the new environment. However, it is the differences between national business systems that also create the potential for cross-border diffusion in the first instance, as MNCs seek to gain a competitive advantage through transferring practices perceived as delivering improved performance across their operations. Are the practices that they seek to diffuse drawn from a wide range of countries, or are some countries likely to be the main 'suppliers' of such practices?

The hierarchy of economies and the diffusion of practices

In Chapter 4, we reviewed the evidence concerned with the influence of a multinational's original home base, arguing that there is a detectable 'country of origin' effect. That is, the ways that MNCs manage their international workforces are disproportionately influenced by their roots in the domestic business system. However, we also noted that this effect is not set in stone but rather evolves over time; in other words, it provides a strong influence on the decisions of actors in key positions, but leaves open the scope to draw on elements of other business systems in which the multinational operates. The way in which they seek to do so is shaped in part by the relative strength of these various national economies. A strongly performing economy is likely to attract attention from actors in senior positions in firms in other countries, creating a dynamic of emulation at the international level. This idea has been developed by Smith and Meiksins (1995) who argue that the international economy contains a hierarchy of national economies. Those countries whose economies have performed strongly are at or near the top of this hierarchy, and this 'dominant' position creates interest among actors in other countries in emulating the practices associated with these 'dominant' economies. A part of this interest can be in HRM, such as methods of work organization, systems of pay and appraisal, or practices in relation to employee development.

One example of these 'dominance effects' is the role of the US economy in the post-war period. The USA emerged from the Second World War with its military and political position enhanced and its economy relatively unscathed. Thus US firms were in a strong position to grow in international markets, and did so partly through exporting and partly through engaging in foreign direct investment (FDI). The consistent growth in the US economy and the strength of many big US firms during the 1950s and 1960s led many to refer to the 'Pax Americana'. During this time, elements of the US business system were diffused – albeit often in amended form – to other countries. Hence, US MNCs were active in diffusing practices such as 'Fordist' forms of work organization, approaches to negotiating such as productivity bargaining, and formalized and standardized procedures in many areas of HRM (see Edwards and Ferner 2002 for a review). During this time, therefore, the USA served as a key source from which practices could be diffused.

During the 1980s, however, the performance of the US economy began to falter, and the perception that the US economy was dominant began to evaporate. Indeed, a whole raft of books, articles and reports were concerned with 'American economic decline'. The Japanese economy at this time was enjoying a sustained boom and large Japanese firms came to dominate many sectors. In automotive, for instance, firms such as Nissan, Honda and Toyota set up production sites in Europe and North America and increased their market share in these areas at the expense of indigenous firms. In electronics and financial services, similarly, Japanese firms grew in international markets. The strength of the Japanese economy led to great interest in 'lean production' – a set of practices including worker involvement in teams or groups that had responsibility for product quality and were designed to minimize waste and throughput time. The way in which these practices were implemented in the foreign subsidiaries of Japanese MNCs, and their adoption by Western firms, became the subject of much attention (e.g. Oliver and Wilkinson 1992). Similarly, the German economy had recovered from post-war devastation to a status of one of the world's leading economies. German firms made great strides into international markets, particularly in sectors such as chemicals and engineering. Their success was widely ascribed to the operation of 'diversified quality production', a strategy of serving niche markets with high-quality, customized products involving highly skilled workers (Streeck 1992). Towards the end of the twentieth century and in the first few years of the twenty-first, the situation changed once again, with the new conventional wisdom perceiving the Japanese and German economies to be 'sclerotic' and unable to deal with the challenges of globalization while the US economy has regained its hegemony owing to its flexibility.

The idea of the 'dominance' of particular economies shaping the direction in which practices flow across borders has much intuitive appeal. However, in its simplest form, the dominance effects argument is open to two main criticisms. The first is that it rests on an assumption that rates of economic growth differ markedly between the major developed countries and that these differences reflect divergences in forms of economic organization. In fact, differences in rates of economic growth are not as great as is often assumed. For instance, while the 1970s and 1980s were seen as a period of economic decline by many in the US, the growth rate of the US economy was actually higher than that of Germany, Sweden and the UK. Only compared with the Japanese economy was there a marked difference and even this was less significant than is often supposed (see Table 5.1).

Moreover, even where there are significant differences in economic performance between countries, only part of this can be explained by divergences in forms of economic organization. Some of the explanation lies in the process of 'convergence and catch-up'. Economists such as Krugman (1994) argue that the rapid growth of the

Table 5.1 Real GDP growth 1961–98

	Average annual percentage change		
	1961–73	*1974–84*	*1985–98*
US	4.0	2.2	2.9
UK	3.1	1.3	2.4
Germany	4.3	1.8	2.2
Sweden	4.2	1.8	1.5
Japan	9.7	3.3	2.6

Source: Hall and Soskice, 2001: 20. By permission of Oxford University Press

German and Japanese economies in the post-war period was due to the process of recovery following the decimation of their industrial bases during the war. Similarly, the remarkable growth rates in the 'Asian Tiger' economies up until 1997 was due, according to Krugman, to one-off gains from using existing resources more intensively. Many academics, notably Abramovitz (1994), have criticized Krugman for overstating his case, arguing that the 'social capability' of a national economy – defined as the ability to take advantage of technological opportunities – is an important determinant of its performance. Nonetheless, even Abramovitz accepts that differences between economic growth rates across nations can only be partially explained by this social capability.

A second criticism is that the notion of dominance risks reifying a national economy. That is, the incentive to emulate elements of a particular national business system creates a danger of implying that a country is characterized by a homogeneous set of structures and practices that operate across firms, and that companies in other countries can identify and seek to emulate these. This is, of course, not the case. We saw in Chapter 1 how national business systems contain important intranational variations. In the USA, for instance, managerial style in HRM differs markedly across the economy: between those developed in the 'sun-belt' states such as Texas and those in the 'rust-belt' cities such as Detroit; between 'welfare capitalist' and 'New Deal unionist' firms; between 'high-tech' firms embedded in areas such as the Research Triangle in North Carolina and the 'low-road' firms that compete on the basis of cost minimization. Thus two sets of managers in, say, the UK which both seek to emulate 'American' practice may have in mind quite different things.

These two points question the usefulness of the dominance effects approach. However, despite these criticisms, it retains some utility. We see dominance effects as a way of categorizing commonly held views by managers – as a management ideology, in other words. Viewed in this light, the notion of dominance captures the interest that exists among organizational actors, particularly senior managers, in emulating practices which originate in other countries. One particularly useful aspect to the concept is in helping to distinguish different forms of diffusion. In MNCs from 'dominant' or 'hegemonic' countries this effect is likely to reinforce the country of origin effect, giving rise to 'forward' diffusion in which practices are diffused from home to host countries. Thus, as we have seen, during the 1980s and 1990s much attention centred on the way in which Japanese MNCs exported some practices characteristic of the Japanese business system, notably 'lean production' and its associated employment practices, and the subsequent adoption by local firms of such practices (e.g. Whitley et al. 2003).

Conversely, in MNCs that are not from 'dominant' or 'hegemonic' countries, diffusion can occur in the opposite direction; this has been termed 'reverse diffusion' and involves practices originating in foreign subsidiaries and subsequently being adopted in the domestic operations. This is particularly likely in MNCs in which key actors perceive their country of origin to exhibit weaknesses and other countries in which the firm has subsidiaries to have 'solutions' to these weaknesses. Where this is the case, these actors can use their foreign subsidiaries' practices in 'dominant' systems, such as the USA. Alternatively, they can look to other countries that have been open to the influence of these dominant systems through high levels of FDI, such as the UK, to learn about new practices.

The shift in the conventional wisdom towards a view that the deregulated, market-based Anglo-Saxon economies have provided a stronger platform for growth than the institutionalized economies of continental Europe and Japan is associated with a growing body of evidence that demonstrates that many continental European firms have adopted structures and practices characteristic of the USA and the UK. For instance, many German MNCs have used their UK subsidiaries as sources of new practices: moving towards adopting performance-related bonuses for managers; identifying and developing 'high potentials' as a way of creating a cadre of 'international' managers; issuing an explicit set of values often referring to the importance of 'shareholder value'; and implementing 'business re-engineering' programmes (Ferner and Quintanilla 1998; Ferner and Varul 2000; Tempel 2001). Similar moves towards the adoption of Anglo-Saxon practices appear to be evident in French MNCs (Mtar 2001) and in the following case study of a Swedish multinational.

Swedco

The issue of the direction in which practices are diffused across a multinational's operations is particularly interesting in the case of Swedish MNCs. The small size of the domestic economy has meant that in order to grow, many firms became multinational at a relatively early stage in their development and subsequently became highly internationalized. Thus, compared to MNCs of most other nationalities, the domestic operations of Swedish MNCs comprise a small proportion of their total sales, assets and employment. Moreover, the nature of the Swedish system of employment relations – the highly centralized system of bargaining, the strength of union organization and high level of union density, the structures promoting co-determination and the tradition of co-operation between management and labour – raises the issue of how such a distinctive system influences a firm's approach at the international level.

Swedco is a highly internationalized firm producing high-tech manufactured goods. It employs tens of thousands of employees, approximately half of whom are outside Sweden, while 95 per cent of the firm's sales are made abroad. The case study involved research into the Swedish, Belgian and UK parts of the firm and sought to address the influence of the Swedish business system over employment relations in the firm and the role of diffusion in reinforcing or eroding this influence.

There is evidence of a distinctively Swedish element to the management of the firm's international workforce, something which shows up in a number of respects. First, in an international context, Swedish workers operate with relatively little direct supervision; indeed, there is no direct translation in Swedish for the word 'supervisor' (Anderson 1995: 72). Managers at the HQ of Swedco describe attempts to spread a 'democratic' approach to decision making throughout the organization. As one put it: 'I want to let my guys loose. I don't want to control them and stand behind their backs. This is typically Swedish, to be a coach.' Second, Hedlund (1981) argues that in Swedish firms it is acceptable to 'bypass the hierarchy' in that organizational actors do not feel constrained by formal authority relationships. One of the UK managers claims that 'the company encourages a Nordic approach to openness. Swedes think nothing of jumping the hierarchy to put forward their ideas.' Third, the tradition of seeking agreement through compromise and negotiation – what Anderson (1995: 76) refers to as the 'quest for accord' – is also evident at the international level in Swedco. One of the Belgian managers argues that this style clashes with what he was used to: 'You cannot always agree or compromise. Sometimes you have to say no. In Belgium, we raise our voices, we explode sometimes. But Sweden says this is something you must not do.' Fourth, the Swedishness of the firm shows up in the stability of ownership. Unlike most big US and UK firms which have fluid ownership structures involving a large number of shareholders each holding a small proportion of the total stock, Swedco has three large shareholders who control nearly three-quarters of the voting shares and have done so for many years. Consequently, in an industry characterized by significant restructuring in recent years, involving a number of 'hostile' takeovers, Swedco has expanded internationally by 'greenfield' investments and through a series of collaborative joint ventures and 'friendly' acquisitions.

This evidence of a country of origin effect is very significant; even in a highly internationalized MNC the nature of the domestic business system shapes the management of the international workforce. However, the evidence also indicates that the country of origin effect is being eroded as senior management seeks to draw on practices originating in other business systems. This process is evident in two areas. The first of these is the development of 'flexible' or 'variable' compensation systems. An international policy working group involving HR managers from across Swedco has recently introduced bonus systems that are linked to individual and company performance. In addition, for very senior managers there is a 'Short Term Incentive Plan' that rewards the achievement of immediate goals. Moreover, four years ago all employees were given the right to subscribe to a convertible debenture scheme, and about 40 per cent of staff worldwide have taken this up. Perhaps most significantly, an individual performance-related pay scheme, in which an employee's performance is assessed against specified targets, affects all employees across the group worldwide. These variable forms of compensation appear to have much in common with practices that have become popular in the USA and UK during the last two decades.

A similar process of adopting 'Anglo-Saxon' style practices is evident in relation to management development. In recent years the HQ has made a concerted effort to develop a cadre of managers from across the company. Subsidiaries have been encouraged to submit suggestions for individuals who should be considered for promotion to positions elsewhere in the firm, a group known as 'high potentials'. The identification of such 'high potentials' as part of an international cadre of managers is, according to Ferner and Varul (1999: 34), a common trait of UK and US MNCs. More generally, in Swedco the UK operations appear to have been particularly influential in the formation of policy on management development. The manager of the firm's 'Management Institute' indicated that the UK subsidiary and UK universities have been influential in developing policy on training programmes and management development:

> 'When I am developing a training programme for managers, I always include the UK. Firstly, it ensures I get the language right but, secondly, there are a lot of good training and management development ideas in the UK that I would like to benefit from. I always bring someone in from the UK site onto the team. We are also developing links with the UK universities such as Cranfield and LSE.'

In sum, while there is evidence of the country of origin being influential over the way Swedco manages its international workforce, there is also evidence that senior managers in the firm perceive the USA and the UK as providing practices in the area of performance management and management development that are seen as desirable. This process of 'reverse diffusion' can be seen as constituting an erosion of the country of origin effect.

For further details, see:
Hayden, A. and Edwards, T. (2001) 'The Erosion of the Country of Origin Effect: A Case Study of a Swedish Multinational Company', *Relations Industrielles/Industrial Relations*, 56(1), 116–40.

Case study question: *Why do you think that senior management in Swedco looked to the US and the UK for new practices in these areas as opposed to, say, Germany or Japan?*

The evidence on the diffusion of practices, whether forward or reverse, raises again the issue of how practices operate differently in the recipient unit. We saw above how the transfer of Japanese-style practices led to changes in the way they operated as they were assimilated into a different institutional context and were interpreted differently by organizational actors at plant level. Similarly, Ferner and Varul note that the evidence concerning the reverse diffusion of Anglo-Saxon practices in German MNCs demonstrates that they were 'being assimilated in such a way as to change their significance' (2000: 137). For example, the Anglo-Saxon emphasis on 'shareholder value' takes on a quite different meaning where shareholders are 'insiders' such as investment banks and families that have had close ties to the firm for a long period. Consequently, the authors argue that 'international "borrowings" from different business systems do not necessarily prefigure homogenisation and convergence among national models' (2000: 137).

Thus the hierarchy of economies creates a dynamic that shapes the direction and form of cross-national diffusion within MNCs, and this has the potential to lead to

significant changes in the nature of HRM in subsidiary units. Given this, it is pertinent to ask whether all MNCs will engage in cross-national diffusion, or whether it is
likely to be found in certain types of MNC. Do the characteristics of MNCs, such as
the way they are structured and organize their systems of international production
and service provision, affect the incidence of diffusion?

Corporate characteristics that promote diffusion

The literature on the diffusion of practices within MNCs has produced some mixed,
even contradictory, findings. For instance, some studies have shown broad similarities between the employment practices of foreign and local firms in a given national
economy, while others have revealed marked differences that are attributed to diffusion from the centre of MNCs. Perhaps the best illustration of this is in Ireland where
the work of Turner et al. (2001), which suggests that foreign-owned firms have
adapted their approach to fit in with the Irish system of industrial relations, contrasts
sharply with other research by Geary and Roche (2001), which claims that the
employment practices in foreign firms differ significantly from those in Irish firms.
How can we make sense of such contrasting findings? One approach is to recognize
that not all MNCs will look to diffuse practices across borders but that some key organizational features make it more or less likely to happen. We adopt this approach,
focusing on key features of MNCs and their environment that give rise to what we
term the 'facilitating characteristics' that promote diffusion.

The first of these is a feature of MNCs of which we have already stressed the
importance – the country of origin. As argued above, MNCs from countries that have
been economically successful have an incentive to diffuse those practices that are
seen as having contributed to this success to their foreign subsidiaries. Hence, this
promotes forward diffusion. Thus there is evidence that many US MNCs transferred
'Taylorist' forms of work organization and formalized payment systems to their
European subsidiaries in the post-war period (e.g. Kogut 1991). More recent evidence
reveals that many US MNCs transfer practices designed to increase the 'diversity' of
their workforces, such as quotas on women in management positions and equal treatment for homosexual employees, apparently in the belief that such diversity policies
form a part of the firm's competitive advantage (Ferner et al. 2004). Similarly, in the
1980s many Japanese MNCs sought to implement 'lean production' and its associated HR practices, such as teamworking and employee involvement in maintaining
quality standards, in their European and North American subsidiaries. We can see
this as testifying to the way that a country of origin gives senior management the
incentive to diffuse practices from their home base. MNCs originating in countries
lower down the hierarchy within the international economy, on the other hand, also
have the incentive to diffuse practices across borders, but in their case practices that
are diffused are more likely to come from their foreign subsidiaries.

A second structural factor that affects the extent to which diffusion occurs is the
nature of a multinational's international management structures. In particular, a

structure that is based on national units, which Porter (1986) calls 'multi-domestic', limits the contact between actors in different countries, thereby constraining the scope for diffusion. In contrast, a structure that is based around international product divisions, which Porter terms 'global', deepens the linkages across borders within the firm. In the personnel/HR function, Marginson et al. (1995) have shown that MNCs with a global structure are more likely to have regular meetings of personnel managers across their sites, to have an international personnel policy committee and to promote the mobility of staff through international assignments. All of these structures have the potential to act as mechanisms through which diffusion occurs. Thus, while a multi-domestic structure limits the scope for the cross-border diffusion of practices, a global structure promotes such diffusion. Many MNCs have moved towards adopting a matrix structure in which international divisions coexist with regional aspects to the structure, normally based around continents. This type of matrix deepens international managerial structures along two dimensions, providing significant scope for the transfer of practices.

Third, the method by which an MNC has grown can have a significant impact upon the likelihood that it will engage in cross-border diffusion. In general, the constraints facing management at the HQ in transferring practices to foreign subsidiaries are greater where the subsidiaries have been acquired. This is because the firm inherits a pre-existing set of practices that may prove difficult to change, and also because the act of acquisition itself may create suspicion and resistance among employees in the acquired units. In firms established through investments on 'greenfield sites', on the other hand, management has greater freedom to introduce practices in operation in other countries. Accordingly, the evidence suggests that MNCs that seek to implement a set of practices that diverge from 'norms' in a particular country grow mainly through greenfield investments in order to facilitate this diffusion.

So far, the discussion has centred on the assumption that senior managers in MNCs will want to diffuse practices across borders but will be constrained from doing so. The country of origin shapes their inclination to diffuse practices across borders, and the firm's structure and method of growth affect the strength of the constraints they face. However, there is a further factor that is arguably more important in shaping whether senior managers in MNCs want to diffuse practices in the first place: the extent to which processes of production and service provision are integrated on an international basis. Some MNCs are not integrated internationally in that their units in different countries operate independently of one another and perform quite different functions. This is the case in conglomerates where there is a high degree of diversification. The lack of integration limits the potential for diffusion since technologies and patterns of work organization differ significantly.

Where international integration does take place it can take two primary forms, each of which has quite different implications for the diffusion of practices. One of these is *standardized production* in which units in different countries perform very similar operations. Examples of this are the large consultancy firms such as Accenture and the firms providing IT services such as IBM, which are increasingly offering standardized services in different countries. In this case, the HQ has a clear incentive to diffuse practices across its operations in order to apply lessons learned in one unit to other units in the company and to develop common policies to encourage the mobility of staff across their operations. Hamill (1984) shows how standardized production is associated with centralization of decision making on industrial relations issues within MNCs, which is likely to result in the transfer of practices, and Marginson et al. (1995) argue that it promotes the development of common policy approaches to labour management.

The other variant of international integration is *segmented production*, which involves units in different countries performing distinct functions within a corporate production process. The way in which this form of integration occurs has been described by Gereffi (1999), who has developed the term 'global commodity chains' (GCCs). Gereffi distinguishes between two types of GCC. First, 'producer-driven commodity chains' are 'those in which large, usually transnational, manufacturers play the central roles in coordinating production networks' (see Figure 5.1). These are characteristic of capital and technology intensive industries such as cars and computers. The way in which the Japanese motor firms have broken up the production of a car so that different parts of the process take place in different Asian countries is an example. Second, 'buyer-driven commodity chains' are 'those industries in which large retailers, designers and trading companies play the pivotal role in setting up decentralised production networks in a variety of exporting countries' (see Figure 5.2). This type of chain is found in labour-intensive consumer goods sectors such as clothing, housewares and consumer electronics. Firms like Nike and The Gap have established this sort of chain. The key aspect of both types of chain is that the incentive to diffuse practices is limited; since the functions performed in different countries are quite distinct from one another, there will be little advantage in developing standardized employment practices.

The way in which segmented production leads to quite different patterns of employment relations in different parts of a production process is evident in studies of Japanese MNCs. For instance, Wilkinson et al. (2001) studied the plants in Malaysia and Japan of two producer-driven chains controlled by Japanese firms and found that the differences in the organization of work and related HR practices 'largely reflected the position of the plants in the international division of labour'

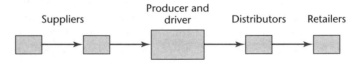

Figure 5.1 Producer-driven chains

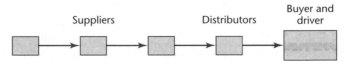

Figure 5.2 Buyer-driven chains

(2001: 686). The Malaysian plants were characterized by: short cycle times; a highly disciplined, cheap and largely unskilled workforce; workers performing a repetitive, narrow range of tasks; little in the way of employee development; and the absence of union representation. In the Japanese plants, in contrast: there was more research and development (R&D) and more 'experimental' work; the workforce was better qualified and better paid; workers were engaged in process improvements and in 'multitasking'; training involved induction followed by six-month on- and off-the-job programmes; and the plants were all unionized. These differences by plant meant that the scope for diffusion of 'best practice' was mainly confined to the technical aspects of the organization of production. While there are obviously some HR consequences of transfer in this area, the cross-border diffusion of practices did not extend to areas such as recruitment, payment systems, development or representation.

This approach to identifying the factors that promote or hinder the transfer of practices has been 'structural' in that it has focused on key organizational characteristics and highlighted the way in which the cross-border transfer of practices is more likely to occur in some MNCs than in others. The country of origin, the way a multinational is structured, the way in which it established its foreign subsidiaries and the nature of production integration all either constrain or facilitate the transfer of practices across borders. Hence, this approach is potentially more productive than those that group all MNCs together and compare them with local firms. However, one weakness in the approach is that it risks implying that outcomes, in this case the diffusion of practices, follow unproblematically from environmental and organizational factors. As argued in Chapter 4, we should not assume that actors in the HQ can exert control over their international operations; rather, the authority of the HQ is commonly contested and challenged. Thus the structural approach should be complemented with attention to the way in which organizational actors at a variety of levels exercise choices, which may either encourage or obstruct diffusion. This 'political approach' highlights the ways in which organizational actors can draw on their sources of power in order to further their own interests, and it is revealing about the processes through which diffusion takes place.

The process of diffusion

Management at the HQ of a multinational may see clear benefits in transferring practices across their international operations. In order to facilitate the transfer of knowledge and expertise across its sites, the HQ may establish a range of formal mechanisms that bring together actors from different parts of the multinational. These formal mechanisms can take the form of regular meetings and conferences of managers whose coverage is wide-ranging, or working parties and task forces with more particular remits.

However, as we saw in Chapter 3, transferring expertise through the formal architecture of a network may not be straightforward since managers at subsidiary level may seek to maximize their independence and look to block diffusion as a part of this,

and use the sources of power they possess in their dealings with HQ. It may be imperative, for example, that the firm has an operating plant in the market it wishes to serve;
this is a requirement in many service industries, of course. Generally, a local operating
presence will require expertise concerning the local environment and market and the
dependence of the HQ on local managers is a source of power for the latter group.
Furthermore, within a foreign subsidiary of an MNC, 'domestic' managers may be able
to lessen the influence of expatriates through their greater familiarity with the language and culture of the host country, as was illuminated by Broad's (1994) study of a
Japanese transplant in Wales. The ability of managers at unit level to form alliances
with other local stakeholders can also be a source of power for this group in dealing
with higher-level managers. Belanger et al. (2003) found that managers in one of the
Canadian sites of ABB formed an uneasy alliance with the union in order to shape the
site's response to the corporate restructuring programme.

Of course, managers at HQ level also possess sources of power that can be used to
overcome resistance at local level and ensure that plants engage in diffusion. One of
these is the formal authority that comes from their position in the managerial hierarchy, which can lead to formal directives or edicts on practices to be adopted at plant
level. There are numerous examples of this in the literature; perhaps most famously,
IBM's 'Blue Book' was used to stipulate policy in a number of areas of HR, such as
single status and employee representation. More generally, most MNCs have formal
policies and guidelines on issues such as the deployment of staff on international
assignments. However, there are significant constraints on the extent to which MNCs
issue formal policies and guidelines on employment practice. Coller (1996) argues that
this is because such 'direct control' involves the costs of, first, restricting the ability of
plant managers to respond flexibly to the local environment and, second, demotivat-
ing them through constraining their involvement in policy making. In a similar vein,
Ferner (2000: 521) argues that 'formal "bureaucratic" controls depend for their effective operation on informal systems and the power relations they embody'.

Indeed, the literature suggests that many MNCs seek to rely on a range of more
informal ways of influencing employment practices at plant level. These include
forms of personal control such as developing the mobility of key staff across the company. Employees on international assignments fulfil a range of roles, but one of these
is to take with them experience and knowledge of particular organizational practices.
In some cases international assignees are given a specific brief to oversee the implementation of a particular practice or system. Bureaucratic forms of control can also be
underpinned by 'social' control, such as attempts by senior managers to forge a distinctive 'corporate culture' that shapes the operation of the mechanisms identified
above. One aspect of this is moves by the corporate HQ to ensure that there are
common 'rules of the game' across the firm, such as shared understandings over the
importance of sticking to formal budgetary targets (Ferner 2000).

This more 'unobtrusive' form of control, as Coller (1996) terms it, has much in
common with the 'transnational' strategy and structure outlined by Bartlett and
Ghoshal (1998). This involves the creation of a network of actors from different
countries, with each node of the network performing a distinct function and sharing

expertise with other parts of the network. As we argued in the Chapter 4, however, this vision of a network underplays the potential resistance to diffusion across the firm and the role of the centre in breaking down this resistance. Accordingly, the formal mechanisms that are established in order to facilitate transfer may also be complemented by the HQ threatening formal sanctions against those actors at unit level not engaging in transfer. The generation of internal competition between plants for new investment and new orders is a key way in which this can take place, as we saw in the Chapter 4. This internal competition creates pressure on managers and worker representatives at plant level to adopt practices favoured by the HQ. The HQs of such firms can also reduce the degree to which they are dependent on any one plant through sourcing the same product or component from more than one location, reducing the uniqueness of any particular plant, which allows them to use internal competition for investment and orders in order to pressurize actors at plant level into adopting practices that operate successfully elsewhere within the group.

In many cases, these kinds of 'coercive comparisons' are not possible, however. The principal reason for this is that the market in one country cannot be served from another location. As noted above, this is the case in many service industries, such as retail and catering, which require a physical presence in the market. Where coercive comparisons are not feasible, managers at the HQ may seek to use an alternative sanction, namely control over managerial careers. There is some evidence that the pay and promotion prospects of plant managers are influenced in part by their willingness to engage in the sharing of best practice across sites (see the following case study). Thus the HQ ensures that a network of managers moving around the organization takes with them knowledge of practices that have operated successfully in one part of the organization and disseminate this information to other plants.

Engineering Products: networking … but with the centre in charge

How does diffusion across a multinational occur? In particular, in what circumstances will subsidiary managers be inclined to both share innovations they have developed with other plants and adopt practices pioneered by others? As we have seen, many writers on international human resource management (IHRM) argue that the diffusion of practices can and should occur through the operation of a network of plants across countries. The workings of such a network in facilitating diffusion was the subject of a recent case study of a UK multinational in the engineering sector that we call Engineering Products. The firm is nearly 100 years old and has had international operations for several decades. In recent years it has reduced the number of product lines it offers and now operates three primary divisions, the largest of which, automotive components, is the area studied. This division is a first-supplier to the large car assemblers, and is both highly integrated in the sense that it produces standardized products and highly internationalized in that it is spread across a number of countries. Indeed, only 15 per cent of the division's employees are based in the UK.

The division has a number of structures capable of transferring expertise and knowledge across borders, many of which the HR function has played a key role in creating. One key aspect of this is the management of overseas assignments. At any one time, the division has around 60 people from various functions on long-term assignments of over a year in countries that are not their own. Spending time on an international assignment has become a key criterion in deciding whom to promote to senior positions within the firm. In addition to these long-term assignments, there are a number of other individuals on short-term visits of a few weeks or months, some of whom travel to learn about a practice operating elsewhere and others who travel to 'spread the word' about something developed in their unit. The division also has a number of mechanisms designed to bring together specialists from different functions: the Manufacturing Councils facilitate exchange of information between manufacturing managers and engineers; the International College of Engineering runs training courses on practices and technologies favoured by the HQ; while the HR function convenes regular meetings (at least twice a year) to discuss developments in HR practice and the scope for harmonizing these across countries.

There is little evidence that the centre has used these mechanisms to exercise 'direct' control: there are few formal guidelines on HR practice across their international assignments and respondents at both plant and HQ level were keen to emphasize that the degree of central intervention in decision making is limited. However, there is compelling evidence that the mechanisms identified above were used by those at the centre of the division to exercise unobtrusive control in order to bring about the flow of practices across the firm's plants. There are a number of instances of this diffusion. First, the US operations pioneered a set of 'key competencies' that engineers across the firm should possess. Managers in the USA were given the task of devising a training programme that would deliver these competencies, to be implemented by the International College of Engineering. Second, the French plant developed a form of organizing the factory floor that involved dividing it into a series of small production units, each with its own support services. The aim was to develop a stronger focus among the workforce on serving an 'internal customer': the next unit in the production process. This practice was diffused through the chief executive of the French plant being accorded the status of 'internal consultant', roaming from one subsidiary to another advising plant managers on the implementation of this system. Third, a form of cellular assembly was developed in the Spanish plant involving the reorganization of the assembly line into a series of U-shaped cells. Within these cells workers are required to perform a range of tasks and responsibility for quality and output levels is shared among team members. A team of Spanish engineers who had developed this practice was sent on a string of short-term assignments to the other plants, while the Spanish plant built and installed the U-shaped cells.

What tactics was the centre able to use to ensure that the sites engaged in the cross-national transfer of practices? A two-pronged approach was evident. The primary way in which the HQ created an imperative on actors at plant level to adopt practices favoured by the centre was to exercise 'coercive comparisons'. In recent years, the firm's customers had moved away from a system whereby their own plants commissioned components from suppliers in their own country towards their HQ placing orders with the HQs of a select band of suppliers who are themselves multinationals. In effect, this strengthened the hand of senior managers in their dealings with the plants since they were able to allocate production to those sites that produce the best-quality products at the lowest cost. This source of power created an imperative on plants whose performance was poor to adopt practices favoured by the centre. One respondent at the divisional HQ described the way in which this pressure had led to the 'greater coordination of manufacturing processes to make sure that the world's best practices are shared and adopted across the organisation'. He went on to state that if, in a hypothetical case, one of the subsidiaries refused to accept that a practice favoured by the HQ should be implemented, the centre would initially try to 'persuade them and then instruct them and eventually fire the chief executive'.

However, while this pressure may be effective in ensuring that plants adopt practices diffused from elsewhere, it might make actors at plant level reluctant to share innovations with those in other plants for fear of undermining their own competitive position. Thus the second element of central influence was to give individuals at plant level an incentive to provide practices for the rest of the group by making it clear that doing so would enhance their own prospects for pay rises and promotion. Instances of this are the French and Spanish managers who had identified the improvements in work organization: not only were they given short-term international assignments as a 'reward' but it was also evident that this would count in their favour if they were to apply for positions outside their own plant.

For further details, see:
Edwards, T. (1998) 'Multinationals, Labour Management and the Process of Diffusion', *International Journal of Human Resource Management*, 9(4), 696–709.

Case study question: *Why do you think that the HQ relied primarily on competition between sites and control over managerial careers as opposed to more direct forms of control?*

It appears that in many MNCs diffusion occurs through networking between plants, underpinned by the HQ retaining control over investment decisions and the prospects of plant managers. This is the process that we have referred to as 'networking within hierarchy' in earlier parts of the book (Edwards et al., 1999).

Conclusion

This chapter has considered several issues relating to the transfer of practices across borders: the extent to which practices can be transferred and can operate in a new environment; the key patterns in terms of the direction of transfer; the types of MNC most likely to engage in diffusion; and the processes through which diffusion takes place. In dealing with these issues, we have integrated into the analysis the role of both nationally distinct business systems and the internal politics of multinationals. Indeed, the interdependence between these two sets of factors has been, and will continue to be, a theme of the book; groups of actors within MNCs derive some of their power and influence from their familiarity with their local or national context, while the actions of large MNCs have the potential to shape the evolution of national systems. This approach comes even more to the fore in our analysis of cross-border mergers and acquisitions in Chapter 6.

Review questions

1 Why are some HR practices more diffusible than others?

2 What are the limitations to the concept of 'dominance' effects in shaping the transfer of practices across borders?

3 What are the different ways in which production or service provision can be integrated in MNCs and what are the implications for the transfer of practices?

4 Do you think that MNCs will look to engage in transfer of practices to an ever-increasing extent in the future?

Further reading

Edwards, T., Rees, C. and Coller, X. (1999) 'Structure, Politics and the Diffusion of Practices in Multinational Companies', *European Journal of Industrial Relations*, 5(3), 286–306.

This article discusses 'structural' and 'political' approaches to the diffusion of employment practices across borders within MNCs and argues that the two approaches can be integrated.

Ferner, A. (2000) 'The Underpinning of Bureaucratic Control Systems: HRM in European Multinationals', *Journal of Management Studies*, 37(4), 521–39.

This paper tackles the nature of formalized, 'bureaucratic' forms of control in MNCs and argues that their efficacy is dependent on the informal workings of firms.

Smith, C. and Meiksins, P. (1995) 'System, Society and Dominance Effects in Cross-National Organisational Analysis', *Work, Employment and Society*, 9(2), 241–67.

The term 'dominance' effects was first articulated in this paper. It provides an interesting discussion of dominance in the context of other influences on firms operating across borders.

Wilkinson, B., Gamble, J., Humphrey, J., Morris, J. and Anthony, D. (2001) 'The New International Division of Labour in Asian Electronics: Work Organization and Human Resources in Japan and Malaysia', *Journal of Management Studies*, 38(5), 675–95.

The way in which Japanese MNCs 'segment' their international operations so that the various parts to the production process take place in different countries is elaborated upon. The authors argue that this segmentation (though they do not use this term) is a key driver of the nature of HR practices in place at each site.

References

Abramovitz, M. (1994) 'The Origins of the Postwar Catch-up and Convergence Boom' in J. Fagerberg, B. Verspagen and N. von Tunzelmann (eds) *The Dynamics of Technology, Trade and Growth*, London: Edward Elgar.

Anderson, B. (1995) *Swedishness*, Stockholm: Positiva Sverige.

Bartlett, C. and Ghoshal, S. (1998) *Managing Across Borders: The Transnational Solution*, Boston: Harvard Business School Press.

Belanger, J., Giles, A. and Grenier, J. (2003) 'Patterns of Corporate Influence in the Host Country: A Study of ABB in Canada', *International Journal of Human Resource Management*, 14(3), 469–85.

Broad, G. (1994) 'The Managerial Limits to Japanisation: A Case Study', *Human Resource Management Journal*, 4(3), 52–69.

Coller, X. (1996) 'Managing Flexibility in the Food Industry: A Cross-National Comparative Case Study of European Multinational Companies', *European Journal of Industrial Relations*, 2(2), 153–72.

Dickmann, M. (1999) 'Balancing Global, Parent and Local Influences: International Human Resource Management of German Multinational Companies', unpublished Ph.D. thesis, London: Birkbeck College.

Dickmann, M. (2003) 'Implementing German HRM Abroad: Desired, Feasible, Successful?', *International Journal of Human Resource Management*, 14(2), 265–83.

Edwards, T. (1998) 'Multinationals, Labour Management and the Process of Diffusion', *International Journal of Human Resource Management*, 9(4), 696–709.

Edwards, T. and Ferner, A. (2002) 'The Renewed "American Challenge": A Framework for Understanding Employment Practice in US MNCs', *Industrial Relations Journal*, 33(2), 94–111.

Edwards, T. and Ferner, A. (2004) 'Multinationals, National Business Systems and Reverse Diffusion', *Management International Review*, 24(1), 51–81.

Edwards, T., Rees, C. and Coller, X. (1999) 'Structure, Politics and the Diffusion of Practices in Multinational Companies', *European Journal of Industrial Relations*, 5(3), 286–306.

Ferner, A. (2000) 'The Underpinning of Bureaucratic Control Systems: HRM in European Multinationals', *Journal of Management Studies*, 37(4), 521–39.

Ferner, A. and Quintanilla, J. (1998) 'Multinationals, National Business Systems and HRM: the Enduring Influence of National Identity or a Process of "Anglo-Saxonisation"', *International Journal of Human Resource Management*, 9(4), 710–31.

Ferner, A. and Varul, M. (1999) *The German Way? German Multinationals and the Management of Human Resources in their UK Subsidiaries*, London: Anglo-German Foundation for the Study of Industrial Society.

Ferner, A. and Varul, M. (2000) '"Vanguard" Subsidiaries and the Diffusion of New Practices: A Case Study of German Multinationals', *British Journal of Industrial Relations*, 38(1), 115–40.

Ferner, A., Almond, P., Clark, I., Colling, T., Edwards, T., Holden, L. and Muller, M. (2004) 'The Dynamics of Central Control: Transmission and Adaptation of "American" Traits in US Multinationals Abroad: Case Study Evidence from the UK', *Organization Studies*, 25(3), 363–91.

Geary, J. and Roche, W. (2001) 'Multinationals and Human Resource Practices in Ireland: a Rejection of the "New Conformance Thesis"', *International Journal of Human Resource Management*, 12(1), 109–27.

Gereffi, G. (1999) 'International Trade and Industrial Upgrading in the Apparel Commodity Chain', *Journal of International Economics*, 48, 37–70.

Gray, J. (2002) *False Dawn: The Delusions of Global Capitalism*, 2nd edn, London: Granta.

Hall, P. and Soskice, D. (2001) *Varieties of Capitalism: The Institutional Foundations of Comparative Advantage*, Oxford: Oxford University Press.

Hamill, J. (1984) 'Labour Relations Decision Making in Multinational Corporations', *Industrial Relations Journal*, 15(2), 30–34.

Hayden, A. and Edwards, T. (2001) 'The Erosion of the Country of Origin Effect: A Case Study of a Swedish Multinational Company', *Relations Industrielles/Industrial Relations*, 56(1), 116–40.

Hedlund, G. (1981) 'Autonomy of Subsidiaries and Formalization of Headquarters-Subsidiary Relationships in Swedish MNCs' in L. Otterbeck (ed.) *The Management of Headquarters-Subsidiary Relationships in Multinational Corporations*, Aldershot: Gower.

Kogut, B. (1991) 'Country Capabilities and the Permeability of Borders', *Strategic Management Journal*, 12, 33–47.

Krugman, P. (1994) 'The Myth of Asia's Miracle', *Foreign Affairs*, November–December, 62–78.

Maccoby, M. (1997) 'Just Another Car Factory? Lean Production and its Discontents', *Harvard Business Review*, November–December, 75(6), 161–68.

Marginson, P., Armstrong, P., Edwards, P. and Purcell, J. (1995) 'Managing Labour in the Global Corporation: A Survey-Based Analysis of Multinationals Operating in the UK', *International Journal of Human Resource Management*, 6(3), 702–19.

Martinez, M. and Weston, S. (1994) 'New Management Practices in a Multinational Corporation: the Restructuring of Worker Representation and Rights', *Industrial Relations Journal*, 25(2), 110–21.

Mtar, M. (2001) 'French Multinationals' International Strategy', Ph.D. thesis, Coventry: University of Warwick.

Oliver, N. and Wilkinson, B. (1992) *The Japanization of British Industry: New Developments in the 1990s*, Oxford: Basil Blackwell.

Porter, M. (1986) *Competition in Global Industries*, Boston: Harvard Business School Press.

Smith, C. and Meiksins, P. (1995) 'System, Society and Dominance Effects in Cross-National Organisational Analysis', *Work, Employment and Society*, 9(2), 241–67.

Streeck, W. (1992) *Social Institutions and Economic Performance: Studies of Industrial Relations in Advanced European Capitalist Countries*, London: Sage.

Tempel, A. (2001) *The Cross-National Transfer of Human Resource Management Practices in German and British Multinational Companies*, Mering: Hampp.

Turner, T., D'Art, D. and Gunnigle, P. (2001) 'Multinationals and Human Resource Practices in Ireland: a Rejection of the "New Conformance Thesis": a Reply', *International Journal of Human Resource Management*', 12(1), 128–33.

Whitley, R., Morgan, G., Kelly, W. and Sharpe, D. (2003) 'The Changing Japanese Multinational: Application, Adaptation and Learning in Car Manufacturing and Financial Services', *Journal of Management Studies*, 40(3), 643–72.

Wilkinson, B., Gamble, J., Humphrey, J., Morris, J. and Anthony, D. (2001) 'The New International Division of Labour in Asian Electronics: Work Organization and Human Resources in Japan and Malaysia', *Journal of Management Studies*, 38(5), 675–95.

Chapter 6

Cross-border mergers and acquisitions

Tony Edwards and Chris Rees

Key aims

This chapter has the following key aims:

● to examine the pressures on firms to integrate HR policies in the two parties to a merger, focusing on the role of the nationality of the parent firm in shaping this process;

● to consider the features of host countries that influence the nature of restructuring in the post-merger period;

● to highlight the 'political' dimension to cross-border mergers and acquisitions, including the role of a range of groups within a firm that will seek to influence the character of the new firm.

Introduction

Cross-border mergers and acquisitions (M&As) are of particular concern to those interested in international human resource management (IHRM). The process of merging two firms, whether they be from different countries or not, raises a number of human resource (HR) issues: the details of the merger and its likely implications for employees must be communicated; management must decide on the extent to which it will seek to integrate pay and benefit policies; and the employment consequences of the restructuring that follows most mergers must be confronted. The impact and consequences of a merger or acquisition, particularly the nature of restructuring, depend in large part on the rationale for it and the context in which it takes place. For example, a merger based on adverse trading conditions, overcapacity and the desire to cut costs is much more likely to lead to large-scale redundancies than one based on an expansion into new markets. The impact and consequences of cross-border M&As are also likely to be strongly shaped by national effects. These national effects show up in two ways in cross-border M&As: first, in terms of the orientation of the parent or larger firm in the merger, something we have termed the 'country of origin' effect in earlier chapters; and, second, the way that HR issues are handled differently at national level, or 'host country effects'. We consider both aspects of these national effects in this chapter.

The 1990s witnessed a boom in cross-border M&As, with their value increasing from $150 billion in 1990 to $1,080 billion in 2000. Much of this increase was concentrated in the last few years of the decade with annual increases averaging very nearly 50 per cent between 1996 and 2000 (see Figure 6.1). This period was one in which there were a string of very large deals: DaimlerChrysler in automotive; AstraZeneca in pharmaceuticals; TotalFinaElf in oil; and so on. In the year 2000 alone there were 175 cross-border mergers that were valued at more than $1 billion. M&As in general, and cross-border M&As in particular, are highly cyclical in that they appear to increase sharply during an economic expansion and reduce sharply during a recession. Hence, the value of cross-border M&As fell by around two-thirds between 2000 and 2003. Even at this reduced level, however, the value was still more than three times its level of ten years earlier (UN 2004). Thus cross-border M&As have been one of the principal ways in which firms have reorganized themselves internationally.

Cross-border M&As can transform companies in terms of their scale, structure and geographic orientation. A prime example is Vodafone, which has acquired either partial stakes in, or full ownership of, mobile phone operators in twenty-eight countries across five continents. Its most notable, some would say notorious, acquisition was that of Mannesmann in Germany, where Vodafone secured control in early 2000 following a bitterly contested, hostile takeover bid. This battle involved many of the great and the good in Germany, including the Chancellor Gerhard Schröder, voicing their disquiet about the encroachment of undesirable 'Anglo-Saxon' business practices. Vodafone's string of acquisitions in the last five years have made it the biggest mobile phone operator in the world, with a presence in most developed economies and a growing presence in some developing economies. Currently, only approximately 14 per cent of Vodafone's customers are in the UK.

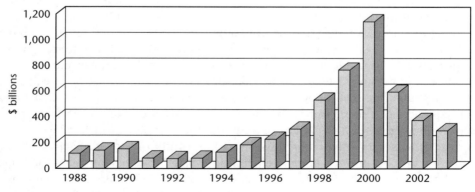

Figure 6.1 Growth in cross-border M&As
Source: data from UN (2004)

A further example of a company that has been transformed by cross-border M&As is Vivendi. Until the middle of the 1990s, the firm was known as Generale des Eaux, was highly concentrated in France and operated in stable, regulated and unglamorous sectors such as water provision and waste disposal. During the second half of the 1990s the group was renamed Vivendi and was transformed, mainly through a series of acquisitions in quite different sectors, such as cable television, music and film. Its largest acquisition was of Universal in the USA. Jean Marie Messier, the chief executive officer (CEO) during this period, regarded this as the jewel in the company's crown, and formally split the rump of the original business into Vivendi Environment, floating a chunk of the shares on the stock market, but retaining full control over Vivendi Universal. Shares in the reshaped firm soared briefly and the company's successful transformation appeared to be complete. However, Vivendi's fortunes have turned down markedly in the last few years, with the massive debts that were incurred in the acquisition spree no longer looking manageable in the context of a share price that has plummeted. In July 2002 Messier was forced to resign, and the company embarked on a series of sell-offs to reduce debt.

Vivendi is not an isolated case in terms of the problems it encountered following overseas acquisitions. Many sources of evidence testify to the poor financial performance experienced by firms that have engaged in a series of cross-border M&As. For instance, a report by KPMG (the international audit and consultancy firm) into cross-border M&As in Europe found that the majority of deals had failed to improve financial performance. The report argued that 'the process of entering into M&A transactions is often less than perfect, with key elements left too late and post-completion integration tackled haphazardly' (KPMG 1999: 23). The greater likelihood of cultural differences between parties to a cross-border merger when compared with domestic mergers may bring more acute challenges that help explain this disappointing performance. However, differences between the parties may also bring greater potential for learning. Stahl et al. (2004: 90–92) argue that this may explain why, while cross-border M&As are associated with poor performance, they actually compare favourably with domestic M&As.

The importance of cross-border M&As as drivers of corporate restructuring demands a close inspection of the processes involved. Throughout this chapter we make use of our own empirical research into cross-border M&As to illustrate the points (Rees and Edwards 2003). This research has taken the form of 12 mini-case studies looking at the handling of HR issues in the UK arm of firms formed through a cross-border merger, and four more in-depth studies that have examined operations in the USA, Spain, Germany and France. For reasons of confidentiality, the companies are often referred to by pseudonyms.

The national orientation of the parent in cross-border mergers and acquisitions

One of the key issues facing a firm that has been created through a cross-border merger is the extent and process of integration between the two firms. One pressure to integrate comes from the incentive to present a uniform face to global clients. In some service industries, such as management consultancy, and in some manufacturing industries, such as automotive components, firms are selling principally to other MNCs requesting a service or product that has few differences across countries. This necessitates the firm standardizing many aspects of its own operations, including HR issues such as work organization, training and service delivery. In other cases, cross-border M&As are justified to shareholders on the basis that they will allow significant cost cutting to take place. This requires the merged firm to remove duplicate functions and shed excess capacity, another force towards integration. A further reason why merged firms will look to integrate their HR policies across borders is that this will promote the mobility of staff across the company. Standard pay scales and benefits policies, at least for managerial and professional workers, is one way of facilitating such mobility.

However, in Chapter 1 we noted a number of significant differences in the framework of employment relations across countries. The distinctiveness of 'national business systems' shows up in a number of respects. One aspect of this is in relation to managerial backgrounds. In France and Germany it is common for senior managers to have technical backgrounds, whereas in the UK and the USA finance and accounting backgrounds dominate. This has implications for the sort of control mechanisms adopted at firm level. Historically, many large French and German firms have favoured a 'functional' corporate structure in which senior managers are involved in a range of technical and operational matters in the various units. In contrast, most UK and US firms have strongly favoured a 'multi-divisional' structure in which the HQ merely exercises financial controls over divisions which operate with devolved responsibilities (Mayer and Whittington 2002). A further difference between countries concerns the use by firms of 'internal labour markets' in which recruitment is undertaken to fill junior positions with more senior positions being largely filled from internal promotions: while this has been a common practice in Japan, in other countries, such as the UK, there is much greater recourse to the external labour market and, consequently, much greater inter-firm mobility of labour. The laws and institutions that afford employees the right to be consulted about, and to influence, decisions that affect their job security, pay prospects and the nature of their day-to-day work also differ markedly from country to country, with one contrast being between the highly regulated and codified system of employee representation in Germany and the more deregulated US system.

One illustration of how national differences are evident in a firm formed through a cross-border merger is provided by Vaara et al. (2003) in their study of the Scandinavian financial services group Nordea. The authors cite the views of managers within the organization and show how 'national stereotypes' were constructed and endured. While these did not represent an 'absolute truth' concerning how people behaved, they did help those within the organization to make sense of why others behaved as they did. Thus 'according to these "strong" stereotypes, Swedes were frequently seen as consensus-driven, Finns as action-oriented, Danes as negotiating merchants and Norwegians as people who go straight to the point in decision-making' (2003: 62).

These national differences are central to understanding the competing pressures on firms as they acquire or merge with those in other countries. The differences create pressure for national 'differentiation' of HR policies, for a company's approach to be responsive to the peculiarities of national systems. This is developed below. National differences are also significant, however, for the way they shape the extent and nature of integration. As we saw in Chapters 2, 3 and 4, most international firms are embedded in their original country in a range of ways: finance is raised and ownership is concentrated predominantly at home; senior managerial positions are filled largely by nationals of the home country; the government in the country of origin often has close ties with, and influence over, large MNCs; and so on. This embeddedness gives rise to a 'country of origin' effect in the way MNCs manage their workforces. Thus we might expect this effect to inform the way that the dominant firm in a cross-border merger or acquisition seeks to integrate the less dominant or acquired firm into the wider organization.

Indeed, the available evidence suggests that MNCs are significantly influenced by their original nationality in this respect. One illustration is a study by Faulkner et al. (2002) that examined acquisitions of UK firms by foreign MNCs. Over the period 1985 to 1994, the researchers used a postal survey to examine the nature of post-acquisition change in 201 cases where the parent firms were US, Japanese, French or German. While they found that there were some changes that appeared to occur whatever the nationality of the parent firm – most firms had sought to establish a clear link between pay and performance, for example – their findings also revealed significant differences by nationality in the handling of HR issues in the post-acquisition period, particularly in relation to recruitment, development and termination practice.

One of the clearest findings was the preference among US firms for formal and regular appraisals, with these being used to ensure good performance; consistently substandard performance could easily lead to 'separations' under such systems. More generally, US firms exhibited a centralized, forceful and hands-on approach to integration, including an emphasis on trying to shape the culture of the acquired unit. Japanese firms also exhibited some distinctive ways of integrating acquired firms: they were less likely to rotate managers between different tasks; they regarded seniority as an important criterion for promotion; and they took a slower, more considered approach to change than the Americans. French acquirers also appeared to introduce some nationally specific practices in the post-acquisition period, such as emphasizing formal qualifications as criteria for promotion. The authors also argue that there was a 'glass ceiling' for promotion for non-French managers. German acquirers tended to emphasize technical expertise in recruiting, but generally they adopted a highly decentralized approach to decision making on HR issues and, relatedly, placed less emphasis on using human resource management (HRM) in an integrative way.

Where the acquiring firm is clearly bigger than the acquired unit, this 'country of origin' effect seems to show through clearly. However, what happens where the two parties to a merger are of a comparable size? In such cases the orientation of the merged firm is less clear-cut. This is a significant issue because in the last few years a number of cross-border mergers have involved broadly similar-sized firms, creating what has been termed 'bi-national' firms. Bi-nationals are so-called because the merger results in them having strong roots in two rather than one business system. This shows up in a number of ways. In terms of the ownership of merged firms, the overwhelming focus on one financial system that is characteristic of most MNCs is strongly eroded. For example, prior to its merger with Chrysler in 1998, Daimler's main shareholder was the Deutsche Bank, which held 22 per cent of the company's shares and had played the traditional role of banks in German firms of holding a large stake for a long period and supplying representatives to sit on the board of directors. Following the merger, this stake was reduced to 13 per cent and the newly merged firm had an almost equal number of US as German shareholders. The roots that bi-national firms have in two systems also show up in the cosmopolitan nature of the management board. It is common for the board in a firm formed through an agreed merger to be comprised of proportionate numbers of managers from each party to the merger. For example, with the creation of Astra-Zeneca, the top four managerial positions were divided up between two Britons and two Swedes. The international expansion of formerly state-owned companies has reduced a further source of national influence from the parent, namely that of the state. France Telecom, for example, has undertaken a string of acquisitions overseas, funded by raising finance on the financial markets in France and elsewhere, thereby reducing its ties with the French state. More generally, the wave of cross-border M&As in the late 1990s was one force towards the increased international spread of MNCs, something that is picked up in the growth of the United Nations' (UN) Transnationality Index (see Chapter 3).

In the case of bi-nationals created through cross-border M&As, is it possible to predict how the management of people will be handled? In particular, are there likely to be discernible national effects? Three possibilities exist. First, two national management styles may continue to be evident some time after the merger, with full integration between the two parties to the merger being weak. If quite different styles do exist, there may be tensions between the two. Second, an integrated style may emerge following the merger that is a hybrid of the two styles. Third, an integrated style may also emerge based on one of the styles characteristic of one of the two firms. The case study on HealthCo that follows shows how all three of these possible scenarios can be evident in a bi-national firm.

The case study on HealthCo has demonstrated not only the influence of the home country business systems of the main parties to a cross-border merger but also the influence of host country systems in shaping the effects of a merger. It is to this that we now turn.

HealthCo

The pharmaceuticals and healthcare sector witnessed a number of mergers in the late 1990s. One of these brought together a UK company with one that was predominantly US, forming a new group that has very strong bases in the UK and in the USA, as well as a notable presence in a number of other countries. The firm, HealthCo, is officially registered as a UK company, but has a split stock market listing in the UK and the USA, has an HQ that is split across the two countries and has a mix of nationalities on the company's management board – Americans and Britons in almost equal numbers, while other nationalities are represented too. The firm is therefore an excellent one in which to investigate the way in which a company formed through a cross-border merger has a detectable country of origin effect. Is it possible to detect particular national influences over the management style of HealthCo or is this a cosmopolitan, globally influenced firm? If the former, does the UK or US influence show up more strongly?

The evidence from nearly 40 interviews in HealthCo suggests that it has been strongly influenced by the US system, something that shows up in a number of respects. First, the firm has a number of global HR policies on issues such as performance-related pay. The influence of the centre was much more marked in the predominantly US party to the merger than in its UK counterpart, which was described as being like an 'absentee parent' by a number of Americans. A relatively centralized approach to decision making on HR issues is a characteristic feature of US MNCs more generally (see Ferner et al. 2004). Second, in the manufacturing side of the business all of the sites were required to introduce a process known as 'Lean Sigma', which is a way of identifying waste and potential economies in the organization of production. A US firm of consultants led the introduction of this process. Third, since the merger the firm has introduced a new policy on the length of time that 'contingent', or temporary, workers can be employed continuously. Responding to a legal ruling in the USA, the firm imposed an 18-month maximum time limit on the use of such workers in the USA and the UK, even though the law in the UK is different. Fourth, in relation to 'diversity' the US operations are clearly perceived as being more advanced than those in other countries and have served as the model on which practices in other countries have been developed, such as 'diverse marketing teams'.

In short, the merger has created a firm with no clear-cut national 'centre of gravity', but one that is shifting towards the USA. The interviews demonstrate that this shift appears to be partly explained by the attractions of the US system to senior managers, such as the widespread perception of it as a fast-moving, dynamic system and one that is 'more advanced' in some areas, such as diversity. One manager summed up this influence: 'All our competitors, or the majority of our competitors, are in the States. So you know 70 per cent of our competition is in the United States so role models of how people behave in our industry seem very influenced by the US.'

However, the influence of the HQ, which we have argued is distinctively US, is of course mediated by the dominant features of the various host country systems that the firm operates within. For example, the pace at which restructuring has taken place has been swifter, with less consultation, in the US than in Germany, partly reflecting the legal requirements for negotiation with employee representatives in Germany. The central influence was also constrained by country-level managers who were reluctant to give up their autonomy, something that was particularly marked in countries with operations belonging to the UK party to the merger.

Source: Edwards et al. (2004)

Case study question: *To what extent can the concept of 'dominance' effects help explain the direction HealthCo took following the merger?*

Restructuring at national level and the legacy of distinctive national systems

The regulation of M&As has some common aspects across countries. This is particularly so within the EU where there is a common legal framework setting out a minimum set of employee rights during M&As. This framework stems from the EU Acquired Rights Directive (77/187/EEC), which was revised in 1998 (98/50/EC), concerning the safeguarding of employees' rights in the event of a transfer of ownership of companies. In essence, the acquiring firm must respect most of the obligations that the acquired firm had towards its employees. In particular, the Directive states that:

- terms and conditions existing in a collective agreement must be observed until such an agreement expires or is replaced with a new one;
- a transfer of ownership does not of itself constitute a justifiable reason for dismissals (though that does not mean that none will occur – they can take place for 'economic, technical or organizational reasons');
- the status of employee representatives should be preserved following a merger or acquisition;
- these representatives are entitled to be consulted as to the likely or planned economic and social implications of the transfer, with this consultation occurring 'in good time' before the transfer is carried out.

The Directive has been implemented into national law in all EU member states, with only limited variation at national level. Thus where M&As bring together firms from different EU countries there is to some extent a common legal framework governing the process.

Despite this EU-wide framework, there are marked differences in the extent of regulation across EU countries since some have additional provisions concerning employee participation in M&As (see EIRO 2001). In the Netherlands, for example, there are a number of institutional means through which employees' rights are protected, notably through the Merger Code and the Works Council legislation. These require that management in the companies involved in a merger inform both sets of works council representatives and also inform union representatives. Management must provide the works council with information concerning the likely impact of the merger, provide a justification of its decision and show that it has taken account of workers' interests. Crucially, works councils have the right to seek external expert assistance and can challenge management's proposals; if they do so, then the proposals must be postponed for a month, during which time the works council can go to a Labour Court to challenge the decision. If this court feels that the management has not done enough to safeguard employees' interests, it can prevent management's plans being implemented. In addition, a merged firm wishing to make redundancies must get the approval of a District Employment Services Authority, and the firm's supervisory board must approve any major changes involved in post-merger restructuring. Even after the recent revisions to the Merger Code, which have marginally weakened the position of unions and works councils in the target company and made hostile takeovers slightly easier, it is clear that Dutch workers enjoy considerable legal and institutional protection during M&As.

In Spain, there are also national-level provisions safeguarding employees' rights, though these are not as strong as those in the Netherlands. Spanish firms are obliged to consult with both works councillors and trade unionists. In particular, the Workers' Statute gives employee representatives the right to be consulted on the same basis as shareholders; since shareholders must be informed in writing at least one month before a general shareholders' meeting at which the merger proposals are to be discussed, so workers must be informed at the same time. Moreover, where a merger or acquisition involves 'any incidence that affects the volume of employment' worker representatives must be given at least 15 days to issue a report containing their views, and this must be received and considered by management before a merger is consummated, though they are not obliged to implement its proposals. However, while worker representatives do not have the power to block or even delay job losses involved in a merger, where collective redundancies of roughly 10 per cent of the workforce are not agreed by worker representatives and management, the plans must go for approval to a 'labour authority' at either local, regional or national level, whichever is most appropriate.

In the UK, by contrast, the ability of employees to influence the merger process is weaker and the framework protecting employees' rights is more minimalist. The European Directives were transposed into UK law through the Transfer of Undertakings (Protection of Employment) Regulations (1981), known as TUPE. This Act, which has subsequently been amended to comply with the new European directive, gives employees the basic rights of consultation that exist across the EU. In addition, legislation on collective redundancies also gives employees the right to be consulted 90 days before any such redundancies are made. However, beyond these provisions, any influence that employees possess stems from their bargaining power in relation to their employer, either in an organized way through the influence of unions or through their possession of skills that mean they are of value to their employer. In essence, therefore, managers have a freer hand in the UK to make changes following a merger than they do in most European countries.

Differences in the regulation of M&As within the EU are even greater when compared with other countries, such as those in North America and Asia. Variations in legal frameworks are only one element, of course, of wider differences in systems of employment relations. These differences encourage the decentralization of decision making on HR issues in firms formed through a cross-border merger. In other words, 'host country effects' significantly shape the handling of HR issues.

The importance of these national-level institutions and regulations shows up in a recent study of Franco-German mergers. Corteel and Le Blanc (2001) argue that 'social issues' – by which they mean pay, working time, holidays, pensions and so on – are governed by a national logic, and that these are 'lastingly rooted at national level'. Thus in the companies they examined, the differences between the French and German operations in terms of pay, benefits and working time arrangements that existed prior to the merger continued to exist following the merger. Managers had not sought to integrate practices in this area, principally because they recognized the importance of national-level regulations and the strength of the 'social partners' in the two countries.

Our own current research confirms this picture. Interviews with HR managers in the British arm of 12 firms that have been involved in a cross-border merger or acquisition (of which HealthCo is one) highlighted how remuneration is strongly conditioned by national-level factors. Pay and benefits is clearly one of the areas where differences in practices become immediately apparent following a merger. The MNCs have a strong incentive to integrate these policies, particularly where they want employees to be geographically mobile. However, a key constraint on managers is that integration will only be readily agreed by employees if it takes the form of 'upward harmonization'. Thus host country effects lead to the creation of a 'patchwork quilt' of various sets of pay and conditions across borders.

The difficulties in integrating remuneration policies across sites in different countries also exist, albeit to a lesser degree, between sites within countries. The TUPE regulations in the UK, and the role of unions in securing collective agreements in many organizations, mean that levels of pay and benefits continue to differ across sites that formerly belonged to different firms. An IT services company in our research, which had gradually taken on groups of workers from a range of other firms through the subcontracting of their IT functions, now has 27 sets of terms and conditions in its British operations. In a French industrial firm, managers were quite clear that while they would like pay levels to be similar across their operations in France, there is little prospect of employee representatives agreeing to this. Thus the 'patchwork quilt' exists within as well as between countries.

The way in which cost savings are made is also something that is strongly shaped by host country effects. As we indicated above, many cross-border mergers are motivated by a desire to reduce costs through removing duplicate functions and concentrating activities in particular locations. However, the ease with which plants can be closed and employees made redundant differs across countries. Corteel and Le Blanc (2001) present a fascinating case that demonstrates this, namely the merger between the German-owned Quante and the French firm Pouyet. Following this merger, the IG Metall union in Germany and the unions in France were successful in preventing any cutbacks leading to compulsory lay-offs in France or Germany.

However, the firm did close a plant in the UK, where workers did not have the same legal protection. For Corteel and Le Blanc 'it is reasonable to argue that … a logic aiming at preserving national employment levels to the detriment of employees located on other territories prevailed'.

The implication of Corteel and Le Blanc's argument is that a range of groups are able to shape the restructuring process that follows a cross-border merger. Restructuring is not simply the product of systematic planning by senior management. Nor is it simply the result of a rational trade-off between the advantages of integrating policies across borders on the one hand versus differentiating policies to national level on the other. Rather, it is a highly political process in which a variety of groups look to defend or advance their own interests and use whatever sources of power they control to do so. We now consider this political dimension in more detail.

The political dimension to cross-border mergers and acquisitions

Much of the writing on M&As in general and cross-border M&As in particular stresses the importance of managers following plans, guidelines and checklists if they are to make a merger a success. For instance, Schuler et al. (2003) provide a series of guidelines for HR practitioners to follow, such as 'state-of-the-art HR policies and practices should be used' (2003: 70). Similarly, Stahl et al. (2004) identify a number of HR issues that have to be confronted in a cross-border merger, such as 'assessing culture in the due diligence phase' and 'undertaking a human capital audit'. While such guidelines may to some extent be useful to practitioners, in this section we emphasize the internal disputes that arise within MNCs concerning the nature of integration and restructuring in the post-merger period.

M&As, whether domestic or cross-border, are a time when organizational structures and styles are 'unfrozen' and new ones are created. During this process, there are many individuals and groups within the organizations concerned who will look to defend or advance their own interests. A merger is a time when a lot is 'up for grabs': the structure of the merged firm must be determined; key positions need to be filled; the units that are to close or suffer the deepest cuts have to be identified; and so on. While the forces of competition and the demands of the financial markets mean that there are external demands that pressurize companies into prioritizing certain outcomes, the process of reaching the eventual course of action is a highly political one. A range of organizational actors possess some scope to influence the overall direction of the firm and, hence, this direction is not solely the product of a rational process of planning by senior managers responding to external pressures; it is also the product of a series of internal negotiations and compromises.

This perspective on organizations generally is well developed in the academic literature on strategy making and organizational change. As we saw in Chapter 4, the processual approach to strategy emphasizes the range of sources of power that exist within organizations, with these not solely residing with those actors at high points in the formal hierarchy. Thus writers such as Mintzberg are sceptical about the mainstream view that strategy making is a rational and objective process. Instead, they see strategies as emerging from a series of negotiations, compromises and 'bodges'. As a consequence, the outcomes of strategy can include goals other than just the maximization of profits for the organization as a whole and can reflect such considerations as the desire of a powerful group to safeguard the future of a unit in which they work. This political perspective helps us understand organizations of any sort, but seems essential to incorporate into an analysis of cross-border M&As. This is partly because mergers are times when a range of issues need to be resolved, as argued above, but also because cross-border M&As involve new operations in different business systems and the divergence of interests within such operations is likely to create fertile ground for political activity.

This perspective is also evident in the literature on MNCs, which are seen by some as 'loosely coupled political systems' (Forsgren 1990). The detailed case study work of Belanger et al. (1999) into ABB is testament to the resources controlled by those in operating units of a large multinational. As we saw in Chapter 4, on occasions these resources can be used to obstruct policies issued by the corporate centre. These political processes should be seen as central to the way that the firms as a whole react to developments and challenges from the context in which they operate. As Edwards et al. (1993: 3) put it: 'Political processes are not separate from structural forces, but represent the working out of responses to them.'

Our own case study work highlights a number of ways in which the process of merging firms across borders is highly political. Where international mergers bring together firms of roughly equal sizes, perhaps the most obvious example is the composition of the senior managerial team. If a merger is billed as a 'merger of equals' it is important symbolically for the top management team to be comprised of equal numbers from both firms. For example, in the UK arm of the large French industrial firm referred to above, the issue of proportionate 'balance' in choosing people for senior positions was seen as crucial. This was influenced by the French parent company, where balance between the three companies that had merged was highlighted explicitly by the CEO as central to its success. In a different company, one manager argued that this process of dividing up the positions according to the proportionate size of the companies could mean that the most able and best qualified people were not always selected – or as he put it, 'you can end up with a complete dingbat in a senior position'. Despite this, even this manager saw achieving balance as necessary for the merger process to be seen as fair by employees of both 'legacy' companies. In other words, achieving balance may mean that the firm does not appoint the best person for the job, but this is often deemed a price worth paying in order to create an impression of fairness.

The way in which senior managerial posts are distributed was identified by Vaara and Tienari (2003) in their discussion of the creation of Nordea. Because of the sensitivity to the mergers being seen as one party being dominant, both to those in the organizations and to those outside, particularly the national governments, it was seen as essential that they were portrayed as 'mergers of equals'. For this impression to be created it was agreed that there should be 'an even distribution of positions in board and executive management' (2003: 95). While this was largely seen as legitimate in the immediate post-merger period, it soon became evident that maintaining this balance was creating tensions with other priorities that the firm had developed, such as stressing the importance of competencies in selecting managers for key positions and increasing the proportion of women in senior levels of management.

The political dimension to cross-border mergers also shows up in the struggle for influence by organizational actors from different functions. Of great relevance here is the role of those in the HR function; a perennial concern for HR practitioners in the UK and in many other countries is their relatively low status within organizations, leading to the danger from their perspective of being marginalized during major organizational changes such as international M&As. In one of the IT companies in our study, the HR director indicated that the function had not been involved in key strategic decisions during an acquisition, such as the choice of partner and the speed with which it would be integrated, nor had it even had much influence over many of the HR issues thrown up by the acquisition, such as the consultation process and recruitment to key positions within the acquired unit. However, in other cases it was evident that HR practitioners have used the merger or acquisition as an opportunity to raise the profile of HR within the organization. One example was the persistent efforts by an 'HR Partner' at an American financial services group to convince other managers, particularly those with an accountancy background, of the benefits of involving her in the setting up of joint ventures in various European countries. These efforts took the form of stressing the impact on the bottom-line of mishandling HR issues, such as the legal penalties of contravening the Acquired Rights Directive and supplementary national regulations.

A further question that is an aspect of many cross-border M&As, and is highly political, is that of where the main brunt of cost cutting is to be felt. Based on their study of Franco-German mergers, Corteel and Le Blanc (2001) argue that a company's overall workload is governed by a 'national fair balance rule'. This rule means that orders from customers are distributed among the firm's sites not only according to the costs and performance of these sites but also according to what is seen as just. In other words, these decisions are governed partly by 'rationality' but also by 'fairness'. The impetus for this often stems from informal deals that were struck during the merger negotiations; these deals were not binding following the merger, but breaching them would risk creating serious grievances in the units that came off worse. As one of their respondents put it: 'If we were willing to work, politically, we had to distribute the load in a fair way.' However, their data also point to the limits of the 'national fair balance rule', particularly the way it is limited to certain territories. As discussed above, the British plant of the firm formed through the merger of Quante and Pouyet was closed, partly in order to preserve employment levels at the French and German operations. Moreover, the authors also stress that the rule can become strained over time, leading to its renegotiation.

Overall, this line of analysis indicates that it is the diffusion of control of resources across a range of groups within a merged organization that results in the process being so highly political. One of these resources that is controlled by staff at unit level within MNCs is knowledge of, and expertise in, local institutions and regulations. This knowledge and expertise can be used to advance or protect their own interests. The Corus case study considered below illustrates the interdependence between local institutions and regulations on the one hand and the influence of different groups within merged firms on the other.

Corus

The merger of British Steel with Hoogovens in June 1999, forming the Anglo-Dutch group known as Corus, provides an interesting example of what can happen when firms from two quite different business systems join together. One key difference between the two countries concerns the nature of employee relations; as we have seen, the Dutch system affords employees more scope than their UK counterparts to influence the restructuring that follows a merger. This has had significant implications for relations between different units of the firm in general, and for the form that cost cutting has taken in particular.

The merger took place in the context of overcapacity in the sector. Other mergers between steel firms have occurred, notably that between Usinor of France, Arbed of Luxembourg and Aceralia of Spain, with a prime motive being the opportunity to realize cost savings through removing duplicate functions. At the time of the Corus merger, managers promised shareholders that savings of £194 million a year would result. It was evident that this would mean large-scale redundancies.

By early 2001, with the market for steel turning markedly down, it was apparent that Corus would be suffering very large financial losses. In February of that year, management announced that 6,000 employees in the UK operations would be losing their jobs. The union representing most of the UK workforce, the Iron and Steel Trades Confederation (ISTC), pressurized the company to amend its plans, advancing counter-proposals that included buying a plant from the company and short-time working to tide the company over until the market picked up. However, the legal framework in the UK meant that these proposals would have to find support from managers if they were to have any impact, and the company was adamant that it should press on with its original plans. Meanwhile, in the Netherlands redundancies were also taking place. Only six months after the merger, there had been a 'wildcat' (unofficial) strike at the huge and profitable Ijmuden plant following the announcement that the steel manufacturing department would be shut with the loss of 590 jobs. In 2001 it was announced that 1,100 further jobs would be cut as the company's losses became apparent.

During the first two years or so of the post-merger period it appeared that employee representatives were liaising more closely across the two countries. When the axe fell on 6,000 British workers in early 2001 the Dutch Trade Union Federation (Federatie Nederlandse Vakbeweging, FNV) wrote to the ISTC, pledging support for its campaign of opposition to the cuts. Moreover, the Dutch union hinted that it might support a boycott at the Ijmuden plant of any work that was to be transferred from the UK to the Netherlands.

Even after the large-scale cuts of 2001, the company's troubles have continued. The share price at the end of 2002 stood at less than half of its value at the time of the merger. This added to the pressure on senior managers, and in response the company signalled a move away from its 'multi-metal' strategy by proposing to sell its aluminium business to Pechiney of France. This met strong resistance from employee representatives, and also revealed tensions between the different parts of the business across the two countries. According to press reports, many in the Dutch part of the firm had come to resent the merger, seeing it as a takeover of a profitable Dutch business by an ailing UK one. In late 2002, it became evident that the Dutch supervisory board, which is made up of a mixture of managers and employee representatives, was threatening to use its power to veto the proposed sale of the aluminium business. Members of the board were concerned that the proceeds from the sale of this part of the business, which stemmed mainly from Hoogovens, were to be used to pay off group debt rather than reinvested in the Dutch part of the business. The implication was that further cuts would have to occur in the UK if the supervisory board was to approve the sale. Indeed, the chair of the board Leo Berndsen is reported to have said that if senior managers 'don't tackle structurally the problems in the UK, Hoogovens will become Corus's cash cow'. The supervisory board did indeed use its power to bock the sale, temporarily throwing the company's future into doubt. Management's response was to seek further rationalizations in the UK part of the business, involving yet more redundancies.

The dispute over the sale of the aluminium business demonstrates the way in which actors at local level within MNCs can draw on their embeddedness in the local institutional framework and use it as a source of power within the company. As we have already seen in this chapter, the ability of UK workers to shape management's plans during and after a merger is much more limited than that of their Dutch counterparts. The significance of the role of the Dutch supervisory board in particular, and the institutions and regulations in the Netherlands more generally, is evident not only in the way that they have limited the restructuring in the Netherlands itself, but also in the knock-on effects on restructuring in other countries.

Case study question: *Why will the concerns of employee representatives be different in other types of cross-border mergers?*

Conclusion

The material in this chapter has both theoretical and practical implications. Theoretically, we have argued that the extent and form of integration between firms engaged in a cross-border merger will be shaped by the national business system of the dominant firm, but will also be constrained by the peculiar features of the various national systems in which the merged firm operates. We have also argued, however, that the integration process, and the restructuring that is a key part of this integration in most mergers, is also a highly political process. In particular, we have attempted to show that the structural aspects of national systems on the one hand and the political processes within merged organizations on the other are interdependent. As we hope is now clear from this and earlier chapters, this approach is not only relevant to the issue of cross-border M&As, but is also integral to the way we understand the operation of multinationals more generally.

In practical terms, the preceding analysis of cross-border M&As has far-reaching implications. One of the central findings in much research on international mergers, as we have seen, has been their high failure rate. The severe problems at Vivendi are an example of the problems experienced by firms that have engaged in a string of acquisitions, and the difficulties at Corus are a further illustration. In light of the above material concerning both the quite different regulatory contexts in which M&As take place across countries and the highly politicized nature of the post-merger period, it is perhaps not surprising that such problems and difficulties are so widespread. An appreciation of the nature of the likely challenges on the part of both 'deal-makers' and those such as HR practitioners who are involved in the subsequent integration is essential if cross-border mergers are to achieve the aims of those who initiate them.

Review questions

1 Why are cross-border M&As more complex than domestic ones?

2 In what ways do national effects condition the post-merger restructuring process?

3 In what ways is the process of restructuring 'political'?

4 If you were asked to highlight the key issues to an HR manager who is about to go through their first cross-border merger, what would you tell them?

Further reading

Faulkner, D., Pitkethly, R. and Child, J. (2002) 'International Mergers and Acquisitions in the UK 1985–94: A Comparison of National HRM Practices', *International Journal of Human Resource Management*, 13(1), 106–22.

> This article reports the findings of a study of foreign acquisitions of UK firms, studying the impact of these acquisitions on HR practices.

Rees, C. and Edwards, T. (2003) *The HR Implications of International Mergers and Acquisitions*, Chartered Institute of Personnel and Development (CIPD) Research Report, London: CIPD.

> This report summarizes a research project carried out for the Chartered Institute of Personnel and Development in the UK. It provides detail on 12 case studies of a variety of mergers, acquisitions and joint ventures.

Stahl, G., Pucik, V., Evans, P. and Medenhall, M. (2004) 'Human Resource Management in Cross-Border Mergers and Acquisitions' in A-W. Harzing and J. Van Ruysseveldt (eds) *International Human Resource Management*, London: Sage.

> This chapter provides an interesting discussion of how cross-border M&As present opportunities for firms to learn from the diversity of their operations and then some detail on the key HR issues that firms encounter in the post-merger period.

Vaara, E. and Tienari, J. (2003) 'The "Balance of Power" Principle: Nationality, Politics and the Distribution of Organizational Positions' in A. Soderberg and E. Vaara (eds) *Merging Across Borders: People, Cultures and Politics*, Copenhagen: Copenhagen Business School Press.

This is a very interesting discussion of the way in which senior managerial positions were distributed in the creation of the Scandinavian financial services group Nordea.

References

Belanger, J., Berggren, C., Bjorkman, T. and Kohler, C. (1999) *Being Local Worldwide: ABB and the Challenge of Global Management*, Ithaca, NY: Cornell University Press.

Corteel, D. and Le Blanc, G. (2001) 'The Importance of the National Issue in Cross-Border Mergers', paper presented to the conference on 'Cross Border Mergers and Employee Participation in Europe', Ecole des Mines, Paris, 9 March.

Edwards, P., Ferner, A. and Sisson, K. (1993) 'People and the Process of Management in the Multinational Company: A Review and some Illustrations', *Warwick Papers in Industrial Relations*, No. 43, Coventry: Industrial Relations Research Unit (IRRU).

Edwards, T., Coller, X., Ortiz, L., Rees, C. and Wortmann, M. (2004) 'How Important are National Industrial Relations Systems in Restructuring in Multinational Companies? Evidence from a Cross-Border Merger in the Pharmaceuticals Sector', paper presented at the conference on 'The Diffusion of Organisational Practices in Multinational Companies' held at IESE Business School, Barcelona, 15– 17 July.

EIRO (European Industrial Relations Observatory) (2001) 'Industrial Relations Aspects of Mergers and Takeovers', http://www.eiro.eurofound.ie/2001/02/study/TN0102401s.html

Faulkner, D., Pitkethly, R. and Child, J. (2002) 'International Mergers and Acquisitions in the UK 1985–94: A Comparison of National HRM Practices', *International Journal of Human Resource Management*, 13(1), 106–22.

Ferner, A., Almond, P., Clark, I., Colling, T., Edwards, T., Holden, L. and Muller, M. (2004) 'The Dynamics of Central Control: Transmission and Adaptation of "American" Traits in US Multinationals Abroad: Case Study Evidence from the UK', *Organization Studies*, 25(3), 363–91.

Forsgren, M. (1990) 'Managing the International Multi-Centre Firm', *European Management Journal*, 8(2), 261–67.

KPMG (1999) *Unlocking Shareholder Value*, London: KPMG.

Mayer, M. and Whittington, R. (2002) 'For Boundedness in the Study of Comparative and International Business: The Case of the Diversified Multidivisional Corporation' in M. Geppert, D. Matten and K. Williams (eds) *Challenges for European Management in a Global Context*, Basingstoke: Palgrave Macmillan.

Rees, C. and Edwards, T. (2003) *The HR Implications of International Mergers and Acquisitions*, Chartered Institute of Personnel and Development (CIPD) Research Report, London: CIPD.

Schuler, R., Jackson, S. and Luo, Y. (2003) *Managing Human Resources in Cross-Border Alliances*, London: Routledge.

Stahl, G., Pucik, V., Evans, P. and Medenhall, M. (2004) 'Human Resource Management in Cross-Border Mergers and Acquisitions' in A-W. Harzing and J. Van Ruysseveldt (eds) *International Human Resource Management*, London: Sage.

UN (United Nations) (2004) *World Investment Report: The Shift Towards Services*, New York: UN.

Vaara, E. and Tienari, J. (2003) 'The "Balance of Power" Principle: Nationality, Politics and the Distribution of Organizational Positions' in A. Soderberg and E. Vaara (eds) *Merging Across Borders: People, Cultures and Politics*, Copenhagen: Copenhagen Business School Press.

Vaara, E., Risberg, A., Soderberg, A. and Tienari, J. (2003) 'Nation Talk: The Construction of National Stereotypes in a Merging Multinational' in A. Soderberg and E. Vaara (eds) *Merging Across Borders: People, Cultures and Politics*, Copenhagen: Copenhagen Business School Press.

Chapter 7

Internationalization and developing countries: the case of China

Miao Zhang, Tony Edwards and Christine Edwards

Key aims

This chapter has the following key aims:

- to consider the impact of internationalization on the developing countries in general and on China in particular;
- to consider the human resource implications of the way that foreign multinational companies manage their Chinese operations;
- to consider the motivation for multinational companies to transfer practices from their operations in developed countries to developing countries;
- to examine the way that Chinese firms have begun to internationalize;
- to examine how Chinese firms manage human resource issues in their foreign subsidiaries and the implications of this for the parent company.

Introduction

Throughout this book the material has related mainly to multinational companies (MNCs) and developed nations. We have looked at multinationals from the USA, Germany, Sweden and the UK, and where we have examined their foreign operations we have concentrated on their sites in other developed countries. To some extent this is justified by the geographic patterns of economic activity in general and of foreign direct investment (FDI) in particular. However, in recent years flows of FDI and trade have become less concentrated in developed nations. This is potentially very significant for three main reasons. First, the large 'institutional divides' that exist between developed countries appear to be even greater when developed and developing nations are compared. For example, forms of labour market regulation have important differences within the European Union, but these differences are minor compared with those between European and Asian countries. Second, including developing nations in the analysis is also significant because of the position that production sites in these countries occupy within internationally integrated production processes. For many MNCs, plants located in developing nations carry out labour-intensive parts of the production process that require largely unskilled workers who can be employed at very low cost. Third, there is considerable controversy surrounding the role of MNCs and development, with some observers arguing that foreign companies act as a spur to growth and assist developing nations to upgrade their economies, and others arguing that they stifle development and exploit vulnerable workers. The human resource (HR) implications of internationalization into developing nations are the focus of this chapter.

There is no universally accepted definition of the term 'developing nations'. The distinction between a developed and developing nation essentially rests on differences in living standards. While it is self-evident that some countries such as the USA have very good living standards and are therefore developed and others such as Mozambique are characterized by widespread poverty and are therefore developing, it is also clear that the distinction becomes less clear among other countries. For example, 30 years ago some South-East Asian nations such as Singapore and Korea would have been classified as developing; the rapid growth that they have experienced leads some observers nowadays to refer to them as developed. Many official statistics gloss over this by making simple distinctions according to regions. For example, the United Nations Centre on Trade and Development classifies countries from North America and Western Europe together with a collection of other countries around the world – Australia, New Zealand and Japan, for instance – into the developed category and those from Africa, Asia, Latin America and the Caribbean, the Pacific, and Central and Eastern Europe into the developing category.

We focus on one developing country: China. China is an excellent country in which to explore these issues. This is partly because of the rapid social and economic changes taking place. For approximately four decades following the Long March and accompanying rise of the Communists to power in the late 1930s, China was almost completely closed to the international economy. During this period, state planning through the famous Great Leap Forwards was central to the organization of economic activity; privately owned firms were highly restricted and FDI was frowned upon. Following the death of Chairman Mao in 1976, however, government policy began to change, and in 1982 the Open Door policy was introduced. This welcomed foreign companies into China and was followed by a series of economic reforms that have accorded a much greater role to private enterprise and market forces. The radical nature of the shift in government policy was officially confirmed at the Communist Party Congress in November 2002 when the outgoing President Jiang Zemin argued: 'The world is changing. We must adapt ourselves ... [and] conscientiously free our minds from the shackles of outdated notions, practices and systems, from the erroneous and dogmatic interpretations of Marxism.' In the last 15 years or so the Chinese economy has boomed, growing at around 10 per cent a year on average. The integration of China into the global economy was cemented by the country's entry into the World Trade Organization (WTO) in 2001 and many argue that FDI has become one of the main forces for change.

The internationalization of the Chinese economy has been dramatic. In value terms, the stock of inward FDI increased thirteen-fold during the 1990s; as a share of total FDI this rose from 1.1 per cent in 1990 to over 6 per cent by 2003 (see Table 7.1). China now receives very nearly a third of all new foreign investments made in developing nations. Western firms subcontracting production to Chinese firms is a further key way in which the country is becoming integrated into the international economy. For instance, China is the largest producer of footwear in the world with companies such as Nike and Reebok increasingly sourcing from the country. Internationalization has taken the form not only of outside involvement in China but also of Chinese companies investing in other countries. The annual investments made by these companies abroad increased from virtually nothing in 1980 to more than $37 billion by 2003 (UN 2004) (see Table 7.2). The impact of FDI and trade is readily apparent in urban China, with the pervasion of Western dress and fast-food outlets – Beijing holds the dubious honour of being host to the largest McDonald's restaurant in the world – and mobile phone and car ownership increasing rapidly. Business practices, including those in the employment sphere, have also been subject to significant change.

Table 7.1 **Growth of FDI into China (stocks)**

	1980	1985	1990	1995	2000	2003
Value ($ billions)	1.1	6.1	20.7	134.9	348.3	501.5
% of total	0.1	0.6	1.1	4.5	5.7	6.1

Source: UN (2004)

Table 7.2 **Growth of FDI out of China (stocks)**

	1980	1985	1990	1995	2000	2003
Value ($ billions)	–	0.1	2.5	15.8	25.8	37.0
% of total	–	0.002	0.1	0.2	0.4	0.5

Source: UN (2004)

Foreign multinational companies in China

The impact that multinationals have on the economies of developing countries has been the subject of much debate. One group of observers, who we refer to as the *optimists*, argue that the consequences of MNCs entering a developing country are largely positive. This group see foreign direct investment as an important source of job creation, both directly and indirectly through the spillover effects on local firms supplying the multinational with components and services. The optimists also see MNCs as an important conduit through which new ideas, technologies and systems can be transferred to a developing nation. Moreover, multinationals have both the resources and the incentive to behave as good 'corporate citizens': since they often rely on a brand name, the optimists argue, they will seek to protect the image of the brand by behaving as a responsible actor in society through, for example, avoiding environmental damage. The implications of this analysis for the behaviour of MNCs as employers are positive. The technological superiority of multinationals enables them to offer better rates of pay than local firms, the optimists argue. Indeed, studies that have compared pay levels between the two groups of firms do generally find that MNCs offer a wage premium; Dunning (1993: 381–82) cites studies from the Philippines, Mexico, Kenya, Argentina, Korea, Uganda, Nigeria, Malaysia and India which show that the foreign affiliates of MNCs pay more than local firms. It should be noted, however, that not all studies produce this finding; a few claim that MNCs pay less than local firms and several find no statistical difference between the two groups, but Dunning argues that the majority of studies point to higher pay being offered by MNCs. Of course, the senior executives of MNCs are keen to stress the beneficial terms and conditions of employment that their firms offer. Phil Knight of Nike, for example, has claimed that for 'the last 25 years, Nike has provided good jobs, improved labour practices and raised standards of living wherever we operate' (Klein 2000). In China, it is evident that remuneration levels in foreign MNCs are higher than in the state-owned firms that still account for the majority of employment. Frenkel (2001) argues that in the Guangdong province, foreign-owned firms and joint ventures between foreign and Chinese firms offer wages that are on average 125 per cent to 145 per cent higher than those available in their state-owned counterparts. More specifically, in the four factories supplying two US sports shoe manufacturers that he studied, working conditions were relatively favourable, owing in part to the impact of the voluntary codes of conduct that the two firms had established in order to protect their corporate image.

A further set of observers, the *pessimists*, take a quite different view of the impact of MNCs on economic and social life in developing countries, arguing that far from promoting economic development, multinationals tend to stifle it. They point out that FDI does not create much new employment since much of this takes the form of acquisitions of existing firms. Even where new operations are set up from scratch through 'greenfield investments', many of the jobs associated with these would have been created by local firms anyway. These adverse consequences are exacerbated by the nature of the activities that are located in developing nations, which are predominantly the routinized, low-technology stages of the production or service provision process. Moreover, critics of MNCs argue that these firms are 'footloose': their geographic scope enables them to shift resources across borders as economic conditions change, and they can use this ability to drive a particularly hard bargain with their workforces over pay and conditions and with the government over tax rates and the nature of regulations. One popular illustration of this line of argument is Naomi Klein's (2000) book *No Logo*. Klein argues that the story of the expansion by MNCs into developing countries has been one of large, powerful firms exploiting the vulnerable and the poor. By concentrating increasingly on marketing their brands and outsourcing the manufacturing of their products, she contends, 'it stands to reason that the people doing the work of production are likely to be treated like detritus – the stuff left behind' (2000: 197). She provides a number of illustrations of how Western clothing firms have taken advantage of those who are desperate for work in China: pay rates as low as 13 cents an hour in a plant supplying Esprit; a working week as long as 84 hours in a Wal-Mart controlled site; allegations of corporal punishment in a plant supplying training shoes to Nike; and so on (2000: 474).

A third group of observers, those who are *ambivalent*, argue that the impact of MNCs on developing nations is more limited than either of the other two groups suggest. This perspective stresses that while there are many competing influences on multinationals, one of the most significant pressures is to adapt to the various national systems in which they operate. Far from being powerless, governments generally retain a good deal of sovereignty and possess the ability to regulate the labour market, for example, in distinctive ways. Some MNCs might lobby politicians seeking reforms in their favour, others may threaten to shift their operations to another country, but many MNCs pragmatically accept that issues such as patterns of working time are governed by legal regulations that vary from one country to another. Moreover, as we have seen, dominant values and attitudes in a society differ markedly across borders, and while powerful MNCs may be able to override these to some extent, the costs of doing so are significant and lead MNCs to adapt their employment practices to fit the culture concerned.

A fourth perspective stresses the *contingent* nature of the impact of MNCs. This argument is based on the notion that the effects of MNCs depend on the type of multinational in general and the nature of their operations in the country in question. As we saw in Chapter 5, some academics have used the concept of 'global value chains' to analyse the way in which MNCs carry out the different parts of the production or service provision process across countries. Where this is the case, the position of the Chinese sites within the global division of labour will be a key influence on the impact that the multinational has on the local economy and on the nature of the employment in its subsidiaries. In this vein, Kaplinsky (2000) argues that 'barriers to entry' within the production or service provision process are crucial. That is, those parts of the process that another unit can easily mimic and consequently can be shifted to another location have low or no barriers to entry, whereas those that have specialist knowledge or expertise that is difficult for other units to acquire enjoy significant barriers to entry that protect their position. Thus, sites protected by barriers to entry stand to gain from the globalization of production and services while those that 'are stuck in activities with low barriers to entry lose, and in a world of increasing competition, the extent of these losses will increase over time' (2000: 15). Thus, the impact of MNCs is highly *contingent* on particular circumstances.

So how can we make sense of the way that MNCs manage their workforces in developing countries? Are they largely innovative and progressive, bringing with them sophisticated forms of organizing work and offering relatively high rates of pay? Alternatively, are they ruthless and exploitative, using their power to drive down wages to extremely low levels and to intensify the pace of work? Are they neither of these things, but instead behave pretty much like local firms in terms of the pay they offer and practices they deploy? Or is the impact of MNCs much more contingent on particular circumstances?

While a comprehensive answer to these questions is difficult, one way of shedding some light on it is to examine the ideas introduced in Chapter 5 concerning the function of a multinational's operations in a particular country and how they relate to those in other countries. One way in which MNCs can expand internationally is to create a diverse range of operations, with those in one country bearing little resemblance to those in others. This approach can arise out of a deliberate attempt by the headquarters (HQ) to diversify into a range of sectors, or it can be the result of significant variation at national level in the nature of consumer tastes and regulations within a product market. These divergences in the nature of product market conditions from one country to another are important in sectors such as retail banking and in electricity and water provision, which are normally the subject of stringent regulations. In these circumstances, MNCs tend to create stand-alone operations in the countries they invest in, with these exhibiting significant differences from one another. Plants will tend to be of a stand-alone nature for reasons other than just product market differences. Many MNCs are concerned to be seen to be behaving like local firms. As we saw in Chapter 3, one motivation for becoming multinational is to overcome the marketing disadvantage of being seen as 'foreign'; where this is the case, the firm has an incentive to ensure that it resembles local firms in a range of ways, including its employment practices. Where a multinational has a series of such stand-alone operations, the HQ has little incentive to attempt to transfer practices across sites since the technological context and patterns of work organization differ significantly. Consequently, these MNCs tend to adopt a decentralized approach to decision making on HR issues, and it is in these MNCs where adaptation to the national system concerned is the most likely outcome. This is the scenario emphasized by those who are *ambivalent* about the impact of MNCs.

A second way in which MNCs expand internationally is to model their new operations on existing ones. This approach of expansion through the creation of 'mini-replicas' produces a standardized process of production or service provision in which units in different countries perform very similar functions, with many employment practices being transferred to the new foreign subsidiaries. In Chapter 4 we gave the example of IT services firms, such as IBM and Accenture, which are increasingly serving clients that are themselves multinational, and which demand a similar type of service across their international operations. Where a multinational builds a standardized process of production or service provision, complete adaptation to the host country is unlikely; rather, the multinational is likely to differ markedly from local firms. The way in which it does so, however, depends on the model of employment relations on which international growth is being standardized. Where a pharmaceuticals firm, for instance, sets up a new research and development (R&D) site that is to liaise closely with others within the firm, it is likely to deploy similar processes for training staff and may want to make systems of reward compatible with those in other sites in order to facilitate the transfer of staff across sites. In this situation, standardization is likely to lead to the creation of relatively well-paid, high skill jobs and the transfer of practices in the area of training and development that contribute to the economic health of the country. This is the type of scenario that the *optimists* highlight.

In contrast, where a fast-food firm opens a new restaurant based on the practices operating in other countries, the nature of employment created is likely to be of much poorer quality: work processes are often deskilled in the big multinational chains; pay rates tend to be as low as the company can get away with and yet still attract enough employees; and unions or other forms of employee representation tend to be resisted fiercely. In this context, standardized production at the international level results in the transfer of practices that appear to offer little in the way of economic development, and it is these types of firm that are likely to use their power to exploit poorly protected workers in developing nations, something that the *pessimists* emphasize.

Of course, where a multinational looks to expand into other countries by transferring home country practices, it is to some extent constrained by the dominant features of the host country into adapting to prevailing practice. The legal, institutional and cultural characteristics of a host country shape the nature of employment practice in MNC affiliates in a range of ways. For instance, Ding et al.'s study (1997) of foreign-owned firms in the Shenzen region of China found that the influence of 'Chinese socialist ideology' was significant in limiting differences in pay between managerial and non-managerial staff. Another characteristic of the Chinese system that foreign firms encounter is the tradition of *guanxi*, which is the expectation that relationships will be characterized by reciprocation. The mutual expectations and trust that exist within *guanxi* connections take time to develop since they are constructed gradually within business networks. They are reliant not on formal institutions such as the law but rather on trust and personal connections. A foreign multinational in China may challenge the reliance on *guanxi*, but to some extent must accept it as the way in which organizations operate in China. This is a second scenario that those who are *ambivalent* about the impact of MNCs tend to emphasize.

These host country influences are rarely so strong as to close off all scope for MNCs to transfer practices, however. Something that was also illustrated in Ding et al.'s findings is that many MNCs have moved away from practices that have a long history in China, such as lifetime employment. Similarly, Gamble's study (2003) of a British multinational retailer transferring practices into China demonstrated the way in which the firm transferred certain HR practices into its Chinese operations. For example, the parent company was very keen to ensure that the management structure was relatively 'flat' as opposed to 'hierarchical'. As Gamble notes, the firm was 'probably unwittingly doing something quite radical in the host country context' (2003: 385).

The third form of international expansion is for MNCs to construct an internationally integrated production process in which each site within the chain plays a distinct role. This is what we term 'segmented' production and differs from standardized production in that the nature of the activity that each plant conducts is specific to itself (or a small number of sites within the firm). As we have seen, the concept of 'global value chains' (Kaplinsky 2000) is useful in understanding this form of integration. A key part of this concept is that MNCs break up the production process into a series of activities, outsourcing some and retaining others within the firm. Crucially, MNCs have some scope to concentrate their different activities in countries that have a comparative advantage in performing them. For example, firms like Nike and The Gap have played key roles in establishing production networks across countries, carrying out the design and marketing activities in the developed economies and conducting the more labour-intensive production activities – often through one or more tiers of subcontractors – in developing nations. Many other products, such as cars and computers, are also manufactured through integrated chains with different parts of the production process taking place in different countries. It is this approach that leads to the *contingent* view of the impact of MNCs in that the mix of benefits and costs depends on the part of the firm's activities that is located in a particular country and the way this is integrated into the rest of the firm.

The way in which segmented production leads to quite different patterns of employment relations in different parts of a production process is evident in studies of Japanese MNCs. For instance, Wilkinson et al. (2001) studied the plants in Malaysia and Japan of two producer-driven chains controlled by Japanese firms and found that the differences in the organization of work and related HR practices 'largely reflected the position of the plants in the international division of labour' (2001: 686). The Malaysian plants were characterized by: short cycle times; a highly disciplined, cheap and largely unskilled workforce; workers performing a repetitive, narrow range of tasks; little in the way of employee development; and the absence of union representation. In the Japanese plants, in contrast: there was more R&D and more 'experimental' work; the workforce was better qualified and better paid; workers were engaged in process improvements and in multitasking; training involved induction followed by six months of on- and off-the-job programmes; and the plants were all unionized. Where there was transfer of 'best practice' it was mainly confined to the technical aspects of the organization of production; while there are obviously some HR consequences of transfer in this area, the cross-border diffusion of practices did not extend to areas such as recruitment, payment systems, development or representation. In cases where MNCs construct segmented chains of production or service provision, therefore, the nature of employment practices is likely to reflect the characteristics of the plant and, more specifically, the function that it plays within the wider production process. For countries such as China, their place within a segmented production process is commonly as the receiver of low-skill and low-pay jobs. In a study of 20 Japanese-owned plants in China, Taylor (2001) argues that the lack of transfer of home country practices to the Chinese plants was partly explained by the parent firms' motivation for locating in the country being to reduce costs. As he put it, 'where location decisions are made to save wage costs, sophistication of labour is not of primary interest' (2001: 614). Multinationals such as Nike are often cited as examples of those that lead to this situation. In these cases, therefore, the predictions of those who adopt a *contingent* perspective chime with those of the *pessimists* concerning the negative impact of MNCs.

The *contingent* view can also lead to much more *optimistic* predictions, however. Some writers have stressed the way in which the subsidiaries of MNCs manage to engage in 'upgrading' (Dorrenbacher and Gammelgaard 2004); that is, their role is enhanced from a low status to one of high status within the company. For instance, Egelhoff et al. (1998) provide data demonstrating that subsidiaries of MNCs can enhance their role through building up unique value-creating resources and Birkinshaw and Hood (1998) show how some units within MNCs can acquire 'charters' from the HQ to fulfil a role outside of their immediate geographic market. The implication is that where subsidiaries manage to upgrade their role in this way, their claim on resources is likely to be enhanced and the future of the site will be more secure. This in turn is conducive to much more favourable terms and conditions of employment.

In sum, consideration of the extent and nature of linkages between various parts of a multinational's operations provides one way of making sense of the polarized debate about the impact that MNCs have on developing nations in general and the way they manage their workforces in particular; these outcomes are *contingent* on particular circumstances. In this section we have concentrated on the way a multinational constructs its international operations. This is not to argue that this factor is the only contingent factor that shapes these outcomes: the timing of internationalization, the nationality of the parent firm and the sector that it operates in are also important factors. Nor do we mean to argue that it will be straightforward to categorize MNCs neatly into one of the three types of international production processes outlined above; often a mix of these three forms is evident, something that shows up in the following case study on AutoPower.

AutoPower in China: a story of independent operations, standardization or segmentation?

In Chapter 4 we considered the case of the US engine manufacturer, AutoPower, a firm that has its origins in a small Midwestern town and now employs around 30,000 people across 12 countries. We saw that the company is embedded in the US business system in a range of ways and that this shapes the way it manages its operations in the UK, such as the paternalistic management style that has been typical of many family-controlled firms in the USA and the emphasis on promoting diversity. It was evident from the material discussed in Chapter 3 that the company had sought to transfer a particular management style and associated employment practices to its operations in the UK. On the basis of research on AutoPower in China we are also able to examine the role that the company's Chinese plants play in the wider company. Are they relatively independent from the rest of the group, perhaps because the Chinese business system is so different from that of the USA? Alternatively, the parent firm may seek to apply the same global policies to the Chinese operations that it does to those in the UK. A further possibility is that the Chinese plants are accorded the role of carrying out particular parts of the production process and are consequently highly distinctive. In fact, the answer is a mixture of all three of these possibilities.

To some extent the Chinese plants operate independently from the rest of the company. The firm's investments in China were governed primarily by the sizeable and growing market in that country, and the need to be physically located in the country to serve this market, rather than the attractiveness of cheap labour. The firm's presence in the country pre-dates that of most other MNCs, stretching back to within a couple of years of the introduction of the Open Door policy, and much of the output is sold in China. This 'market-seeking' investment means that the firm's Chinese operations are to some extent independent of the parent firm since they generate most of their own business. This independence also stems from the scale of the cultural and institutional differences between the US and China, which has restricted the ease with which foreign multinationals can introduce their preferred practices. These constraints have been strengthened in the case of AutoPower by the (recently reformed) condition imposed by the Chinese government that foreign investors in 'strategic' industries work with a Chinese partner in a joint venture, meaning that the firm must consider the expectations and preferences not only of Chinese workers but also of managers in the partner firm. This has further increased the stand-alone status of the plants in China. Accordingly, in some areas of human resource management (HRM), such as the ways in which management communicate with their workforces and differences in pay rates between sites in different parts of China, there is little obvious influence from the parent firm.

However, it is also clear that the parent firm is anxious to develop a high degree of standardization in the way its subsidiaries operate through the issuing of a number of global HR policies. We saw in Chapter 4 how the system of teamworking, involving operators working flexibly within a cell, was diffused across the firm's operations, reflecting a belief that the system had universal benefits. The firm's commitment to diversity, reflecting both the political importance of the issue in the USA and the ideological leanings of the founding family, has led to the development of a number of global policies and targets for the subsidiaries to aspire towards. The 'domestic partner' benefits, in which unmarried and same-sex partners of the firm's employees received the same benefits as wives and husbands, was seen as too controversial in China and so was not implemented, but the operations are coming under increasing pressure from the HQ to increase the number of women and members of minority ethnic groups in the workforce, particularly in managerial positions. Thus in a number of ways, the Chinese plants are subject to strong pressures towards standardization, even if these sometimes clash with the cultural and institutional features of the Chinese business system.

Recently, the firm has revamped its policy on performance management, resulting in less scope for local deviation from the firm's commitment to a 'forced distribution' in which managers must assess the performance of all of their subordinates and place 10 per cent into a 'high-flyers' category, 80 per cent into a 'solid' category and 10 per cent into a 'poor' category – the so-called '10-80-10' that Jack Welch made famous at General Electric. This has been viewed with some suspicion in China, where many managers and employees dislike the way in which the system exposes poor performers and especially the way it puts those in the bottom category 'at risk'. This attempt to standardize HR practices across borders could be associated with the *optimistic* or *pessimistic* view of MNCs and their impact, depending on one's evaluation of the merit of the performance management system.

However, such attempts to transfer practices come up against significant constraints. In relation to the practice of the performance management system, the buoyancy of the job market in many parts of China, especially the big cities, has given local managers a 'buffer' in operating the system because the natural turnover that it creates lessens the pressure to cut the bottom 10 per cent each year. Indeed, there were some indications that the system could be operated in a way that was not intended by corporate managers, since those employees that leave the organization voluntarily can be classified as being in the bottom 10 per cent whatever their actual performance. A further illustration of the way in which Chinese managers are able to pay lip-service to corporate policies and in fact do things differently is in relation to annual pay rises. In each of the two years prior to our research, the corporation had imposed a pay freeze on 'exempt staff' (those not covered by collective agreements). In the booming job market of Beijing this caused enormous recruitment and retention problems since annual wage rises were around 7 per cent. Following a number of discussions, the corporate HQ refused to make an exception for the Chinese part of the company. The Chinese managers reacted by using the Employee Supplementary Fund – a fund that has been built up by employer and employee contributions over time with the purpose of funding 'welfare' projects for company employees – to pay for benefits for employees, such as mortgage subsidies. This is intended to compensate for the absence of a pay rise and prevent people leaving. It should be stressed that this is entirely legal, but is done without the knowledge of the HQ. Such evidence gives some weight to the *ambivalent* view of MNCs; whether the HQs know it or not, its attempts to standardize are often adapted so as to minimize their impact.

To complicate matters further, there is also a sense in which the production process within AutoPower is segmented internationally. While each of the plants carries out most of the steps in the production of an engine, some of the functions are concentrated in one part of the company. The production of filters for the engines is focused on particular plants but, perhaps more significantly, R&D is conducted mainly at a site in the company's original base in the Midwest of the USA. An illustration in relation to the HR function is the recent creation of a 'shared services' centre to be located in India that will act as a focal point for a range of enquiries that employees may have about their holiday leave, pension contributions and so on. This will involve removal of the responsibility for providing this service from the country-based HR teams. In these ways, the firm is moving towards segmenting some aspects of its activities. The implication is that the incentive to adopt standard practices across countries will diminish as this segmentation increases, though currently the production process for engines still has many common features internationally. It is this tendency towards segmentation that is stressed by those who hold a *contingent* view.

It is evident that the organization of AutoPower's production process internationally has elements of all three factors identified in this chapter. Perhaps the strongest of these is the company's commitment to standardized production and many associated practices. However, the pressures on affiliates to stand alone are also evident, albeit limited, and there is also a limited tendency towards segmenting their production process. The firm's approach to managing its international workforce is influenced by the mix of these pressures.

Case study question: *On balance, which of the optimistic, pessimistic, ambivalent or contingent views do you find most convincing?*

The internationalization of Chinese firms

The internationalization of developing countries through FDI, as we argued in the introduction to this chapter, can occur both through inward investment but also through outward investment. Thus, if firms in a developing country lack certain capabilities, such as the ability to conduct research and development activity to generate advanced technologies, investments abroad represent a potential channel through which this ability can be obtained (Duan 1995; Feng 1996). Subsidiaries established in other countries can serve as mechanisms through which firms learn about the practices prevalent in advanced capitalist societies and the 'rules of the game' of operating in international markets. In other words, firms based in developing countries can use their foreign subsidiaries as ways of 'catching up' with what they perceive as their more advanced counterparts in developed countries through absorbing knowledge and experience (Zhang and Edwards 2004).

There is some empirical evidence that suggests that some MNCs from developing countries are investing into more developed countries in order to gain access to channels of distribution, to foreign technology and to management skills. For example, Lee (1993) found that firms from the Philippines use their sites in developed countries to collect information and resources. He writes:

> 'A gradual widening of investment destinations saw a number of foreign investments in developed countries. The scale of the latter could not be quantified but included significant FDI in banking to serve the needs of Philippine companies involved in international trade, and to gain access to low cost funds and financial information.' (1993: 309)

Lee argues that the substantial improvement in the performance of Philippines MNCs is related to the technology transfer from subsidiary to parent via outward investment. In a similar vein, Young et al. (1996) suggest that MNCs from developing countries are using their subsidiaries in developed countries to gain crucial experience concerning operating in international markets; the practices of these countries are not only used locally but also diffused back to their home firm or other subsidiaries as a way to facilitate their 'catch-up' process.

The internationalization process of Chinese MNCs has been different from those of other developing countries in a number of respects. In particular, there has been a 'leapfrogging' of the stages in the internationalization process followed by firms of other nationalities. The internationalization sequence of Chinese MNCs has been shaped by changes in Chinese economic policy since the end of the 1970s (Zhang and Van Den Bulcke 1995; Young et al. 1996; Branine 1997). Prior to this period, Chinese MNCs operated almost solely in the domestic arena, which was characterized by a centrally planned economic system with little integration into the international economy except for limited exporting and importing of goods (Zhang and Van Den Bulcke 1994). With the introduction of the Open Door policy, and the shift from a centrally planned to a market-orientated business system in the 1980s, China saw economic integration with the rest of the world as a way of achieving the nation's 'four modernizations': modernization in industry, agriculture, science and technology, and defence (Warner 1996). In this context, there have been two key pressures on Chinese MNCs. One is derived from the competitive pressure of gradually opening up the domestic market, in particular the entry of foreign-owned companies. For example, the state-owned trading MNCs lost their monopolies with the expansion of foreign trade in 1984 (Brown and Branine 1995). The other arose from the need to participate in international economic markets. To deal with this new situation, new business activities that went beyond importing and exporting grew, including overseas sites engaged in production and service provision. Many Chinese firms have pursued new corporate strategies, focusing on diversification and internationalization (Zhang and Van Den Bulcke 1994; Benson and Zhu 1999).

However, a study by Lan and Young (1996) suggests that the degree of technology transfer associated with inward FDI in China has been fairly restricted, due to factors such as limited host country technological capacities and poor partner firm assimilation capabilities. As we saw in the previous section, foreign MNCs experience a number of barriers to transferring HR practices to their Chinese sites; for example, AutoPower's appraisal system was operated by Chinese managers in a quite different way to that intended by corporate-level managers. Arguably, senior managers of Chinese nationality are more likely to be aware of, and sensitive to, the peculiarities of the Chinese system, allowing them to more accurately anticipate how a practice may operate.

Outward investment, therefore, serves as a potentially important additional route through which new practices spread to China (Duan 1995; Young et. al. 1996). Young and his colleagues (1996) point out that outward investment to developed countries enables Chinese enterprises to access international markets and to absorb those countries' management practices more directly and efficiently. Duan (1995), in his research on Chinese MNCs, stresses that FDI and 'transactional management' have become an essential part of China's internationalization process. He argues that competing in international markets will force Chinese companies to improve their technological and managerial competencies, and that FDI by Chinese firms 'has become the most important channel through which advanced technological innovations are being developed and shared' (1995: 387). Recently, the policy of 'walking out the gate of the county' has been formally advocated by the Chinese government, which has encouraged more Chinese firms to invest abroad, especially in the developed countries. In particular, many state-owned companies in China, which have a long history of conducting international trade, have pursued new business strategies, shifting from only exporting or importing to investing in developed countries to obtain local advanced product technology and knowledge about a range of practices.

Moreover, Zhang and Van Den Bulcke (1994), in a survey of Chinese MNCs, indicate that in contrast to other multinationals from developing nations, which generally invested in neighbouring, 'downstream' developing counties that had lower levels of industrialization and technological capabilities, Chinese multinationals have tended to invest more in 'upstream', higher-income industrialized countries. Luo et al. (1993) estimate that about 70 per cent of Chinese overseas subsidiaries are established in developed countries. Furthermore, other authors have found that a strategy of 'total participation' in international competition is emerging in some Chinese MNCs (Luo et al. 1993; Duan 1995). For these MNCs, outward investment is not only used to access international markets but also to fully participate in global competition. This evidence suggests that the subsidiaries of Chinese MNCs operating in developed countries are likely to play an important role in the internationalization process of Chinese enterprises as a whole. Accordingly, Zhang and Edwards (2003) argue that Chinese MNCs can use a strategy of 'absorptive localisation' in those subsidiaries operating in developed countries to absorb what they perceive to be advanced management practice and to diffuse these practices to domestic plants and other foreign subsidiaries as a way of 'catching up' with their more internationalized competitors.

Research by Zhang (2001; see also Zhang and Edwards 2004) has shed light on the extent and nature of cross-organizational learning activities that have taken place within Chinese MNCs. She found that the six Chinese MNCs in her study actively use the UK as a base in which to accumulate their experience of international business and management in general and of international human resource management (IHRM) in particular. In all of these companies, young Chinese managers were given assignments in the UK operations, partly as an attempt by the firm to gather expertise on the 'rules of the game' in Western capitalist societies, especially in relation to employment practices. In some cases, these assignments were part of a formal development programme and those returning to China at the end of their assignment were on occasions given a specific task of transferring some of their expertise into the domestic operations. Complementing this was the transfer of UK staff to China on shorter assignments that were also motivated by a desire to transfer to China a set of practices operated in the UK. One illustration is of recruitment practices. In one of the companies studied by Zhang and Edwards (2004), the UK sites had been identified as employing a particular approach to recruitment that could beneficially be transferred to the Chinese sites. This appeared to be clear evidence of 'reverse diffusion'.

However, the impact of the transfer back to China was less than had seemed apparent. In practice, the sheer weight of job applications meant that the Chinese sites did not have the resources to use to approach as it was operated in the UK, and selection continued to be made according to personal contacts, in the tradition of *guanxi* in China. As one manager put it:

> 'We did use a recruitment process which is similar to the one I learnt in the UK, but before the interviews the candidates for most posts have been decided already. For the positions which are above the middle managerial level, it is still decided by the government rather than from the labour market or organisation.' (Quoted in Zhang and Edwards 2004)

We have seen that outward investment from a developing country into a developed country could be prompted by multiple motives, some of which are the opportunities to absorb technology, obtain information and assimilate international management experience not available in the domestic environment. However, in practice, the realization of these opportunities is not a straightforward process. In particular, the huge differences between national business systems and international development stages constrain the competencies of many Chinese MNCs. The following cases of two subsidiaries of CFS illustrate this.

CFS: adaptation, absorption or retention?

CFS is a state-owned financial enterprise with over 1,000 domestic branches and 500 foreign branches. There are two subsidiaries operating in the UK, one of which, Old-CB, has a long history in the country, while the other, New-CB, has only two years' operating experience in Britain.

Old-CB was established in the 1940s. Until the 1980s, it was a representative agent of the government and carried out financial services for Chinese exporting and importing businesses. It was strongly controlled by the government and had little link with the UK market. As a result, most staff in this branch were Chinese expatriates and very few were recruited locally. Most management practices were modelled on practices in China rather than those in the UK. For example, the staff in this subsidiary were employed with the 'job for life' status that was enjoyed by most professional employees in China. Moreover, the salary rose in line with age and tenure rather than performance, and there was only a modest gap in salary between top managers and the most junior staff.

The parent company, CFS, began to lose its monopoly position in China during the 1980s as the government gradually opened up the domestic market. Simultaneously, the firm began to expand internationally. As the oldest overseas branch, Old-CB was accorded a key role in extending the company's business into international markets from the early 1990s, losing its 'agent' status and becoming more autonomous. Its main task became to learn how to do business in a competitive environment, and a key part of this involved greater use of local managers and the adoption of local management practices in some areas. One such area is in the pay structure, with pay being linked to individual performance and the gap in pay between the highest and lowest earners rising significantly. Crucially, this subsidiary took on the role of training managers from the home country and other subsidiaries, setting up a training centre to run courses on a range of aspects of doing business in market environments. So far, the subsidiary has trained more than 1,000 Chinese managers, including most top-level managers and heads of departments.

In relation to the important issue of training, therefore, the subsidiary has taken on a 'vanguard' status within the wider company, and it is evident that practices in this area are being 'reverse diffused'. However, the subsidiary does not have complete autonomy, and is still strongly controlled by the parent firm. Many top managers and over half the staff are Chinese or have a Chinese background, and a Chinese management style is still evident. British management practices have been applied mainly in the areas that are strongly shaped by the demands of the local labour market and regulations, such as the recruitment process and pay for non-managerial staff, but a Chinese influence was detectable on other types of HR practice. For example, the importance of harmony in work relations is still stressed, and the selection and pay packages of senior managerial positions remain controlled by the parent company.

New-CB's establishment was a key part of the global strategy of the parent company. At the beginning of its establishment, this subsidiary was intended to become the HQ in Europe, in charge of the business of all other related subsidiaries and branches. According to the description of one of the founders of this subsidiary, the UK was perceived as advanced in HR terms, making it an ideal base for this plant. CFS invested significantly in the subsidiary in the hope that it would serve as the basis for learning for the wider firm, and whether it made a profit or not was seen as secondary to its key task of absorbing local management practices.

In the first two years of its existence, this subsidiary used a strategy of 'localization' in HRM. That is, most top managers and all middle managers were British and HRM policies and practice were based on those of local companies. For example, recruitment, remuneration and appraisal systems were all modelled on those in place in similar organisations in the UK. Moreover, practices operating in this subsidiary were subsequently diffused to the HQ and to other sites. One example is that of an appraisal system that had been implemented at the site after senior staff learned about it in operation in a similar local UK company. Knowledge of this practice was passed to the HQ and given the status of 'best practice', with other subsidiaries expected to implement it. Thus this subsidiary also had a 'vanguard' role in transferring practices within the company.

From these two cases, it is clear that this Chinese multinational attempted to use a strategy of 'localization' to absorb UK management practice. However, the extent to which this process of 'reverse diffusion' occurred was constrained by various factors. For example, following the Asian financial crisis in 1997 the subsidiaries' business was severely impacted and the parent company changed its previous plans, reducing the size and security of New-CB, and the HQ moved to establish greater control over staff remuneration, reducing the autonomy it previously enjoyed. Currently, this subsidiary is focusing on its own survival and cost-reduction programme, rather than serving as a site for others to learn from. In this respect, the case study has much in common with that of AutoPower, considered in Chapter 4 as well as in this one, in which attempts to establish a network of HR managers working collaboratively across borders was derailed by adverse trading conditions.

Source: See Zhang (2001)

Case study question: *Why might the internationalization process of Chinese companies such as CFS differ from those of other nationalities?*

Other sources of evidence indicate that the experience of CFS is not unique. In their research on HRM in Chinese state-owned companies, Benson and Zhu (1999) found that social and political factors, such as the 'rule of law', the lack of transparency in decision making and the inefficiency of the administrative system that characterize the operations in the home country constrain the adoption of international standardized HRM in these companies. They claim, thus, that there is a long way to go before these enterprises will be able fully to absorb HR practices from other countries.

Conclusion

In this chapter we have considered some of the HR issues that arise in MNCs in developing nations. To some extent, these are quite different from those facing MNCs originating in, and investing in, developed nations. For example, the scale of variations between national business systems in developed and developing nations tends to be much greater than those between developed economies. A further key factor in identifying the issues that are pertinent to developing countries is the role that sites in these countries often play within MNCs, namely that of low-cost production sites for labour-intensive operations. However, we have also seen that many of the issues that featured in earlier chapters are also pertinent to developing nations. The most obvious of these is the tension between the incentive that MNCs have to engage in the transfer of knowledge and expertise about organizational practices on the one hand and the barriers to effecting such transfer on the other. This points to the need to consider in more detail the nature of the management of knowledge at the international level, something that we turn to in Chapter 8.

Review questions

1 What are the main challenges that a multinational entering the Chinese market should expect to encounter?

2 Why will the nature of production processes in China – 'stand-alone', 'standardized' or 'segmented' – vary by sector?

3 Why might we expect Chinese MNCs to behave in different ways from, say, US MNCs?

4 What does the evidence reviewed in this chapter tell us about a multinational's ability to transform itself through learning from the practices in place in its foreign subsidiaries?

Further reading

Benson, J. and Zhu, Y. (1999) 'Markets, Firms and Workers in Chinese State-owned Enterprises', *Human Resource Management Journal*, 9(4), 58–73.

This paper sheds some light on the extent of change in Chinese state-owned firms, detailing the erosion of many long-established traditions in China.

Frenkel, S. (2001) 'Globalization, Athletic Footwear Commodity Chains and Employment Relations in China', *Organization Studies*, 22(4) 531–62.

A relatively upbeat account of the impact of multinational firms in the production of training shoes, arguing that employment conditions compare favourably with most alternative forms of work.

Gamble, J. (2003) 'Transferring Human Resource Practices from the United Kingdom to China: The Limits and Potential for Convergence', *International Journal of Human Resource Management*, 14(3), 369–87.

An interesting case study of a UK retailer and its attempts to transfer many HR practices from its UK to its Chinese stores.

Taylor, B. (2001) 'The Management of Labour in Japanese Manufacturing Plants in China', *International Journal of Human Resource Management*, 12(4), 601–20.

This article provides detailed evidence of the nature of employment practices in some Japanese MNCs in China.

References

Benson, J. and Zhu, Y. (1999) 'Markets, Firms and Workers in Chinese State-owned Enterprises', *Human Resource Management Journal*, 9(4), 58–73.

Birkinshaw, J. and Hood, N. (1998) 'Multinational Subsidiary Evolution: Capabilities and Charter Change in Foreign-owned Companies', *Academy of Management Review*, 23(4), 773–95.

Branine, M. (1997) 'Change and Continuity in Chinese Employment Relationships,' *New Zealand Journal of Industrial Relations*, April, 77–94.

Brown, D. and Branine, M. (1995) 'Managing People in China's Foreign Trade Corporations: Some Evidence of Change', *The International Journal of Human Resource Management*, 6(1), 159–73.

Ding, D., Fields, D. and Akhtar, S. (1997) 'An Empirical Study of HRM Policies and Practices in Foreign-Invested Enterprises in China: The Case of Shenzen Special Economic Zone', *International Journal of Human Resource Management*, 8(5), 595–613.

Dorrenbacher, C. and Gammelgaard, J. (2004) 'Subsidiary Upgrading? Strategic Inertia in the Development of German-Owned Subsidiaries in Hungary', paper presented at EGOS (European Group of Organizational Studies) conference, Ljubljana, 1–3 July.

Duan Y.C. (1995) *Management and Strategies of China's Multinational Enterprises*, Beijing: China Development Press.

Dunning, J. (1993) *Multinational Enterprises and the Global Economy*, Reading, MA: Addison Wesley.

Egelhoff, W., Gorman, L. and McCormick, S. (1998) 'Using Technology as a Path to Subsidiary Development', in J. Birkinshaw and N. Hood (eds) *Multinational Corporate Evolution and Subsidiary Development*, Basingstoke: Macmillan Press.

Feng, Y. (1996) 'Book Review: Management and Strategies of China's Multinational Enterprises', *The Journal of Developing Areas*, 30, 387–90

Frenkel, S. (2001) 'Globalization, Athletic Footwear Commodity Chains and Employment Relations in China', *Organization Studies*, 22(4), 531–62.

Gamble, J. (2003) 'Transferring Human Resource Practices from the United Kingdom to China: The Limits and Potential for Convergence', *International Journal of Human Resource Management*, 14(3), 369–87.

Kaplinsky, R. (2000) 'Spreading the Gains from Globalisation: What can be Learned from Value Chain Analysis', IDS Working Paper No. 110, http://www.ids.ac.uk/ids/bookshop/wp/ wp110.pdf

Klein, N. (2000) *No Logo*, London: HarperCollins.

Lan, P. and Young, S. (1996) 'Foreign Direct Investment and Technology Transfer: A Case Study of FDI in Northeast China', *Transnational Corporation*, 5.

Lee, A.E.K. (1993) 'The Impact of Foreign Direct Investment upon Parent Companies' Competitiveness: An Empirical Study on Singaporean Industrial Multinational Enterprises', Ph.D. thesis, University of Strathclyde, Glasgow.

Luo, L., Chen, Y. and Yang, R. (1993) 'Some Consideration on the Management of Chinese Multinationals', *World Economy*, 5, 46–50.

Taylor, B. (2001) 'The Management of Labour in Japanese Manufacturing Plants in China', *International Journal of Human Resource Management*, 12(4), 601–20.

UN (United Nations) (2004) *World Investment Report: The Shift Towards Services*, New York: UN.

Warner, M. (1996) 'Chinese Enterprise Reform, Human Resources and the 1994 Labour Law', *International Journal of Human Resource Management* 7(4), 779–96.

Wilkinson, B., Gamble, J., Humphrey, J., Morris, J. and Anthony, D. (2001) 'The New International Division of Labour in Asian Electronics: Work Organization and Human Resources in Japan and Malaysia', *Journal of Management Studie*s, 38(5), 675–95.

Young, S., Huang, C.H. and McDermott, M. (1996) 'Internationalisation and Competitive Catch-up Process: Case Study Evidence on Chinese Multinational Enterprises', *Management International Review*, 36(4), 295–314.

Zhang, H. and Van Den Bulcke, D. (1994) 'International Management Strategies of Chinese Multinational Firms', *Discussion Paper* No. 1994/E/17, Centre for International Management and Development, University of Antwerp.

Zhang, H. and Van Den Bulcke, D. (1995) 'Rapid Changes in the Investment Development Path of China', *Discussion Paper* No. 1995/E/21, Centre for International Management and Development, University of Antwerp.

Zhang, M. (2001) 'Multinationals, the Internationalisation Process and Human Resource Management Strategy: A Case Study of UK Subsidiaries of Chinese MNCs', Unpublished Ph.D. thesis, Kingston University.

Zhang, M. and Edwards, C. (2003) 'Multinationals, HRM Strategy and the Influence of "the Country of Origin": Evidence from Chinese MNCs Operating in the UK', in the proceedings of IIRA 13th World Congress, Berlin, 9–12 September.

Zhang, M. and Edwards, C. (2004) 'The Motivation, Facilitation and Limitations of HRM Practice Diffusion: A Study of Chinese Multinationals', paper presented at conference on 'Multinationals and the International Diffusion of Organisational Forms and Practices', 15–17 July, Barcelona.

Part Three

The management of international human resource practices in multinational companies

Chapter 8

Knowledge management and international human resource management

Stephen Gourlay

To an increasing extent, the success of multinational companies (MNCs) is considered to be contingent upon the ease and speed by which valuable knowledge is disseminated throughout the organization (Hedlund 1986; Bartlett and Ghoshal 1998; Gupta and Govindarajan 1991). Thus creation of knowledge in a spatially dispersed multinational organization and tapping into advanced local knowledge wherever it can be found are necessary conditions for success in the global marketplace (Gammelgaard et al. 2004: 195).

Key aims

This chapter has the following key aims:

- to become familiar with key concepts relating to knowledge and knowledge transfer;

- to understand the way that knowledge transfer can occur within multinational companies;

- to analyse the key implications of knowledge transfer for international human resource management.

Introduction

The idea that 'knowledge' is a significant factor of production has been discussed since the late 1940s (Hayek 1945) but it was not until the 1990s that a 'paradigm shift' in business management occurred and 'knowledge management' (KM) entered business vocabulary (Scarborough et al. 1999). The reasons for this shift are complex, lying in the perceived threats and opportunities of the late 1980s, in particular the maturation of information processing technology, companies' difficulties following downsizing, growing attention to customers, the emergence of the resource-based perspective on business strategy and the increasing economic significance of information or knowledge-intensive products and, consequently, of knowledge workers (Covin and Stivers 1997).

KM practice and theory was initially dominated by information systems and computing disciplines, resulting in a focus on using computer technologies to capture, store and disseminate knowledge, and on specific issues such as data mining and intranet design and use (Scarborough et al. 1999; Thomas et al. 2001). This emphasis led to a focus on *explicit* knowledge (books, databases and so on) and to a neglect of *tacit* knowledge (knowledge people have but cannot express) (Johannessen et al. 2001). KM journals and texts also focus on topics such as strategy and, more recently, customer relationship management (e.g. Tissen et al. 1998; Tiwana 2000). There is, however, also a persistent minority who emphasize the importance of people, and hence, usually implicitly, of human resource management (HRM). Thus it has been argued that effective management of knowledge requires managers to attend to the context of work and the management of networks of relationships among people, since knowledge itself cannot be managed (Sierhuis and Clancey, 1997). Others advocate managing knowledge through 'communities of practice' (Brown et al. 1991) or 'self-organizing teams' (Nonaka 1994). Nevertheless, despite the fact that behaviour is clearly central to widely quoted models such as that of Nonaka and Takeuchi (1995), and reviews of KM projects have drawn attention to the importance of human social and cultural factors (e.g. Davenport et al. 1998), KM writing and practice still largely ignore the human dimension (Swan et al. 2002).

From the perspective of international human resource management (IHRM) research this oversight is even more marked. A review of the field covering the 20 years to 1997 (Clark et al. 1999) did not even consider KM or the related area of organizational learning. This is somewhat surprising since the issue of knowledge transfer has received considerable attention in international business and strategy literature, and is clearly important in the context of international partnerships, mergers and acquisitions (Bresman et al. 1999; Simonin 1999; Bhagat et al. 2002) and in the transfer of organizational practices across borders that we covered in Chapter 5. There are, however, signs that knowledge issues are receiving attention from an IHRM perspective. Kamoche (1995, 1997) calls for a reorientation of IHRM research to adopt an organizational learning perspective, while Bender and Fish (2000) discuss the issues of KM and transfer in the context of expatriate management. Moreover, Schuler (2001) writes at length about the importance of learning and knowledge issues for international joint ventures, while Wong (2001), Novicevic and Harvey (2001) and Hocking et al. (2004) contribute to the growing discussion. Despite this growing interest, the issue is relatively neglected in IHRM and in this chapter we seek to get to grips with the basic concepts of 'knowledge' and 'knowledge transfer' before going on to consider the implications for human resources (HR) across countries.

Since the focus on KM issues in an international context has been on knowledge transfer, it is useful to begin by looking at that field to consider what implications it holds for IHRM. It will be apparent, however, that knowledge transfer research faces some critical conceptual difficulties. To respond to these, and thereby to provide a sound theoretical basis for considering the potential relationship between IHRM and KM, a perspective on 'knowledge' will be outlined in the following section. This model supports the notion of complementary but distinct roles for HR and behavioural disciplines on the one hand, and IS/IT (information systems/information technology) perspectives on the other. It also provides a sound basis for discussing the implicit role of IHRM practices for KM, including knowledge transfer.

Knowledge and knowledge transfer

Defining what knowledge is may seem a straightforward task. Indeed, in much of the writing on KM it is used interchangeably with 'information'. For example, Myers (1996: 2) calls organizational knowledge 'processed information', and Davenport et al. (1998: 43) see knowledge as 'information combined with experience, context, interpretation and reflection ... a high-value form of information'. While the simplicity of such definitions is seductive, they raise further questions, namely how such 'processing' transforms information into knowledge, or how information acquires 'high value'. Garavelli et al. (2002) point out that the transformation of information into knowledge requires the activity of a cognitive system, and that it is wrong to assume that knowledge grows by the accumulation of 'knowledge objects'. Currently we do not have agreement on defining knowledge and a satisfactory definition is perhaps 'elusive' (Bresman et al. 1999: 444).

Knowledge transfer has been defined as the 'process through which one unit (e.g. group, department or division) is affected by the experience of another', particularly when this brings about measurable changes in the receiving unit (Argote and Ingram 2000: 151, 154). Since knowledge itself is difficult to measure, a change in performance is often taken as a proxy measure for a change in knowledge. If 'knowledge transfer' is the process of transferring knowledge between a unit that possesses it and one that does not, the way knowledge is treated will have important consequences for our understanding and treatment of this process.

Although there is no agreed definition of knowledge, a number of important distinctions can be made and are generally accepted:

- Perhaps the most common distinction among different types of knowledge is between explicit or codifiable knowledge on the one hand, and tacit or uncodifiable knowledge on the other (Argote and Ingram 2000: 153, 157; Nonaka and Takeuchi 1995). The former can be readily identified, is often in written form and consequently can be transferred relatively easily; the latter, in contrast, is difficult to summarize, is more context-dependent and, therefore, cannot easily be transferred.
- A further distinction of great importance is between human, social and structured knowledge. Human knowledge includes both explicit and tacit knowledge. Social knowledge concerns relationships between individuals and groups, and is largely tacit, such as cultural norms. Structured knowledge, on the other hand, concerns organizational processes, routines and rules, and is largely explicit (Bhagat et al. 2002).
- Knowledge is also described as being 'embedded' in 'repositories', which can take a number of forms. These repositories can range from characteristics of the workplace or organization, such as established organizational practices, the corporate

culture, documents and the physical structure of the workplace. Repositories can also be individual employees (Argote and Ingram 2000: 152–53). The tacit/explicit distinction is important here because tacit knowledge can only be 'embedded' in people while explicit or codified knowledge can be 'embedded' in the other repositories.

● Knowledge can be conceived either as an object or as a process. From the object perspective, knowledge is considered as something 'that can be directly observed, stored and successively reused or transferred' (Garavelli et al. 2002: 270–71). On the other hand, the process view treats knowledge as 'a more dynamic matter, a flow of interacting changes taking place in the people involved in a learning process' (Garavelli et al. 2002: 270). This view emphasizes learning as something that happens to and in people and sees inherent difficulties in 'translating' knowledge-as-object into particular competences or behaviours.

The consensus of much of the writing in this field is that knowledge that is tacit, social and embedded in people is generally more difficult to capture, absorb and transfer than knowledge that is explicit, structured and embedded in formal organizational characteristics. This shows up both in work on knowledge transfer between operating units in the same country and in cross-border knowledge transfer. These challenges raise the issue of how knowledge is transferred.

How is knowledge transferred?

If knowledge is embedded in 'repositories' or 'reservoirs', it is logical to propose that it can be transferred 'by moving a knowledge reservoir from one unit to another or by modifying a knowledge reservoir at a recipient site' (Argote and Ingram 2000: 155). Argote and Ingram argue that moving networks is difficult because they are necessarily integrated with other units while networks involving people are 'the most problematic knowledge conduits'.

While Argote and Ingram emphasize transfer of knowledge reservoirs, others emphasize communication. Szulanski (2000: 11) suggests that most research on knowledge transfer is underpinned by the 'signalling metaphor' (Shannon and Weaver 1949). This specifies the basic elements of a transfer: source, channel, message, recipient and context. Knowledge transfer, according to this model, requires the processes of encoding the knowledge by or from a source, its transmission through a channel in a message, and its decoding by a recipient (Szulanski 2000; Garavelli et al. 2002). Implicitly, this metaphor underlies the 'reservoir' model of knowledge transfer – the reservoir being an analogue of a message. For brevity, these notions will be referred to as as the 'container' metaphor since they envisage that knowledge can somehow be packed into some kind of container to be transferred. Thus Bonaventura (1997: 85) describes knowledge as being embodied in a document that is a 'multi-media container'.

While this model of communication has been extremely useful for understanding some technical aspects of signalling, it was criticized long ago as being inadequate for dealing with *human* communication processes (Cherry 1966; Reddy 1979). More recently, and in the context of knowledge transfer research, Garavelli et al. (2002) also point to its failure to recognize the centrality of human cognitive processes for knowledge and knowing. In the language of the container metaphor, this approach is silent on the critical processes of how knowledge is put into the containers or how it is taken out of them.

Recognition of these difficulties goes some way towards explaining why knowledge transfer is widely regarded as a complex, time-consuming and difficult process. While many seem to regard the transfer of explicit knowledge (documents and the like) as relatively easy or unproblematic, Garavelli et al. (2002: 271) point out that even 'if knowledge is successfully materialized in an object ... when the object has again to be translated in a competence, it can generate behaviors very different from those expected'. This implicitly draws attention to the interpretation of documents by readers, the significance of which is supported by models of the reading process (Gourlay 2003). It would thus seem that transfer of any and all forms of knowledge is critically dependent on social, cultural and cognitive factors – all of which, in some form or other, are factors about which HRM is directly and explicitly concerned in a variety of ways.

Knowledge and situated cognition

Situated cognition is an interdisciplinary perspective that emphasizes the roles of feedback, mutual organization and emergence in shaping intelligent behaviour (Clancey, 1997a: 1–5). It has had only a marginal influence on KM through the concept of 'communities of practice' introduced by Lave and Wenger (1991), but we argue that it has the potential to help generate a deeper understanding of KM. The adjective 'situated' indicates the concern to see every action as intrinsically connected with the context or situation in which it occurs (Clancey 1997a). There is a very close parallel here with the concept of economic activity being 'embedded' in distinctive national contexts, something that has been a major theme of the book.

One aspect of the situated cognition approach to knowledge is that at any one time we can regard an individual as possessing dynamic cognitive schemes that have developed during that individual's life. Saying these schemes are dynamic emphasizes the idea that they exist and are maintained and developed through being activated by transactions between the organism and its environment. They are also developed through brain processes operating to a degree independently of overt experiences (Freeman 2000). In so far as they are accessible to consciousness, and can be named (thus bringing them within the linguistic sphere), they can also be recorded, and become 'explicit knowledge'. Knowledge in various forms is thus continuously, dynamically developed through transactions. Descriptions can be made that subsequently form part of an organism's environment, thus entering into further transactions.

The concept of situated knowledge can be broken down into three distinct senses of 'situated': functional or social, behavioural or psychological, and structural (neural) or interactive (Clancey 1997a: 25). First, the *functional* or social perspective emphasizes the idea that 'knowledge of activities ... is with respect to social relationships and purposes' (Clancey 1997a: 27). For example, studies of negotiated order (e.g. Strauss et al. 1963) and ethnographies of work (e.g. Orr 1990, 1996) illustrate how the process of collective formation of working procedures is developed and sustained. From this perspective, 'knowledge is inherently social in content' (Clancey 1997b: 14). Second, the *behavioural* or psychological sense of 'situatedness' concerns activities over a shorter time span than the functional or social. Cognition is behaviourally situated in that 'perception, movement, and conceptualization are changing with respect to each other moment-by-moment' (Clancey 1997b: 12). Thus cognition is 'grounded' in everyday activity and behaviour is shaped by continuous reflection on, and feedback from, what has just been done. In this sense, cognition is a process of continual readjustment of the next step in the light of what has just been accomplished. Knowledge is therefore local, contextual and continuously changing (see also Thelen 1995). Finally, the *structural* or interactive dimension of 'situatedness' concerns the 'physical structure of knowledge' (Clancey et al. 1998: 6). Clancey argues that at the neural level, 'perception, conception, and action are physically coordinated' (Clancey 1997a: 24). Cognition is situated, from this perspective, because conceptualizing is linked to sensori-motor co-ordination.

Thus on the one hand we find individuals enter into situations bearing 'prior knowledge' developed throughout their lives so far. Prior knowledge is neurally situated and will be selectively 'energized' or 'activated' as the individual engages in activities (transactions). This process is situated both socially (the general context), and behaviourally (the specific context of the activity). Here we can say that the individual's 'knowledge' is intimately bound up with the actions they are engaged in. On the other hand, an entirely different activity involves reflecting on other activities (specifically or in general) to produce descriptions of those activities, often intended to convey how to perform the activities reflected on. In other words, having ridden your bicycle, or developed a strategic plan for IHRM, you look back at *those* activities, and engage in a new one – the production of descriptions of those activities. Such reflection is a more extended activity than might occur while doing something, and results in the production of symbolic representations of the activity reflected on that can be shared or stored as artefacts like documents, books or computer records. Such descriptions can function as tools for further inquiry (Clancey 1997b) and action, and their use (planning) is also situated not only in relation to the proposed activity (and its perceived social context), but also to the individual's prior knowledge. Eliciting descriptions from people may require special effort and thus will need managing. Similarly, storing, searching, maintaining, and providing access to the descriptions and the artefacts containing them will require considerable effort, activities which have been called 'information management' (Orna 1990). Finally, as Garavelli and his colleagues (2002) point out, the effects of document use often depart from what was intended, and so also require managing.

The foregoing perspective suggests it is important and useful to distinguish knowledge as situated from knowledge representations or descriptions. This distinction, however, has largely been overlooked in KM discussion, and certainly does not inform KM frameworks. It seems a useful distinction to make since it enables us to hold in one conceptual frame the information processing approach, with its emphasis on documents and the like, and the 'people centred' approach, which stresses knowledge as 'embodied' in people and their social relationships. We no longer have two opposing approaches.

Implications for knowledge transfer

Returning to the question of knowledge transfer, we can perhaps regard people as 'containers' of knowledge, but this is only true of knowledge situated at the neural level, of prior knowledge. Such knowledge develops only as a result of ongoing person-in-context behaviour and experience (as well as unconscious brain processes). The question of how such knowledge 'gets into' its neural container can thus be answered: through experience, entailing various forms of learning.

An emphasis on prior knowledge, however, would risk overlooking the significance of the behavioural and social levels of situation. This is an unreasonable oversight since while we can make an analytical distinction between the three levels, in practice all three are integrated. To put this differently, the transfer of knowledge by transferring people depends for its efficacy on also transferring, or replicating, sufficiently similar behavioural and social contexts. In extreme cases, transfer might involve whole work units and their relevant social relations and this would greatly facilitate the transfer of knowledge, but such kinds of transfer are so rare, especially across borders, as not to be an issue. But again, if the social context of work cannot be transferred, this indicates that the container approach is not a viable one for understanding the issues involved in the process.

These points have obvious relevance in IHRM with transnational staff transfers, whether from centre to subsidiaries or partners, or, as has recently been highlighted, from partners and subsidiaries to headquarters units (Edwards and Ferner 2004). A technician installing and setting up familiar plant in a new country may face few problems with the plant itself (neural and behavioural level knowledge and activity) but any problems are likely to be particularly acute where relations with the host culture (organizational and wider culture – the sites or sources of socio-cultural knowledge) are concerned. Regarding people as containers of knowledge is thus at best extremely compressed shorthand for a complex and often indeterminate process.

The transfer of one or more individuals to a new environment is, however, probably only of minor significance for knowledge transfer in general because we are less concerned with migration and resettlement of employees than with the transfer of knowledge from temporary emigrants (expatriates) to local people. In other words, knowledge transfer is less concerned with the transfer of people and their effective functioning in new contexts (except over the short run) than with transfer from one person to another.

From the perspective of situated cognition, such transfer is clearly unthinkable – outside science fiction we cannot perform neural transplants. 'Knowledge transfer' evidently involves the question of how someone with a particular prior knowledge operating in one behavioural and social context comes to be able to behave in certain respects like someone else whose prior, behavioural and socio-cultural knowledge is different. Rather than referring to 'knowledge transfer,' it would perhaps be better to talk about 'learning', an approach that would certainly indicate the need for an HR role in the process.

The situated approach to learning emphasizes experience and therefore in the case of knowledge transfer indicates that the potential recipient must perform the activities about which they are seeking to acquire knowledge in order to acquire it. Assuming their prior knowledge does not prevent this from happening (it will certainly influence the learning process) and assuming no deficiencies in the design of the activity or technology, then the outcome of the learning process is likely to depend a great deal on the new social context. Transfer will depend on whether the 'donor' can find niches in the host socio-cultural context that permit replication (or improvement) on the previous levels of technical efficiency, i.e. whether the host culture can be changed or whether it proves too strong to permit transfer/learning.

While the cultural and behavioural dimensions are clearly important, emphasizing them tends to encourage the view that knowledge management/transfer problems will be overcome if people recognize these essentially psychological barriers and remove them. This overlooks what might be termed more structural factors, particularly those involving the division of labour and organization of work. Lam's (1997) study of two firms' attempts to share knowledge reveals how what could be called 'knowledge structures' are dependent on, and maintained by, the division of labour and tasks (see the following case study, 'A tale of two firms'). Where these differ, knowledge transfer may be difficult or impossible, or at best only operate in one direction. The way work was organized engendered different modes of knowledge generation and maintenance between the UK and Japanese firms. This study also suggests that the above argument about the relative ease of setting up a plant in a new country is oversimplistic. That scenario can only work where the division of labour and tasks is the same in both the 'home' and 'away' situations. More generally, Lam's study reinforces the point that the neural/behavioural levels cannot in practice be treated separately from the social. All three levels, and particularly the behavioural and social levels, are tightly integrated.

A tale of two firms: structural obstacles to knowledge sharing across borders

A comparison of two electronic engineering firms, one UK, the other Japanese, by Lam (1997) provides an interesting illustration of the difficulties of knowledge transfer where the organization of work, and consequent 'knowledge structures', differ. The study focused on the product design process, and particularly on the role of graduate engineers. In both countries companies employ graduate engineers, and the design process in each firm involves a similar set of roles: product design, development, testing, quality assurance and production, with a corresponding formal division of labour. The ways in which the firms treat graduate engineers after recruitment, the design process and the practical operation of the division of labour, however, differ significantly between the two firms, with important consequences for knowledge sharing.

UK graduate engineers receive a highly specialized training at university, and on recruitment tend to be deployed on productive work as soon as possible according to their specialization. Thus in the UK case study company, although design work is the responsibility of a team, each engineer works in a relatively isolated way on 'their' parts of the overall design, specializing in areas of individual expertise.

The engineers' training encourages the idea of a hierarchy of design work, with theoretical conceptual work at the top, and the organization of work maintains this approach. Individuals within the design team are responsible for their own parts of the task, and the design team as a whole is responsible for producing the design that others 'downstream' will implement. Product development, testing, quality control and manufacture are all seen as dependent downstream activities that have no role in design. Work in the UK factory is thus characterized by a strong division of labour, both as regards formation of skills (graduate design engineers are unlikely to have had any significant practical engineering skills) and ongoing organization of work.

One consequence of this approach is that control and co-ordination of downstream activities takes on special significance. This is largely achieved through written documentation – detailed, highly specific blueprints, guidelines and procedure documents that the downstream groups are expected to follow. Design and process knowledge is thus clearly divided between written (explicit) form and a largely overlooked tacit form. Emphasis is placed on the explicit knowledge for work co-ordination and communication. While Lam says nothing about tacit knowledge in the UK firm, it is reasonable to assume that it is present. Furthermore, it seems likely that it would be highly segmented – each task/functional group (and sub-groups within those groups) would have its own tacit knowledge about its range of tasks – and there would be no tacit knowledge concerning particular design processes as a whole.

The Japanese firm also recruits graduate engineers but they are not expected to contribute to productive work immediately. Instead they spend some time following a systematic process of job rotation, getting to know the organization and acquiring a range of organization-specific skills by on-the-job learning. Once deployed in engineering roles they tend to rely more on practical know-how than theoretical knowledge.

Development teams are quite large, and include people from a wide range of backgrounds and functions, such as planning, design and development, quality control and production. Design and manufacturing are seen as closely linked and manufacturing has a high profile on the design teams. The design engineers are responsible for planning and design, but as a development group. Moreover, they do not initially produce a complete design. The design process is explicitly iterative, and the designers begin with a relatively loose specification intended to be open to mutual and continual adjustment until the decision to go to production is made. Product development is thus characterized by strong cross-functional linkages and reciprocal flows of information and exchange of ideas across phases of development and functions and roles. In particular, production and manufacturing staff have an active role to play in the overall development process, providing input to the design, not just implementing the designers' blueprints.

This 'overlapping' design process requires intensive and frequent communication for its success. Decisions are made by agreement among all the team members, a process that often requires lengthy project co-ordination meetings. Face-to-face communication is the principal means of communication and co-ordination in the Japanese firm. Indeed, Japanese managers feel not only that they are not very good at producing documentation, but also that they lack a 'high-level' abstract technical language for describing their designs.

Design and process knowledge in the Japanese firm exists in both explicit (documentary) and tacit forms, but here the tacit is far more important, even dominant. Documents are produced as negotiable guidelines until a final design has been agreed utilizing the input of all involved in the process. Co-ordination is achieved not through specifying what 'downstream' functions have to do, but through discussion and negotiation through which all parties develop an understanding of what they are doing, and how their part contributes to the whole. Critical knowledge thus resides in social networks involving a wide range of roles and functions.

These two firms were linked in a technological partnership, and wanted to engage in co-operative working and knowledge sharing. What they did not realize was that these different 'knowledge structures', based on different work traditions and ways of organizing work, made knowledge transfer very difficult. In fact, the relationship was not just difficult, but one-sided. UK design engineers lacked the practical working experience of their Japanese counterparts, and thus the corresponding production knowledge. They relied on documents to understand design, but since the Japanese documents were often intentionally open and incomplete, they could not easily understand them, lacking the more practical knowledge (let alone the tacit knowledge relating to a particular project) to interpret the documents. The Japanese, for their part, felt they lacked an equivalent language for producing the kind of documents the UK engineers were used to. UK engineers thus found it very difficult to learn from working with the Japanese but the latter were able to learn from the British because they could understand and interpret the detailed documents the latter produced.

For further details, see:
Lam (1997) 'Embedded Firms, Embedded Knowledge: Problems of Collaboration and Knowledge Transfer in Global Cooperative Ventures', *Organization Studies*, 18(6), 973–96.

Case study question: *You have been asked to advise a Japanese company that is establishing a subsidiary in the UK on the challenges it will face in transferring knowledge from the firm's domestic operations to its UK sites. What advice would you give?*

Knowledge management in multinational companies

The case study described above raises a number of important issues for MNCs. Much of the writing on multinationals assumes that a key source of competitive advantage can be their ability to transfer knowledge across their sites. The concepts of 'situated cognition' in particular and the 'embeddedness' of economic activity in general suggest that this process will rarely be straightforward, and in this section we consider a number of aspects of the activity of MNCs that are relevant to the discussion.

One issue of great importance is the way that the knowledge that key actors in the firm view as central to its competitive position shapes the way the firm expands overseas. This idea is central to the Uppsala model of the growth of MNCs that we covered in Chapter 3, the basic idea of which is that the internationalization of the firm is a gradual process that arises from a series of incremental decisions rather than a few grand leaps forward. Since firms lack the knowledge crucial to operating effectively in other business systems due to the 'psychic distance' between countries (Johansson and Wiedersheim-Paul 1975), they tend to enter new markets through a series of incremental steps that become less risky as the firm acquires new knowledge. The tortuous nature of this process and the decades that it has taken the Swedish MNCs studied by the Uppsala authors to move through the steps they outlined become easier to understand when knowledge is seen as dependent on situated cognition rather than merely as information that can be transferred unproblematically between 'containers'.

A related issue is the method of growth. Many instances of growth through investment in 'greenfield sites' appear to be motivated by a desire to transfer knowledge that already exists within the firm. This was a central reason why many Japanese MNCs as they expanded into the UK went to some lengths to locate their sites in entirely new locations, often in 'new towns' with little history of industrial activity. Growth through mergers and acquisitions (M&As), in contrast, can result in the firm expanding much more quickly than the Uppsala model can explain. One motivation for this is that a merger or acquisition brings with it a body of knowledge, partly about the new market and environment in question but also knowledge that is seen as transferable to other parts of the firm. Thus one motivation for growing by acquisition is to acquire new knowledge and transfer it across borders. As we saw in Chapter 6, many cross-border M&As result in disappointing performance, suggesting that acquiring and transferring knowledge is rarely a source of easily realizable competitive advantage. This too is easier to understand in the light of the discussion of knowledge in this chapter.

A subsequent issue concerns the nature of the structures within MNCs that are effective in encouraging knowledge transfer. As we saw in Chapter 4, much of the writing in this area centres on the idea of networks of 'multi-centred' firms (Forsgren 2004; Hedlund 1986). For example, Cantwell and Mudambi (2004) argue that what is crucial to the value-creation process is the MNC's ability to leverage its internal network of subsidiaries in order to integrate knowledge bases that are geographically dispersed. Perhaps the best-known exponents of this view are Bartlett and Ghoshal (1998) and their idea of the 'transnational' organizational form as the solution to managing across borders. There are some indications that MNCs are increasingly moving towards such networks with multiple centres of excellence (see the case study 'GlaxoSmithKline and centres of excellence in research and development').

In emphasizing the idea of networks, however, there is a danger that the difficulties in transferring knowledge are downplayed as integrating knowledge from dispersed networks may be more difficult than it seems. Bartlett and Ghoshal (1998), for example, appear to pay insufficient attention to the willingness of actors in different parts of the MNC to identify and share innovations from which other parts of the firm can benefit (see Chapter 4). One way that HR can try to inhibit networks in subsidiaries from becoming too locked into their local contexts regarding knowledge development, a key HR role according to Gammelgaard et al. (2004: 204), is to create special rewards for those groups. Typically this might involve linking the identification of valuable innovations to material rewards, such as bonuses, for individuals or groups. Another way is to give individuals or groups responsibilities beyond their own operating unit, such as the status of 'internal consultant' (Edwards 1998). However, rewarding individuals within networks, or the networks themselves, can have contradictory effects. On the one hand, actors in the subsidiaries may be willing to absorb new ideas and innovations from other parts of the firm only because to resist doing so would jeopardize the future of their unit. On the other, it may create an unwillingness to share knowledge that has been developed locally as to do so may erode the competitive position of the unit. As Lado and Wilson (1994) point out, it is all too easy to implement good HR practices only to find that they incidentally inhibit learning and thus knowledge transfer. A key HR challenge for MNCs becomes how they can set up the incentive structures that facilitate knowledge sharing and thus transfer, something that we examined in relation to the transfer of HR practices in Chapter 5. Bringing about the transfer of knowledge in MNCs not only has to overcome the barriers arising from situated cognition but also has to overcome motivational barriers.

It is implicit in the foregoing that the significance of motivational factors relates primarily to *explicit* knowledge transfer since people can only be motivated to transfer (or withhold) that of which they are consciously aware. However, irrespective of the motivational issues arising from multi-centre networks of relatively independent (if not in some sense competing) units, there is the likelihood that they will also inhibit the transfer of tacit knowledge. Collins's studies of knowledge sharing in scientific communities where there were no motivational disincentives to sharing knowledge illustrate this well. In two quite different articles, Collins (1974, 2001) explores the difficulties scientists faced in successfully replicating published experiments reported by others. Tacit knowledge was evident in that the successful teams could perform certain experiments, but failed to transmit that knowledge to others through scientific publications designed precisely to facilitate such communication. It turns out that their inability stemmed from the fact that they were unaware of the real reasons for their success. In both cases, features of the experimental set-up regarded as marginal or routine practice, and hence overlooked in reporting the results, were critical to the success of the experiment. This was only discovered when teams worked together, and each gradually learned what the critical factors were.

The implications for knowledge transfer in any context where independent teams are concerned is obvious: personal contact and shared experiences between individuals on different teams are essential to the transfer of tacit knowledge. Since no one can predict whether or not significant tacit knowledge will attach to some innovation until after the event (when other teams fail to replicate results) this suggests a need for a continual exchange of personnel between teams such as those formed by

GlaxoSmithKline (see the following case study). As Arvidsson and Birkinshaw argue (2004; see also Szulanski 2000), capabilities developed locally are often 'sticky', hard to identify and do not flow easily between subsidiary units. Special measures are required to ensure that they do flow, and practices of Japanese engineers reported in Lam's (1997) case study illustrate one possible approach to remedying this problem.

GlaxoSmithKline and centres of excellence in research and development

In late 2000 a merger between GlaxoWellcome and SmithKline Beecham created the second biggest pharmaceuticals firm in the world, known as GlaxoSmithKline (GSK), which employs around 100,000 people. The merger itself presented opportunities for the firm to achieve cost saving through removing duplicate functions. More generally, there are many advantages that go with being a very large firm in this sector, notably the scope that exists for economies of scale to be realized. One illustration of this is in research and development (R&D) where a large firm can spread the risks of a particular project not generating a new drug by having a greater number of projects running at the same time. There are also disadvantages of being so large – or diseconomies of scale, in other words – notably that a big firm can become proceduralized in such a way that stifles innovation. In the R&D field, where GSK has 15,000 staff, this was a real danger.

GSK's response to the need to realize economies of scale but avoid the diseconomies of scale was to split up the intermediate phases of the R&D process into small, semi-autonomous working units that are termed 'Centres of Excellence for Drug Discovery' or CEDDs. Six of these were established soon after the merger and a seventh has been added subsequently, with each one dedicated to a specific therapeutic category of research. Each one of these units is tasked with the responsibility of bringing a chemical compound to the point where it can begin large-scale clinical trials, at which stage it is passed on to another group of scientists within the firm. As the company itself puts it:

'While harnessing the power of our size to capture new knowledge about how diseases develop and progress, we are also drawing upon the energy, drive and nimbleness of small groups of scientists to make the discoveries which will lead us to the development of new, safe and effective medicines'
(http://science.gsk.com/process/drugs.htm – accessed 13 December 2004).

The company hoped that this structure would help it to emulate the entrepreneurial spirit of the much smaller bio-tech firms. To help facilitate this spirit the CEDDs were given a high degree of autonomy from other parts of the firm with the heads of the units able to buy in compounds from inside and outside the firm and bid for funds from the centre of the firm. In addition, when they were successful in bringing new drugs to clinical trials the staff would be richly rewarded. The head of the R&D division of the firm, Tachi Yamada, has repeatedly insisted that he wants to see GSK create as many millionaire scientists as the bio-tech sector does.

There were a number of consequences for the HR function in the management of the CEDDs. Perhaps the most obvious of these was the facilitation of international communication and the handling of international assignments since the CEDDs comprise research laboratories at a number of sites in the USA, the UK and Italy. An additional issue for the HR function was to ensure that the CEDDs had in practice the autonomy that was intended by their creators. This was a challenge because the firm in general, and corporate HR function in particular, was developing a range of policies that applied across the firm and thus the push for greater autonomy went against the grain of the way the company was moving. More specifically, the move towards autonomous units had to be balanced against the need for a degree of consistency in HR policies, particularly in relation to pay, since it was envisaged that some researchers might move from one CEDD to another over time – vast differences in pay levels and in ways of calculating bonuses and performance-related rewards might impede such mobility.

Case study question: *What advice would you give to GSK, or any similar firm, regarding making best use of its R&D knowledge assets? How might it manage the implicit tension between controlling and motivating research scientists, and managing tacit knowledge effectively?*

Knowledge management and international HRM

The foregoing discussion raises a number of very important issues for IHRM. Perhaps the most obvious one concerns the precise mechanisms through which MNCs facilitate the transfer of knowledge across their sites. A crucial distinction in this respect is between codifiable (explicit) and implicit (or tacit) forms of knowledge. Notwithstanding some of the issues surrounding the relatively neglected question of how explicit knowledge transfer happens (Gourlay 2003), a body of evidence testifies to the way that it can be transferred across sites in the form of written documents such as manuals of 'best practice', codified databases and standardized frameworks (Edwards and Ferner 2004). For example, Coller's (1996) case study of a European food multinational testifies to the existence of a document known as 'Best Proven Practice' that contains any improvement made by an operating unit and which is then publicized to all other units in the division. Similarly, in a German electrical engineering company a special team comprising those from the HQ and seconded managers from operations around the world conduct systematic management audits of 'best practices' from across the firm (Ferner and Varul 1999).

While such mechanisms may be effective for codifiable forms of knowledge, they are manifestly inappropriate for tacit forms of knowledge. Linsday et al. (2004) argue that knowledge embedded in people is particularly important for MNCs in the service sector since these firms are heavily dependent on knowledge that is locationally embedded and context specific. It is the mobility of people across the multinational that is the primary channel through which tacit knowledge can be transferred. People-based mechanisms of transfer can be formalized – as is the case with the use of international HR committees in many MNCs – or relatively informal, such as the use of open-ended expatriation, fixed-term assignments, short business trips, informal contacts, international workshops and so on. Harzing (2001) has developed the metaphor of expatriates as corporate 'bumble bees', travelling across countries and taking with them knowledge that has rubbed off on to them from other sites. Studies of international assignments have tended to show that such learning and transfer does not occur instantly or even quickly, but rather becomes more likely the longer a person spends on an assignment in another country (e.g. Hocking et al. 2004). This is, of course, consistent with our earlier analysis of situated cognition and the challenges facing individuals in accessing knowledge in a quite different setting.

Thus the focus on international assignments is likely to remain a key part of IHRM, in part reflecting what IHRM practitioners currently do but also because temporary transfers, and exchanges, of staff between organizations and units within partnerships and joint ventures remain important practices, particularly for the purpose of knowledge transfer. In this context, KM interventions indicate that there should be a focus on enhancing their learning and its transfer back to the next generation of transferees, and on incorporating individual learning into an organizational learning system. This might involve a number of interventions. First, for example, individuals' awareness of the learning opportunities, both for themselves (and perhaps their families) and the organization can be developed as part of the preparation for the assignment. Second, conditions in the organization to which the individual is going can be evaluated against, for example, the organizational learning mechanisms model (Popper and Lipshitz 1998). If possible, changes can be sought that will enhance the learning opportunities for the expatriate. The same can, of course, also be done by the host organization, independently or in tandem with the organization from which the expatriate is coming. Finally, when, if not before, the individual returns to their 'home' organization, policies and processes can be in place to facilitate learning from them, and thus deriving a contribution to the organization's knowledge from each particular experience.

Another area that is obviously relevant to the issue of knowledge transfer is the issue we covered in Chapter 5, namely the transfer of practices across borders. We saw that there are a number of constraints on the ability of a multinational to transfer a practice across its sites, meaning that the practice may need to be altered so that it can be implemented in the new business system. In this context, we raised the issue of 'transmutation', by which we mean the way in which a practice may not operate in precisely the same way in the new unit when compared with the original unit as actors in the recipient unit seek to adapt it to pre-existing models of behaviour, assumptions and power relations. Thus the formal substance of a practice may be diffused but the operation of this practice may differ between countries (Edwards and Ferner 2004; see also MacKenzie's (1996) argument about the *reinvention* as distinct from *transfer* of, in particular, tacit knowledge). Edwards and Ferner provide an illustration of the adoption by some US automotive firms of Japanese forms of work organization, arguing that in implementing lean production and its associated practices, US-based companies have attached less emphasis on the devolution of responsibility to teams of operators which characterizes the nature of teams in Japan, and instead have retained the distinctive supervisory relationships characteristic of their US-based operations. This becomes easier to understand once one is familiar with the concept of situated cognition, as we now are; it shapes people's understandings and behaviour in ways of which they themselves are not always conscious.

More generally, a perennial concern of HR departments worldwide is that they are of relatively low status compared with other functions such as finance and operations. Thus the HR department tends to exert relatively little influence on 'strategic' issues and finds itself marginalized in cases of major organizational change. In some countries, this reflects particular features of the institutional context. For instance, Ferner and Varul (2000) argue that the German HR system has tended to make German personnel specialists experts in the 'juridified' system of bargaining and co-determination but has precluded them spreading their wings into more 'strategic' aspects of the firm's international operations. Even in UK MNCs, however, the HR function is often not as influential as many within it would like it to be. In this context, the issue of KM and knowledge transfer offers an opportunity for those within the HR function to upgrade their status and exert more influence. As we have already noted, it is widely accepted that a multinational's competitive position is shaped by the knowledge it has within the boundaries of the firm and the way that it transfers this across its operating units. In this context, those in the HR function may be able to carve out a niche for themselves as experts in this area, stressing their understanding of the way that knowledge is 'situated' or 'embedded' and the challenges presented by attempts to transfer this across the firm. Thus KM can become a way in which HR practitioners are able to portray themselves as well placed to contribute to core issues that help the firm to 'create value'.

Other implications for practice are more far-reaching, implying the extension of IHRM to managing HR and related issues on an inter-organizational and international scale instead of only on an organizational and domestic scale. This has been suggested by Novicevic and Harvey (2001) who argue that IHRM should become strategic IHRM, or SIHRM. But the role development implicit here is more fundamental. In so far as HRM, strategic or otherwise, focuses on issues such as pay, conditions, rewards, contracts and the employment relationship in general, it often tends to treat questions regarding employee development and training as subsidiary. Knowledge and learning issues, however, require a new focus on these topics, a shift to looking at the development potential of, and developing appropriate policies and practices for, the whole unit. The emphasis of such policies would obviously vary depending on the nature of the inter-organizational relationship. Where the relationship is one of partnership, or some other co-operative form, a policy for the whole unit would probably be possible and sensible. If, on the other hand, the relationship is more predatory, then the emphasis would more likely be on human resource development (HRD) planning for the whole unit, but from the perspective of the dominant part of that unit – on what the leading or dominant company can gain in knowledge and learning terms, regardless of the subordinate companies.

Conclusion

At the beginning of this chapter, KM was described as comprising two foci or rival camps: the dominant one emphasizing IT-based methods and solutions; and a subordinate one drawing attention to the centrality of human behaviour to knowing and thus KM. From the former perspective, it is apparent that behaviour is critical to the success of IT-based KM projects (Davenport et al. 1998; Scarborough et al. 1999; Thomas et al. 2001), which is also obvious in so far as databases are only useful if they are used, maintained and developed, all of which require motivated people. In so far as skills required for influencing and managing behaviour are found in HR departments, and it is their role to advise if not carry out measures to influence behaviour, this implies an important and necessary role for HR even with an IT-centred approach to KM.

On the other hand, if the wider approach to KM, outlined above is adopted, it is clear that managing behaviour, learning and knowledge cannot be separated from one another. Managing behaviour means to manage learning and knowledge, regardless of the intentions behind the management process or policy. As Lado and Wilson (1994) point out, HR practices can hinder and inhibit learning, and thus undermine, if not destroy, the very resource they aim to manage. The issue for HR practitioners thus becomes that of how to manage better in order to enhance the possibilities for individual and organizational learning. A number of measures have been suggested, as was indicated earlier. Even if the wider perspective on knowledge is rejected as being too broad, the literature on knowledge transfer clearly shows that human behavioural processes are a critical factor, something authors like Garavelli et al. (2002) have articulated.

This chapter has also shown that knowledge transfer issues are particularly important for MNCs. The transfer of knowledge always comes up against the challenges that result from it being 'situated' in a particular context, but in an international context these challenges are all the greater. Thus the scope of IHRM research could usefully be extended to look in more detail at KM and learning aspects. In particular, it is clear that a central issue for IHRM concerns how individuals develop and how they learn, and it is to this issue that we turn in Chapter 9.

Review questions

1 What is the key difference between explicit or codifiable and tacit or implicit forms of knowledge and what are the implications of the distinction for the way that knowledge can be transferred across operating units?

2 In what ways can cognition be described as 'situated'? How useful is this concept when considering knowledge transfer in MNCs?

3 In what ways do differences in national business systems affect the transfer of knowledge across borders?

167

Further reading

Garavelli, A.C., Gorgoglione, M. and Scozzi, B. (2002) 'Managing Knowledge Transfer by Knowledge Technologies', *Technovation*, 22, 269–79.

This article provides a useful discussion of some issues in knowledge transfer theory.

Gupta, A. and Govindarajan, V. (2000) 'Knowledge Flows within Multinational Corporations', *Strategic Management Journal*, 21(4), 473–96.

This is one of the most widely cited papers on knowledge management in MNCs.

Kamoche, K. (1997) 'Knowledge Creation and Learning in International HRM', *International Journal of Human Resource Management*, 8, 213–25.

This is an interesting discussion of how learning takes place in MNCs.

Lam, A. (1997) 'Embedded Firms, Embedded Knowledge: Problems of Collaboration and Knowledge Transfer in Global Cooperative Ventures', *Organization Studies*, 18(6), 973–96.

This article provides detailed case study evidence on the difficulties that a Japanese and UK firm had in transferring knowledge between their operations.

References

Argote, L. and Ingram, P. (2000) 'Knowledge Transfer: A Basis for Competitive Advantage in Firms', *Organizational Behavior and Human Decision Processes*, 82, 150–69.

Arvidsson, N. and Birkinshaw, J. (2004) 'Identifying Leading-Edge Market Knowledge in Multinational Corporations' in V. Mahnke and T. Pedersen (eds) *Knowledge Flows, Governance and the Multinational Enterprise: Frontiers in International Management Research*, Basingstoke: Macmillan.

Bartlett, C. and Ghoshal, S. (1998) *Managing across Borders: The Transnational Solution*, Boston: Harvard Business School Press.

Bender, S. and Fish, A. (2000) 'The Transfer of Knowledge and the Retention of Expertise: The Continuing Need for Global Assignments', *Journal of Knowledge Management*, 4, 125–37.

Bhagat, R.S., Kedia, B.L., Harveston, P.D. and Triandis, H.C. (2002) 'Cultural Variations in the Cross-Border Transfer of Organizational Knowledge: An Integrative Framework', *Academy of Management Review*, 27, 204–21.

Bonaventura, M. (1997) 'The Benefits of a Knowledge Culture,' *Aslib Proceedings*, 49, 82–89.

Bresman, J., Birkinshaw, J. and Nobel, R. (1999) 'Knowledge Transfer in International Acquisitions', *Journal of International Business Studies*, 30, 439–62.

Brown, J.S., Collins, A. and Duguid, P. (1991) 'Organizational Learning and Communities-of-Practice', *Organization Science*, 2, 40–57.

Cantwell, J. and Mudambi, R. (2004) 'Multinational Enterprises and Competence-Creating Knowledge Flows: A Theoretical Analysis' in V. Mahnke and T. Pedersen (eds) *Knowledge Flows, Governance and the Multinational Enterprise: Frontiers in International Management Research*, Basingstoke: Macmillan.

Cherry, C. (1966) *On Human Communication. A Review, a Survey and a Criticism*, Cambridge MA, and London: MIT Press.

Clancey, W.J. (1997a) 'The Conceptual Nature of Knowledge, Situations and Activity' in P. Feltovich, R. Hoffman and K. Ford *Human and Machine Expertise in Context,* Menlo Park, CA: The AAAI Press.

Clancey, W.J. (1997b), *Situated Cognition: On Human Knowledge and Computer Representations*, Cambridge: Cambridge University Press.

Clancey, W.J., Sachs, P., Sierhuis, M. and van Hoof, R. (1998) 'Brahms: Simulating Practice for Work Systems Design', *International Journal of Human-Computer Studies*, 49(6), 831–65 (copy at Cogprint: Cognitive Sciences Eprint Archive: http://cogprints.soton.ac.uk/ – accessed 23 November 1999).

Clark, T., Gospel, H. and Montgomery, J. (1999) 'Running on the Spot? A Review of Twenty Years of Research on the Management of Human Resources in a Comparative and International Perspective', *International Journal of Human Resource Management*, 10, 520–44.

Coller, X. (1996) 'Managing Flexibility in the Food Industry: A Cross-National Comparative Case Study in European Multinational Companies', *European Journal of Industrial Relations*, 2(2), 153–72.

Collins, H.M. (1974) 'The TEA Set: Tacit Knowledge and Scientific Networks', *Science Studies*, 4, 165–86.

Collins, H.M. (2001) 'Tacit Knowledge, Trust, and the Q of Sapphire', *Social Studies of Science*, 31, 71–85.

Covin, T.J. and Stivers, B.P. (1997) 'Knowledge Management in Focus in UK and Canadian Firms', *Creativity and Innovation Management*, 6, 140–50.

Davenport, T.H., De Long, D.W. and Beers, M.C. (1998) 'Successful Knowledge Management Projects', *Sloan Management Review*, Winter, 43–57.

Edwards, T. (1998) 'Multinationals, Work Organisation and the Process of Diffusion: A Case Study', *International Journal of Human Resource Management*, 9(4), 696–709.

Edwards, T. and Ferner, A. (2004) 'Multinationals, Reverse Diffusion and National Business Systems', *Management International Review*, 24(1), 51–81.

Ferner, A. and Varul, M.Z. (1999) *The German Way? German Multinationals and the Management of Human Resources in their UK Subsidiaries*, London: Anglo-German Foundation for the Study of Industrial Society.

Ferner, A. and Varul, M.Z. (2000) 'Internationalisation and the Personnel Function in German Multinationals', *Human Resource Management Journal* 10(3), 79–96.

Forsgren, M. (2004) 'The Use of Network Theory in MNC Research' in V. Mahnke and T. Pedersen (eds) *Knowledge Flows, Governance and the Multinational Enterprise: Frontiers in International Management Research*, Basingstoke: Macmillan.

Freeman, W.J. (2000) *How Brains Make Up Their Minds*, London: Orion Books (Phoenix).

Gammelgaard, J., Holm, U. and Pedersen, T. (2004) 'The Dilemmas of MNC Subsidiary Transfer of Knowledge' in V. Mahnke and T. Pedersen (eds) *Knowledge Flows, Governance and the Multinational Enterprise: Frontiers in International Management Research*, Basingstoke: Macmillan.

Garavelli, A.C., Gorgoglione, M. and Scozzi, B. (2002), 'Managing Knowledge Transfer by Knowledge Technologies', *Technovation*, 22, 269–79.

Gourlay, S.N. (2003) 'Knowledge Transfer and Reading: Implications of the Transactional Theory of Reading for Research and Practice', paper presented at 'Organizational Knowledge, Learning and Capabilities', 4th Conference, Barcelona, Spain, 13–14 April.

Gupta, A. and Govindarajan, V. (1991) 'Knowledge Flows and the Structure of Control within Multinational Corporations', *Academy of Management Review*, 16(4), 768–92.

Gupta, A. and Govindarajan, V. (2000) 'Knowledge Flows within Multinational Corporations', *Strategic Management Journal*, 21(4), 473–96.

Harzing, A-W. (2001) 'Of Bears, Bumble-bees and Spiders: The Role of Expatriates in Controlling Foreign Subsidiaries', *Journal of World Business*, 36(4), 366–79, available at http://www.harzing.com/papers.htm#spiders

Hayek, F.A. (1945) 'The Use of Knowledge in Society', in P.S. Myers (ed.) *Knowledge Management and Organizational Design*, Boston and Oxford: Butterworth-Heinemann.

Hedlund, G. (1986) 'The Hypermodern MNC – a Heterarchy?', *Human Resource Management*, 25(1), 9–35.

Hocking, J., Brown, M. and Harzing, A. (2004) 'A Knowledge Transfer Perspective of Strategic Assignment Purposes and their Path-Dependent Outcomes', *International Journal of Human Resource Management*, 15(3), 565–86.

Johannessen, J-A., Olaisen, J. and Olsen, B. (2001) 'Mismanagement of Tacit Knowledge: The Importance of Tacit Knowledge, The Danger of Information Technology, and What To Do About It', *International Journal of Information Management*, 21, 3–20.

Johansson, J. and Wiedersheim-Paul, F. (1975) 'The Internationalisation of the Firm: Four Swedish Cases', *Journal of Management Studies*, 305–22.

Kamoche, K. (1995) *Knowledge-Creation and Learning in International HRM*, Birmingham: Department of Commerce, Birmingham Business School.

Kamoche, K. (1997), 'Knowledge Creation and Learning in International HRM', *International Journal of Human Resource Management*, 8, 213–25.

Lado, A.A. and Wilson, M.C. (1994) 'Human Resource Systems and Sustained Competitive Advantage: A Competency-Based Perspective', *Academy of Management Review*, 19(4), 699–727.

Lam, A. (1997) 'Embedded Firms, Embedded Knowledge: Problems of Collaboration and Knowledge Transfer in Global Cooperative Ventures', *Organization Studies*, 18(6), 973–96.

Lave, J. and Wenger, E. (1991) *Situated Learning: Legitimate Peripheral Participation*, Cambridge: Cambridge University Press.

Lindsay, V., Chadee, D., Mattson, J. and Johnston, R. (2004) 'Knowledge Flows in International Service Firms: A Conceptual Model' in V. Mahnke and T. Pedersen (eds) *Knowledge Flows, Governance and the Multinational Enterprise: Frontiers in International Management Research*, Basingstoke: Macmillan.

MacKenzie, D. (1996) *Knowing Machines. Essays on Technical Change*, Boston: MIT Press.

Myers, P.S. (1996) *Knowledge Management and Organizational Design*, Boston and Oxford: Butterworth-Heinemann.

Nonaka, I. (1994) 'A Dynamic Theory of Organizational Knowledge Creation', *Organization Science*, 5, 14–37.

Nonaka, I. and Takeuchi, H. (1995) *The Knowledge-Creating Company*, New York and Oxford: Oxford University Press.

Novicevic, M.M. and Harvey, M. (2001) 'The Changing Role of the Corporate HR Function in Global Organizations of the Twenty-First Century', *International Journal of Human Resource Management*, 12, 1251–68.

Orna, E. (1990) *Practical Information Policies: How to Manage Information Flow in Organizations*, Aldershot: Gower.

Orr, J.E. (1990) 'Sharing Knowledge, Celebrating Identity: Community Memory in a Service Culture', in D. Middleton and D. Edwards (eds), *Collective Remembering*, London: Sage.

Orr, J.E. (1996) *Talking About Machines. An Ethnography of a Modern Job*, Ithaca, NY and London: Cornell University Press.

Popper, M. and Lipshitz, R. (1998) 'Organizational Learning Mechanisms: A Structural and Cultural Approach to Organizational Learning', *Journal of Applied Behavioral Science*, 34, 161–79.

Reddy, M.J. (1979) 'The Conduit Metaphor – a Case of Frame Conflict in Our Language About Language', in A. Ortony (ed.) *Metaphor and Thought*, Cambridge: Cambridge University Press.

Scarborough, H., Swan, J. and Preston, J. (1999) *Knowledge Management: A Literature Review*, London: Institute of Personnel and Development.

Schuler, R.S. (2001) 'Human Resource Issues and Activities in International Joint Ventures', *International Journal of Human Resource Management*, 12, 1–52.

Shannon, C.E. and Weaver, W. (1949) *The Mathematical Theory of Communication*, Urbana: University of Illinois Press.

Sierhuis, M. and Clancey, W.J. (1997) 'Knowledge, Practice, Activities and People', in proceedings of the 'AAAI Spring Symposium on Artificial Intelligence in Knowledge Management', 142–48.

Simonin, B.L. (1999) 'Ambiguity and the Process of Knowledge Transfer in Strategic Alliances', *Strategic Management Journal*, 20, 595–623.

Strauss, A., Schatzman, L., Ehrlich, D., Bucher, R. and Shabsin, M. (1963) 'The Hospital and its Negotiated Order', in E. Friedson (ed.) *The Hospital in Modern Society*, New York: Macmillan.

Swan, J., Robertson, M. and Newell, S. (2002) 'Knowledge Management: The Human Factor', in S. Barnes (ed.) *Knowledge Management Systems*, Oxford: Thomson.

Szulanski, G. (2000) 'The Process of Knowledge Transfer: A Diachronic Analysis of Stickiness', *Organizational Behavior and Human Decision Processes*, 82, 9–27.

Thelen, E. (1995) 'Time-Scale Dynamics and the Development of an Embodied Cognition' in R.F. Port and T. van Gelder (eds) *Mind as Motion: Explorations in the Dynamics of Cognition*, Cambridge, MA: MIT Press.

Thomas, J.C., Kellogg, W.A. and Erickson, T. (2001) 'The Knowledge Management Puzzle: Human and Social Factors in Knowledge Management', *IBM Systems Journal*, 40, 863–84.

Tissen, R., Andriessen, D. and Deprez, F.L. (1998) *Value-Based Knowledge Management*, Amsterdam: Addison Wesley Longman.

Tiwana, A. (2000) *The Knowledge Management Toolkit*, Upper Saddle River, NJ: Prentice Hall.

Wong, M.M.L. (2001) 'Internationalizing Japanese Expatriate Managers: Organizational Learning Through International Assignment', *Management Learning*, 32, 237–51.

Chapter 9

International management development

Jean Woodall

Key aims

This chapter has the following key aims:

- to outline the changing scope of international management development and international manager roles;
- to explore more fully the significance of learning theory for international management development, something that is of obvious importance given our discussion of knowledge management in Chapter 8;
- to outline specific international management development interventions that are commonly used;
- to reflect on future developments.

Introduction

Much has been written about the selection and preparation of managers for international roles in global organizations, and much of the literature is of a rather descriptive and prescriptive nature. In general, the focus tends to be on identifying high-potential employees for expatriate assignments and devising executive development programmes for them. Unfortunately, this leads to a very narrow perspective on international management development (IMD), as there are a number of other factors that need to be considered.

The first of these factors is the organizational context within which the international manager operates. Multinational companies (MNCs) can have quite diverse structures – they are not simply headquartered in a 'home' country with foreign operations run by expatriates. The scale of the operations controlled by MNCs and their global reach have given 'host' and 'third' country nationals a more significant role in the management process. Also, the rapid changes in company fortunes as a consequence of globalization mean that the international manager will face a potentially shorter, more uncertain career as operations are switched between countries. This has serious implications for the range of roles required of international managers (as outlined in the next section), and in turn starts to raise issues about the nature of the IMD provided. Should it be confined purely to executive development for a select group of high-potential expatriates? Or is this something that should be extended to include other managers at all levels, in different roles and at different stages of their careers? Finally, what does this mean for host country and even third country nationals who hitherto might not have been included within IMD activity?

Another factor concerns the scope of activities that are included in IMD. It involves more than simple training and development and also comprises succession planning and performance management, and even extends into personal and family welfare. In particular, it is important to situate IMD within the context of management learning. Unfortunately, however, much of the debate on IMD has taken place in isolation from the insights on learning that have emerged over recent years (Briscoe and Schuler 2004; Sparrow et al. 2004; Tayeb 2004). These insights can be summarized as follows:

- the importance of responding to individual learning styles (Kolb 1983);
- the growing significance of informal and incidental learning that takes place through everyday work activities as opposed to formal off-the-job training sessions (Marsick and Watkins 1990); there is also evidence that work experiences of a negative as well as a positive kind can be very important for individual learning and career development (McCauley et al. 1994);
- linked to this, the growing awareness of the ways in which formal work-related activities can be harnessed as learning tools;
- the growing interest in organizational and team learning as well as individual learning;
- a growing awareness that the wider organizational culture and the specific learning culture of the organization can encourage or inhibit individual, team and organizational learning;
- the potential contribution of information and communications technology (ICT) to individual, team and organizational learning as well as knowledge transfer; in particular, this underpins the enthusiasm for knowledge management (KM) and corporate universities.

The changing scope of international management development

Until the 1990s, the international manager was typically a senior-level corporate employee who was mid-to-late career, male and Caucasian, and who had a 'trailing spouse'. Usually 'he' was embarking on an international assignment of at least two years, which was often presented as a reward towards the end of a long career with the organization. The pre-departure development would be confined to a 'briefing' from existing expatriates returning or visiting the home country, occasionally supplemented, by the opportunity to make a short visit to the overseas site. Formal international development programmes that included a wider range of pre-departure support were rare. Indeed, the administration of international human resource management (IHRM) was usually separate from corporate management development activities and mainly preoccupied with arranging international salary packages and dealing with relocation issues such as visas, work permits and housing. This model was developed largely by US multinationals, although it was also widely adopted in the UK.

However, by the mid-1980s it was becoming clear that this 'neo-colonial' model was exhibiting serious flaws (Scullion 1993). First, the rate of expatriate turnover was much higher than in comparable management groups, with hidden indirect costs to the business as well as the expense of replacement and development. This in turn led to shortages in the supply of international executives, thereby severely constraining the potential for overseas business development. The expatriate with 'trailing spouse' (usually female, although males are increasingly facing this predicament – see Selmer and Leung 2003) was being replaced by dual career couples who exhibited a greater reluctance to embark on an international assignment unless it offered career development for both partners. This was also related to changing patterns of female employment and family life, so that expatriates with school-age children were reluctant to disturb the children's education or to send them home to boarding school. Furthermore, traditional stereotypes and host country social conventions reinforced women's continued under representation among the ranks of international managers (Harris 2004). Finally, there was growing evidence that the process of repatriation was not a satisfactory experience for most managers, who on their return often experienced culture shock, lost career opportunities and even unemployment.

These trends were still evident at the start of the twenty-first century. Forster (2000) argues that the idea of the 'international manager' as originally conceived is now a myth. It is rather a 'loose description of someone who is potentially or currently abroad on a one-off international assignment' (2000: 126). Short-term travel assignments are increasingly used by European, Japanese and US MNCs and involve people drawn from a wide range of business functions – human resource managers, corporate lawyers, engineers, computer programmers and hardware designers, and finance, marketing and sales personnel. Forster's study of 500 expatriates in 36 UK companies showed that a substantial number of respondents experienced psychological difficulties in adjusting to a foreign culture, and even more so at the stage of repatriation. He saw this as contributing to a declining interest in continuing an international career, and concluded that the form of international assignments would need to change from a long-term stay overseas to more frequent short-term cross-border job swaps, short assignments or participation in multicultural virtual project teams. This would require managers with international competencies, who were able and willing to undertake such short assignments. It would mean that the frequency of traditional expatriate postings with male employees and trailing female spouses would become less common in the future (Forster 2000). Thus if international managers are required to carry out a greater variety of roles, it is important to consider what has led to this.

International manager roles: the development implications

The popular conception of the role of the international manager as a mid-career expatriate who relocates overseas in order to assume a senior management position in a subsidiary of the parent company needs to be dispelled. Managers now need to fill different roles at various stages of corporate international development (Hendry 1994; Woodall and Winstanley 1998). Although organizations do not progress in linear fashion through various stages of international development, it is helpful to analyse these different stages in order to perceive the different role requirements of international managers.

Where an organization only has limited overseas relationships, such as export through an agent or foreign distributor moving on to the setting up of a foreign sales subsidiary or branch office, only those individuals directly concerned may need development. Yet this will not necessarily be just for the expatriates, but may also be required for the host country nationals (HCNs). In addition, sales representatives from the parent company, who have previously not contemplated an international role, may well require intensive cultural awareness and, possibly, language training. However, when a company opens up foreign subsidiaries in individual countries, the initial requirement is for a senior expatriate management team, with a gradual extension of management positions to host country nationals. At the next stage, setting up a regional business, managers from the various subsidiaries need to meet frequently to share ideas and information, and often to brainstorm and agree solutions. Thus development that facilitates cross-cultural communication is essential. In a mature regional business, succession planning becomes important in order to prepare potential expatriate managers as well as host and third country nationals. Finally, the transition towards a highly internationalized business requires managers who are able to share information and be willing to work as team members across functional and country-regional lines, exhibiting the so-called 'helicopter' quality (the ability to demonstrate cultural sensitivity and to rise above cultural constraints).

However, globalization has witnessed an intensification of focus on international development, and the growing use of international joint ventures and cross-border alliances provides a method of exploiting synergies and minimizing risks. At the same time, middle-level technical and commercial staff may suddenly find themselves with greater international responsibility and exposure to international partners. This means that management development has to be provided not only speedily, but also in a cost-effective manner to minimize risk. All these differing requirements of international managers indicate how diverse the needs for management development are. So, inasmuch as it is possible to identify clear international manager roles, it is useful to consider the role specifications developed by Sparrow (1999):

- the home-based manager who has a central focus on different markets and players;
- multicultural team members who work on a series of international projects;
- internationally mobile managers who undertake frequent but short visits to numerous overseas locations while remaining loyal to the parent culture;

- employees in specialist non-management roles that involve international activity or transfer of knowledge (e.g. sales, training, buying, engineering, etc.);
- expatriates who carry the parent organizational culture, but who undertake lengthy assignments representing the parent in a limited number of host countries;
- transitional managers who move across borders on behalf of the organization, but who are relatively detached from any organizational headquarters.

This variety of management roles has implications not only for the type of development required, but also for the skills to be developed. However, before looking at these skills and the interventions used to develop them, it is important to reflect more fully on management learning.

Learning theory and international management development

At the start of this chapter we mentioned the relative neglect of research evidence on learning by specialists in IMD. It is ironic that many MNCs were introducing many innovative human resource development (HRD) practices, but that these were confined to their domestic operations. Their international management development policies remained immune to such innovation. This was certainly the case until the early 1990s, but has since changed. Particularly in the USA, the growing interest in developing international managers has led many MNCs to draw upon wider theoretical insights into learning gained from the academic world (Maznevski and DiStefano 2000; Black and Gregersen 2000). The framework underpinning IMD initiatives now draws heavily upon a number of key principles. Among these are: that adults learn most effectively when the learning is embedded in meaningful experiences; that behavioural skills are improved through observation and practice and with feedback from others; that learning also requires the ability to search for and identify new patterns of thinking so that individual cognitive frameworks are able to accommodate new assumptions; that most learning is informal and incidental, rather than planned and formal; and that challenging experiences, often quite negative in nature, can be powerful learning tools. We shall now examine each of these in turn, and indicate their significance for the development of international managers, highlighting potential IMD interventions that will be dealt with more fully in a later section of this chapter.

The effectiveness of learning embedded in meaningful experiences

The four-stage model of learning outlined by David Kolb (1983) has been an extremely influential tool for employee development in the USA and the UK over the last 20 years. The four stages of the learning cycle, experiencing, reflecting, conceptualizing and experimenting, have been used to demonstrate that effective learning involves multiple interactions with experience and passing through all four stages.

However, at the same time, Kolb's research revealed that individual learners display learning style preferences that corresponded to each stage of the learning cycle: the activist, reflector, theorist and pragmatist learning styles. The implications of this are twofold. First, effective learning requires some correspondence between experience and learning style: the 'activist' who is forced to listen to a long lecture will not learn well, but might respond very well to a practical assignment (the reverse would be true for the 'theorist'). Second, the individual learning style preference can be an obstacle to learning from certain types of learning experience. Again, the 'activist' will avoid reflecting on their activities and drawing conclusions from this, leading to potential mistakes. Thus, it is important to assist individuals to become aware of their individual learning styles and to identify ways of ensuring that their learning is effective.

Another set of learning theories that recognize the importance of meaningful experience to learning are to be found in 'humanistic' adult learning theory, and in particular the work of Knowles (1989) and Rogers (1969). Both are much more focused on the emotional and personal development aspects of learning than Kolb. Rogers argues that in an ever-changing environment, teachers and trainers must become 'facilitators' of learning, setting a climate of trust, eliciting individual and group aims, providing access to resources, accepting and sharing emotional as well as intellectual contributions and, above all, accepting their own limitations as teachers. Similarly, Knowles, in his principles of adult learning – self-styled as 'andragogy' – stresses the importance of a leaner-centred, experience-based approach that takes into account the wider life experiences and personal motivations of learners.

Therefore experiential learning theory tells us that international management development programmes should offer a variety of learning opportunities that make it possible for the manager to draw the most out of their experience. This means that the design of such programmes should start to go beyond pre-departure awareness training, and build in real-life experiences with opportunities to stand back, reflect, draw conclusions and try out alternative courses of action and behaviours. It explains why a number of international leadership development programmes now take place over a number of years, not only prior to departure but also during the overseas assignment. Work-related projects, mentoring schemes and international seminars become important tools for ensuring that programme participants can draw upon all stages of the learning cycle.

Developing behavioural skills in an interactive context

A further principle of learning is the recognition that it is as much a social as an individual experience. The Kolb model is focused on the individual, but the work of Bandura (1977) has shown the importance of the process of learning through observation and imitation. Feedback from others can provide a 'reality check' for the potential perceptual distortions to which we all can succumb. In addition, the identification of positive and negative role models provides another cognitive 'prod' to encourage the adoption of positive, and avoidance of negative, behaviours. Above all, a supportive social environment with strong social cohesion is important to enable the learner to feel that they can take reasonable risks in their behaviour with others.

This has been recognized in the design of international leadership programmes. While a great deal of attention has been devoted to the *identification* of international leadership competencies (see below), it is quite clear that their development requires an appropriate environment for practice. So, a group-based international leadership development programme will provide the opportunity for acquiring the essential skills of learning, managing relationships (including communication, motivation, decision making, conflict management) and managing uncertainty. This will be done in an environment where the development of strong social cohesion and trust will enable participants to explore and experiment without creating the potential for intention to be misinterpreted. Ultimately, therefore, they will achieve the mastery of these skills before they acquire the leadership responsibility (Maznevski and DiStefano 2000). Often, however, the acquisition and development of these skills will be the 'spin-off' from working with colleagues on a shared task or problem.

For this reason, it is increasingly common for such international leadership programmes to include an element of action learning. Action learning was popularized by Revans (1982) in the 1960s as a method that is learner-led rather than trainer-led, and yet is able to provide a great deal of structure to the learning process with minimal direction. Revans believes that the most effective managerial learning takes place within the context of real-life problems that are of a non-routine nature and that present a challenge to the manager concerned. Action learning aims to create a collective learning experience through the creation of learning sets of five or six people that meet to discuss, and question each other about, the challenging, work-related problems to which they have each been assigned. They negotiate the use of their meeting time, and are usually assisted by a facilitator who will point them in the direction of an appropriate source of expertise and will assist with group learning, when requested. The key point is that managers are motivated to take responsibility for their own learning and to focus on action rather than just analysis. While supportive, the learning set culture is not 'soft'. There is emphasis on 'learning by doing' and working together to reframe problems. There is only limited tolerance of failure. Such learning sets can be built in towards the latter part of an international leadership development programme, and can be a useful tool in consortium programmes of several organizations. They are also an important means of support for the international manager once they are alone back in their post.

Learning as the ability to reframe cognitive maps

The quality of an inquisitive and challenging mindset is often found in the lists of international management development competencies. However, while it is easy to identify this ability, it is much more difficult to know how it can be developed. Thus it is not surprising that many companies with long histories of extensive international activity, such as Unilever and Colgate Palmolive, pay a great deal of attention to global leadership attributes when hiring or promoting people. The ability to reframe mental maps in a rapid and dramatic manner is essential if international managers are to become aware that what is considered to be 'best practice' in one country is not necessarily the same in all countries. Thus international managers need to be able to do more than solve problems – they need to be able to reframe them.

Argyris's work (1990, 1994) has drawn attention to the limitations of a narrow definition of management learning tied to problem solving, as this leads managers to over-focus on identifying and correcting errors in their external environment, rather than to question and confront the way in which the problem is defined. Similarly, managers may not be able to learn from a successful experience as it often leads to the complacent assumption that the same behaviour will result in the same outcomes in all circumstances, and may well encourage overconfidence in their individual ability. Drawing heavily on theories of group dynamics and personal change, Argyris describes how even highly intelligent professionals and managers will explicitly espouse theories – private assumptions – that they think they use every day, but which in fact they do not. Furthermore, managers and professionals are usually unaware of the assumptions that they do use to design and manage their actions. In this situation, the difference between 'espoused theory' and 'theory in use' means that unwittingly they screen out certain information. Consequently their attempt to manage and control their environment results in the adoption of 'defensive routines' as they display 'skilled incompetence' in their efforts to avoid surprise, embarrassment or threats. The outcome is 'single-loop learning', in which the response to a problem does not involve any change in assumptions, norms and values. To avoid skilled incompetence, managers have to learn new skills, and especially to question and confront their assumptions, and to explore and take calculated risks. This will enable 'double-loop learning' to occur. Yet Argyris observed that managers and professionals can be among the most resistant to double-loop learning because of their strong task-focus and desire to avoid failure.

Thus the need to provide an environment to encourage double-loop learning is essential for successful international management development programmes. Such programmes now usually incorporate this in a workshop format or in one-to-one coaching. It involves three stages (Black and Gregersen 2000), starting with *unfreezing* activities that will shake up the old mental map. Remapping involves presenting the participants with a noticeable contrast of interpretation or behaviour. This is the principle behind the use of cultural assimilators in cross-cultural awareness training (see below). The second stage takes this further through placing the international manager in a situation where they are forced to confront these contrasts. This will be most effective where it involves a real work assignment or project. The third stage involves presenting them with a conceptual framework that indicates the variables that change between countries and cultures. The key is ensuring that managers are provided with frequent opportunities, either in a group or with a coach, to develop their double-loop learning skills.

Taking advantage of informal and incidental learning and making use of developmental challenges

There is thus a paradox presented by the above principles. Effective learning needs to be embedded in meaningful experiences, but managers often engage in defensive routines that only result in single-loop learning. Furthermore, individuals may not be aware that they are learning. Marsick and Watkins (1990) noted that much learning is 'incidental' as well as 'informal'. While informal learning can be planned or intentional, incidental learning is usually the by-product of some other activity, such as carrying out a task or interactions with other people. As such it is neither planned nor intentional, but rather is tacit, taken for granted and implicit in everyday management assumptions and actions. There is much evidence that adults are more likely to learn from non-routine rather than from routine experiences (Marsick and Watkins, 1990; McCall et al. 1988). This obviously raises the question of how international managers can best take advantage of the opportunities for incidental learning. In the first place, the nature of their work means that formal learning opportunities are difficult to access, but opportunities for informal and incidental learning abound. This has two implications for IMD. First, the manager has to be exposed to new experiences, but at the same time usually needs help to recognize these as learning opportunities.

Furthermore, the nature of the learning opportunities may not always be positive. Research undertaken to identify the developmental components of managerial jobs (McCauley et al. 1994) highlighted that several developmental challenges are highly negative in nature – such as having to manage a business turnaround, cutbacks, or a troublesome boss or colleague. International managers are probably more likely to encounter such negative experiences. The challenge then becomes how to learn from them. However, what is clear is that individual managers require support to encourage them to reflect, either privately, in a group or with a counsellor. Again, research (Wood-Daudelin 1996) has shown that those managers who had a personal counsellor or were part of a group were much better able to recall and analyse their learning from a highly developmental experience.

The implications for IMD are that managers need to be sensitized to the opportunities for incidental learning and to be open to the fact that this might well occur by means of negative as well as positive experiences. However, if such learning is to occur then individual managers will need support to encourage them to reflect. This is why many MNCs now use action learning sets and individual mentors as ways of enabling this.

International management development initiatives

Given the tremendous diversity of international manager roles, the reluctance of many managers to embark on a long-term expatriate career and the above-mentioned insights from theories of managerial learning, there have been a number of new initiatives in IMD programmes since the early 1990s. These include:

- the identification of international leadership competencies as a basis for developing managers for international assignments;
- cross-cultural awareness training;
- multicultural team building and development;
- IMD for women.

We will consider these initiatives below.

Identifying and developing international leadership competencies

Most models of leadership have been generated in the USA, and there is general agreement that they have been helpful in assisting US managers to lead in a domestic context where the focus is on the use of hierarchical structures and institutional position. However, the rise of globalization has shown how culture impacts on norms and values, and therefore European, Asian and Latin American leadership models are often very different from US approaches (Morrison 2000). The dangers of establishing an 'ethnocentric' leadership model have been recognized (Adler and Bartholomew 1992; Black and Porter 1991), and Yeung and Ready (1995) found significant differences in the national emphasis on key leadership capabilities. So while Australians believe that global managers needed to lead change, Korean and Japanese leaders disagree. Similarly, French employees value leaders who would be skilful in managing internal and external networks, but this was far less important for US, German, Australian, Italian, Korean and UK managers. Also, the current US vogue for transformational leadership models does not translate easily to many parts of the world, especially Asia where authoritative, decisive and forceful action is prized. Nonetheless, this has been ignored by some specialists in IMD who are preoccupied with the search for generic competencies (Barham and Wills 1992; Wills and Barham 1994). They argue that those who possess the ability to deal with ambiguity and uncertainty, who are analytical, risk-taking, action-oriented, multidimensional figures, and who are not aggressively defensive, but are in touch with their own emotions and sensitive to the needs of others are more likely to succeed as international managers than those who do not possess these attributes.

Yet a review of the research literature on global leadership (Morrison 2000) shows that evidence supporting the need for such qualities is inconclusive and very ambiguous in focus, covering such topics as competencies, cultural differences, the impact of nationality on managerial values and the impact of culture on management style. In addition, the scientific rigour varies from descriptive to analytical studies and from convenience samples to large-scale, multi-country surveys. Thus it is not surprising that many international businesses, such as PricewaterhouseCoopers, resort to developing their own company-specific models (Hoeksema and de Jong 2001). However, sometimes the manner in which these competencies are derived is not particularly rigorous, relying on an unvalidated 'wish list' generated by senior executives (Connor 2000; Alldredge and

Kellogg, Brown and Root

Kellogg, Brown and Root (KBR) was formed in 2001 when Halliburton, the US firm, brought together three business units dealing with defence and civil infrastructure, oil and gas projects, and petrochemical projects into one subsidiary. KBR has global revenues of nearly $6 billion and operates in over 100 countries. It has a workforce of 45,000, of which 12,000 are located in the UK.

The attraction and retention of managerial talent was seen as vital to the formation of effective teams appropriate for the different projects. However, a previous attempt to 'export' a competency framework developed at the Houston headquarters of Halliburton had been unsuccessful. During 2002 and 2003, KBR drove through a massive project to create a global competency framework. This was achieved by the creation of global steering groups clustered around over 100 'job families'. The outcome was a series of definitions of the core skills of individual jobs. These job-specific competencies were supplemented by 39 'transferable managerial behaviours' applicable to most KBR managers, whatever their country of location. The system is supported by an online database, and forms the basis of both performance management and career planning, by enabling senior management across the whole company to search for talent in other countries. The link to the corporate intranet assists younger managers to plan their careers by accessing information on the skills needed for their current job or for any post, anywhere in the company.

Source: Carrington (2003)

Case study question: *What difficulties might a management development scheme like that developed in KBR encounter in practice?*

Nilan 2000), but the involvement of a large number of managers from across the organization is essential in order to build commitment to such competence schemes. A typical example of how this is done is illustrated in the case of Kellogg, Brown and Root.

In addition, the revision of 3M's global competencies in the mid-1990s provides an interesting case study of how the HRM team simultaneously managed to achieve buy-in from the senior executives by getting them to use their everyday language to draft the competency labels and definitions (see Table 9.1). Rigour was achieved by ensuring that all the competencies were behaviourally anchored using critical incident technique (Alldredge and Nilan 2000).

While there is considerable controversy over the nature of global leadership competencies, there does appear to be more consensus over developing managers to use them. Global organizations concerned to expand capacity are aware of the acute shortage of new general managers and are concerned to identify people earlier in their careers. Thus corporate leadership development programmes providing training and workshops at intervals over a period of two years or more are now common (Neary and O'Grady 2000; Connor 2000). A typical programme structure is outlined in the box on page 184.

Table 9.1 3M leadership competencies

FUNDAMENTAL

- *Ethics and integrity* Exhibits uncompromising integrity and commitment to 3M's corporate values, human resource principles, and business conduct policies. Builds trust and instills self-confidence through mutually respectful, ongoing communication.

- *Intellectual capacity* Assimilates and synthesizes information rapidly, recognizes the complexity in issues, challenges assumptions, and faces up to reality. Capable of handling multiple, complex, and paradoxical situations. Communicates clearly, concisely, and with appropriate simplicity.

- *Maturity and judgment* Demonstrates resiliency and sound judgment in dealing with business and corporate challenges. Recognizes when a decision must be made and acts in a considered and timely manner. Deals effectively with ambiguity and learns from success and failure.

ESSENTIAL

- *Customer orientation* Works constantly to provide superior value to the 3M customer, making each interaction a positive one,

- *Developing people* Selects and retains an excellent workforce within an environment that values diversity and respects individuality. Promotes continuous learning and the development of self and others to achieve maximum potential. Gives and seeks open and authentic feedback.

- *Inspiring others* Positively affects the behavior of others, motivating them to achieve personal satisfaction and high performance through a sense of purpose and spirit of cooperation. Leads by example.

- *Business health and results* Identifies and successfully generates product, market, and geographic growth opportunities, while consistently delivering positive short-term business results. Continually searches for ways to add value and position the organization for future success.

VISIONARY

- *Global perspective* Operates from an awareness of 3M's global markets, capabilities, and resources. Exerts global leadership and works respectfully in multicultural environments to 3M's advantage.

- *Vision and strategy* Creates and communicates a customer-focused vision, corporately aligned and engaging all employees in pursuit of a common goal.

- *Nurturing innovation* Creates and sustains an environment that supports experimentation, reward risk taking, reinforces curiosity, and challenges the status quo through freedom and openness without judgment. Influences the future to 3M's advantage.

- *Building alliances* Builds and leverages mutually beneficial relationships and networks, both internal and external, which generate multiple opportunities for 3M.

- *Organizational agility* Knows, respects, and leverages 3M culture and assets. Leads integrated change within a business unit to achieve sustainable competitive advantage. Utilizes teams intentionally and appropriately.

Source: Alldredge and Nilan (2000)

This structure is very common among leading global companies, including British Airways, Unilever, IBM, DaimlerChrysler Aerospace (De). Usually the content of the programme will cover a number of themes such as global strategy, leadership style and behaviour, culture and organizational capabilities, and in some programmes there is further emphasis on cross-cultural training or multicultural team building (see below). However, as already outlined in the previous section on learning, the

A typical global leadership development programme

- **Annual appraisal** in all operating units used as the basis for identifying 'hi-pos' (high potential younger managers)
- Names forwarded to a **global database**
- **Assessment centres**, often held bi-annually
- **First workshop**, using diagnostic instruments (e.g. Myers-Briggs Type Indicator, 360-degree feedback, self-assessment) and one-to-one executive coaching to create an individual personal development plan with action points
- Use of **other interactive learning techniques**, such as case studies, break-out group assignments, team-building interactions, and project work, to encourage networking
- Following the first workshop, **action learning projects** of either an individual or group nature are assigned to be worked on between the first and second workshops
- **Second workshop**, at which the outcomes of the action learning projects are presented, often to senior management
- Periodic **international management seminars** at later stages.

major aims of such programmes are to encourage participants to reframe their cognitive maps and to provide opportunities for guided reflection upon experience and exposure to peers from other cultures. It is also very common in the USA for programmes to be developed in collaboration with university business schools and for programmes to be hosted in a variety of locations. However, Townsend and Cairns (2003) argue that the development of globally capable managers requires experiential development that goes beyond competency. This is necessary to move beyond simple skill and knowledge acquisition to the development of understanding and self-efficacy.

The problem is that such leadership development programmes are costly, as are expatriate assignments. They are thus only available to a small proportion of organizational personnel and, as we have seen, the number of employees involved in international business activities is increasing. While short-term travel assignments are increasingly used by European, Japanese and US multinational firms, there is little strategic use of these experiences for development purposes. Too often the managers are 'cocooned' and isolated from the host country experience, staying in an international hotel and having little opportunity to socialize with host country nationals. Oddou et al. (2000) provide many examples of how the experience could be enhanced for such managers.

Cross-cultural awareness training

The growth in expatriation by the 1990s was accompanied by an alarming increase in the number of curtailed assignments. In the USA this was estimated to have reached up to 50 per cent (Eschbach et al. 2001). While there are many reasons for international assignment failure (see above), culture shock was viewed as a major contributory factor. Culture shock has been described as

> 'an adjustment reaction syndrome caused by cumulative, multiple, and interactive stress in the intellectual, behavioural, emotional and physiological levels of a person recently relocated to an unfamiliar culture, and is characterized by a variety of symptoms of psychological shock.' (Befus 1988)

The experience of culture shock usually follows an initial 'honeymoon' on arrival, and results from a frustration with the host culture as it becomes apparent to the manager that past behaviours are inappropriate but what is desirable is not apparent. This is where cross-cultural awareness training plays a major role. There is evidence that integrated cross-cultural training that begins prior to departure, is designed for trainees in a specific context and continues intermittently during the foreign posting is the most effective means of doing this (Eschbach et al. 2001).

Research indicates that in both the USA and Europe, between half and two-thirds of companies are providing cross-cultural training for their international managers (Bennett et al. 2000). Companies such as Monsanto, GE, Motorola and Fujitsu place a great deal of emphasis on such cross-cultural training. There are many techniques that can be used. It involves more than the provision of factual information on the host country, and should move into the psychological and emotional domains to develop an awareness of the cultural differences. A 'cultural general assimilator' (Brislin 1998) is a frequently used technique. This is an instrument based on over 100 critical incidents that capture the experiences, feelings and thoughts that all who embark on an overseas experience in a different culture might encounter. The incidents are grouped into eight categories: host customs, interaction with hosts, settling in, tourist experiences, the workplace, the family, schooling and returning home. The use of the cultural general assimilator is usually more effective after exposure to the culture, and the critical incidents present an opportunity for discussion and exchange of views. They can then be used as the basis for a number of interactive exercises, including role play.

In general, cross-cultural training tends to be seen mainly as a tool for assisting international managers to adjust to the host culture, and ignores the need to develop mutually respectful and trustful relations with members of the host culture both within and outside the company. However, it is also a major means for helping managers develop so that they can perform effectively. The failure of international assignments is not only to be measured in the costs of early repatriation. Delays in start-up of an international project, low productivity, disrupted relations with local nationals, damage to the company image and lost opportunities can all be averted by cross-cultural training delivered both prior to, and subsequent to, departure. It is generally argued that pre-departure training should occur between three and five weeks before leaving, and should be followed up between eight and twelve weeks after arrival. The content and delivery methods for a typical cross-cultural training programme are outlined in the box below.

A model cross-cultural training programme

Content

- General and country-specific cultural awareness
- Area studies, history, geography, politics, economics
- Frameworks for understanding and valuing cultural differences
- Planning for a successful international assignment
- Intercultural business skills for working effectively in the local environment
- Understanding cultural variations for those with regional responsibilities
- Business and social customs in the host country
- International transition and stress management
- Practical approaches to culture-shock management and lifestyle adjustment
- Information on daily living issues
- Special issues: partners and families abroad
- Repatriation as a pre-departure issue.

Training delivery methodologies

- Led by a multicultural team of facilitators, including both host nationals and international managers who have recently returned
- Learner-centred, taking account of individual learning styles
- Methods to enhance cultural self-awareness (e.g. culture general assimilator, culture inventories)
- Interactive methods, such as case studies, critical incidents, simulations, video, role play and guided discussion
- Mentors (both recently returned international managers and host nationals)
- Access to an executive coach after arrival.

Cross-cultural training is not only needed for those who depart on international assignments, but is also needed for home-based employees who are in face-to-face or 'virtual' contact with other nationals. More specialized training in subjects such as cross-border communication and teamwork, cross-cultural negotiations and region-specific business briefings may also be needed.

Multicultural teamworking

International businesses increasingly rely on multicultural teamworking as more and more organizations get involved in joint ventures and partnering arrangements. Companies that make extensive use of international teams include ABB, Unilever, HSBC, Shell, IBM, Deutsche Bank and SAP. The types of team can vary enormously in terms of their duration, composition and location. They can be home or overseas based, as well as 'virtual' and transnational (Snell et al. 1998). This means that managers need to be able to understand and cope with the processes of communication and decision making in different settings. Problems can arise in multicultural teams around the different ways in which decisions are taken, tasks are allocated and work co-ordinated. Also attitudes to time (especially deadlines and punctuality), the ways in which meetings are conducted, how poor performance is evaluated, how conflict is resolved and how negotiation takes place are other key issues.

Such teamworking requires an understanding of cross-cultural differences in organizational behaviour – especially communication, motivation and decision making (Adler 1997; Smith 1992; see also the following case study: 'Clashes between French and UK approaches to management development'). Thus while the standard techniques of development are required, the processes for arriving at common understanding and 'norms' are likely to require slower and more explicit discussion of processes. The problem is that in many international organizations team development tends to be delivered in an ad hoc manner, and the constraints of business deadlines often allow little time for team development to take place. Furthermore, the growing sophistication of ICT and a reluctance to contemplate travel and relocation mean that international organizations are expecting their international teams to function very soon after start-up. However, the desirable team member qualities, such as adaptability, ability to communicate, commitment to membership, openness to others and understanding of the wider business context, cannot be developed remotely. They require an initial period of intensive contact and regular follow-up meetings.

In most cases such teams require a leader, and care is required in selecting and developing the leader, especially when the team operates as a part-time parallel organization to the rest of the core business. Such team leaders require sophisticated group management skills and the capacity to act as a role model. They must also have the ability to manage the team's external environment – cultivating relations with the management sponsors of the team and with different parts of the parent organization. Very often there will be multiple leaders in virtual teams.

Clashes between French and UK approaches to management development

A theme of this book has been the 'embeddedness' of economic and social activity in distinct national contexts and management development is the same as any other activity in the way it is shaped by the national context. An interesting situation in which to investigate this is through a cross-border merger or acquisition since in these circumstances differences in practice become immediately evident. A case study of a merger between a UK and a French firm in the retail sector enables us to shed some light on this issue. In this merger, the UK party was slightly larger and eventually established full control through a hostile takeover. Management development was seen as the way in which the new firm would become integrated, but the case reveals ways in which prevailing practice differed markedly and proved difficult to change.

The French approach to management development is strongly shaped by the education system and the resulting conception of the role of senior managers. In France the most able students are selected for the *Grandes Ecoles*, the most elite institutions within higher education which provide a primarily theoretical rather than practical approach to learning. It is almost exclusively from this route that people can achieve the position of *cadres* – this is similar to management in the UK but differs significantly in that the latter has a broad role incorporating a number of dimensions such as the management of people, whereas the former is narrower, confined mainly to a strategic planning role. The term *cadres* is more than a professional description, rather it is a social group or class that is highly conditioned and homogeneous, with all members sharing a similar educational and social background. In the *cadres*, it is the ability to think logically and analyse situations in an abstract way that is more highly valued than practical action. The impenetrability of the *cadres* leads to organizations being highly hierarchical; the importance of boundaries between different levels remain sharply distinct, with the *cadres* typically adopting an authoritarian management style.

In the UK, in contrast, the managerial class is much more difficult to define and is much more diffuse. There has been a tendency to emphasize a 'professionalized' approach, with the focus on accountancy qualifications. Recently, MBAs have become more popular as the influence from the USA grows. The MBA is quite different from the French Diploma from the *Grandes Ecoles*; it is less theoretical and much easier to obtain. Consequently, UK individuals can move up into management positions and get promoted up the management hierarchy more easily than can their French counterparts. A further key difference is that in the UK management is more about applying a set of techniques than about abstract reasoning, and generally applicable skills are seen as central. This emphasis on generally applicable skills means that there is a high degree of mobility across firms.

In the case study firm, in order to try to establish a common bond at the top with a shared identity, a uniform management development programme was introduced. This rested in part on the Anglo-American concept of 'high potentials' in which uniform systems of measurement and of identifying and developing managers were central. Those who were categorized as high potential would be fast-tracked into management positions, and this was to be applied to French managers as well. A serious culture clash was the result. Principally, this revolved around the differing attitudes towards measuring potential; while the Brits saw it as very important in distinguishing between individuals, in France it is something that is taken for granted among the *cadres*. The French simply refused to operate the system. Boussebaa and Morgan (2004) quote a French manager's reaction to a presentation from the UK HQ on management development: 'This is utter rubbish. We don't need this stuff. We simply don't operate this way on this side of the Channel and your plans are simply meaningless to us.' For their part, UK managers viewed the French as 'backward in terms of MD', an approach that needed to be 'corrected'.

A related conflict was over the issue of developing talent. The UK firm sought to carry out management development centrally, through 'executive education' at business schools. A cultural clash was evident at these courses, with the British looking for practical information and the French looking for abstract ideas. These attitudes were reflected in training sessions held in both countries; when they were held in the UK the French appeared to be cynical and detached about the low intellectual level of the material; when they were held in France the British appeared frustrated at the lack of practical relevance.

Overall, five years of integrated management training aimed at producing a shared identity among managers was ultimately unsuccessful. Differing attitudes remained, with this resulting in management style and practice varying between the two countries. Ultimately, the story is one of deep-rooted differences in management training and development enduring even in the face of concerted attempts to change underlying attitudes.

Source: based on Boussebaa and Morgan (2004)

Case study question: *What does this case study tell us about attempts by MNCs to develop unified management development programmes?*

International management development for women

It has been estimated that women make up between 2 per cent and 15 per cent of international managers (Harris 2004), and in both the UK and the USA the proportion of expatriates who are women has remained constant at around 2 per cent to 3 per cent (Scullion 1993; Adler et al. 2000). There has been a tendency to assume that societal norms, domestic arrangements and women's preferences are the main obstacle. However, Adler (1984) has debunked these and other commonly held myths about women's lack of interest in international management, and Harris (2004) indicates the critical influence of home country organizational policies on women's prospects in international management. In particular, the interplay of formal company policies and informal processes can have an effect upon women's perceptions of the opportunities available. While the majority of UK and US companies have espoused equal opportunity policies, this certainly does not translate into a growing proportion of women in international management. This is ironic in the light of the research on international management competencies (Barham and Devine 1991), which shows that women tend to be more sensitive to cultural differences and are therefore more able to work effectively with managers from other countries. However, the barriers to their participation are not necessarily within the control of women managers themselves. The major obstacles often lie in the unacknowledged assumptions and prejudices held by senior managers and within the policies for career and succession planning. These can be difficult to overcome. The way in which a major US consumer foods company addressed the underrepresentation of women in senior-level international management positions is illustrated by the following case study, drawn from the work of Adler et al. (2000), showing the process that led to the development of a Women's Global Leadership Forum.

In sum, this case illustrates a highly sophisticated exercise in organization development that required raising awareness among senior male managers in a non-threatening manner as much as activities to develop women themselves.

A special international management development initiative for women

Bestfoods is amongst the largest US branded food companies. It is headquartered in New Jersey, has operations in more than 60 countries, and markets its products in more than 110 countries. It also earns 60 per cent of its revenue from non-US sources, and is projecting continued future growth. Bestfoods' leadership is as global as the company's operations; almost half of the 20 corporate officers came from outside the USA in the mid-1990s, with eight nationalities represented among them. They need to attract the best global talent to succeed in operating both locally and globally. With women making more than 80 per cent of decisions for Bestfoods' products, the corporate officers believed that the company would not survive unless it understood women's needs. This was perceived to be a problem if women continued not to be represented at the most senior level, as well as broadly throughout the company. By 1997, 14 per cent of the board of directors, 16 per cent of corporate officers and 13 per cent of directors and vice presidents were women. In the light of this the Director of Diversity and Development encouraged the CEO to hold a Women's Global Leadership Forum off site.

The sponsorship of the CEO plus endorsement from the strategic management team was used to good effect, and a programme was devised for 60 senior women participants drawn from 25 countries. The aims were to identify and develop talent, and to provide a network. Particularly valuable was a survey of all senior management about perceptions of how men and women pursued their career strategies. This was very revealing. While men gave a low priority to action on international management development for women, and perceived the barriers to women's advance as self-imposed, they also showed considerable discomfort with ambitious women and with having to report to a woman. Consequently many women felt isolated and perceived that they needed to adopt a style with which men would be comfortable. This had implications for the design of the development programme for international women managers. As well as considerable emphasis on raising cross-cultural awareness and team building, this programme also devoted much effort to sessions on handling power and negotiation and to encouraging networking and the identification of mentors, both from among other senior women and, particularly, from among other senior male managers. Senior managers sat in on a presentation of the survey findings and were also invited to presentations from individual women managers recommending further action to improve women's involvement in international management.

Source: Adler et al. (2000)

Case study question: *How effective do you think firm-level initiatives such as those deployed at Bestfoods can be in removing barriers to women making advances in international management?*

Future developments

While the previous discussion has focused on the main interventions in the field of IMD, there are some potential new developments on the horizon. One review (Brewster et al. 2001) of the implications of globalization for HRM has shown that the fastest increase in internationalization has been among small and medium-sized enterprises. To date there has been little research on IMD for this sector. Furthermore, increasing competition is forcing many global organizations to cut back and often outsource IMD activities. In some cases independent consultancies have emerged specializing in particular aspects of IMD, such as cross-cultural awareness training or executive coaching. However, several leading international management schools such as London Business School, INSEAD, IMD and several 'Ivy League' US business schools have expanded their international manager programmes and also work closely with the corporate sector to deliver customized executive development. Furthermore, developments in ICT and the growing interest in KM across the corporate sector have brought a new perspective to IMD, in which sophisticated software and 'corporate universities' play a major role (Prince and Stewart 2002). The potential for accelerating communication is enormous, but can only be realized if organizations adopt a strategic approach. This involves a precise analysis of the company's international involvement and the ways in which it is likely to develop, before considering what is required of international managers. The current policies and practices for developing international managers need to be open to critical scrutiny before alternative methods are proposed, and the wider implications for corporate careers for women and host country nationals as well as for white male expatriates need to be addressed.

Review questions

1 How have the roles of international managers changed in the last two decades or so?

2 What aspects of learning theory are useful tools for thinking about IMD?

3 What would you regard as the key competencies that international managers should have? To what extent will these vary according to the context?

4 Do you think that technological developments, particularly in relation to international communication, will mean that firms will need to rely on international managers more or less in the future?

Further reading

Chartered Institute of Personnel and Development website: http://www.cipd.co.uk/subjects/intlhr/manageia.htm

The Chartered Institute of Personnel and Development (CIPD) in the UK provides a range of practical sources of information on the subject of international development.

A flavour of these, together with some further references and links, can be found at the above web address.

Forster, N. (2000) 'The Myth of the "International Manager"', *International Journal of Human Resource Management*, 11(1), 126–42.

This article challenges a number of myths that are associated with managers who operate at the international level.

Harris, H. (2004) 'Women's Role in International Management', in A-W. Harzing and J. Van Ruysseveldt (eds) *International Human Resource Management*, London: Sage.

This chapter provides an excellent overview of the research into women and international management.

Morrison, A. (2000) 'Developing a Global Leadership Model', *Human Resource Management*, 39, 2 & 3, 117–31.

This article reviews the evidence concerned with the factors that affect the nature and success of global leadership.

References

Adler, N. (1984) 'Women Do Not Want International Careers and Other Myths About International Management', *Organizational Dynamics*, 13(2), 66–79.

Adler, N. (1997) *International Dimensions of Organisational Behaviour*, 3rd edn, Cincinnati: South Western Press.

Adler, N. and Bartholomew, S. (1992) 'Managing Globally Competent People', *Academy of Management Executive*, 6(3), 52–65.

Adler, N., Brody, L.W. and Osland, J.S. (2000) 'The Women's Global Leadership Forum: Enhancing One Company's Global Leadership Capability', *Human Resource Management*, 39, 2 & 3, 208–25.

Alldredge, M.E. and Nilan, K.J. (2000) '3M's Leadership Competency Model: An Internally Developed Solution', *Human Resource Management*, 39, 2 & 3, 133–45.

Argyris, C. (1990) *Overcoming Organizational Defenses: Facilitating Organizational Learning*, Boston: Allyn and Bacon.

Argyris, C. (1994) *On Organizational Learning*, Oxford: Blackwell.

Bandura, A. (1977) *Social Learning Theory*, Englewood Cliffs, NJ: Prentice Hall.

Barham, K. and Devine, M. (1991) *The Quest for the International Manager: A Survey of Global Human Resource Strategies*, London: Economist Intelligence Unit.

Barham, K. and Wills, S. (1992) *Management Across Frontiers: Identifying the Competencies of Successful International Managers*, Berkhamstead: Ashridge Management Research Group.

Befus, C.P. (1988) 'A Multilevel Treatment Approach for Culture Shock Experienced by Sojourners', *International Journal of Inter-Cultural Relations*, 12, 381–400.

Bennett, R., Aston, A. and Colquhoun, T. (2000) 'Cross-Cultural Training: A Critical Step in Ensuring the Success of International Assignments', *Human Resource Management*, 39, 2 & 3, 239–50.

Black, S. and Gregersen, H. (2000) 'High Impact Training: Forging Leaders for the Global Frontier', *Human Resource Management*, 39, 2 & 3, 173–84.

Black, J. and Porter, L. (1991) 'Managerial Behavior and Job Performance: A Successful Manager in Los Angeles May Not Succeed in Hong Kong', *Journal of International Business Studies*, 22, 291–317.

Boussebaa, M. and Morgan, G. (2004) 'Organising Across Borders: Differences in British and French Conceptions of Management and their Impact on a Management Development Programme', paper presented at a conference on 'Multinationals and the International Diffusion of Organizational Forms and Practices', Barcelona, 15–17 July .

Brewster, C., Harris, H. and Sparrow, P. (2001) *Globalisation and HR*, London: Chartered Institute of Personnel and Development (CIPD).

Briscoe, D. and Schuler, R. (2004) *International Human Resource Management*, London: Routledge.

Brislin, R.W. (1998) 'A Culture-General Assimilator: Preparation for Various Types of Sojourns', in J.B. Keys and R.M. Fulmer (eds) *Executive Development and Organizational Learning for Global Business*, Binghampton, NY: International Business Press.

Carrington, L. (2003) 'Nine Day Wonder', *People Management*, 12 June, 42–43.

Connor, J. (2000) 'Developing the Global Leaders of Tomorrow', *Human Resource Management*, 39, 2 & 3, 147–57.

Eschbach, D.M., Parker, G.E. and Stoeberl, P.A. (2001) 'American Repatriate Employees' Retrospective Assessments of the Effects of Cross-Cultural Training on Their Adaptation to International Assignments', *International Journal of Human Resource Management*, 12(2), 270–87.

Forster, N. (2000) 'The Myth of the "International Manager"', *International Journal of Human Resource Management*, 11(1), 126–42.

Harris, H. (2004) 'Women's Role in International Management', in A-W. Harzing and J. Van Ruysseveldt (eds) *International Human Resource Management*, London: Sage.

Hendry, C. (1994) *Human Resource Strategies for International Growth*, London: Routledge.

Hoeksema, L. and de Jong, G. (2001) 'International Co-ordination and Management Development: An Application at PricewaterhouseCoopers', *Journal of Management Development*, 20(2), 145–58.

Knowles, M. (1989) *The Adult Learner: A Neglected Species*, Houston: Gulf Publishing Company.

Kolb, D. (1983) *Experiential Learning: Experience as the Source of Learning and Development*, Englewood Cliffs, NJ: Prentice Hall.

Marsick, V. and Watkins, K. (1990) *Informal and Incidental Learning in the Workplace*, London: Routledge.

Maznevski, M. and DiStefano, J. (2000) 'Global Leaders Are Team Players: Developing Global Leaders Through Membership on Global Teams', *Human Resource Management*, 39, 2 & 3, 195–208.

McCall, M.W. Jr., Lombardo, M. and Morrison, A. (1988) *The Lessons of Experience: How Successful Executives Develop on the Job*, Lexington, MA: Lexington, Books.

McCauley, C., Ruderman, M., Ohlott, P. and Morrow, J. (1994) 'Assessing the Developmental Components of Managerial Jobs', *Journal of Applied Psychology*, 79, 544–60.

Morrison, A. (2000) 'Developing a Global Leadership Model', *Human Resource Management*, 39, 2 & 3, 117–31.

Neary, D. and O'Grady, D. (2000) 'The Role of Training in Developing Global Leaders: A Case Study at TRW Inc', *Human Resource Management*, 39, 2 & 3, 185–93.

Oddou, G., Mendenhall, M. and Bonner Ritchie, J. (2000) 'Leveraging Travel as a Tool for Global Leadership Development', *Human Resource Management*, 39, 2 & 3, 159–72.

Prince, C. and Stewart, J. (2002) 'Corporate Universities – An Analytical Framework', *Journal of Management Development*, 21(4), 794–811.

Revans, R. (1982) *The Origins and Growth of Action Learning*, Bromley: Chartwell Bratt.

Rogers, C. (1969) *Freedom to Learn*, Columbus, OK: Charles E. Merrill.

Scullion, H. (1993) 'Creating International Managers: Recruitment and Development Issues', in P. Kirkbride (ed.) *Human Resource Management in Europe: Perspectives for the 1990s*, London: Routledge.

Selmer, J. and Leung, A.S.M. (2003) 'Provision and Adequacy of Support to Male Expatriate Spouses', *Personnel Review*, 32(1), 9–21.

Smith, I. (1992) 'Organizational Behaviour and National Cultures', *British Journal of Management*, 3, 39–51.

Snell, S., Snow, C., Davison, S. and Hambrick, D. (1998) 'Designing and Supporting Transnational Teams: The Human Resource Agenda', *Human Resource Management*, 37, 2, 147–58.

Sparrow, P. (1999) 'International Recruitment, Selection, and Assessment', in P. Joynt and R. Marlin (eds) *The Global HR Manager: Creating the Seamless Organisation*, London: Chartered Institute of Personnel and Development (CIPD).

Sparrow, P., Brewster, C. and Harris, H. (2004) *Globalizing Human Resource Management*, London: Routledge.

Tayeb, M. (2004) *International Human Resource Management: A Multinational Company Perspective*, Oxford: Oxford University Press.

Townsend, P. and Cairns, L. (2003) 'Developing the Global Manager Using a Capability Framework', *Management Learning*, 34(3), 313–27.

Wills, S. and Barham, K. (1994) 'Being an International Manager', *European Management Journal*, 12(1), 49–58.

Wood-Daudelin, M. (1996) 'Learning from Experience Through Reflection', *Organizational Dynamics*, 24(3), 36–49.

Woodall, J. and Winstanley, D. (1998) *Management Development: Strategy and Practice*, Oxford: Blackwell.

Yeung, A. and Ready, D. (1995) 'Developing Leadership Capabilities of Global Corporations: A Comparative Study in Eight Nations', *Human Resource Management*, 34(4), 529–47.

Chapter 10

Recruitment and selection of international managers

Fiona Moore

Key aims

This chapter has the following key aims:

- to outline the factors that influence the recruitment and selection of international managers;
- to consider how the recruitment and selection of international managers differs from that of more locally based managers;
- to examine in greater detail issues of gender, ethnicity and cross-cultural variation in the recruitment and selection of international managers;
- to discuss the implications of the globalization debate for recruitment and selection for international assignments.

Introduction

Recruitment is an extremely significant issue in international human resource management (IHRM), for the simple reason that a failed expatriate assignment can be a catastrophic waste of money and time for both the manager in question and their company. Unfortunately, however, most companies tend to use an informal and/or generic recruitment and selection programme when selecting their international staff, and ignore the impact that the tension between local embeddedness and the drive to global integration has on the question of who to recruit and how.

In international management, it has been said that 'managers who are unwilling or incapable of generating global learning practices significantly reduce the effectiveness of an organisation' (Berrell et al. 2002: 92). In other words, selecting the wrong person for an expatriate assignment can give the organization a bad image, cause friction with host-country employees, reduce profits or give a new business venture a bad start. All writers on the subject of expatriates also agree that 'expatriate failure', i.e. when an expatriate is unable to complete his/her assignment successfully, has a huge financial cost for the company. In a 1995 survey, Forster (2000: 128-9) estimates that the total cost of moving a single US expatriate to the UK for two years, including selecting, training and monitoring the assignee, was at least £250,000 (about $460,000). This figure does not include the cost of housing and other material benefits. The cost of sending a third-country national (see below), as many companies are currently doing, is not a great deal lower, and may in some cases be even more expensive. The frequency of expatriate failure is thus cause for concern among many managers. As Berrell et al. (2002) note that the first step in developing a successful management and development programme is to recruit and hire the right people for the job, we shall consider how these practices can be used to minimize expatriate failure.

One of the key problems of many expatriate recruitment and selection programmes is that they tend to focus on standard, traditional hiring practices, albeit with some cosmetic alterations. However, many researchers are coming to realize that, given the differences between companies and the contested nature of globalization, this approach is detrimental to good performance. Bartlett and Ghoshal (1997) point out that at each managerial level, managers may play similar roles and have similar responsibilities, but their activities will be of a different size and scope. This holds true for international management as well, if not more so: although they may all broadly be 'managers', they have different situations and different responsibilities in different locations, and cannot be treated as a single category. Furthermore, as Berrell et al. note, 'There is... a shortage of managerial talent capable of operating internationally... the globally friendly senior manager is a scarce and, therefore, an expensive commodity' (2002: 92). International human resource managers are thus best advised to abandon 'generic' hiring practices in favour of more specialized ones.

This chapter builds on the issues raised in Chapter 9 on international management development (IMD). We will first consider the issues surrounding the development of a successful recruitment programme and the selection of international managers that enable firms to find the right person for the job. We will then look at two case studies of the recruitment and selection of Japanese international managers, with a view to comparing and contrasting the two situations. We will then examine broader issues of diversity, developing themes referenced elsewhere in this book by considering issues of gender, ethnicity and intercultural training in recruitment. Finally, we will address the question of whether the concept of the 'international manager' is a help or a hindrance in this regard, before drawing some general conclusions about recruitment and selection in the era of globalization.

The main theme of this chapter, therefore, is that when recruiting and selecting international managers, companies need to consider their organizational needs and goals, the needs and goals of the candidates involved, the nature of the global and local pressures on the corporation and the circumstances of the assignment, and then tailor their programme accordingly. We will now define some general concepts in recruitment and selection before going on to address issues within this field in greater detail.

Key concepts and definitions

Recruitment can broadly be defined as the practice of deciding what the company needs in a candidate and instigating procedures to attract the most appropriate candidate for the job. In recruitment, the human resource manager will need to identify the key traits of the required individual (through working out a *job description* and *person specification*) and, through advertising and/or approaching individuals who might be suitable, find people with these traits. Recruitment thus involves identifying the needs of the company regarding the position to be filled, and attracting suitable candidates for the job.

Selection, by contrast, involves choosing the right candidate for the position from those who have been recruited. It involves testing and evaluating the skills and attributes of these individuals to determine which are the best for the job at hand. Selection should be, according to the ACAS guidelines, 'effective, efficient and fair' – effective in picking the right person, efficient in doing it with minimal fuss and expense, and fair in that it should preclude discrimination (Beardwell et al. 2004). This holds true as much when selecting international managers as when selecting those who will be working closer to home.

Finally, a word on how we will here define the *international manager*. The term is, broadly speaking, used to describe a manager who is sent on an international assignment; the stereotypical image most people have of such a manager is of a fairly young, elite individual who takes an international assignment for about three years before returning home. Increasingly, writers are also coming to use the term 'international manager' to mean someone with a more or less completely global orientation, who specializes in international assignments; Leonard (2002) identifies what she calls 'transpatriates', individuals who operate globally rather than in specific local cultures. Nick Forster, however, argues against this, noting that both the stereotypical expatriate and the 'transpatriate' are the exception (only about 8 per cent of any given company at any point in time), and that the concept of 'expatriation' includes more variety, including permanent migrants, short-term assignments, cross-border job swaps and multicultural project teams (2000). He further notes that many international recruitment and selection programmes make a basic a priori assumption that managers fit the above stereotypes, and treat them accordingly, regardless of whether they fit the model or not, to the detriment of both individual and firm. In this chapter, therefore, we will define an international manager in broad terms as a manager on an assignment that requires working and living for a time outside of their home country, recognizing that this definition includes a good deal of variation. We will now examine the issues involved in recruiting such individuals for an international assignment.

Criteria for recruitment

As noted above, international recruitment involves defining what the assignment entails and what sort of person is needed for it, and then considering how to attract that person. This process has, however, been given little attention, to the point where Dowling and Welch (2004) identify four myths that have grown up surrounding the recruitment of international managers:

1 There is a universal approach to management.
2 People can acquire multicultural behaviours without outside help.
3 There are common characteristics shared by all successful international managers.
4 There are no impediments to mobility.

In fact, both managers and assignments can vary widely in terms of what they need and the characteristics required. We will here outline the factors affecting the criteria for recruitment, considering the role of the company, the nature of the assignment, the needs of the person and the legal issues, and the amount and type of training and development required.

The company

As we saw in Chapter 4, companies have different needs and strategies in the international sphere, and different relationships to the global and the local. When recruiting international managers, these strategies are arguably the first thing that should be taken into account, with particular regard to what sort of expatriate would best fit with the company's strategy.

Bartlett and Ghoshal (1993) note that companies tend to take different forms when operating across national borders, depending on the degree to which the company aims for global integration versus embeddedness in various national contexts. These differences have an impact on the type of person needed for expatriate assignments in each case. A more centralized multinational company (MNC), for instance, would, generally speaking, want expatriates with a strong head-office focus, who are able to transfer knowledge to, and maintain control of, subsidiaries and branches. A more decentralized company would favour managers who are flexible, entrepreneurial and capable of making crucial decisions on their own. More globally-oriented companies might want managers who can integrate and serve as a 'bridge' between different markets; those approaching Bartlett and Ghoshal's 'transnational' model would need someone capable of thinking in both global and local terms (see Harzing 2001b). There is also the question of what the company expects the subsidiary or branch to achieve over the course of the assignment, which has a bearing on the skills required of the expatriate.

The selection of expatriates is also affected by more nebulous factors. The company's culture, for instance, may favour a more flexible outlook or a more regimented one (certain international hotel chains, for instance, refuse to allow any deviation from a certain set of standard management procedures); a company may favour either promoting talent from within the company or hiring people with the relevant skills from elsewhere (also called 'growing their own' versus 'poaching'). A company's international image is also significant: certain German banks, for instance, want to be seen as 'German' wherever they are, and so favour placing particularly German-focused people in key international management positions, while certain German manufacturing corporations wish to cultivate a more international image and consequently favour hiring third-country nationals or Germans with considerable international experience. 'Soft', qualitative factors might thus affect the question of who to hire for an international assignment.

Money is also an issue. Before deciding on who to recruit, the company must consider how much it wants to spend on the assignment, how much it is willing to invest in the training and development of the manager and whether it would be willing to provide financial or other incentives to successful candidates. The issue of how much to spend on the manager's family is also an issue (see below). These criteria affect, for instance, whether one hires a manager with the relevant technical skills but few intercultural abilities, with the aim of training them in the latter area, or whether one looks for a manager with both sets of skills (who might demand a higher price). It also might raise issues of equal opportunities, which will be discussed in greater detail below. When recruiting international managers, therefore, the strategy, culture and financial position of the company must first be taken into account.

The nature of the assignment

Next, the nature and length of the assignment must be considered. An expatriate assignment lasting only a few months, for instance, requires less preparation and causes less disruption to the lifestyle of a manager than one lasting for three years; similarly, an assignment involving travel to a variety of countries requires a different sort of preparation to one that simply involves moving to another country. The circumstances of the assignment might also be significant, as one would need different skills and capabilities for each of the following common reasons for expatriation:

- teaching a new process;
- helping a branch through a matrix integration;
- setting up a new branch or representative office;
- assisting with a joint venture;
- facilitating knowledge transfer between a subsidiary and its head office.

When recruiting candidates, therefore, HR managers must consider the following questions:

- What are the needs of head office from the expatriate?
- What sort of role does the expatriate need to play in the assignment?
- How long will they be required to play it?

Once these questions have been answered, a clearer picture of the type of candidate required may emerge.

Furthermore, it is not only the needs of the head office that have to be taken into account under these circumstances. Whether or not the subsidiary's needs are being considered affects how the expatriate will be treated by their new colleagues, how well they will be able to carry out their duties and, ultimately, the success of the assignment. This can be seen in a study of performance management by Li and Karakowski (2001). They conducted a laboratory study of Asian-American and Caucasian-American subjects, in which they were shown videotapes of a group of students making a decision on an investment project, and were then required to evaluate the behaviour of particular individuals in the videotape. The results demonstrated that their standards of performance appraisal differed significantly: what one group considered appropriate behaviour for a manager, the other considered inappropriate, with, for instance, Caucasian subjects approving of behaviour that Asian subjects considered aggressive. Consequently, a person who is hired according to their compatibility with head office behavioural norms and practices might find their actions a severe liability in other national contexts. Furthermore, Berrell et al. note that involving the management of the subsidiary in the recruitment and selection of the international staff to be assigned there encourages trust between both parties (2002: 93). They also advise that there should be overlap between the new expatriate taking over and the incumbent leaving, both as a mark of respect and to allow the new assignee to get used to the particular circumstances of the assignment. Thus the nature of the assignment and the needs and wishes of the subsidiary must be considered when recruiting managers for international assignments.

The person

It is equally crucial to consider the nature and motivations of the sort of person the company requires for the international assignment. Managers do not always take international positions for the same reasons, but may do so from a combination of motivating factors, including the following:

- *Career advancement*: some managers hope that the assignment will either advance their careers at home or make them more desirable on the job market.
- *Financial incentives*: some managers are interested in the remuneration and other benefits that may accompany an international assignment.
- *Interest in the area*: many people who put their names forward for international assignments have prior experience of, and a fondness for, the country to which they will be assigned. As will be noted below, this has both advantages and disadvantages.
- *Interest in travel*: it is worth noting that many expatriates are young (25–35), single or in new relationships, and childless – that is to say, at a stage of their professional development when an international assignment might seem like a fun and exciting thing to do.

It is worth considering these motives when advertising the position, as they may provide ideas as to how to attract the right person; it is worth considering, for instance, what sort of compensation package would be most attractive or whether a prior knowledge of the country would prove beneficial. Furthermore, it is worth considering whether or not the candidate's interests, aims and goals are in fact aligned with those of the company or in conflict; while Harzing's studies of expatriates reveal that many are sent abroad as a more or less formal means by which head office can maintain control over the branches (2001a, 2001b), a more qualitative study reveals that expatriates tend to view building an international career as more important, and may become disillusioned and leave the company when this career fails to materialize (Moore 2005). Finally, people who are interested in the assignment only for financial or career-related reasons may not actually be interested in the assignment, and may consequently find themselves unable to deal with the stress. It is also worth considering whether or not an expatriate would consider accepting such an assignment again: while much of the business literature considers this to be the case, in Forster's 1996 survey of expatriates only about 13 per cent replied that they would consider undertaking further international assignments (Forster 2000).

The personal qualities of the candidate should also be taken into account. Crucial to many assignments is the ability of an individual to adapt to particular circumstances. This is an essential skill for international managers, which may be even more important than previous knowledge of the country/region to which the candidate will be sent. This also affects the nature and amount of guidance from head office that will be required. The problem is that adaptability, being a psychological attribute, may be difficult to measure. It may also stem from character traits that are not highly valued in business. As Gregersen et al. (1996) note, often adaptability is the result of qualitative skills like empathy and the ability to compromise and get along with other people as opposed to skills like competitiveness, aggression and so on, rather than of practical, quantitative skills. Consequently, managers with the right abilities may be ignored or passed over because the recruiters do not consider their personality appropriate for a key management position.

It is often debated whether prior experience of working in the country of assignment is an asset or a liability. On the plus side, prior experience can save the company money as it could mean that linguistic and intercultural training will not be required; Selmer (2004) notes that many European MNCs currently establishing a presence in China are deliberately selecting managers who speak at least one Chinese language, as these languages can be expensive and time-consuming for Westerners to learn. On the negative side, however, there is always the possibility of the manager becoming biased towards the subsidiary's culture rather than maintaining a degree of impartiality or, when the assignment is over, deciding that they want to stay in the country and quitting their job.

Finally, it is worth considering the personal skills of candidates. As noted above, expatriates tend to show a certain demographic similarity, which is surprising when one considers the wide variety of assignments currently being conducted. This similarity suggests that there is a hidden problem in that companies are not making use of a diverse array of skills and experiences, but simply hiring people who are interested. As noted below in the section on gender and ethnicity, there are also reasons why a qualified manager might not put themselves forward for an assignment. Companies thus may need to think about how to attract candidates who might not otherwise apply for the job and engage in more imaginative recruitment practices.

Legal issues

Legal issues also play a significant role in developing international recruitment pro-grammes. When outlining the recruitment criteria, managers should consider what the hiring regulations are in the home country and in the host country, especially whether regulations exist forbidding companies from hiring non-local staff unless they can prove that they are essential. It is also worth considering how long a person can legally work in the country of assignment, and whether it has any legal impedi-ments to the immigration of certain groups (see the section on gender and ethnicity below). The hiring of third-country nationals and the potential development of 'transpatriates' raises particular issues in legal terms, especially when taking into account how the company can provide such individuals with social security, a pen-sion and other essential benefits (Polak 2002). The salary and benefits package offered to a candidate must also include compensation for a number of things – finding a new house, differences in standard of living, cost of relocating any spouse and chil-dren – and must also be compatible with the legal and social security systems of home and host countries.

However, it should also be noted that legal issues are subject to change over time. Since 11 September 2001, for instance, US visa requirements for foreign expatriates have become much more stringent. By contrast, formerly restrictive areas such as China are becoming more and more accommodating to expatriates. Legal issues thus not only vary according to circumstances but also change over time.

As no two international assignments are the same, it is therefore not advisable for managers to attempt to come up with a universal formula for expatriate managers when developing criteria for recruitment, but rather to consider the individual cir-cumstances of the assignment, the ideal characteristics of the manager required and the degree to which the organization is willing to compromise. We shall now con-sider issues involved in the selection of the appropriate candidate.

Selection

As with recruitment, how the selection of candidates for international positions is undertaken varies from company to company and from situation to situation. We will here consider some of the more common methods of selecting candidates, and their advantages and disadvantages, as well as some of the issues that they raise.

Informal methods

Traditionally, little consideration has gone into the specific requirements of an inter-national assignment, and instead candidates have been selected informally, based on personal contacts. Harris and Brewster (1999) call this the 'coffee-machine' system of selection, and present a scenario in which the selection of the candidate results from a manager saying to a colleague as they take a coffee break, 'We need someone to take over the Beijing assignment,' and the colleague responding, 'Well, Perkins has been to China, he might do it.' To play devil's advocate for a moment, it was mentioned above that what often makes or breaks an international assignment is not so much the formal qualifications of the assignee as the 'intangibles' – the assignee's ability to get by in a particular situation. Under such circumstances, a colleague's feelings about the candidate's suitability might be as reliable a guide as anything else.

Unfortunately, however, one has little way of knowing whether any given manager's judgement in this area is particularly sound. Perkins's manager might be putting forward a suitable candidate, but he might equally be trying to do a friend a favour or to rid himself of a troublemaker or ambitious subordinate. It is also not a particularly fair method of selection, in that better candidates might be passed over simply because they don't happen to know the manager getting the coffee at that particular time. Similar objections exist to the common practice of using seniority as the main consideration (Berrell et al. 2002), as seniority does not necessarily mean capability, particularly in the international arena. Selection on the basis of connections or seniority thus has a number of problems, and is strongly discouraged as a means of selecting an international manager.

Formal methods

Formal methods, while more reliable, are not entirely problem free. Selection on the basis of past experience, for instance, is often deemed a reliable guide to future performance. However, simply because a manager has performed well in the home context or in a particular host country environment, it does not follow that they will do well wherever they are assigned. Indeed, as countries and people change over time, it does not even necessarily mean they would do well in the country of their first assignment! Past experience is thus, as Bartlett and Ghoshal note, not necessarily an indicator of future performance capability:

> 'One problem is that profiles that have been generated often include an inventory of personality traits, individual beliefs, acquired skills and other personal attributes and behaviours assembled … with little logical linkage to bind them. Furthermore, these profiles are often developed based on surveys of current managers or analysis of the most successful individual performers in the existing context.' (1997: 104)

The use of such criteria: first, fits the previous needs of the corporation, not the current needs; second, does not take individual variation into account; and, finally, encourages people to formulate a kind of 'ideal type' of manager that actually bears little relation to the realities of individual managers. So, although past experience is useful, it is not a predictor of future success.

There is also the case of selection by skill. As noted in the previous chapter, it is unfortunately common among MNCs to treat international experience or global awareness as a kind of 'bolt-on'; if you need a manager for a car factory, for instance, you select a good engineer and give him some intercultural training. The problem is that some skills and experiences cannot be formally taught. The author's own research at a large Anglo-German MNC, for instance, revealed the case of a German expatriate who was competent at his job, but whose lack of ability to communicate with the staff of the UK office to which he was assigned resulted in mutual alienation and a rapid declaration of expatriate failure. While one might discover hidden inter-cultural capabilities in some international assignees, it is best to treat these as pre-existing skills and abilities rather than as something that can be 'downloaded into' any suitable person.

Formal selection methods may thus be as problematic as informal ones, depending on the criteria for selection; while they may be used as criteria for making the initial selection, other methods will be needed subsequently to determine the best candidate.

Tests and examinations

In theory, at least, formal tests and assessments are more objective than the selection methods we have considered above, in that they are less based on advantageous friendships or on formal criteria which may or may not be good indicators of future performance. As expatriate assignments become more common, and consequently more consideration goes into the selection of candidates, more emphasis is being placed on using formal tests, examinations and so forth.

Some of the means of selection are fairly familiar, such as:

- *Interviews*: when interviewing a candidate for an international assignment, it is advantageous to have a variety of people from different parts of the organization consider the candidate – even, perhaps, to have them assessed by people from both head office and the office to which they may be assigned. In this way, a more balanced assessment of the candidate's skills can be obtained.
- *References/résumés*: as noted above, success in one international assignment does not necessarily guarantee success in another. As also noted, some assignments require a global orientation rather than previous experience. References and past experience are thus not always the best means of selection, although they can provide a useful indication of the candidate's skills and background.

In addition, more specialized means of selection may be used:

- *Selection tests*: these are often used for non-international assignments; however, in the case of selecting an expatriate, they may also include tests for linguistic ability, intercultural ability, psychological fitness for expatriation, and other, perhaps assignment-specific, criteria.
- *Assessment centres*: these, again, are often used for selecting for non-international positions. However, they can be useful in assessing abilities such as flexibility, quick thinking, coping with multi-ethnic teams and handling difficult situations. In the future, we may increasingly see assessment centres specifically geared towards international assignments. However, as Berrell et al. note, the key problem with selection is that 'it is exceedingly difficult to simulate cultural influences' (2002: 92), meaning that it is doubtful that an assessment centre would prove to be a better guide than any other to the candidate's potential fitness for the assignment.

● *Specific monitoring of disadvantaged groups*: this is a legal requirement in some cases, and should be practised even when it is not, for reasons discussed below. The purpose is to ensure that the selection is effective, efficient and fair for all candidates.

Whatever criteria are used initially to select candidates, they should be followed up with tests and assessments. It is worth bearing in mind, however, that tests can also show bias, as can examiners, when selecting candidates.

Third-country nationals

As some more globally integrated companies are now beginning to recruit cross-nationally rather than simply looking for an applicant at the head office, more complex and specific criteria for selection are needed. Such expatriates are known as third-country nationals (TCNs), as opposed to being from the home or host country of the MNC. The advantages of selecting such individuals are that the firm can hire the best person for the job, regardless of their head office connections or their place of origin; they are also widely believed to be more impartial than head office employees sent to branches (or vice versa) and, given that there are three rather than two cultures involved, to find it easier to cultivate a global mentality. However, they are also harder to recruit, and it can be harder to allow for cultural differences in the selection process and to arrange for training, compensation and so forth. It is also worth questioning whether it really is easier to develop a global mentality in this way rather than by any other. Thus, the decision on whether to select TNCs or not will depend to a large extent on the individual assignment and the company.

Selecting for specific abilities and competencies

Finally, MNCs will want to select candidates with specific abilities and competencies that might prove useful in the assignment. The fact that, as mentioned above, many MNCs starting operations in China select expatriates on the basis of their ability to speak Chinese can be a mixed blessing: on the one hand it saves the cost of training, but on the other hand it might mean that a better performer in other areas is passed over. Although Berrell et al. (2002) say that companies engaged in international joint ventures benefit from actively recruiting people who have lived for extended periods in the other culture so that they can facilitate knowledge transfer and develop intercultural learning, it might be less useful in other areas in which knowledge transfer is less of an issue than particular technical skills or the ability to be a negotiator. Overall, managers need to have 'effective cross-cultural communication, a capacity to be non-judgemental, empathy, flexibility and a high tolerance for ambiguity' (Berrell et al. 2002: 92), but quite what these entail in the particular circumstances of the assignment is more ambiguous.

Entrepreneurial skills are often cited as advantageous in international managers, as these managers may find themselves developing a new venture virtually on their own or steering an established branch on a particular course. However, the importance of these skills depends on how isolated the branch is, how much of a controlling role the expatriate has been given and the company's overall strategy vis-à-vis its branches. Ultimately, then, the importance of particular skills to the assignment is very much down to the individual circumstances of the company and the manager in question.

In sum, then, selection, like recruitment, is very much dependent on the particular context of the assignment: the needs of the company, the skills of the candidates and the role the manager will play in the organization. It is advisable to use both traditional and non-traditional selection methods to find the right individual for the position.

Hamada versus Sakai

Japanese expatriates are a particularly interesting group to consider in the context of recruitment and selection because the economic circumstances, expectations of expatriates and attitude to globalization of Japanese MNCs has, generally speaking, changed dramatically over recent years. By comparing and contrasting two studies of Japanese expatriates conducted ten years apart, Hamada's 'Under the Silk Banner' (1992) and Sakai's *Japanese Bankers in the City of London* (2000), we can see how the needs, circumstances and attitudes of the expatriates and their companies change over time in response to outside events, impacting on the recruitment and selection of international managers.

Hamada's study was based on interviews with Japanese expatriate managers in the mid-1980s. At this time the emphasis in Japan was strongly on the idea of managers as 'company men', who would remain loyal to the company, making it the focus of their personal lives as well as their business activities (see Rohlen 1974) and of strongly centralized companies focused on a Japanese head office. Japan was also internationalizing rapidly after a period in which business was largely domestic. Consequently, companies tended to prefer a model of expatriation based on a group of Japanese expatriate top managers and senior managers controlling the branch, with local junior managers and staff handling the situation on the ground.

At the same time, the Japanese managers were concerned about the personal impact of the internationalization process. Hamada's interviewees were reluctant to go overseas and concerned about losing their social networks within the company: under the traditional Japanese corporate system, senior employees look after and encourage the careers of their juniors, who in turn support their seniors, but staff posted overseas find themselves struggling to maintain their position within this network. Women were virtually non-existent within this cadre: Alice Lam (1992), writing at the same time as Hamada, noted that women were usually passed over for expatriate positions on the grounds that they would be expected to leave the company once they married and became pregnant. The wives and children of expatriates often stayed in Japan; given that Japanese men were expected to form their social lives around the company, this is not too surprising, but the perceived difficulty of making an overseas move was also a factor.

In terms of recruitment and selection, then, Japanese companies had a strong stake in ensuring that the people sent abroad were loyal and focused on Japan and the head office. There was the additional problem, however, that the international assignment might induce feelings of disloyalty in managers cut off from their networks and families. Furthermore, the fact that overseas postings were not regarded as avenues for career advancement meant that they had difficulty attracting the best staff for such positions. Japanese companies in the 1980s were thus forced to rely on employee loyalty to maintain successful expatriate assignments.

By the time of Sakai's study, however, much had changed. During the 1990s, Japan had undergone a severe financial crisis, which had a similarly drastic effect on traditional Japanese company structure. In addition, the intervening years had seen the development of a cohort of what Goodman (1993) calls 'international youth' – Japanese children raised wholly or partly abroad, who are consequently more internationally focused. Japan had thus become more flexible and globalized as a result of its experiences.

Consequently, among Sakai's interviewees, we see more interest in an international career among Japanese managers; as the system collapses and reforms itself, managers feel less bound by the old social hierarchies and traditions of company loyalty, and seek non-traditional employment patterns, including going abroad. We also see more flexible approaches to international management: a notable portion of Sakai's interviewees were either Japanese already settled in England who were recruited to Japanese banks or expatriates who settled and became locals. Although women are still discriminated against, the loss of the 'career for life' among male employees has put women on a more equal footing with the men. With the 'international youth' becoming a more and more prestigious group, families are becoming less concerned about going abroad. In view of these changes, the head offices are more inclined to allow their subsidiaries more control over their own affairs, resulting in a relaxation of the Japan-centric international management practices.

Furthermore, Sakai's study clearly shows that the Japanese companies' relationship to home and host countries changes over time. In the 1960s, she notes, banks focused for the most part on domestic concerns and providing financial support for Japanese companies overseas; in the 1970s they became more focused on the international, due to financial and political pressures from Japan to expand into other economies. Following the collapse of the Japanese 'bubble economy' in the 1990s, the banks have again changed their practices, hiring more foreign employees (and, apparently, allowing them greater status within the organization); layoffs and redundancies have become more common. Many of her interviewees felt that the Japanese national business culture was changing to become more like that of the USA or the UK: no lifetime employment, a focus on generalists rather than specialists and less of a sense of belonging to the company. With these changes, patterns of recruitment and selection have also changed, from wanting staff who are focused on head office, loyal to the company and technically skilled, to more flexible patterns focusing increasingly on intercultural skills and linguistic abilities.

The case of the two studies of Japanese expatriates thus demonstrates that the needs and strategies of both companies and expatriates change over time and under different circumstances; the requirements of the company and the concerns of the expatriate were quite different in Hamada's and Sakai's studies. Finally, the main lesson that we can learn is that recruitment and selection patterns for international managers can, and should, vary depending on the circumstances of the individual assignment.

For further details, see:

Goodman, R. (1993) *Japan's 'International Youth': The Emergence of a New Class of School Children*, Oxford: Clarendon Press.

Hamada, T. (1992) 'Under the Silk Banner: The Japanese Company and its Overseas Managers', in Takie Sugiyama Lebra (ed.) *Japanese Social Organization*, Honolulu: University of Hawaii Press, 135–64.

Lam, A. (1992) *Women and Japanese Management: Discrimination and Reform*, London: Routledge.

Rohlen, T.P. (1974) *For Harmony and Strength: Japanese White-Collar Organization in Anthropological Perspective*, Berkeley: University of California Press.

Sakai, J. (2000) *Japanese Bankers in the City of London: Language, Culture and Identity in the Japanese Diaspora*, London: Routledge.

Case study question: *What impact do you think the changes in expatriation in Japanese companies will have on (a) what the manager expects from the company and (b) the company's criteria for recruiting a suitable candidate?*

Gender and ethnicity in recruitment and selection

Although women can have advantages over men in certain expatriate assignments, even sometimes in countries where female managers are not the norm, women have a harder time winning expatriate assignments. This is partly because of the belief that they will not be taken seriously in less egalitarian countries, and partly because they traditionally take on more of the family's childcare responsibilities. This is a pressing problem for many companies, both because of increasing equal opportunities legislation in many countries and because MNCs are increasingly concerned to hire the best candidate for the job. We shall here consider some of the issues involving both gender and ethnicity in international recruitment and selection.

The problem

As noted in Chapter 9, international management has long remained the preserve of white male employees – or, as Davison and Punnet (1995: 418) put it, the preserve of male employees of the 'elite race' (Japanese males in Japanese firms, German males in German firms, and so forth). This is despite the fact that demographics in the home countries of these firms have been changing; in North America, for instance, equal opportunity initiatives have meant a relative rise in the numbers of women and ethnic minorities in management, which is not reflected in the same firms' international management practices. Also, Davison and Punnett (1995) note the development of a catch-22: although most if not all firms recognize that they can benefit from diversity and that firms that avoid systematic discrimination are more effective internationally, they still maintain discriminatory hiring practices. Despite advances in equal opportunity practices, then, women and ethnic minorities are still discriminated against in international management.

These practices may, furthermore, actually be *preventing* women and ethnic minorities from obtaining international posts. Davison and Punnet (1995) argue that many companies try to take a 'gender and race blind' approach to hiring, but, rather than therefore being able to pick the best candidate for the job, they frequently damage the assignment. In the first place, to try to ignore gender and race is to deny the real fact that discrimination exists. Linehan and Walsh (1999) note that of their sample of female international managers, none had been asked or suggested by their colleagues for the assignment; all had deliberately put their names forward. Second, this approach ignores the advantages that gender and race may bring to the assignment, particularly as this is a situation in which intangible assets may count more than visible ones, and in which an innovative approach may be necessary. To be 'colour blind' is thus not to grant everyone an equal chance, but to ignore the realities of the workplace.

This is all the more significant because discrimination in recruitment is often the result of unconscious biases rather than any systematic process. Thomas (1990) notes that there is an overwhelming number of white male managers in US corporations because the senior management of such corporations also tend to be white men, who are more favourably disposed towards people who resemble themselves and with whom they can empathize. This is supported by Davison and Punnet's (1995) study, which suggests that female and black candidates are more favourably viewed by female and black assessors than by white and/or male assessors. Unconsciously, managers may decide that a female candidate would be 'unambitious', or think that a black manager would 'have trouble fitting in', or be reluctant to choose a woman for an assignment seen as involving an element of risk; women are also often seen as being more likely to have 'split loyalties', as they attempt to balance their role within the company with their role within their families. Alternatively, managers may not consider any of these people at all if they do not fit their stereotype of what an international manager looks like. This stereotype is reinforced by the fact that most of the literature on organization studies regarding expatriates assumes the baseline norm to be a married, white (and generally American) man (Linehan and Walsh 1999), which is problematic in and of itself when one considers that, even now, large numbers of expatriates do not fit this description.

In addition, Linehan and Walsh suggest that male senior managers may feel threatened by an ambitious woman. They argue that as 'the role of the expatriate involves even more uncertainties than that of the domestic manager, and as uncertainty increases the need for trust, this is perceived as having further implications for limiting women expatriate managers' (1999: 523). Furthermore, they note that studies of uncertainty suggest that people under those conditions are more inclined to fall back on stereotypes than otherwise, which would further preclude the hiring of candidates stereotyped as unambitious or unreliable. The strongest barrier to the selection of women and ethnic minorities as international managers would thus seem to be unconscious prejudice.

Finally, it is also worth noting that different countries have different regulations on discrimination, equal opportunities and positive discrimination. When engaging in the selection of international managers, it is thus advisable to be aware of the regulations in the home and the host country regarding the hiring of disadvantaged groups, and to take these into account. One should also consider the International

Labour Organization (ILO) regulations concerning race and gender, in particular the ILO Convention Concerning Discrimination in Respect of Employment and Occupation (Convention 111). In many places there can be significant benefits to being seen to be an equal opportunities employer.

Hiring women and ethnic minorities: the pros and cons

Aside from the legal argument, another reason to recruit women and ethnic minorities as international managers is that they may have advantages that white male managers do not. Adler and Izraeli (1994) cite the case of an American female manager who did very well in Japan, despite the fact that the Japanese indigenous business culture is strongly male-biased, because an American woman was seen as a novelty or curiosity, and so her contacts were better able to remember her than more conventional male expatriates. It may also be the case that in a male-dominated business culture businessmen may not see a female manager as a potential rival, and thus may be more open with her than with male managers. Taylor et al. (2004) cite the case of a black American female interviewee, who said that due to her experience of discrimination in her home country, she was less upset than her white male colleagues when she faced discrimination in Japan. Linehan and Walsh (1999) note that as managers come to realize that relational skills and intercultural competencies may be worth more than technical skills as success factors in the international business arena, the stereotype of women as better relators and facilitators than technicians may come to work to the advantage of female managers. There are thus a number of inherent advantages to recruiting women and ethnic minorities as international managers.

There are, however, also disadvantages. Discrimination can be a source of stress, particularly when a woman or minority ethnic manager moves from a more egalitarian business culture to a more segregated one; American women in Germany, for instance, found what they saw as the 'casual sexism' of their German colleagues offensive (British women, however, did not, indicating that what is seen as acceptable forms and levels of discrimination vary from culture to culture) (Taylor et al. 2004; see Burrus 1997 for a case study of an American female manager attempting to operate in the male-dominated Swiss business environment). This can also lead to situations of cross-cultural misunderstanding, in which a local manager may cause offence to an international manager without realizing it, or vice versa, due to differences in attitude to gender and ethnicity. Furthermore, in some cases, discrimination goes beyond simple bias and stereotyping; in some countries, for instance, women may not be allowed to travel without a male escort, and in the apartheid-era in South Africa, a black manager would have been barred from dealing with white colleagues. It is also possible that a male trailing spouse will face more problems than a female one, due to the lack of an extant support group and finding himself in a non-traditional social role (that of stay-at-home spouse and/or parent) at the same time as he moves to a foreign setting, and so forth, which may cause problems within the assignment.

When selecting women and ethnic minorities as international managers, one must bear in mind both the particular advantages and disadvantages that they face; one should not, however, let the disadvantages blind one to the potential benefits of such a choice.

Family

For expatriate managers of both genders, the happiness of a spouse and children can have a strong impact on their morale and adaptability. Even in the most traditional expatriate situation, the attitudes of the family can be crucial to its success or failure; in a now-classic article, Steinmetz (1965) focuses on the role of wives in the traditional expatriate assignment, and the fact that the happiness of the expatriate's family can impact on his own attitude. It is therefore important for the MNC to ensure that the expatriate's family members are also adequately provided for.

Furthermore, as dual-career couples increasingly become the norm, situations may arise in which one spouse may be forced to choose between their partner's expatriate assignment and their own career. As Forster notes, 'It is often relocating partners who have the most to lose from a move abroad – particularly if this means they have to give up work or … put their careers on hold' (2000: 131). Despite the fact that some companies are now trying out compensation policies for spouses, including hiring an executive search consultant to find a new job for the spouse in the area to which the manager is being assigned, Forster's research indicates that the majority of trailing spouses simply give up employment altogether for the duration of the assignment (see Table 10.1).

Table 10.1 Career patterns of partners of expatriates

Before the move		After the move	
Part time	32%	Part time	9%
Full time	34%	Full time	11%
Not employed	34%	Not employed	80%

Source: Forster (2000: 131)

Forster also notes that people who might otherwise be suitable candidates for an international assignment are increasingly refusing the offer or failing to put their names forward because they do not want their partner to be forced to choose between the assignment and their own job. When hiring international managers of whatever gender, then, the situation and welfare of the family should be a key consideration.

Whereas in the past, most of the literature has assumed expatriates to be white and/or elite males with families, and while managers have consequently focused their selection processes on this group, it should not be assumed that such individuals are therefore the best candidates for an international assignment. Human resource (HR) managers must thus be particularly careful in the case of international assignments to ensure that the recruitment and selection process is egalitarian and that it takes into account the particular strengths and weaknesses of women and ethnic minorities in this situation, and that they consider the impact of the move on the expatriate's family.

The myth of the international manager?

In this final section we will briefly consider whether the case of international recruitment and selection supports or contradicts the theory that 'international managers' are emerging as a distinct group in the business world, what the implications are for recruitment and selection in either case and the potential implications for how we think about globalization.

There is currently a lot of support in international business for the idea that the increasing recognition of international management as a distinct case within recruitment and selection is furthering the emergence of the 'international manager' as a distinct class (Gregersen et al. 2004; Selmer 2004). By selecting less for practical or technical skills, and more for such things as 'intercultural ability' and 'global awareness', it is possible that MNCs are in fact developing a cadre of people who specialize in international management, and who ultimately will become a group who go from assignment to assignment, like diplomats (Forster 2000). While this seems an extreme case, it is also possible that, through the processes of convergence, expatriate managers around the world may come to regard themselves as a distinct group with particular social capabilities. It is also possible that selecting for such traits would favour the international cultural elite described by Micklethwait and Wooldridge (2000) – people from all over the world who mix and marry internationally, attend elite universities like Harvard and Oxford, then go on to careers with big MNCs in whichever country is hiring – developing the kind of global elite described by Sklair (2001).

If this is in fact the case, then the possibility of such a group developing should form a key part of any MNC's international recruitment and selection programme. HR managers should target individuals who meet Sklair (2001) and Micklethwait and Wooldridge's (2000) profiles, encouraging them to try for international assignments, and also seek out individuals who are in local management but who have the attitudes and orientations to join this elite. Recruitment and selection should also focus less on the particular *national* context of the assignment, and more on the international development of the manager.

On the other hand, there is considerable evidence to support Forster's rejection of the development of such a managerial class in an article tellingly entitled 'The Myth of the "International Manager"' (2000). As noted in Chapter 9, Forster argues, following the more general arguments of Hirst and Thompson (1996), that managers are not, and can never be, 'rootless'; everyone has to come from somewhere and go to somewhere else, and few people (to say nothing of their families) are psychologically capable of moving from region to region at regular intervals, adapting to new cultures every few years. The most successful international managers, he notes, are not the ones who keep on moving, but the ones who like their assignment so much they opt to stay in the country: MNCs 'may be becoming more international but their staff are not' (2000: 126). Again, the processes of globalization can be seen to be encouraging divergence as much as they do convergence. Furthermore, it has been suggested by researchers such as Bartlett and Ghoshal (1993) and Tomlinson (1999) that globalization is as much a state of mind as anything else; a manager can remain locally rooted, and yet be global or international by virtue of their orientations, values, beliefs and uses of communications and transportation technology, suggesting that if a globalized managerial elite is emerging, it will not be defined in terms of people's international assignments, but more in terms of their attitudes and activities.

If this is the case, HR managers must be more flexible in terms of international recruitment and selection, thinking less in terms of developing the individual over the long term and more in terms of the particular position to be filled and the specific requirements and competencies needed for it. While this need not preclude companies from developing general guidelines and policies for international management, they must also recognize that this term covers a wide and diverse field.

While it is possible that international managers may be developing into a distinct group, the situation, as always in globalization, is probably more complex, involving processes that encourage both convergence and divergence. Although it may be a good idea to keep an eye on the potentialities of international management and to develop the skills of particular managers in this area, the important thing for managers is to focus on the specific circumstances of the assignment in question and the particular pressures involved.

Conclusion

In sum, the one certain thing in international recruitment would seem to be the *lack* of certainty. While one can identify certain general skills and abilities that can be useful under particular circumstances, the nature of globalization and the political manoeuvring that the implementation of IHRM policy involves mean that it is impossible to identify hard-and-fast criteria for all expatriates, or for that matter all expatriate assignments. Each situation must therefore be taken on its own merits. The strategy of the company, the MNC's relationship with home and host country cultures, the tension between global and local interests within the MNC and the agendas of the candidate and their family all need to be taken into account; and the recruitment and selection programme needs to be designed accordingly. As Bartlett and Ghoshal put it, 'instead of forcing the individual to conform to the company's policies and practices, the overall objective is to capture and leverage the knowledge and expertise that each organisational member brings to the company' (1997: 114).

Key points to remember in international recruitment and selection are as follows:

● Be flexible; remember that things change rapidly in the global sphere and that a variety of different political and cultural pressures are involved.
● Consider carefully the nature of the assignment, the cultures of the home and host countries, the company's needs and the expatriate's needs and the subsidiary's needs before developing a recruitment programme.

- Don't be gender/race blind, but remember the problem of unconscious prejudice – ask yourself what you really need, and be wary of discrimination.
- If there are problems, or even expatriate failure, the key thing is to *learn* from the experience. If you do, this can offset the short-term cost by producing long-term improvement.
- Don't be afraid of taking risks – it can prove beneficial in the long run!

Recruitment, selection and development in the international sphere are thus very much context dependent, and it is consequently very difficult to predict who will do well. However, with care and consideration, it may be possible to greatly reduce the risk of failure and produce successful international managers.

Review questions

1 How important are cultural factors as opposed to past knowledge and experience for international assignments? Discuss the pros and cons of hiring an expatriate based on each criterion.

2 Develop an advertisement to recruit an international manager for one of the corporations described in any of the books in the References section for this chapter. Be sure to take all possible considerations into account.

3 You are an HR manager at a large MNC. You are asked to help select a candidate for an international assignment to a country where local women face a considerable amount of discrimination. The two candidates are equally qualified; one is a man with no intercultural experience at all, the other is a woman with considerable past experience in the country in question. Which would you choose and why?

4 'There is no such thing as an international manager; therefore, there is no point in developing specialized programmes for the recruitment and selection of international managers.' Argue for or against this statement, with reference to Forster (2000).

Further reading

Bartlett, C.A. and Ghoshal, S. (1997) 'The Myth of the Generic Manager: New Personal Competencies for New Management Roles', *California Management Review* 40(1), 92–116.

While not specifically dealing with recruitment and selection, this article challenges the received 'one-size-fits-all' approach to international management and argues for a more customized approach.

Dowling, P. and Welch, D. (2004) *International Human Resource Management: Managing People in a Multinational Context*, London: Thompson, Chapter 4.

This chapter provides a comprehensive, if brief and slightly managerialist, overview of the issues involved in international recruitment and selection.

Linehan, M. and Walsh, J.S. (1999) 'Recruiting and Developing Female Managers for International Assignments', *Journal of Management Development*, 18(6), 521–30.

This a good consideration of the issues involved in the recruitment and selection of women in international management.

Sklair, L. (2001) *The Transnational Capitalist Class,* Oxford: Blackwell.

This is the primary source for the argument in favour of the emergence of a distinct transnational class; it is interesting and well written, but should be taken with a grain of salt.

References

Adler, N. and Izraeli, D. (1994) *Competitive Frontiers: Women Managers in a Global Economy*, Oxford: Blackwell

Bartlett, C.A. and Ghoshal, S. (1993) *Managing Across Borders: The Transnational Solution*, London: Random House

Bartlett, C.A. and Ghoshal, S. (1997) 'The Myth of the Generic Manager: New Personal Competencies for New Management Roles', *California Management Review*, 40(1), 92–116.

Beardwell, I., Holden, L. and Claydon, T. (2004) *Human Resource Management: A Contemporary Approach*, London: Prentice Hall.

Berrell, M., Gloet, M. and Wright, P. (2002) 'Organisational Learning in International Joint Ventures: Implications for Management Development', *Journal of Management Development*, 21(2), 83–100.

Burrus, K. (1997) 'National Culture and Gender Diversity within One of the Universal Swiss Banks', in A. Sackman (ed.), *Cultural Complexity in Organizations: Inherent Contrasts and Contradictions*, London: Sage, 209–27.

Davison, E.D. and Punnett, B.J. (1995) 'International Assignments: Is There a Role for Gender and Race in Decisions?' *International Journal of Human Resource Management*, 6(2), 412–41

Dowling, P. and Welch, D. (2004) *International Human Resource Management: Managing People in a Multinational Context*, London: Thompson.

Forster, N. (2000) 'The Myth of the "International Manager"', *International Journal of Human Resource Management*, 11(1), 126–42.

Goodman, R. (1993) *Japan's 'International Youth': The Emergence of a New Class of Schoolchildren*, Oxford: Clarendon Press.

Gregersen, H.B., Hite, J.M. and Black, J.S. (1996) 'Expatriate Performance appraisal in U.S. Multinational Firms', *Journal of International Business Studies*, 27(4), 711–39.

Gregersen, H.B., Harrison, D.A., Black, J.S. and Ferzandi, L.A. (2004) 'You Can Take it With You: Individual Differences and Expatriate Effectiveness', in N. Boyacigiller and T. Kiyak (eds) *Proceedings of the 46th Annual Meeting of the Academy of International Business*, East Lansing, MI: Academy of International Business, 185.

Hamada, T. (1992) 'Under the Silk Banner: The Japanese Company and Its Overseas Managers', in T.S. Lebra (ed.) *Japanese Social Organization*, Honolulu: University of Hawaii Press, 135–64.

Harris, H. and Brewster, C. (1999) 'The Coffee-Machine System: How International Selection Really Works', *International Journal of Human Resource Management,* 10(3), 488–500.

Harzing, A-W. (2001a) 'An Analysis of the Functions of International Transfer of Managers in MNCs', *Employee Relations*, 23(6), 581–98.

Harzing, A-W. (2001b) 'Of Bears, Bumblebees and Spiders: the Role of Expatriates in Controlling Foreign Subsidiaries', *Journal of World Business*, 36(4), 336–79.

Hirst, P.Q. and Thompson, G. (1996) *Globalization in Question: The International Economy and the Possibilities of Governance*, Cambridge: Polity Press.

Lam, A. (1992) *Women and Japanese Management: Discrimination and Reform*, London: Routledge.

Leonard, O. (2002) 'Away Winners', *Financial Management*, March, 42.

Li, J. and Karakowski, L. (2001) 'Do We See Eye-to-Eye? Implications of Cultural Differences for Cross-Cultural Management Research and Practice', *Journal of Psychology*, 135(5), pp. 501–17.

Linehan, M. and Walsh, J.S. (1999) 'Recruiting and Developing Female Managers for International Assignments', *Journal of Management Development*, 18(6), 521–30.

Micklethwait, J. and Wooldridge, A. (2000) *A Future Perfect: The Challenge and Hidden Promise of Globalisation*, London: William Heinemann.

Moore, F. (2005) 'Governing the Outposts? Exploring the Role of Expatriate Managers in a German Multinational Corporation', in M. Mayer and M. Geppert (eds) *Global, National and Local Practices in Multinational Corporations*, London: Palgrave.

Polak, R. (2002) 'Retirement Programs for Cross-Border Transfers', *Compensation and Benefits Management,* 18(3), 24–28.

Rohlen, T.P. (1974) *For Harmony and Strength: Japanese White-Collar Organization in Anthropological Perspective*, Berkeley: University of California Press.

Sakai, J. (2000) *Japanese Bankers in the City of London: Language, Culture and Identity in the Japanese Diaspora*, London: Routledge.

Selmer, J. (2004) 'Do You Speak Chinese? Language Proficiency and Adjustment of Business Expatriates in China', in N. Boyacigiller and T. Kiyak (eds) *Proceedings of the 46th Annual Meeting of the Academy of International Business*, East Lansing, MI: Academy of International Business, 104.

Sklair, L. (2001) *The Transnational Capitalist Class*, Oxford: Blackwell.

Steinmetz, L.L. (1965) 'Selecting Managers for International Operations: The Wife's Role', *Management of Personel Quarterly*, 4(1), 26–30.

Taylor, S., Napier, N.K. and Blair, A. (2004) 'Women Expatriates Working in Germany: Factors of Success', in N. Boyacigiller and T. Kiyak (eds) *Proceedings of the 46th Annual Meeting of the Academy of International Business*, East Lansing, MI: Academy of International Business, 186.

Thomas, R.R. (1990) 'From Affirmative Action to Affirming Diversity', *Harvard Business Review*, March–April, 107–17.

Tomlinson, J. (1999) *Globalization and Culture*, Cambridge: Polity Press.

Chapter 11

International pay and reward

Guy Vernon

Key aims

This chapter has the following key aims:

- to outline the commonalities and differences of the national environments faced by multinational companies in terms of reward structures;
- to consider the key drivers of cross-national variation in these structures;
- to outline the approaches of multinational companies to reward in this context;
- to consider the strategic space for international reward;
- to consider the issue of how this might best be used in pursuit of improved performance.

Introduction

As is often observed, with many tangible resources increasingly easy to obtain, the management of people appears increasingly central to the achievement of competitive advantage. Pay, or extrinsic reward, is of obvious centrality in the employment relationship: to the recruitment, retention and motivation of employees. Moreover, as Kessler and Purcell (1995) note, it is often expressive of management style and of symbolic importance.

Within the multinational company (MNC), reward constitutes an area of human resource (HR) policy in which an overall direction, harmonization or even standardization appears very much less subject to processes of local implementation than other areas. The administrative nature of pay arrangements, and the relative simplicity of administering pay across national borders, appears to lend itself better than many other aspects of human resource management (HRM) to deliberate multinational strategy. If HR is not to be subservient to other functions, acting on a mere operational level within a framework that these other functions have established, but rather to be active in forging deliberate corporate strategy, then pay arrangements must be central to this strategic role. Indeed, even if HR is to be meaningfully aligned with corporate strategy, the approach to pay must be central.

Yet the international situation of MNCs implies that they must steer a careful course between Scylla and Charybdis in their approach to reward. On the one side lurk dangers of an unthinking universalism in the approach to pay and pay systems, most of all a universalism that is ethnocentric, involving the extension of practices from the country of origin to all countries of operation. On the other side the danger is of an unthinking conformity with existing or typical practice in the various countries of operation. In this context, a strategic approach to pay appears to have much potential.

Despite the focus on expatriate, international, or at best senior subsidiary managers in the existing literature on international reward, and indeed even now in much management discussion, there seems much potential in reflecting on the reward of non-managerial employees. Even if there has been little or no change in the general stance of MNC managements since the late 1980s – when Wood and Peccei (1990) found a lack of interest among the managers of UK MNCs in the cross-national standardization of pay structures – this does not eliminate the space for such strategic contemplation. An international strategic role for HR, extending beyond the treatment of expatriates, does not require a commitment to such standardization. MNCs are increasingly subtle in their contemplation of strategies on pay that extend not only across national borders but also beyond the small management group to non-managerial employees (who comprise the majority of the workforce and in most cases the vast bulk of the pay bill).

This chapter overviews the issues arising in the international management of reward. In so doing it gives careful attention to the available evidence. The chapter begins by outlining the international and comparative situation with regard to reward. It then moves to consider MNC responses to the prevailing cross-national variation in conditions. Building on this, the discussion then turns to consider the space that is actually available to MNCs for international reward strategy. An important issue is how this space might best be used in the promotion of performance; thus, evidence on 'best practice' is the subject of the following section. Finally, some conclusions are drawn about the lessons concerning the role that HR may play in the shaping of strategy in this vital area.

Cross-national variation in reward structures

MNCs face variations across their countries of operation, not only in average pay but in the reward structures and pay arrangements that are common and accepted. This section aims to shed light on the extent of these differences.

Pay inequality

While a plethora of statistics on pay arrangements are available, those that are both comparable across nations and available for a large number of nations are much harder to come by. However, such data are available on the distribution of gross earnings across national workforces: the extent of earnings inequality (OECD 2001). More specifically, these data show the gap in pay between those towards the top of the earnings distribution, those on average (median) earnings and those towards the bottom.

Figure 11.1 shows for a number of OECD (Organization for Economic Co-operation and Development) nations a gauge of the spread of the overall earnings distribution of full-time employees: the ratio of earnings towards the top of the earnings distribution to the earnings of those towards the bottom. More specifically, it shows the ratio of the earnings of those at the 90th percentile of the earnings distribution (in the relatively comfortable position that only 10 per cent of employees earn more than them) to the earnings of those at the 10th percentile (in the relatively uncomfortable position that only 10 per cent earn less than them). A good deal of similarity might be expected in these ratios across nations, particularly perhaps in the advanced industrialized nations to which these data relate. We might expect convergence in these ratios, perhaps particularly in the 1990s in the wake of the fall of state socialism, the explosion of multinational activity and indeed the resurgence of the USA as an economic power. The evidence, though, is rather at odds with such a view. In the 1990s, those towards the top of the earnings distribution in the USA earned four-and-a-half times as much as those towards the bottom. In the Nordic countries the ratio was barely two-and-a-quarter: half as great. The UK lies between these extremes, though it is becoming increasingly separated from the continental European situation. Generally, the enormous differences between nations show no signs of narrowing.

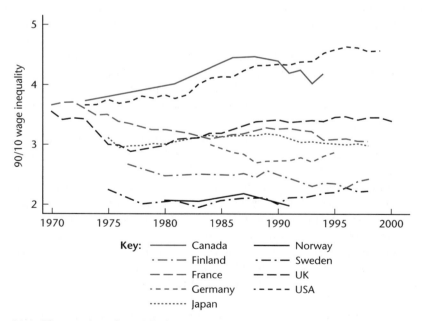

Figure 11.1 Time series plot of 90/10 wage inequality
Source: based on data from OECD (2001)

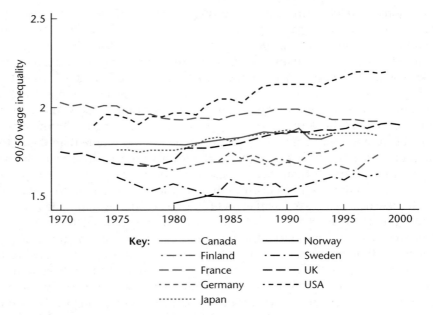

Figure 11.2 Time series plot of 90/50 wage inequality
Source: based on data from OECD (2001)

Figures 11.2 and 11.3 provide a little more detail, showing the ratios of earnings of those at the top to the average, and of those at the average to those at the bottom. This shows that the bulk of the cross-national variation in the overall earnings ratio is the result of variation at the bottom of the distribution: in the extent to which the relatively low paid are short of the average earner. Variation at the top contributes less to the cross-national differences in the overall ratio: that is to say, there is greater cross-national commonality in the relative pay of those towards the top of the distribution and those on average earnings.

What underlies such enormous cross-national variation? Recent work (Rueda and Pontusson 2000; Pontusson et al. 2002; Rueda 2003) shows that there is a remarkably strong relationship between the (national) density of union membership and the compression of bottom-end earnings inequality in particular, but also overall earnings inequality. Even *within* the oft-distinguished groups of social market economies (principally northern Europe), and liberal market economies (Anglo-Saxon nations) density bears a strong relationship with earnings inequality. Moreover, indices of the centralization of collective bargaining also bear a strong relationship to bottom-end earnings compression in particular. Whatever the precise interpretation of these findings, it seems clear that collective bargaining is of much relevance to nations' earnings structures. This work also shows that greater government employment and statutory regulation of wages significantly shape earnings inequality, especially at the bottom end.

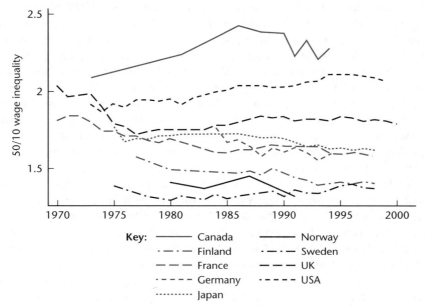

Figure 11.3 Time series plot of 50/10 wage inequality
Source: based on data from OECD (2001)

Much more progress has been made in establishing influences on bottom-end earnings inequality, and thus on overall earnings inequality, than in establishing influences on top-end inequality specifically. The cross-national relationships to top-end inequality established in the literature are much fewer, weaker and more difficult to interpret. However, there is a relationship between the political alignment of governments and top-end inequality, with social democratic government associated with lower top-end inequality and Christian democratic or neo-liberal government associated with greater. This may be principally due to the relevance of the alignment of governments for the income tax rates applied to higher earners, with greater rates discouraging the establishment of a pronounced differential even in gross payments between median and higher earners (Pontusson et al. 2002). It may, however, be that social democratic government generally creates (or indeed expresses) a more diffuse climate in which the offering of enormous differentials is socially illegitimate (even if not considered illegitimate by senior managers themselves).

Pay systems

So much for cross-national variation in the earnings distribution. What of pay systems more specifically? Discussion of pay systems is complicated by the prevalence of a variety of terminologies, variously employed across, and even within, national boundaries. Essentially, though, we may distinguish between three bases of pay, or elements of pay packages, that are variously present in the cases of different employees. First, and predominantly for most employees, is a rate for the job, which may include allowances for unsociable hours, etc. Second, competence-based pay, assessed by qualifications or relevant experience, or a seniority element, based upon age or tenure, which is often seen as related. Finally, and subject of the most intense discussion, most particularly in the Anglo-Saxon world, variable pay or pay for performance. This may take the form of bonuses or special payments related to individual, team, departmental or organizational performance. This performance itself may be assessed in a multiplicity of ways: 'hard' objective or 'soft' subjective.

The predominant conventional wisdom is that the USA is the true home of pay for performance, and most particularly individual performance-related pay, the nation of innovation from which the practice spread to Europe (Almond 2004). Indeed, notions of high-performance work systems, which are generally seen as involving some degree of pay for performance (e.g. MacDuffie 1995), sometimes specifically individual, have been much discussed in the USA and have had at least some impact on pay practice. Barton and Delbridge (2004) note the limitations of the evidence but suggest that team, establishment or department-based reward is rather more common in the USA than in the UK. Of course, the UK itself is typically seen as an extreme within Europe in terms of its take-up of pay for performance of all forms; as we shall see, this is in some respects justified by the evidence. It is doubtless the case that pay for performance is quite common in the USA, and merit pay specifically quite common even for manual employees (Shibata 2002). There is, however, rather less evidence of the importance of pay for performance in the USA than there is assertion of its centrality.

The situation in Germany, the most cited example of a social market economy and a society often counterposed with that of the USA, is rather unexpected (see Schulten 2000). Just over half of all private sector establishments, which themselves comprise more than three-quarters of all employment in Germany, offer some form of payment by results, and just under half offer pay related to wider company performance to at least some of their employees. Payment by results (individual and collective) is not confined to white collar employees, but applies to manual employees almost equally. Indeed it seems that the situation of manual employees has changed rather little in this regard over the last couple of decades, while there has been a shift towards payment by results in the case of white collar staff. In contrast, pay based on company performance tends to be confined to the upper levels of the organizational hierarchy, with around 15 per cent of all private sector employees receiving such payments. Typically, moreover, payment by results is much more important to employees' incomes than pay based on company performance, though this is not the case for those at the top of organizational hierarchies, as might be expected.

Evidence for Sweden, often grouped with Germany as a social market economy, but in many respects more densely institutionalized, also makes interesting reading (see Kjellberg 1998). At the beginning of the 1990s, almost 15 per cent of both manual and non-manual employees received some form of pay for profits. As in Germany, though, payment by results seems of more significance to the workforce generally, with 60 per cent of manual employees in the highly unionized metal and engineering sector subject to some form of payment by results, often on a team basis, in 1994. Pay for performance is, however, much less developed not only in the very substantial public sector but also in private services. Moreover, it seems that through the 1990s the weight of pay for performance in employees' incomes has generally waned, with job and competence based elements of pay in recent ascendancy.

This evidence suggests that pay for performance is significant, but meaningful comparison of the situation in one nation to that in another is difficult. However, a collaborative project spanning a number of European nations has established that certain cross-national comparisons are possible on the basis of national surveys conducted at the turn of the millennium (Emans et al. 2003).

The nature of the surveys is such that it is difficult to establish the comparative coverage of pay for performance. Emans et al. (2003: Table 11), drawing on a Chartered Institute of Personnel and Development (CIPD) survey, estimate that around 70 per cent of British employees within the private sector and around 25 per cent within the public sector are subject to some form of pay for performance. This implies coverage of close to 60 per cent across the UK economy as a whole, a figure that has some support from elsewhere: while subject to other difficulties, the evidence of the Workplace Employment Relations Survey, designed to be representative of the situation of employees, suggests that generic pay for performance covered almost 60 per cent of the UK workforce as a whole (see Gilman 2000). In the other nations for which comparable questions are asked in national surveys, prevalence is much lower than in the UK, at around 40 per cent for the private sectors of Italy and the Netherlands (Emans et al. 2003: Table 11). Generally, prevalence is a little higher among managerial among non-managerial employees.

Alternative data, on the coverage of pay for performance among organizations, are also available for some nations (Emans et al. 2003: Table 15). The different basis of the data is of potential importance if the surveys of organizations are not scrupulously designed to represent the experience of the typical employee, as it may be the case that a relatively small number of firms employ certain pay practices, but that these tend to be the larger firms, such that the coverage of employees is nonetheless high. For example, the evidence available for the UK and also for Germany suggests that the larger the firm, the more likely the use of some form of pay for performance – see Gilman (2000) and Schulten (2000). Data available for Finland are not only based on a survey representative of Finnish employees, but are of particular interest given Finland's status as a member of the Nordic nations. Although the nature of the categorization of practices and employees makes comparisons a little problematic, it is clear that the coverage of pay for performance is at very least as great as that in the Netherlands, and most likely stands at around 50 per cent across the workforce as a whole (Emans et al. 2003: Table 1). This raises the possibility that the coverage of pay for performance in the Nordic nations may even approach that in the UK.

Perhaps surprisingly, cross-national comparisons of the prevalence of specific forms of pay for performance are rather easier to make. Emans et al. (2003: Table 12) show that an element of pay based on specifically individual performance applied to around a third of British private sector employees, but only around a quarter of Dutch. The prevalence of specifically individual performance-related pay (PRP) is only around half as great in the public sector in each case.

Comparisons between Finland and the UK are the most striking, however. Across the economy as a whole (including the public sector), the available data suggest that a quarter of all UK employees are subject to individual PRP. Yet some 23 per cent of Finnish manual employees and some 40 per cent of lower-level clerical employees are subject to merit pay *specifically*. The proportions are still higher for upper clerical employees/managers. While merit pay is the predominant form of individual PRP in Finland, other forms are of course present, such that one may say with much confidence that a minimum of a third of Finnish employees have some form of individual PRP (Emans et al. 2003: Tables 1, 12 and 15). There is thus little doubt that the prevalence of individual PRP is greater in Finland than in the UK. This is a remarkable finding given common presumptions about the Nordic nations in contrast to the Anglo-Saxon.

Some comparisons regarding the linking of pay to team or organizational performance are also possible. Linking pay to team or organizational performance is much more widespread in the UK than in the Netherlands, affecting around 50 per cent of private sector employees in the UK but only 20 per cent in the Netherlands. Such systems are uncommon outside the private sector. Again, while comparison is not unproblematic, it seems that such pay systems are at least as prevalent in Finland as in the UK. However, it seems that in Finland such reward is based much more commonly on performance at sub-organizational level: at the level of teams or departments.

These detailed and specific comparisons, while limited by the number of countries on which certain data are available, are the most meaningful comparative evidence we have, and highlight substantial cross-national variation in the prevalence of pay for performance, some of it of a surprising nature. There is an important limitation of the discussion so far, however. It concerns only the prevalence of pay for performance, not its significance in the typical financial reward package. The limited data available give some indication of this. Even in the private sector, despite fairly extensive coverage, pay for performance of all types accounted for less than 10 per cent of the base pay of Italian employees in 2001 (Emans et al. 2003). Data for Belgium, about which the prevalence of pay for performance is very difficult to determine, suggest that it is still less important in terms of the financial reward package as a whole.

Perhaps more importantly, anecdotal evidence suggests that in practice there is an extremely tight bunching of the actual payouts from pay for performance. The payout to individuals from PRP tends to vary little across teams or departments in practice, and the payout to teams or departments varies little within each organization in practice. Assessed performance must be very extreme for it to make a substantial difference to an employees' income. Generally speaking then, while pay for performance now quite commonly forms an element of the pay of employees across Europe, it tends to be a very limited element and, moreover, an element that is, in practice, very insensitive to variations in the performance on which it ostensibly depends.

Certainly, though, pay for performance not only applies to most senior managers and executives but also constitutes a sizeable proportion of their pay. Most commonly by far this takes the form of pay based on organizational performance. In Belgium, despite its almost total irrelevance to most employees, it represents more than 40 per cent of base salary for executives (Emans et al. 2003). Although systematic data are difficult to come by, it appears that, quite generally across Europe and North America at least, pay for performance is of much importance in the pay of the most senior managers. Even here, though, there must be doubts about the extent to which this pay for performance is actually linked to performance since bunching in actual payments appears common.

As we have seen, research on the influences shaping the earnings structure has focused on the significance of the nature of nations' institutional environment. Given the importance of the institutional environment for the earnings structure, it seems likely that it is of at least some relevance for the nature of pay systems more specifically. However, to date, attempts to explore the bases of cross-national variations in pay systems have usually pursued cultural explanations. Assertions about the nature of a particular nation's culture are sometimes ill-based and simplistic, evidence about the relevance of a particular pay system is sketchy, and the claim that there is some link between the two is left unsubstantiated by any contrast with the situation in other nations. The relationship between national culture and pay systems remains, however, intriguing.

Schuler and Rogovsky (1998) present a stimulating quantitative effort to explore the link between national culture and indicators of national prevalence of pay systems across a dozen nations from across and beyond the advanced industrialized world. They, like many other of the leading commentators in the area (e.g. Newman and Nollen 1996), depend on the influential cultural classification of Geert Hofstede, derived from his massive survey of global IBM employees in the early 1970s. Hofstede argues that there are essentially four dimensions of national culture: power distance, masculinity, individualism, and uncertainty avoidance (see Chapter 2). Schuler and Rogovsky's data on pay systems are drawn from several international surveys conducted in the late 1980s and early 1990s.

They find that nations that are characterized by greater uncertainty avoidance, most commonly the Latin nations, tend to feature pay systems in which seniority and some notion of skill weigh heavily. There is, moreover, less focus on specifically individual performance related pay in such nations. Conversely, nations with lower uncertainty avoidance, notably the 'Anglo-Saxon' nations, tend to focus less on seniority or skill, and more on specifically individual PRP. They present a similar pattern of findings for the focus on employee share ownership or options, in this case among each of four categories of employees (manual, clerical, technical, managerial).

Schuler and Rogovsky (1998) also find that nations characterized by greater individualism, most strikingly the Anglo-Saxon nations, tend to have a greater focus on pay for performance generally, and still more strongly a focus on individual pay for performance. Nations with less individualism, most prominently Spanish or Portugese-speaking countries, tend to focus less on pay for performance, generally lying at the opposite end of the spectrum. The findings for the focus on share ownership or options are similar, with this relationship again holding within each category of employees.

They also show that nations characterized by greater 'masculinity', in the sense of a focus on assertiveness regarding the acquisition of wealth in contrast to a focus on personal relationships, tend to have more focus on individual bonuses, which applies to most categories of employees. Thus more 'masculine' nations, principally the Anglo-Saxon ones but also Germany and to a remarkable extent Japan, generally tend to feature individual PRP among professional and technical staff, clerical staff and manual employees. The contrast here is with the general situation in the less masculine Scandinavian nations, and indeed the Netherlands, which tend to have a lesser focus on such payments for these non-managerial employees. Interestingly, though, there was no relationship between the focus on individual bonuses for managers specifically and nations' masculinity.

Thus, there are substantial indications here of some link between Hofstede's uncertainty avoidance, individualism and masculinity dimensions and pay systems. In contrast, Schuler and Rogovsky find that only the focus on employee share ownership or options is related to the fourth of Hofstede's dimensions: power distance. Nations with the greatest tolerance of status differentials, generally the Latin, tend to feature less of such a focus, while those with the lowest power distance, the Anglo-Saxon and Scandinavian, tend to feature more.

It should, however, be noted that this general overview lumps nations together in a manner that may obscure important differences. Moreover, pay systems can change quickly even across a nation, conceivably as culture itself changes, such that the snapshot Schuler and Rogovsky present of the situation around 1990 may be misleading if considered in isolation. Of course, Hofstede's characterization of culture should not itself be considered uncritically. Culture is a diffuse concept, and inherently difficult to measure. Moreover, to a significant extent, nations consist of clusters of sub-cultures. Most fundamentally, it may not only be that national culture is multidimensional in the manner that Hofstede allows but also that it is contradictory, certainly if considered in the sort of fairly simple terms that he employs in specifying his dimensions. The matter of such contradictions in national culture will be taken up later.

Multinational companies and international reward

While their principal purpose has often lain elsewhere, many studies have dealt in part with the approach to compensation of MNCs. Existing research demonstrates that MNCs differ in their responses to the conditions they find in their various nations of operation, and different MNCs seem variously responsive to these conditions.

There seems little doubt that MNCs' approaches to reward generally involve greater homogeneity in their treatment of management, and most of all international cadres of management, across their countries of operation. There has been an increasingly powerful tendency for convergence in the precise compensation practice employed for managers within the corporate boundaries of MNCs, regardless of the country of operation or assignment. Moreover, the total value of managers' compensation packages, however calculated, is becoming increasingly detached from that of non-managerial employees. Where MNCs are Anglo-Saxon in origin, this is very often a matter of the diffusion of compensation systems from domestic to foreign operations (e.g. Björkman and Furu 2000). Where they are not, it is a matter of the general dominance of such Anglo-Saxon approaches to the compensation of management, an influence attributable at least in part to the general perception of the success and centrality of the USA in terms of productivity, competitiveness and profitability/shareholder value.

There is also evidence of some convergence of practice across multinationals, regardless of their countries of origin or of sector. The compensation of senior managers, and most particularly of the international cadre that multinationals are now particularly keen to promote (Wigham 2003), is subject to increasing homogeneity across the corporations of the advanced industrialized world. Individual PRP is of significance for managers, and pay systems linked to subsidiary or corporate performance or specifically to share prices are of significance for the pay of senior managers (e.g Lowe et al. 2002). This is true to an extent even in the companies of the traditional exemplars of organized capitalism, such as Germany or even, although less so, Sweden. This should, however, not be taken as indicating complete homogeneity, except perhaps as an intended strategy among some senior HR specialists. The country of origin of corporations, among other influences, continues to matter to an extent.

Björkman and Furu's (2000) interesting study concerns the payment systems applied to the top managers of 110 foreign-owned subsidiaries in Finland, focusing in particular on the significance of pay for performance as a proportion of fixed income. They show that on average pay for performance constitutes somewhere between 11 per cent and 25 per cent of the fixed income of such managers, but that there is marked variation, with some managers facing almost no pay for performance while others face pay for performance of more than 50 per cent of their base fixed salary. They show that pay for performance constitutes a greater proportion of base salary where the Finnish operations are sales subsidiaries, a lower proportion where they are production or research and development (R&D) subsidiaries. They also show that in subsidiaries that are treated as centres of excellence, managers tend to be more subject to pay for performance. Moreover, US ownership tends to imply a greater use of pay for performance. This careful study shows that variation in the pay systems applied to subsidiary managers remains. Moreover, it is not only that there is variation according to the role of the subsidiary in the activities of the multinational. The nationality of the multinational remains of relevance to the pay system applied.

With regard to the lower-level, or less high-flying, employees of MNCs, the situation is still more complex. There are certainly examples of MNCs that have determinedly pursued the introduction of uniform systems across their national operations. In part, MNCs have sought to do this by operating outside the systems of pay determination that predominate in their countries of operation. Muller (1998) notes that several Anglo-Saxon multinationals operating in Germany have opted out of employers' associations, so remaining outside of the industrial bargaining that remains the general rule and is of particular relevance in some industries.

Perhaps unsurprisingly, fast-food retailers, and perhaps most of all McDonald's, have sought similarity in compensation practice across their outlets, regardless of national location. In the case of McDonald's, this is a matter of exporting an approach to compensation from the domestic, US, operations. Most particularly, this involves avoidance of, and resistance to, meaningful collective bargaining over pay and a focus on containing wage costs. In the case of Germany, it is also a matter of an ongoing struggle to prevent the formation of works councils that would have the right to co-determine pay systems (Royle 2000, 2004).

Nonetheless, as Royle (2000) shows, the real pay levels of McDonald's counter staff, adjusted for the purchasing power of currencies, shows marked variation within Europe, with, for example, real pay typically more than 50 per cent higher in the Nordic nations than in the UK. Even McDonald's has not been able to escape entirely the realities of the political economies or national business systems in which it operates. Even aside from the necessity of legal compliance on some matters, McDonald's must both attract staff and offer them a reward package that they consider legitimate in some sense. This necessitates adjustment to the societal norms and generally prevailing pay practices that institutions have served to shape.

More generally, US MNCs have sought to export specific pay practices to foreign operations. One of the US financial services multinationals studied by Bloom et al. (2003) has determinedly sought to export the equity based incentives that it employs at home to its foreign operations. In the cases of some of its countries of operation, this has been extremely difficult as the ownership of shares by employees is illegal, but the company has circumvented this problem by structuring reward around a formula that reflects equity values. Bloom et al. (2003) also discuss a US high-tech MNC that has sought to standardize compensation across its national operations, though apparently in this case not only exporting practice from the US, but also seeking to draw on prevailing practice in all national locations to forge a globally integrated reward system.

Innovation in pay systems in Sweden

It is not only US-based, or even Anglo-Saxon, MNCs that have recently pursued some standardization of pay systems. Hayden and Edwards (2001) consider the HR practices of Swedco, a large, Swedish-based information and communications technology MNC. In many respects, the approach to HR at Swedco was 'typically Swedish', with managers seeking to foster a democratic approach to decision making, seeing themselves as coaches and facilitators of compromise. A UK manager noted that 'the company encourages a Nordic approach to openness. Swedes think nothing of jumping the hierarchy to put forward their ideas.'

However, Hayden and Edwards note that in the late 1990s an individual PRP scheme was introduced globally, affecting all employees. Such standardization across national borders seems quite at odds with the traditional view of Swedish companies as decentralizing decision making to national subsidiaries. Moreover, the nature of the strategy itself does seem to reflect the influence of Anglo-Saxon approaches to compensation, with their stress on individual pay for performance. This may have been a matter, as Hayden and Edwards themselves claim, of the reverse transfer of practices, if not predominant, then considered legitimate, in the UK operations of Swedco. Alternatively, it may reflect a more broadly based dominance effect of Anglo-Saxon practices on pay strategy in this company at least, an effect that is not dependent on the presence within the organizational boundaries of a UK subsidiary.

This innovation in pay strategy at Swedco might be considered of particular significance given the historically famed particularity of Swedish management approaches, and of the densely institutionalized political economy of Sweden. Indeed it might even be viewed as a demonstration of the ultimate triumph of Anglo-Saxon practice. However, as Hayden and Edwards stress, the very openness to foreign ideas that is characteristic of Swedish managers allows the possibility of learning from the Anglo-Saxon world; in this context, the selective taking of elements of systems common elsewhere may be seen as inherently Swedish. Also, although Hayden and Edwards insist that in this particular case the nature of the pay system did not differ substantially across the nations of operation of the multi-national, they do not offer any detail in this regard; even specifically individual PRP might, in its criteria, application and significance as a share of income, be a rather different beast in different nations.

Developments in this single multinational might not necessarily express any general tendency among Swedish multinationals. Such change as did occur could well have been facilitated not only by the highly internationalized nature of the company, as Hayden and Edwards stress, but also by the nature of the sector: a high-tech and fiercely competitive industry in which hostile takeovers have been common. Moreover, even general change in Swedish practice may be a matter of a slight change in an approach that remains very different to that characterizing Anglo-Saxon companies; indeed the distance between them may not in any sense be declining. Certainly though, the study demonstrates that the application across national borders of elements of pay systems is not confined to US companies. It also shows very clearly that the Swedish political economy, or business system, despite dense institutionalization, leaves space for innovation in pay systems, of which some HR managers at least have taken advantage.

For further details, see:

Hayden, A. and Edwards, T. (2001) 'The Erosion of the Country of Origin Effect: A Case Study of a Swedish Multi-national Company', *Relations Industrielles*, 56(1), 116–40.

Case study question: *Does the Swedco case demonstrate the final victory of Anglo-Saxon pay strategy?*

In sum, there is considerable evidence of MNCs, and in particular US-based MNCs, seeking to export or, perhaps in a more integrative way, standardize pay systems. This is of potential general import given not only the growing importance of MNCs but also, via aggressive acquisition strategies, the increasing predominance of US multi-nationals in particular. There is, however, rather less evidence that even the standardization efforts of US-based MNCs typically result in a commonality of prac-tice on the ground. Indeed, where there has been detailed attention to pay practice as this situation develops, most strikingly in the case of McDonald's, what is apparent is not the homogeneity of compensation but rather, whatever the strategic intention of the corporation, its sensitivity to the prevailing practices of the nations in question. As Edwards and Ferner (2000) note, practices undergo transformation or 'transmuta-tion' when transferred. This transmutation can be substantial. MNCs seeking standardization do not generally secure all that they hope; indeed, the result of a determined standardization may often be rather unexpected.

In a sense, efforts by MNCs to impose universal approaches or practices are indeed noted precisely because they are at odds with a general tendency for MNCs to show at least some sensitivity to the conditions prevailing in their nations of operation, or to quickly develop such sensitivity when obstructed. At the level of non-managerial employees this is perhaps most often a result of unconscious drift rather than a strategic intent to adapt, with national subsidiaries, which have often been acquired relatively recently and are only to a limited degree integrated or even understood by the corporation, allowed to continue much as before in terms of pay practice.

Before its acquisition by Ford, Volvo was famed for its repertoire of approaches to employment relations, HRM and compensation practices (e.g. Berggren 1994). Volvo's sensitivity to local conditions, and preparedness to let subsidiary manage-ments decide on pay systems was very likely exceptional. However, prevailing pay practice at the Swiss-Swedish ABB, until recently an exemplar of the business litera-ture, is revealing. Despite the famed internationalization of the company, and indeed its status as an integrated, global company in the Bartlett and Ghoshal sense (1998 – see also Chapter 4), Belanger et al. (1999) show that HR generally, and pay systems specifically, differed on the ground.

Moreover, it is not only European companies that abstain from the pursuit of stan-dardization. Bloom et al. (2003) record that a 'global high-tech' company that they studied went to such lengths to allow local variation that there were different pay systems even across its five Californian operations. Shire (1994) found that General Motors introduced quite different pay systems in its German and Austrian operations when seeking a shift to teamworking from the early 1990s. The works council in Germany was concerned to preserve the relatively egalitarian wage structure. With German management feeling no particular attachment to the principle of individual incentives within teams, the matter was not pursued. In Austria, where the sectoral agreement was rather less exacting and where the works councils were rather less interested, something much closer to corporate management's original intention was achieved. Moreover, despite a prevailing view in the literature that Japanese compa-nies, like US ones, tend to export domestic practices, Bloom et al. (2003) found that a highly internationalized Japanese MNC sought to be a 'good citizen' right across its extensive operations by complying with prevailing local practice.

The space for international reward strategy

All this, however, concerns what currently prevails rather than what might be forged by multinationals with an international reward strategy. Evidence on the existing approaches of multinationals is not at all the same thing as a picture of what is possible. There may be space for international reward strategy that is only very rarely, if ever, made use of.

The very independence of an MNC from a particular country of operation affords an opportunity to move beyond the common presumptions of a particular nation, presumptions that may be particularly strong with regard to pay. Moreover, MNC status offers opportunities for the imposition of strategy. Where operations are more integrated, strategic action by the headquarters (HQ) or corporate region may be buttressed by implicit or explicit threats that particular facilities or subsidiaries will not be favoured with investment. Regardless of integration, some threat of sale may be employed by the HQ or region for leverage. Moreover, if the subsidiary is developed, perhaps on a greenfield site, rather than acquired, the opportunities of a clean sheet appear to beckon.

However, MNC status confers not only opportunities but also constraints for the HR practitioner, some of which may be insurmountable. The literature is replete with theoretical discussions of the supposed influences of multinationals on the approach to pay that come not from without but from within the company. We may consider these constraints in their entirety as a matter of corporate culture, but this probably obscures more than it enlightens.

As we have seen, there is much evidence that the country of origin of multinationals tends to be related to the nature of their approach to pay. Of course, the extent to which this is expressive of a set of constraints to which HR must submit is far from clear. Certainly, though, as we have seen, different companies from the same country of origin, and indeed involved in similar industries or even activities, do pursue different approaches, something that we might take as indicative of a true space for contemplation and a strategic approach to reward.

Of course, the space enjoyed by HR in contemplating reward strategy is shaped by the standing of HR within the corporation, and indeed the importance attached by senior managers generally to consideration of matters of reward specifically. MNCs that are centralized offer certain opportunities for the strategic use of reward across national boundaries. However, subsidiary managements may resist the suggestion that their pay arrangements should be shaped by HQ. Then, of course, the competencies and attitudes of general, line and HR managers may present varying possibilities in terms of individual negotiations or indeed appraisals, and these may be difficult to surmount. Thus, though we are very far from understanding the extent of their importance in constraining the determined corporate HR or reward manager, there are certainly constraints from within.

With regard to the approach to the pay of higher-level employees, the expatriates, senior managers and general managers of national subsidiaries on which the literature most focuses, the constraints posed by the external environment are quite limited. This is reflected in the relative homogeneity of pay arrangements for such employees. For these employees a balance must be struck between conflicting objectives of organizational uniformity and local conditions in a manner that takes account of the reference groups to which these staff compare themselves. Consideration must be given to the total remuneration package and to purchasing power and taxation for the recruitment, retention, motivation and mobility of international staff. In all this, the key constraint is what is acceptable and motivating to the individuals concerned. However, the varying accounting and tax treatments of payments of stock and the actual legality of pay in the form of stock or specifically options across nations does represent an additional consideration, perhaps particularly since the emergence of corporate governance failings in, for example, Enron (Bloom et al. 2003; Dunn 2004).

For less high-profile employees, though, as we have seen, what lies outside the boundaries of the corporation in the country of operation is typically more strongly related to pay arrangements than what lies within it. MNCs inevitably encounter some national governmental regulations that immediately affect the pay arrangements possible in a particular location. Such substantive regulation – precluding certain forms of pay arrangement – is generally close to impossible to avoid. Thus, statutory pay minima exist, sometimes varying with the age of employees or their status as trainees, in most OECD (Organization for Economic Co-operation and Development) nations and a third of the nations of the established advanced industrialized world (OECD 1998). Self-evidently, such minima only affect the pay of the very worst paid, representing a constraint on MNCs, which in any case tend to pay rather better than domestic companies, only at the margin. In general, the observance of substantive statutory regulation of pay arrangements presents little in the way of constraints to MNCs.

Within the advanced industrialized world at least, collective bargaining and the statutory representation of employees is an issue of much greater significance for an international approach to pay arrangements (which extends beyond top managers) than is substantive statutory regulation. For companies of Anglo-Saxon origin operating in northern Europe in particular, this joint regulation of pay can seem difficult to grasp, perplexing, even forbidding. Enterprises covered by collective bargaining are thus immediately subject to procedural regulation with regard to the development of pay systems, procedural regulation that will result in at least some substantive (joint) regulation of pay arrangements.

However, much more flexibility exists within joint regulation within even those nations that are subject to its denser forms than is commonly thought. As Sisson (1987) notes, confederal or industrial agreements do not, with regard to rates of pay, lay down standards that must be observed. Rather, they lay down minima of various forms. They may also include clauses relating to permissible pay systems. There is then a subsequent negotiation, whether formal, with unions, or informal, with works councils ostensibly independent of unions, at the level of the establishment or (national) enterprise.

Typically, much is left by confederal or industrial agreements to be determined at the level of the establishment or enterprise. Thelen (e.g. 2000) stresses the flexibility involved in German collective bargaining. Schulten (2000) notes that the principal concern of German unions is that there should be negotiation over pay for performance and that it should be in addition to basic pay. Currently, however, the restrictions on pay for performance in German industrial agreements are limited.

In practice then, the joint regulation of pay, in part by sectoral negotiators outside the confines of the enterprise, offers managers much room for manoeuvre, even in northern Europe. This is the case even with regard to the relatively contentious matter of PRP. Nonetheless, a number of companies in Germany have recently demonstrated the possibility of operating beyond the coverage of industrial-level collectively bargained agreements. Withdrawing from employers' associations, some employers of all sizes negotiate company-level agreements independent of the prevailing sectoral agreement (Hassel 1999), a possibility allowed by the very limited legal extension of collective agreements in Germany (Traxler et al. 2001: 185).

The transformation is, however, very far from complete. Interestingly, since 1989 an industry association specifically for fast food has existed in Germany, established essentially by McDonald's after almost two decades of adverse publicity (Royle 2004). Yet collective bargaining is extremely unstable in the sector, with companies sometimes participating in industrial negotiations, sometimes concluding company agreements and sometimes, it seems, not having an agreement at all. Moreover, as noted earlier, McDonald's has determinedly sought to avoid the representation of its German employees in works councils (Royle 2000, 2004).

Whatever the difficulties which result, it is clear that even in the most organized capitalism, individual employers can sometimes opt to shape pay without the immediate procedural confines of joint regulation. This appears at first glance to substantially increase their strategic space with regard to reward. Much of this increase is illusory, however. Inescapably, employers in a particular nation must face the political economy in which they are located. This consists not merely of the institutions of collective bargaining, which they may in some cases be able to circumvent, but the substantial national environment that these institutions have in part shaped. The broader environment, consisting of national culture generally but more specifically including the pattern of employment, the earnings structure and the prevailing systems of pay, inevitably impact all employers. Thus, regardless of their participation in collective bargaining or indeed their efforts to avoid the statutory representation of employees in works councils, employers must recruit, retain and motivate staff; they cannot operate in a vacuum.

Of course, different groups within the workforce of a nation may have different expectations regarding pay. Bloom et al. (2003) stress variability *within* nations in the pay practices to which employees are used. Crucially for MNCs, there is variability also within particular industries and occupational groups. This potentially creates still greater space for pay strategy. Of course, managers need to reflect carefully before situating themselves in a particular pay location within the existing pattern of practices of a nation.

However, a recent study (Lowe et al. 2002) provides interesting indications that the prevalence of a system may not necessarily be a guide to its cultural fit. Examining the attitudes of managers and engineers to pay systems in ten nations, the research finds that pay for performance at this level is quite evenly spread, even across the divide between the established advanced industrialized nations and the newly industrialized countries. However, employees on the American continent particularly would like to see more. Moreover, though variable pay tends to be contingent on group performance rather more in Asian nations than on the American continent, employees across the world are equally keen on such a basis. Perhaps most interestingly, while Anglo-Saxon nations display less emphasis on long-term performance in their pay systems, employees in other nations across the world similarly value such a long-term emphasis. It seems not to be the case that national culture determines the pay systems in operation. At the very least, there are culturally permitted alternatives that have, for some reason, been suppressed by the decisions made by, and often bargaining of, existing employers.

Thus, while there are definite constraints, the complexity and ambiguity of the external environment offer much room for manoeuvre for the HR or reward manager. Most likely, the same is true of the internal environment of the multinational. All this, of course, leaves aside the issue of how the space enjoyed by HR and reward managers, and indeed MNCs more generally, should be used. Strategic approaches to HR should, of course, give some cognisance to the performance implications of various practices. It is to the evidence available on pay arrangements and performance that we now turn.

Best practice in international reward

What then of 'best practice'? Does the knowledge embodied in the literature allow us to draw any general conclusions on the issue of whether there is a 'one best way', a universal best practice, in terms of pay systems? Certainly, given the nature of recent discussion among many managers, not only within but also beyond the Anglo-Saxon world, one might presume the general superiority in terms of performance of both a talent rewarding and a motivating stretch in the earnings distribution. More specifically, one might suppose, despite Enron and WorldCom, that the bottom line delivery of pay for performance focusing in large part on individual contributions, allied to an element of share-price-related compensation, particularly for more senior managers, is well established. However, in this as in so many other areas, commonplaces, even conventional wisdoms, have little or no empirical support.

It seems that notions of the superiority of great pay dispersion, PRP and share-price-related pay have much to do with perceptions of the economic position of the USA, particularly as it resurged in the 1990s. In the terms of Smith and Meiksins (1995), 'dominance effects' appear to be at work; perceptions of the superior performance of US companies and industries in general have led to an interest in the emulation of the employment relations, HR practices and indeed pay systems specifically of the USA. This not only presumes that the superiority of US performance has been established, but also that the distinctiveness of US HR and pay systems have been established. Moreover, it also presumes that it is this distinctiveness that has been crucial to performance.

Little comparative or international evidence on relationships between pay and performance is available. Examination of the influence of the nature of pay systems on the aggregate performance of nations, or even of a broad sector of a nation, has not yet been possible. However, Rogers and Vernon (2003) provide interesting comparative historical evidence on the relationship between the extent of earnings inequality and labour productivity growth across the manufacturing sectors of nine advanced industrialized nations over the period 1970–95.

Taking account of other influences on productivity growth, they find that there is a strong relationship between higher levels of earnings inequality at the top end of the earnings distribution and faster productivity growth, consistent with a broad incentive view. They also find, however, a strong relationship between *lower* levels of earnings inequality at the bottom end of the earnings distribution and faster productivity growth. A compression of earnings inequality at the bottom end, *attenuating* broad incentives, is associated with faster productivity growth, a finding quite at odds with an incentive view. This suggests that while greater inequality is productively motivating at the top end of the earnings distribution, lower inequality is productively motivating at the bottom. It may well be that marked earnings inequality at the bottom-end of the earnings distribution discourages lower-grade employees, provides little incentive for managers to offer them training or indeed to reflect on work organization and leads to a profound and dysfunctional stratification within the organizational hierarchy.

Generally speaking, then, this aggregate evidence suggests that greater inequality at the top end of the distribution but compressed inequality at the bottom is ideal in terms of the promotion of productivity growth at least. To the extent that we may talk of a generic 'best practice' in terms of the stretch of the earnings distribution, it seems that it lies in a compression of pay at the bottom of the distribution and a great spread at the top. Thus, the USA may represent best practice at the top end of the earnings distribution, but it seems to represent worst practice at the bottom. The productivity growth performance of the USA, which is certainly among the best in the advanced industrialized world, seems on this evidence to have little to do with pay arrangements, despite the apparent influence in this regard of the USA through the 'dominance effects' previously discussed.

We might expect, though, that the performance implications of earnings structures, and pay systems more specifically, might be contingent on the cultures prevailing in the nations, at least to an extent. Arrangements that work in one nation may not work as well elsewhere, and indeed it may even be the case that a pay arrangement that delivers in most nations of the advanced industrialized world is nonetheless debilitating in others. To an extent at least, it is surely misguided to speak of a generic best practice, and attention must turn to the congruence of pay arrangements with the national culture concerned.

Again, there is much discussion, some assertion, but little evidence. However, the seminal work of Newman and Nollen (1996), even though it focuses on the global activities of a single, US-based MNC and is now almost a decade old, deserves serious attention. Their statistical analysis examined the relationship, across 176 work units based in 18 (mostly advanced industrialized) nations at the close of the 1980s, between financial performance and the fit between management practices and the national cultures of the host nations, characterized with reference to Hofstede. Among the foci of the authors is what they term 'merit based reward', an encompassing concept relating not only to practice with regard to merit pay but also to the possibilities of promotion, particularly on the basis of individual performance.

Taking account of other influences, their careful work shows strong results regarding the congruence between management practices and host cultures and financial performance. In more masculine national cultures, emphasizing activity and achievement, merit-based rewards are generally associated with superior performance. In more feminine cultures, emphasizing contemplation and interpersonal relationships, merit-based rewards are generally associated with inferior performance. Congruence with national culture in the nature of pay systems appears to matter for performance.

Some managers might hope that national culture can be superseded, through determined effort, by corporate culture in a manner that could obliterate such contingency. Indeed, Newman and Nollen (1996) suggest that the MNC that is the focus of their work does not have a strong corporate culture. Yet this MNC is US based, a characteristic often taken as indicative of a relatively strong corporate culture (e.g. Ferner 1997). Moreover, Newman and Nollen's very study is critically dependent on the limited sensitivity of managerial practice to host culture – if there were always complete adaptation, there would be no differential incongruence of practice with which to compare performance variations. Finally, it may be that efforts by multinationals to secure a stronger corporate culture are in any case counter-productive. Laurent (1983) suggests that employees working in the foreign subsidiaries of multinationals display a more pronounced *national* culture than their compatriots working in purely domestic companies.

What guidance does the available evidence offer HR managers about best practice, then? It seems that to the extent that the objective is productivity or its growth, it is generally the case that while inequality at the top end of the earnings distribution is fruitful, inequality at the bottom end is detrimental. However, productivity or its growth are not the sole, perhaps not the most important, objectives of senior managers. It may or may not be that profitability, or share price, are similarly sensitive to earnings inequality. In any event, this is some way from a commentary on the performance implications of different forms of payment systems more specifically.

Moreover, it is very likely that the general rule with regard to productivity and earnings inequality masks significant cross-national differences in even this relationship. The limited evidence available suggests that financial performance is sensitive to the congruence or fit between host culture and the approach to reward adopted.

Yet a conclusion that the only 'best practice' is constituted by an accommodation of host culture is not justified by a single study of a single multinational that deals only in part with reward.

Conclusion

We have seen dramatic differences across national environments. We have also seen differences in MNC responses. Moreover, we have seen that while there appears much space for a strategic approach to reward that is international in scope, there is limited evidence about the best practice that it might pursue. In short, we have seen that no simple prescriptions are valid.

Principally, it is clear that there is potential at least for strategic HRM across national boundaries with regard not only to management but also to employees more generally. Nation of operation does not narrowly determine the possibilities. It is clear that there is much room for manoeuvre with regard to pay practice, even within highly institutionalized societies. Even in the case of manual staff in manufacturing in nations that are regarded as heavily regulated by collective agreement, much space is left. The ultimate constraint on multinationals is the perceived legitimacy of pay arrangements (and the mechanism by which they are arrived at) in the eyes of the employees concerned. Care must be exercised with regard to the psychological contract.

While UK companies, in contrast to some US companies, have in the past shied away from any standardization of pay arrangements (Wood and Peccei 1990), there is now interest even here in at least a strategic framing of compensation practice. Of course, an approach to pay can be strategic without being standardizing: the options are not wholesale standardization versus national 'business as usual'. Indeed, while an unthinking adoption of predominant local practice is not strategic, an unthinking imposition of the systems of the corporation in its country of origin is not strategic either. There is certainly much space for critical reflection on the pay practice that prevails; Scylla and Charybdis do not leave only one possible route.

The pursuit of performance, however, provides no detailed guide. There is no conclusive evidence in favour of any general proposition about the superiority of certain forms of pay system, no matter how confidently the view is held or indeed how senior the person who holds it. Thus, 'best practice' in pay systems remains elusive. This is not at all comfortable for HR or reward managers seeking to justify a particular pay system or indeed an international strategic place for reward. Uncomfortable or not, this is the reality. Of course, the very limited evidence available does constitute an opportunity for a plethora of cases to be made for a plethora of pay arrangements, and indeed for criticism of all cases.

Already, though, the limited evidence available regarding best practice should heighten our scepticism of certain approaches. Evidence on the aggregate performance of manufacturing sectors suggests that while pay arrangements generating greater earnings inequality in the top half of the earnings hierarchy promote value added, greater earnings inequality in the bottom half is inimical to this. Moreover, evidence on financial performance across the national operations of an MNC suggests that the congruence between reward practice and national culture is of substantial import. At the very least, we may conclude from this that there should be great scepticism about strategic approaches to reward that, perhaps consciously or unconsciously shaped by impressions of practice in the USA, seek to standardize pay arrangements across national boundaries around a model of pay for performance and a steep pay gradient throughout the hierarchy.

Yet the limits of existing knowledge are such that the importance of corporate culture is heightened. HR and reward face significant constraints from within the MNC in shaping a strategic approach to international reward. Critical reflection on pay systems requires a geocentric approach, involving a preparedness to reach across the national boundaries of the multinational organization in the consideration of pay arrangements and determination of strategy. More than this, though, it requires a preparedness to reach beyond the organization, and not just to interpretations or intimations of the US experience. Appreciation of the character of pay systems, and the assessment of their performance implications, requires careful scrutiny.

In sum, there is much space for an international strategic approach to pay arrangements. A strategic approach requires sensitivity to institutions and, perhaps more importantly, the expectations and societal norms that these have in part shaped in the nations of operation. Of course, HR and reward managers must be conscious of pressures from within, in addition to those from without. Corporate strategy and culture shape possibilities, even if not determining developments. HR is best placed of all management functions to appreciate the nature and limits of our knowledge with regard to international reward, to appreciate cross-national diversity in context of operations, to display sensitivity and to allow experimentation. Moreover, HR can play a crucial role in the evaluation of performance and thus the development of more considered pay arrangements.

Review questions

1 What sort of differences exist between advanced industrialized nations in reward practice?

2 How have MNCs responded to the different national conditions that they find?

3 What seems to define the space available for reward strategy?

4 What may we say of 'best practice' in international reward?

5 In what respects is there potential in international reward strategy?

Further reading

Björkman, I. and Furu, P. (2000). 'Determinants of Variable Pay for Top Managers of Foreign Subsidiaries in Finland', *International Journal of Human Resource Management*, 11(4), 698–713.

> This is a careful statistical/econometric study of the influences on the pay systems deployed for subsidiary managers.

Bloom, M., Milkovich, G. and Mitra, A. (2003) 'International Compensation: Learning From How Managers Respond to Variations in Local Host Contexts', *International Journal of Human Resource Management*, 14(8), 1350–67.

> This article considers the often neglected issue of the variation present in institutions and practices even within national borders.

Lowe, K., Milliman, J., DeCieri, H. and Dowling, P. (2002) 'International Compensation Practices: A Ten Country Comparative Analysis', *Human Resource Management*, 41, 45–66.

> This article provides a stimulating demonstration of the gap between the expectations and experiences of higher-level employees with regard to reward.

Newman, K. and Nollen, S. (1996) 'Culture and Congruence: The Fit Between Management Practices and National Culture', *Journal of International Business Studies*, 27(4), 753–78.

> This article provides the seminal statistical contribution on the issue of the importance to the bottom line of cultural sensitivity in reward.

References

Almond, P. (2004) 'The Management of Pay, Wage Classification and Performance in the UK Subsidiaries of US MNCs', Mimeo, Department of HRM, Leicester Business School, De Montfort University.

Bartlett, C. and Ghoshal, S. (1998) *Managing Across Borders: The Transnational Solution*, Boston: Harvard Business School Press.

Barton, H. and Delbridge, R. (2004) 'HRM in Support of the Learning Factory: Evidence from the US and UK Automotive Components Industries', *International Journal of Human Resource Management*, 15(2), 331–45.

Belanger, J., Berggren, C., Bjorkman, T. and Kohler, C. (1999) *Being Local Worldwide: ABB and the Challenge of Global Management*, Ithaca, NY: Cornell University Press.

Berggren, C. (1994) *The Volvo Experience*. London: Macmillan.

Björkman, I. and Furu, P. (2000) 'Determinants of Variable Pay for Top Managers of Foreign Subsidiaries in Finland', *International Journal of Human Resource Management*, 11(4), 698–713.

Bloom, M., Milkovich, G. and Mitra, A. (2003) 'International Compensation: Learning from How Managers Respond to Variations in Local Host Contexts', *International Journal of Human Resource Management*, 14(8), 1350–67.

Dunn, B. (2004) 'One Size Does Not Fit All: Global Equity Compensation in the New World', *Compensation and Benefits Review*. 36(4), 13–18.

Edwards, T. and Ferner, A. (2000) 'HRM Strategies of Multi-nationals: The Organisational Politics of "Reverse Diffusion"', paper presented at conference on 'Multinational Companies and Emerging Workplace Issues: Practice, Outcomes and Policy', Detroit: Wayne State University, 1–3 April.

Emans, B. et al. (2003) 'Pay for Performance in Europe: Prevalence and National Differences', paper presented at European Congress on Work and Organizational Psychology, Lisbon, May 2003.

Ferner, A. (1997) 'Country of Origin Effects and HRM in MNCs', *Human Resource Management Journal*, 7(1), 19–36.

Gilman, M. (2000) 'Variable Pay: The Case of the UK', Mimeo prepared for the European Industrial Relations Observatory.

Hassel, A. (1999). 'The Erosion of the German System of Industrial Relations', *British Journal of Industrial Relations*, 37(3), 483–505.

Hayden, A. and Edwards, T. (2001) 'The Erosion of the Country of Origin Effect: A Case Study of a Swedish Multi-national Company', *Relations Industrielles*, 56(1), 116–40.

Kessler, I. and Purcell, J. (1995) 'Individualism and Collectivism in Theory and Practice: Management Style and the Design of Pay Systems', in P. Edwards (ed.) *Industrial Relations: Theory and Practice in Britain*, Oxford: Basil Blackwell.

Kjellberg, A. (1998) 'Sweden: Restoring the Model?' in A. Ferner, and R. Hyman (eds) *Changing Industrial Relations in Europe*, Oxford: Blackwell.

Laurent, A. (1983) 'The Cultural Diversity of Western Conceptions of Management', *International Studies of Management and Organization*, 13, 75–96.

Lowe, K., Milliman, J., DeCieri, H. and Dowling, P. (2002) 'International Compensation Practices: A Ten Country Comparative Analysis', *Human Resource Management*, 41, 45–66.

MacDuffie, J. (1995) 'Human Resource Bundles and Manufacturing Performance: Organisational Logic and Flexible Production Systems in the World Auto Industry', *Industrial and Labor Relations Review*, 48(2), 197–221.

Muller, M. (1998) 'Human Resource and Industrial Relations Practices of UK and US Multinationals in Germany', *International Journal of Human Resource Management*, 9(4), 732–49.

Newman, K. and Nollen, S. (1996) 'Culture and Congruence: The Fit Between Management Practices and National Culture', *Journal of International Business Studies*, 27(4), 753–78.

OECD (Organization for Economic Co-operation and Development) (1998) 'Making the Most of the Minimum: Statutory Minimum Wages, Employment and Poverty', *Employment Outlook*, Paris: OECD.

OECD (Organization for Economic Co-operation and Development) (2001) Earnings dispersion database.

Pontusson, J., Rueda, D. and Way, C. (2002) 'Comparative Political Economy of Wage Distribution: The Role of Partisanship and Labour Market Institutions', *British Journal of Political Science*, 32, April, 281–303.

Rogers, M. and Vernon, G. (2003) 'Wage Inequality and Productivity Growth: Motivating Carrots and Crippling sticks', Economic and Social Research Council Research Centre on Skills, Knowledge and Organizational Performance, Warwick and Oxford, Working paper No. 40, April.

Royle, T. (2000) *Working for McDonald's in Europe: The Unequal Struggle?* London: Routledge.

Royle, T. (2004) 'Employment Practices of MNCs in the Spanish and German Quick-Food Sectors: Low Road Convergence?', *European Journal of Industrial Relations*, 10, 51–71.

Rueda, D. (2003) 'Government Partisanship, Policy and Inequality in the OECD', presented at the Forum de Ciencia Politica at Pompeu Fabra, Barcelona, 15 January.

Rueda, D. and Pontusson, J. (2000) 'Wage Inequality and Varieties of Capitalism', *World Politics*, 52, April, 350–83.

Schuler, R. and Rogovsky, N. (1998) 'Understanding Compensation Practice Variations Across Firms: The Impact of National Culture', *Journal of International Business Studies*, 29(1), 159–77.

Schulten, T. (2000) 'Variable Pay in Germany', Mimeo prepared for the European Industrial Relations Observatory.

Shibata, H. (2002) 'Wage and Performance Appraisal in Flux: A Japan–United States Comparison', *Industrial Relations*, 41(4), 629–53.

Shire, K. (1994) 'Bargaining Regimes and the Social Reorganization of Production: The Case of General Motors in Austria and Germany', in J. Bélanger, P. Edwards and L. Haiven (eds) *Workplace Industrial Relations and the Global Challenge*. Ithaca, NY: ILR Press.

Sisson, K. (1987) *The Management of Collective Bargaining*, Oxford. Blackwell.

Smith, C. and Meiksins, P. (1995) 'System, Society and Dominance Effects in Cross-National Organizational Analysis', *Work, Employment and Society*, 9(2), 241–67.

Thelen, K. (2000) 'Why German Employers Cannot Bring Themselves to Dismantle the German Model', in T. Iversen, J. Pontusson and D. Soskice (eds) *Unions, Employers and Central Banks*. Cambridge: Cambridge University Press.

Traxler, F., Blaschke, S. and Kittel, B. (2001) *National Labour Relations in Internationalized Markets*, Oxford: Oxford University Press.

Wigham, R. (2003) 'Multinationals Amend Reward Structures for Global Workers', *Personnel Today*, 16 October.

Wood, S. and Peccei, R. (1990) 'Preparing for 1992? Business Led vs. Strategic Human Resource Management', *Human Resource Management Journal*, 2(1), 94–109.

Chapter 12

International employee representation – a case of industrial relations systems following the market?

Keith Sisson

Key aims

This chapter has the following key aims:

- to consider the variety of forms that international employee representation takes;
- to look at the growing significance of international employee representation, paying particular attention to developments in Europe in the wake of economic and monetary union and the directive providing for the setting up of European works councils;
- to seek to explain why, contrary to what might have been expected, the management of some multinational companies seem to be promoting international employee representation;
- to speculate about the prospects for the future.

Introduction

Historically, international employee representation is a topic that has primarily involved trade unions and international organizations such as the International Labour Organization (ILO) and the United Nations (UN). It has been of relatively little interest to the management of multinational companies (MNCs) and, arguably, has had little overall significance, the main achievement being the various codes and statements of the international organizations. However, this situation is changing rapidly. In expanding markets, 'globalization' in general and 'regionalization' in particular have significantly increased the profile of international employee representation, with MNC management increasingly required to take strategic choices about their approach. In the EU member states especially, management in MNCs find themselves having to deal with statutory European works councils (EWCs) and reinvigorated international trade union federations, such as the European Metalworkers' Federation (EMF), which are taking advantage of the changed situation to mount major campaigns targeted at the co-ordination of existing national collective bargaining arrangements. In sectors characterized by standardized products and a great deal of integration, such as automotive, management are themselves adding to the pressures for international employee representation, finding it difficult to resist the temptation of using benchmarking to help discipline the bargaining behaviour of local management workforces, leading to the inevitable response (Sisson et al. 2003). In the changed circumstances, some managers are also finding that it is in their interests to promote a measure of international employee representation – sometimes to demonstrate their 'social responsibility' and in other cases because they need to legitimize major restructuring exercises. The result is an increasing amount of cross-national dialogue raising speculation about the prospects for transnational forms of collective bargaining. In the event, the mounting evidence suggests that these are likely to take the form of 'soft frameworks' and co-ordinated bargaining rather than fully-fledged collective bargaining along the lines of national systems. The latter requires not just a market but a 'strong state protagonist', which is lacking (and likely to remain so) even where the polity has acquired considerable powers of intervention, as in the case of the EU.

A variety of forms

The offspring of inter-governmental organization

As Gumbrell-McCormick (2000: 33) reminds us, trade unions have been talking about the need for unity on the international level in order to pursue effective action since the end of the nineteenth century. It was only in 1919, however, with the formation of the International Labour Organization (ILO), that necessary institutional infrastructure emerged to help to overcome the massive problems of independent action such as the costs of travel and communication. Despite its many weaknesses, the ILO at least offered trade union representatives from different countries an opportunity to meet and discuss common problems and put pressure on the employers and governments for commitments to action. Following the Second World War, the ILO was incorporated into the new structure of the United Nations (UN), which has itself taken a growing interest in the activities of MNCs in the form of the work of its Commission on Transnational Corporations (UNCTC). Another international organization that has become involved is the Organization for Economic Co-operation and Development (OECD), which brings together the world's major industrialized market economies. As well as supporting its own Trade Union Advisory Committee, it has also sponsored the development of guidelines for the corporate behaviour of MNCs in a range of areas including employment, which will be discussed in more detail below.

Just as the formation of the ILO helped to underpin trade union co-operation on the international scale, so too did the emergence of the European Union (EU) and other trading blocs such as the North American Free Trade Association (NAFTA) at regional level. The coming of the EU, which involved a significant political as well as economic dimension, gave a particular boost to international employee representation. Not only is the EU responsible for the directive giving rise to so-called European works councils (EWCs), more of which below, but also for a plethora of committees and other forums around which international union co-operation has been built. For example, there has been an Advisory Committee on Social Security for Migrant Workers since the early days of the Treaty of Rome. Special committees on sectors such as road and rail transport have been added, along with a Standing Committee on Employment and an Employment and Social Affairs Council. Perhaps most important, though, was the social policy protocol agreed by the majority of EU member states at the time of the Maastricht Treaty negotiations in 1991, subsequently given a treaty basis at the Amsterdam inter-governmental conference in 1997: this introduced a wide-ranging structure of social dialogue, and potentially collective bargaining, at both Community and EU sector levels (European Commission 2000: 11-22).

Trade union based

Of course, trade unions have not been solely reliant on the support of international agencies. The basis for independent cross-national trade union collaboration has been the loosely organized federations and their derivatives, which date back to the first half of the nineteenth century. Historically, the main bodies have been divided on political and religious grounds: the International Federation of Free Trade Unions; the World Federation of Labour, which was essentially the forum containing those in the Soviet bloc and with a Communist affiliation; and the International Federation of Christian Trade Unions. Important regional federations include the European Trades Union Congress (ETUC). There has always also been a strong sectoral dimension with international trade secretariats such as the as International Metalworkers' Federation (IMF) and Union Network International, which have their regional affiliates such as the European Metalworkers' Federation (EMF) and UNI-Europa (the European arm of the former International Federation of Commercial, Clerical, Professional and Technical Employees, which now also embraces telecommunications, the media and graphical trades). More informal groupings would include regionally-based organizations such as those to be found bringing together trade unions across the Scandinavian countries.

Company based

The organization of international employee representation on a company basis is not surprisingly a relatively recent phenomenon, with the IMF setting up the first world company councils at Ford and General Electric in 1966. Those covering Nestlé and Unilever followed in the 1970s. The *European Works Council Bulletin* (2000e: 7) lists 47 MNCs where there are worldwide groupings of union and works council representatives that meet regularly and/or remain in continuous contact. Around a quarter (12) involved US companies. Japan had the next highest representation (7), followed by France (6), Germany (4) and Sweden and the UK (3 each). The sector that accounted for the largest number of these arrangements was metalworking (19), followed by transport (6) utilities (5) telecommunications and food (4 each) and the extractive industries, tyres/rubber and other services (3 each).

In the late 1980s to early 1990s, with the process of European integration developing apace, a number of companies began to establish joint forums, often building on these arrangements, with a predominantly European focus. Initially, these were largely restricted to former French state-owned companies such as Bull and Thomson, along with a small number of the larger German companies including Bayer and Volkswagen. By the time of the passage of the EWC Directive in 1994, there were reckoned to be 41 European-scale works councils (Hall et al. 1995: 15–16). Most were to be found in metalworking and chemicals, reflecting restructuring issues, and involved representatives of national works councils as well as, in some cases, full-time trade union officers.

It was the 1994 EWC Directive that was the main catalyst for the emergence of such councils on a more widespread basis. Briefly, this required 'community-scale' enterprises (broadly those with at least 1,000 employees within the states covered, including at least 150 in two or more countries) to establish transnational forums for information and consultation on cross-border issues. Three basic options were given in implementing the directive:

● Under Article 13, they could negotiate an agreement tailor-made to their own requirements up until the implementation date of the directive (i.e. 22 September 1996);

● Under Article 6, they could use the 'special negotiating body' to provide for the implementation of an agreement;

● If they did not take advantage of this, they had to implement the 'default arrangements', which effectively dictated the nature of the arrangements.

According to the *European Works Council Bulletin* (2003: 14-16), 639 MNCs had established EWCs, which is only just over a third of the total of 1,865 MNCs thought to be eligible. Most of those established, between 400 and 450, were the result of Article 13 agreements with the remainder resulting from Article 6. EWCs are disproportionately found in the manufacturing sectors where MNCs tend to have integrated operations across borders, such as metalworking and chemicals, as well as in the broader area of services (see Figure 12.1).

The growing significance of international employee representation

Changing concerns

There has been a long-standing trade union and, to some extent, government interest in preventing undercutting, the process whereby workforces in one country are forced to accept less favourable terms and conditions under the threat of production being transferred. This is the main underlying rationale for international employee representation.

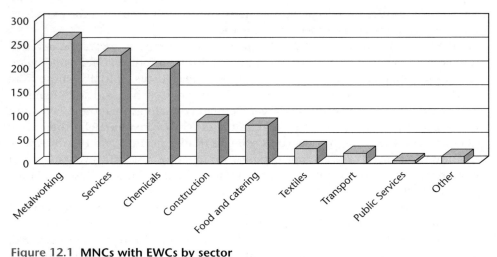

Figure 12.1 MNCs with EWCs by sector

Source: data from *European Works Council Bulletin* (2003)

Such interest has intensified in recent years. In the words of the *European Works Council Bulletin* (2001a: 14), the 'primary reason' for the growth and increasing importance attached to these initiatives is the 'process of economic globalization'.

Critically important is not only that national economies are becoming ever more interlinked with improved transport and communication systems, but also that there is an increasingly global market for capital. Within certain constraints, MNCs are in a position to locate their operations wherever it is most cost-effective to do so, with profound implications for both the processes and the outcomes of industrial relations, which have been based on nation states. As the International Confederation of Free Trade Unions (ICFTU) puts it:

> 'MNEs (multinational enterprises) have the power to disrupt collective bargaining agreements or bargaining structures. With the ever present threat of relocation to countries with low wages, low standards and a low degree of organization, MNEs are in a strong position to put pressure on trade unions and their workforces, as well as their governments, to accept whatever they are proposing.' (2000)

So-called 'regionalization', in the form of the single market project of the EU and the free trade area of NAFTA, has only served to tighten the screw. It is no longer just a question of the 'old' world being threatened by the 'new'. Benchmarking *within* as well as *between* MNCs is increasingly widespread – almost four out of five companies in the UK, the rest of Europe, North America and South East Asia reported practising it by the mid-1990s (Hastings 1997) – with a view to diffusing preferred working practices across locations in different countries. Methods include the regular convening of meetings of managers from different countries, rotation of managerial personnel from one location to another, compilation of manuals of best practice and the setting up of task forces and/or nomination of 'lead' operations with responsibility for directing change. Especially important in encouraging such developments has been the adoption of continent-wide strategies for production and the servicing of markets across Europe involving the formation of international divisions that group operations within the same stream of business across different countries. Shell, Thomson, Unilever and General Motors are amongst those companies that have shifted the emphasis from territorial to international business-based forms of organization (Marginson and Sisson 1996, 1998; Martin and Beaumont 1998).

As industrial relations analysis has long recognized (see, for example, Coller 1996; Coller and Marginson 1998; Marginson et al. 1993, 1995; Mueller and Purcell 1992; Ferner and Edwards 1995), benchmarking is inextricably linked with the use of 'coercive comparisons' to help discipline the behaviour of local management as well as local workforces, particularly in collective bargaining. The collection and analysis of data on performance practices and outcomes is widely used to exert pressure on business unit management within the context of an internal 'market' for investment.

The paradigm case is the automotive sector, characterized by standardized products and a great deal of integration. The European Foundation investigation into so-called 'pacts for employment and competitiveness' (PECs), in which companies offer reassurances on jobs in return for greater flexibility of pay, working time and work organization, revealed that the major motor manufacturers Ford, General Motors, Mercedes-Benz and Volkswagen had negotiated such agreements in a number of European countries (Sisson and Artiles 2000; Zagelmeyer 2000). Significant, too, is the context in which these practices were introduced. In each case the catalyst was a headquarters' review of future investment plans and existing cost structures across its businesses. Typically, national negotiators had been left in no doubt that a failure to introduce them would lead to the withdrawal or postponement of investment in favour of subsidiaries in other countries. The case studies in two countries tracked developments in General Motors Europe. In the case of Vauxhall in the UK and Opel in Germany, the trigger for the negotiation of agreements embracing employment was the so-called 'Vision 96' prepared by the chairman of General Motors Europe in 1992. In this, he proposed the introduction of the system of teamwork organization and associated personnel management practices that had been experimented with at the General Motors-Toyota Nummi 'greenfield' joint venture in California and reflected developments such as 'just-in-time' production arrangements. This was followed by the so-called 'template' study of 1997, in which an international unit compared labour costs in the General Motors operations across Europe, including the Eisenach site in the former East Germany and the new operation in Hungary. The clear implication was that those sites wishing to maintain investment and employment would have to display a determination to make themselves the best in the group. It was only in 1998 that the effects became fully manifest, however. Hancké describes developments at General Motors' operations in Belgium, Germany, Spain and the UK in that year:

> 'The competitive dynamic underlying the process explains this convergence. Management would start by singling out one plant as a pilot bargaining arena for changes in working time or work organisation. The agreement concluded in this 'most favourable' setting (for

management) was then, in the next round, presented to every other plant in the company as a minimum standard. These other plants had no alternative but to follow suit, since they might otherwise find themselves in an unfavourable position in the next round of model planning.' (2000:45)

In the light of these changing concerns, there have been significant recent developments in employee representation on several dimensions. One is the international, where the effort of both government policy makers and trade unions has been directed at seeking to raise standards in the 'new' world. The second is the regional, where the European-based International Trade Secretariats (ITSs) have been especially active in seeking to co-ordinate the bargaining of their national affiliates at the sector level. The third is the company level, where the developing activities of some EWCs have led to considerable speculation about the prospects for cross-national collective bargaining.

International developments – raising the standards

Here there have been a number of examples of trade unions and employers' organizations at the sector level concluding agreements and other joint texts establishing codes of conduct on employment matters. In 1996, for example, there was an agreement aimed at implementing ILO labour standards in the production of FIFA-approved footballs worldwide, and in 1999 a joint statement on child labour in the tobacco-growing industry (*European Works Council Bulletin* 2000b).

The prime focus and impetus have been at company level, however. Codes of conduct drawn up by international organizations that address aspects of industrial relations are of course nothing new, with some dating back to the 1970s. The OECD guidelines for multinational companies, which include an employment and industrial relations chapter, were originally adopted in 1976; the ILO's tripartite declaration on social policy in multinational companies dates back to 1977 and the UN has been attempting to conclude a code of conduct for multinationals since the same year. In June 2000, however, revised OECD guidelines for multinational companies and strengthened procedures for securing their implementation were adopted. In the employment and industrial relations chapter, new provisions related to abolishing child and forced labour and strengthened provisions concerning discrimination and employee information and consultation (*European Works Council Bulletin* 2000c). A month later, under the auspices of the UN, 50 of the world's largest corporations signed a 'global compact' that commits them to observing nine principles, including upholding the right to association and recognition of the right to collectively bargain, abolition of child labour and elimination of discrimination at work.

Renewed activity within inter-governmental organizations reflects both the burgeoning number of codes of conduct adopted within individual MNCs, specifying standards and goals for the company's conduct across the globe, and growing debate around the insertion of 'social clauses' into international trade agreements. While fundamental disagreements between industrialized and developing nations over the inclusion of clauses on labour standards makes any new regulation on these matters through the World Trade Organization (WTO) an unlikely prospect in the immediate future, new regulatory measures have been put in place within the main trading blocs of NAFTA and, rather more so, the EU to limit the scope for social dumping (Teague 2000).

Many of the growing number of codes of conduct adopted by MNCs, either drawn up unilaterally or negotiated with trade unions or other employee representatives (such as works councils), address employment and industrial relations issues. These include child and forced labour, health and safety, freedom of association and the right to bargain collectively, levels of wages and anti-discrimination. A 1998 ILO study identified 215 international codes that identified labour issues, of which over 80 per cent were individual company codes (*European Works Council Bulletin* 2000a). There is considerable variation in the provisions made for the implementation of these corporate codes. Of the company codes covered by a 1999 OECD study, 38 per cent made no provision at all for monitoring implementation through such means as inspections, visits and control procedures (*European Works Council Bulletin* 2000a). Among those that do make provision, the overwhelming majority (59 per cent) specify some form of internal monitoring and just 3 per cent provide for some form of external monitoring, for example by an independent agency. Codes that apply to contractors and subcontractors to the MNC often require the contractor/subcontractor to confirm in writing that the terms of the code will be observed, although the extent of subsequent monitoring is unclear. Enforcement measures, specified in barely a majority of codes, include termination of the contract and working with the contractor/subcontractor to address any identified breach. Unsurprisingly, provisions for monitoring and other means of implementation and enforcement measures are markedly more likely to be specified in codes agreed with trade unions or works councils than those adopted unilaterally (*European Works Council Bulletin* 2000b).

European sector developments – towards co-ordinated bargaining?

At EU sector level, the ETUC and its industry federations have begun to put in place procedures for European-wide co-ordinated bargaining to combat the 'social dumping' that an intensification in benchmarking by MNCs is expected to bring. As Fajertag (2000: 11–13) reminds us, the 9th ETUC Congress in Helsinki in June 1999 adopted a specific resolution on the 'Europeanisation of industrial relations', recognizing 'a need for the European trade union movement to act swiftly to put in place instruments and procedures to promote co-ordination of collective bargaining now that the euro-zone is a reality'. A clear division of labour was also established: the ETUC itself is to be 'competent for overall co-ordination, providing the necessary framework to guarantee the overall coherence of the process'; and the ETUC's industry federations are to create 'the requisite structures and instruments, adapted to the needs of the sector concerned' (for further details, see Marginson and Schulten 1999).

Those already in the process of doing so include the EMF and the constituents of UNI-Europa.

Trade unions have also taken a leaf out of management's book in using benchmarking. The EMF was among the first international union organizations to develop co-ordinated cross-border initiatives in the collective bargaining arena (Schulten 2001). The first major example involves the negotiation of Article 13 agreements setting up EWCs prior to the implementation date of the EWC Directive of September 1996. The EMF drew up a set of minimum standards for agreements, or 'benchmarks' based on 'best practice' observed in agreements already made. This embraced key issues such as provisions for trade union experts to be involved, together with a detailed procedure for their negotiation including the 'signing off' of agreements by the EMF. As a result, relatively few agreements slipped through the net and most of the EMF's negotiating objectives were reached (for further details, see the report of an interview with the EMF's EWC co-ordinator in the *European Works Councils Bulletin* 1997). Since then, in July 1998, the EMF has unfolded a 'working time charter', according to which affiliated unions should aim to conclude agreements for working time that should not exceed an annual maximum of 1,750 hours. On wages policy, it introduced a so-called 'European co-ordination rule' in December 1998, according to which 'the wage policy of trade unions in all countries must be to offset the rate of inflation and to ensure that workers' incomes retain a balanced participation in productivity gains' (for further details, see Sisson and Marginson 2002). In parallel, the EMF has established an electronic database both to facilitate the systematic exchange of bargaining information between affiliates and to monitor progress in implementing the working time target and co-ordination rule.

Trade union resort to benchmarking not only reflects fears about management's use of benchmarking but also the refusal of the employers collectively and internationally to negotiate at EU sector level. For some, the co-ordinated bargaining that it is hoped benchmarking will make possible is an end in itself. Arguably, co-ordinated bargaining makes it possible to have the best of both worlds: to establish guidelines that will help to prevent undercutting and yet, at the same time, give negotiators scope to tailor details to their own situation (for further details of the logic of co-ordinated bargaining, see Sisson and Marginson 2001 and 2002). For others, it is a means to an end – to revive and ultimately go beyond the sector-level social dialogue. In Hoffman's (1998: 145–46) words, the hope is that trade unions will be the 'midwives for the birth of European employer federations at sectoral level', leading eventually to European-level sector collective bargaining.

The difficulties of achieving such a goal should not be underestimated, however. There are immense practical problems in developing effective co-operation between employee representatives from different countries, ranging from the 'expense of holding international meetings, the complications of trade union pluralism, and language barriers' (ICFTU quoted in European Works Council Bulletin 2001a: 15) through to the difficulties that sovereign bodies inevitably appear to have in resolving the collective action problem. Even achieving what might be thought to be the most basic of targets for the purposes of co-ordinated bargaining is not nearly as easy as it may appear. The EMF's seemingly straightforward 'working time charter' is an excellent example. The process of identification involved heated debate about whether the target should be expressed in the form of a yearly figure or a weekly figure (Sisson et al. 2003). The delegates from some countries even wanted to specify daily working time. The German, Belgian and French representatives wanted a ban on Sunday working, but this was unacceptable to their Nordic colleagues because, in the context of batch production, their agreements give scope for workforces to organize working time on a preferred basis, including Sunday working. The debate did not end, though, once the decision to go for a yearly figure had been taken. Should the figure be the highest, the lowest or 'somewhere in the middle'? In the event, 'somewhere in the middle' was chosen. If the lowest level had been chosen, then 'the European house would be built from the lowest brick', which was seen as undesirable. If the highest level had been chosen, on the other hand, it would have amounted to a demand for the 35-hour week, which would have been unrealizable in some countries.

European works councils – opening the door to European-level collective bargaining?

At company level, the spillover effect of management's use of benchmarking has been the deployment of similar comparisons by employee representatives. The European Foundation's investigation into the industrial relations impact of economic and monetary union (EMU) (for further details, see Sisson and Marginson 2001 and 2002) confirmed that trade union representatives found it difficult to make cross-national pay comparisons because of the complexity of different payment structures and tax, national insurance and social security systems, but that issues such as working time were emerging as valid reference points across borders. At GM Vauxhall, for example, international comparisons were successfully used to secure a reduction in working time first in 1995 and subsequently in 1998. Similarly, at Peugeot's UK subsidiary the unions won a reduction in working time following the conclusion of an agreement in France implementing the 35-hour week in the parent PSA group.

It is the prospect of EWCs becoming cross-national negotiating bodies, however, that has aroused most speculation (for further details, see Müller and Hoffmann 2001). Strictly speaking, this is not intended to be their primary role, which is seen as that of social dialogue. Trade unions as well as employers and their organizations are also opposed. As indicated above, trade union initiatives are primarily aimed at cross-border co-ordination on the *sector level* (Marginson and Schulten 1999). There is widespread concern that the assumption by EWCs of a collective bargaining role would help to undermine the already shaky national sector bargaining that has been the key instrument by which trade unions in the great majority of EU member states – the exceptions being the UK and Ireland – have sought to advance basic standards. Even employee representatives in the highly organized automotive sector tend to see EWCs as a means to gain information to be deployed in domestic negotiations rather than co-ordination across countries (Hancké 2000). Equally, the employers' organizations responsible for sector-level negotiations are strongly opposed to cross-border co-ordination of any kind. For their part, the management of MNCs may increasingly be using benchmarking to co-ordinate bargaining over working practices and working time arrangements across countries, but generally speaking have no desire to allow employee representatives to become involved.

Even so, an as yet small number of EWCs have gone on to agree joint texts. Analysing fourteen such texts, concluded by eight EWCs, Carley (2001) notes that in some instances the texts spell out general frameworks for company policy – as at Suez-Lyonnaise des Eaux and Vivendi – with no indication as to how their implementation will be effected or monitored. In others, they commit the signatories to specific actions – such as the establishment of a health and safety observatory at ENI. A further group take the form of framework agreements for lower-level action, with a crucially important distinction between those that are permissive, inciting follow-up at lower levels – such as Danone's 1996 agreement on training and Vivendi's 1999 agreement on safety – and those that are obligatory on the parties at lower levels. Of the latter, the agreements coming closest to traditional 'hard' collective agreements are those concluded during 2000 and 2001 by the EWCs at Ford and GM. In Ford's case, the agreement deals with the status, rights and terms and conditions of employees being transferred into the Visteon spin-off. In GM's case, which is discussed in more detail in the next section, there have been three major agreements, dealing respectively with a new power train joint venture with FIAT and restructuring involving the Vauxhall and Opel subsidiaries.

European works councils in UK- and US-based MNCs

How much influence does the country of origin of a multinational have on the way that a European works council operates? It may be the case that the established patterns of information disclosure and consultation in the original home base are the model on which the EWC is based and that it becomes in essence an extension of this national model. This may occur because of the numerical dominance in most EWCs of worker representatives from the country of origin and also because of the proximity of key figures in the EWC to the main locus of strategic decision making within the company. There is certainly some evidence that in the first EWCs that were set up – mainly French and German – the domestic labour relations model was indeed highly influential on the nature of the EWC.

This issue has recently been examined further in the case of eight UK and US MNCs (Hall et al. 2003). There is some evidence in these case studies of a home country influence. This is particularly marked in the UK firms where a relatively 'restrictive' approach on the part of management is in evidence, with managers keen to minimize the role of the EWC, and a fragmented, largely ineffective approach from employee representatives in the UK. Both of these factors can be traced back to the relative weakness of statutory forms of employee representation in the UK. There are also some indications in US MNCs of management adopting a minimalist approach to EWCs, arguably reflecting the deregulated tradition in the US labour market.

However, the findings also demonstrate that the country of origin is only a very partial guide to the character of EWCs. Country of location factors are also important – the countries that are the largest in terms of the distribution of MNCs across Europe had the most representatives, of course, and therefore also the most influence on the employee side. In addition, a number of company-specific factors, such as the extent to which production is integrated across borders, also shape the way a multinational approaches the EWC. For example, a company with strongly integrated operations is more likely to see benefits in using the EWC as a way of communicating with its international workforces.

For further details, see:
Hall, M., Hoffman, A., Marginson, P. and Muller, T. (2003) 'National Influences on European Works Councils in UK- and US-based Companies', *Human Resource Management Journal*, 13(4), 75–92.

Case study question: *We know from previous chapters that US MNCs are characterized by a strong 'country of origin' effect in the way they manage their international workforces. Why does this seem to be less marked in the area of European works councils?*

The management interest – the two faces of legitimacy

Our focus now turns to the management interest in international employee representation, which rarely receives the attention it deserves. It is perhaps not surprising that MNCs have co-operated to the extent they have with the international agencies or accepted statutory developments such as the EWC. More difficult to explain is why in a number of cases management has seemingly taken the initiative in promoting international employee representation, even being prepared, albeit in a small number of cases, to negotiate with employee representatives on a cross-national basis. Surely, it might be thought, management has very little to gain from doing so. It is not just that any kind of employee representation would appear to affect the balance of power between management and employees. An insistence on decentralization is critical to maintaining the principle of business managers' bottom line responsibility. It also denies the union a platform to raise key issues of strategy at company level, such as investment decisions. Furthermore, it can be used to promote 'attitudinal structuring' and 'integrative bargaining': targeting local union representatives encourages greater identification with the business, along with recognition of the importance of the ability to pay. Critically, it enables headquarters managers to play the 'regime competition' card: the use of benchmarking as a form of 'coercive comparisons' to drive down costs and push up quality in what is essentially an internal market for capital.

In some cases, there have been very specific circumstances at work that help to explain why management has taken a different view. It is no coincidence, for example, that a number of the former state-owned French companies were to the fore in introducing European works councils on a voluntary basis before the EWC directive – this primarily reflected the French domestic political situation. More generally, two sets of considerations would appear to be at work: the first, which is largely external, is a concern for the company's image among society at large; and the second, which is primarily internal, is a desire to secure legitimacy for key restructuring decisions, which might otherwise threaten the much-needed commitment and co-operation of the workforce. Each of these will be considered in turn.

External legitimacy – a concern for corporate social responsibility

As Chapter 13 argues in greater detail, there are good reasons why MNCs are taking issues such as human rights and international standards seriously. In the words of the European Commission's Green Paper *Promoting a European Framework for Corporate Social Responsibility* published in 2001:

> 'Many factors are driving [the] move towards corporate social responsibility:
>
> ● new concerns and expectations from citizens, consumers, public authorities and investors in the context of globalization and large scale industrial change;
> ● social criteria are increasingly influencing the investment decisions of individuals and institutions both as customers and investors;
> ● increased concern about the damage caused by economic activity to the environment;
> ● transparency of business activities brought about by the media and modern information and communication technologies.' (2001: 5)

The key point that MNCs have come to appreciate is that ethical trading campaigns mounted by non-governmental pressure groups can be extremely damaging not only to their image but also to their sales in the event of finding themselves in the dock. Examples include the sports shoe manufacturers Nike and Adidas, which have been accused of exploiting child labour in developing countries (Donaldson 2000). The negotiation of global frameworks, which effectively demand employee representation, is one important way in which they can seek to demonstrate their corporate social responsibility, an issue we analyse in Chapter 13.

Internal legitimacy – maintaining employee co-operation and commitment

Managing the employment relationship, as many commentators have observed, involves maintaining a delicate balance between commitment and control (see, for example, Walton 1985; Edwards 1986). There is also a growing consensus, in the USA (Cappelli et al. 1997: 226) as well as in Europe (European Commission 1997), about the major challenge facing management for the foreseeable future, even if there is no easy answer. To paraphrase Herriot and his colleagues (1998), given the intensifying competition and/or pressure on scarce resources, management has to reconcile two seemingly conflicting requirements: to cut costs to the bone and yet at the same time promote the security, autonomy and teamwork that are the conditions for innovation into new markets, products and services. In the words of the European

Commission Green Paper *Partnership for a New Organization of Work* (1997: 2) again, the challenge is to reconcile 'security for workers with the flexibility which firms need'. In discussions of flexibility there has been a tendency to focus on the external dimension – the ability of the organization to vary its commitments through reductions in the number of employees or changes in their status (e.g. from permanent to temporary) or through subcontracting. The real advances, it is argued, are much more likely to come from internal flexibility leading to improved organizational capacity. In the words of the same European Commission Green Paper:

> 'It is about the scope for improving employment and competitiveness through a better organisation of work at the workplace, based on high skill, high trust and high quality. It is about the will and ability of management and workers to take initiatives, to improve the quality of goods and services, to make innovations and to develop the production process and consumer relations.' (1997: 5)

It is in this context that the legitimacy of management decision making takes on its special significance. Securing the necessary employee co-operation and commitment in this kind of exercise is difficult at the best of times. It can be doubly difficult in ongoing restructuring situations, where considerations such as absenteeism, safety and customer relations can become especially acute. In these circumstances, the legitimacy of management decision making can be profoundly important, helping to explain why managers would want to get the agreement of employee representatives. The alternative, of attempting to proceed unilaterally, is likely to lead to far greater demoralization of the workforce as well as possibly inviting organized resistance, neither of which is likely to be perceived sympathetically by either major customers or headquarters management. The effect is to force local managers and employee representatives into each other's arms, notwithstanding any ideological concerns that they might have.

General Motors

General Motors, which it was earlier suggested was at the forefront of the use of 'coercive comparisons' to promote improved performance, offers an excellent illustration of a growing dialogue between management and unions at the international level. The original agreement establishing the EWC in 1996 does not explicitly provide for the body to have a negotiating role. The EWC has nonetheless been used as the machinery to reach no fewer than three major framework agreements in recent years. The first, in July 2000, deals with the implications of GM's alliance with FIAT (*European Works Council Bulletin* 2000d); the second, in March 2001, is on handling restructuring at Vauxhall, GM's subsidiary in the UK (*European Works Council Bulletin* 2001b); the third, in August 2001, deals with similar events at Opel, which is GM's subsidiary headquartered in Germany (*European Works Council Bulletin* 2001c).

In the latter case, for example, the comprehensive framework agreement ratified in October 2001 extends to more than 80,000 employees in 16 plants in 10 European countries. GM management commits itself to implementing the proposed changes associated with the so-called 'Olympia' programme though continuing dialogue and in socially responsible ways. For their part, employee representatives give their support to the programme in general terms. This covers such matters as a reduction in capacity from 350,000 to 300,000 units, immediate steps to increase productivity levels to 'world-class benchmark' standards, greater flexibility of staffing and working time and the pursuit of partnerships and joint ventures, which could have considerable implications for the existing workforce. The chairman and managing director of Opel is quoted as saying:

> 'I am particularly pleased that management and employee representatives agree on the necessary objectives and specifically on instituting actions that support our company's turnaround and contribute to a successful future of the employees. Combined with the many initiatives to revitalise the Opel brand, grow sales and increase revenues, we have made excellent progress towards strengthening the Opel, Vauxhall and Saab brands. Bringing them to leadership positions in the European automotive industry is our common priority.'
> (*European Works Council Bulletin*, 2001c: 8)

This is a reminder that employee representatives can fulfil the same kind of fundamental managerial functions at the cross-national as they do at the national level. One is the 'agency' function that is especially important where there are large numbers of employees engaged in relatively homogenous activities – management minimizes the time-consuming and costly process of dealing with employee representatives on a country-by-country basis, avoids the inconsistencies that can be a major problem and promotes the opportunities for promoting 'regime competition'. A second is that employee representatives 'voice' the grievances and complaints of employees (Freeman and Medoff 1984). A third, and in many respects the most important, function is in helping to manage discontent by legitimating management decisions.

Case study question: *Will management in all MNCs have a similar incentive to use a European works council in this way?*

Fairly obvious in the light of the discussion, however, is that recognizing the importance of international employee representation very much depends on circumstances. Here the six sets of factors identified by Marginson et al. (2004) as potentially influencing the impact of EWCs on management decision making would appear to be especially important. The first three sets are structural conditions that may serve to facilitate or to constrain the development of an effective EWC, and thereby the nature and extent of its impact. The second three sets bring considerations of agency into play, focusing on management policy and organization, employee-side organization and activity, and the interaction between the management and the employee side.

The first set of factors relate to the nature of the company's business operations:

1 *Business alignment* – the focus, spread and integration of the company's business activities;
2 *Management structure* – the existence and nature of a European management structure;
3 *Industrial relations platform* – the existence of an industrial relations platform through national group-level structures and a pre-existing international network among employee representatives.

These three sets of structural conditions are expected to constrain or facilitate the effectiveness of the EWC, and thereby its impact on management decision making. Beyond this, the nature and extent of an EWC's impact will be determined by the organization and policy approaches of the actors involved – management and employee representatives – and there are three of these conditions:

4 *Management policy* – management's approach to the EWC and the levels and functions of management routinely involved in the EWC, particularly whether it is about minimalist compliance or an enthusiastic embrace;

5 *Employee-side organization* – the organization and cohesiveness of the EWC's employee side, the interaction between the employee side and structures of employee representation at national and local level and the extent to which the employee side mobilizes trade union resources in support of its activity;

6 *EWC interaction* – the nature of the interaction between the EWC (employee side) and management, especially whether it is open, constructive and ongoing, or adversarial.

Marginson et al. (2004) investigated the extent to which EWCs in eight MNCs had an impact on the handling of industrial relations issues. In doing so, they distinguished between the way an EWC might affect the process of decision making on these issues, through shaping the mechanisms through which management co-ordination takes place, for example, and the outcome of the issues. In relation to the latter, they made a further distinction between EWCs affecting the implementation of industrial relations decisions and the substance of them. In short, their findings suggest that it is common for EWCs to affect the process of decision making on industrial relations issues – in six of the eight cases there was convincing evidence of this – but it is rare for the outcome of decisions to be affected – in four of the eight cases there was evidence of an impact on the implementation of decisions but in only one was there evidence relating to the substance of decisions. The variation between companies in these respects was explained by the six factors identified above.

Conclusion and prospects for the future

There are two main conclusions to be drawn about developments in international employee representation from this discussion. The first is that its significance is likely to increase. There is, it seems, a close association between markets and industrial relations systems, as Commons (1909) argued around a century ago. The growth in the number and significance of MNCs, particularly those with integrated operations, has created significant pressures for a countervailing force. These pressures are becoming institutionalized not only through EWCs but in the future may also be institutionalized through the European Company Statute. This is the result of a European directive that from October 2004 has allowed companies to opt to be designated as 'European' (as opposed to German, say) so long as they reach agreement with employee representatives on the nature of industrial relations structures to operate within the firm (EIRO 2002). The managements of many MNCs have themselves recognized the value of such representation – partly to signal to governments and consumers that they are acting responsibly and partly because they need the legitimation that only the involvement of employee representatives can bring for the process of change and ongoing restructuring in which they are involved.

The second conclusion is a qualification of the first. Although the significance of international employee representation is likely to increase, one should not expect it to lead to a fully fledged system, however, along the lines of national systems. Rather 'soft frameworks' and co-ordinated bargaining look set to be the distinguishing features of industrial relations in most MNCs for the foreseeable future. Even in companies such as GM, which would appear to have gone much further down the road of European collective bargaining than most, there is in effect a multi-tiered system, with implementation remaining the responsibility of management and employee representatives at national and local levels. It is not just that there are immense practical problems in developing international employee representation; there is also the fundamental problem that sovereign bodies inevitably have in deciding upon a collective course of action. Just as a single market does not produce a vertically integrated system unless there is a parallel political authority of substance, so one should not expect cross-national company-level industrial relations systems without a highly integrated management structure. A multi-level governance system produces a multi-level industrial relations system.

Review questions

1 What are coercive comparisons and in what circumstances can management at the headquarters of MNCs use them?

2 What is the European Union's rationale for introducing European works councils?

3 What are the main incentives for management to engage in an international dialogue with representatives of their workforce?

4 What are the barriers to employee representatives in different countries forming closer alliances?

Further reading

Hancké, B. (2000) 'European Works Councils and the Motor Industry', *European Journal of Industrial Relations*, 6(1), 35–60.

This article provides a detailed discussion of the operation of EWCs in the motor industry, a sector where one might expect them to have some influence.

Marginson, P., Hall, M., Hoffmann, A. and Müller, T. (2004) 'The Impact of European Works Councils on Management Decision-Making in UK- and US-based Companies', *British Journal of Industrial Relations*, 42(2), 209–33.

The way in which EWCs influence key decisions affecting employment is addressed through a discussion of eight case studies. The paper makes a distinction between the process and the outcome of decision making, arguing that the former is commonly influenced by EWCs but the latter only rarely.

Mueller, F. and Purcell, J. (1992) 'The Europeanisation of Manufacturing and the Decentralisation of Bargaining', *International Journal of Human Resource Management*, 3(1), 15–24.

This article examines the way in which manufacturing processes are becoming increasingly integrated, especially at the European level, and discusses the implications for industrial relations. It uses the term 'coercive comparisons' to depict the strategy that management in integrated MNCs take to collective bargaining.

Sisson, K., Arrowsmith, J. and Marginson, P. (2003) 'All Benchmarkers Now? Benchmarking and the "Europeanisation" of Industrial Relations', *Industrial Relations Journal*, 34(1), 15–31.

This article tackles the issue of benchmarking, arguing that it has a number of dimensions and is a growing aspect of European integration.

References

Capelli, P., Katz, H. and Osterman, P. (1997) *The New Deal at Work*, Boston: Harvard Business School Press.

Carley, M. (2001) *Bargaining at European Level? Joint Texts Negotiated by European Works Councils*, Luxembourg: Office for the Official Publications of the European Communities.

Coller, X. (1996) 'Managing Flexibility in the Food Industry: A Cross-National Comparative Case Study in European Multinational Companies', *European Journal of Industrial Relations*, 2(2), 153–72.

Coller, X. and Marginson, P. (1998) 'Transnational Management Influence over Changing Employment Practices: A Case from the Food Industry', *Industrial Relations Journal*, 29(1), 4–17.

Commons, J. (1909) 'American Shoemakers 1648–1895: A sketch of Industrial Evolution', *Quarterly Journal of Economics*, 24, 38–83, reprinted in R.L. Rowan and H.R. Northrup (eds) (1968) *Readings in Labor Economics and Labor Relations*, Homewood, IL: Irwin.

Donaldson, T. (2000) 'Adding Corporate Ethics to the Bottom Line', *Financial Times Survey – Mastering Management,* 13 November.

Edwards, P. (1986) *Conflict at Work: A Materialist Analysis*, Oxford: Blackwell.

EIRO (European Industrial Relations Observatory) (2002) 'European Company Statute in Focus', http://www.eiro.eurofound.ie/2002/06/feature/eu/0206202f.html

European Commission (1997) Green Paper, *Partnership for a New Organisation of Work*, Bulletin of the European Union. Supplement 4/97. Luxembourg: Office for the Official Publications of the European Communities.

European Commission (2000) *Industrial Relations in Europe 2000*, Luxembourg: Office for the Official Publications of the European Communities.

European Commission (2001) *Promoting a European Framework for Corporate Social Responsibility*, Green Paper. Luxembourg: Office for the Official Publications of the European Communities.

European Works Council Bulletin (1997) 'European Metalworkers' Strategy for EWCs', Report of an interview with Charlie McKenzie, the EMF's EWC Coordinator', Issue 8, March/April, 4–7.

European Works Council Bulletin (2000a) 'Code of Corporate Conduct and Industrial Relations – Part One', Issue 27, May/June, 11–16.

European Works Council Bulletin (2000b) 'Code of Corporate Conduct and Industrial Relations – Part Two', Issue 28, September/October, 7–16.

European Works Council Bulletin (2000c) 'OECD Guidelines for Multinationals Revisited', Issue 29, September/October, 13–16.

European Works Council Bulletin (2000d) 'GM Management and EWC Agree on FIAT Alliance', Issue 29, September/October, 2.

European Works Council Bulletin (2000e) 'Trade Union Councils and Networks in Multinationals – Part One', Issue 30, November/December, 7–10.

European Works Council Bulletin (2001a) 'Trade Union Councils and Networks in Multinationals – Part Two', Issue 32, March/April, 12–15.

European Works Council Bulletin (2001b) 'GM Deal Highlights EWC's Negotiating Role', Issue 33, May/June, 7–11.

European Works Council Bulletin (2001c) 'GM EWC Reaches Agreement on Opel Restructuring', Issue 36, November/December, 8–10.

European Works Council Bulletin (2003) 'Latest EWC Figures', Issue 43, January/February, 14–16.

Fajertag, G. (2000) *Collective Bargaining in Europe 1998–1999*, Brussels: European Trade Union Institute (ETUI).

Ferner, A. and Edwards, P. (1995) 'Power and Diffusion of Organisational Change within Multinational Enterprises', *European Journal of Industrial Relations*, 1(2), 229–57.

Freeman, R. and Medoff, J. (1984) *What Do Unions Do?* New York: Basic Books.

Gumbrell-McCormick, R. (2000) 'Globalisation and the Dilemmas of International Trade Unionism', *Transfer*, 6(1), 29–42.

Hall, M., Carley, M., Gold, M., Marginson, P. and Sisson, K. (1995) *European Works Councils: Planning for the Directive*, London: Eclipse Group Ltd.

Hall, M., Hoffman, A., Marginson, P. and Müller, T. (2003) 'National Influences on European Works Councils in UK- and US-based Companies', *Human Resource Management Journal*, 13(4), 75–92.

Hancké, B. (2000) 'European Works Councils and the Motor Industry', *European Journal of Industrial Relations*, 6(1), 35–60.

Hastings, M. (1997) *Managing the Management Tools*, London: Institute of Management.

Herriot, P., Hirsch, W. and Reily, P. (1998) *Trust and Transitions: Managing the Employment Relationship*, Chichester: John Wiley.

Hoffman, R. (1998) book review of O. Jacoby and P. Pochet (eds) *A Common Currency Area – a Fragmented Area for Wages* in *Transfer*, 4(1).

International Confederation of Free Trade Unions (ICFTU)(2000) *A Trade Union Guide to Globalization*, http://www.icftu.org

Marginson, P. and Schulten, T. (1999) 'The "Europeanisation" of Collective Bargaining', European Industrial Relations Observatory On-line, TN9907201S), http://www.eiro.eurofound.eu.int/about/1999/07/study/tn99072015.html

Marginson, P. and Sisson, K. (1996) 'Multinational Companies and the Future of Collective Bargaining: A Review of the Research Issues', *European Journal of Industrial Relations*, 2(2), 173–97.

Marginson, P. and Sisson, K. (1998) 'European Collective Bargaining: A Virtual Prospect?', *Journal of Common Market Studies*, 36(4), 505–28.

Marginson, P., Armstrong, P., Edwards, P. and Purcell, J. with Hubbard, N. (1993) 'The Control of Industrial Relations in Large Companies', *Warwick Papers in Industrial Relations*, No. 45, Coventry: Industrial Relations Research Unit (IRRU), University of Warwick.

Marginson, P., Edwards, P.K., Armstrong, P. and Purcell, J. (1995) 'Strategy, Structure and Control in the Changing Corporation: A Survey-Based Investigation', *Human Resource Management Journal*, 5(2), 3–27.

Marginson, P., Hall, M., Hoffmann, A. and Müller, T. (2004) 'The Impact of European Works Councils on Management Decision-Making in UK- and US-based Companies', *British Journal of Industrial Relations*, 42(2), 209–33.

Martin, G. and Beaumont, P. (1998) 'Diffusing "Best Practice" in Multinational Firms: Prospects, Practice and Contestation', *International Journal of Human Resource Management*, 9(4), 672–95.

Mueller, F. and Purcell, J. (1992) 'The Europeanisation of Manufacturing and the Decentralisation of Bargaining', *International Journal of Human Resource Management*, 3(1), 15–24.

Müller, T. and Hoffmann, A. (2001) 'EWC Research: A Review of the Literature', *Warwick Papers in Industrial Relations*, No. 65, Coventry: Industrial Relations Research Unit.

Schulten, T. (2001) 'The European Metalworkers' Federation's Approach to a Europeanisation of Collective Bargaining' in T. Schulten and R. Bispinck (eds) *Collective Bargaining Under the Euro: Experiences from the European Metal Industry*, Brussels: European Trade Union Institute (ETUI)/EMF.

Sisson, K. and Artiles, A.M. (2000) *Handling Restructuring. A Study of Collective Agreements on Employment and Competitiveness*, Luxembourg: Office for the Official Publications of the European Communities.

Sisson, K and Marginson, P. (2001) '"Soft" Regulation: Travesty of the Real Thing or New Dimension?' *One Europe or Several? Working Paper* 32/01. Falmer: University of Sussex.

Sisson, K. and Marginson, P. (2002) 'Co-ordinated Bargaining: A Process for our Times?' *British Journal of Industrial Relations*, 40(2), 197–220.

Sisson, K., Arrowsmith, J. and Marginson, P. (2003) 'All Benchmarkers Now? Benchmarking and the "Europeanisation" of Industrial Relations', *Industrial Relations Journal*, 34(1), 15–31.

Teague, P. (2000) 'The Social Dimension to Regional Trading Blocs: Lessons from the EU and NAFTA', paper presented to the 12th International Industrial Relations Association Conference, Tokyo, 29 May to 2 June.

Walton, R.E. (1985) 'From Control to Commitment in the Workplace', *Harvard Business Review*, 63, March/April, 76–84.

Zagelmeyer, S. (2000) *Innovative Agreements on Employment and Competitiveness in the European Union and Norway*, Luxembourg: Office for the Official Publications of the European Communities.

Chapter 13

International corporate social responsibility and employment relations

Sanjiv Sachdev

Key aims

This chapter has the following key aims:

- to understand the concept of corporate social responsibility and its application at the international level;

- to appreciate the role of human resources in developing corporate social responsibility programmes;

- to consider the consequences of corporate social responsibility, particularly the limitations to actual practice living up to its formal aims.

Introduction

In December 2002 the food multinational Nestlé demanded a $6 million payment from the Ethiopian government for business that was nationalized in 1975. At the time, despite the country being in the grip of famine, the Ethiopian government had offered $1.5 million to settle the claim (Denny 2002a). A few days later Nestlé had back-tracked; facing a 'mounting public relations disaster' (Denny 2002b) over its handling of the issue, its chief executive pledged to donate the owed money to hunger relief (although it did not relinquish the original $6 million claim). A few weeks later Nestlé made a further retreat and accepted the Ethiopian government's $1.5 million offer, to be handed to famine relief (Denny 2003). This is an excellent example of the issues that businesses can face in an international climate where there is a growing view that the responsibilities of businesses extend beyond maximization of profits within the confines of adherence to the law.

Corporate social responsibility (CSR) has rapidly risen up the hierarchy of issues that businesses seek to address. In the wake of the Enron crisis, corporate behaviour and governance has been subject to unprecedented attention. In 2001 the UK stock exchange, following the example of the Dow Jones Sustainability Index in 1999, launched the 'ethical index' FTSE4Good (similar indices operate in Japan, France, Italy and Belgium). In the same year the European Commission published a Green Paper on CSR (although momentum has since faltered) and the UK appointed a minister for corporate responsibility and established a website giving examples of good practice and seeking views on the future direction of policy on corporate behaviour. Company reports and corporate websites routinely include sections on CSR, detailing the organization's work on issues such as the environment, human rights and fair trade. According to the World Bank president, James D. Wolfensohn, 'there is also a growing understanding on the part of business leadership that it is not only morally good but good business to invest with a strong sense of social responsibility' (cited in Friedman 1999).

It is estimated that £13.4 billion is spent annually in the UK on investments, goods and services governed by ethical decisions (Doane 2001). Since July 2000 UK pension fund trustees have been required to report on whether they take account of social and environmental matters.[1] In 2001 Germany introduced a similar measure. French law now requires companies to take into account, in their annual reports, the 'social and environmental consequences' of their activity. Belgium now has a national 'kitemarking' scheme so that consumers can identify companies that follow CSR principles. The Netherlands, Denmark and Norway have long-standing environmental disclosure requirements. The 'Fairtrade' brand is now an annual £315 million global niche market and has encouraged public authorities to pursue ethical procurement policies (Vidal 2003). One dollar in every eight invested in the USA is invested in ethical funds (Heertz 2001). In June 2002 the European Parliament agreed a resolution inviting the Commission to consider a directive requiring companies to include social and environmental reporting alongside their annual financial reports. In 2004 the United Nations (UN) issued the draft 'UN Norms' that brings together a range of international human rights instruments in a single code and envisages ways of enforcing them (Maitland 2004). Evidently, there is an international trend towards companies and public authorities becoming more interested in 'ethical' and 'socially responsible' corporate behaviour.

Of the UK companies surveyed in 2000, 75 per cent had a code of conduct, while 62 per cent of respondents from the FTSE 350 or equivalent sized unquoted companies claimed that ethical policies were a priority; in contrast, in 1993 barely 33 per cent of leading companies either had or were developing a code (Carmichael 2001). Similarly in the USA, all Fortune 500 companies have codes of conduct (Heertz 2001). In April 2006 the UK will introduce a new Operating and Financial Review (OFR) for annual reports of larger public companies, including information relating to employees, customers and suppliers as well as social and environmental impacts where this is necessary for shareholders' proper understanding of the company (Sikka 2004: Cowe 2004a), although some non-governmental organizations (NGOs) have complained of the narrowness of these requirements (Eaglesham 2002). As massive users of natural resources, large corporations have become involved in discussions as to their use. Thus Coca-Cola is involved in issues of water scarcity, IKEA with that of

---

[1] The impact of this measure would, however, appear to be very limited (see Cicutti 2002).

deforestation (with Greenpeace and the World Wide Fund for Nature) and Ford with the emission levels and recyclability of its cars (Lloyd 2000; Cowe (2000) argues that Ford's green credentials have been seriously tested, if not undermined, by its pursuit of the sports utility vehicles market). It is argued that 'social responsibility is becoming a generally accepted principle that applies to a growing variety of business partnerships involving multinational and local enterprises in industrialised and developing economies alike' (Diller 1999).

Conceptual confusion

CSR is 'poorly defined' (Murray 2002). It is said to involve 'identifying every aspect of society on which a company has an impact, through its non-core as well as core activities' (Joseph 2001). The range of issues embraced by the term can be extensive – Table 13.1 outlines some of them.

Table 13.1 Issues covered by CSR

● Environmental	● Concern for human rights
● Fair trade	● Philanthropic history
● Organic produce	● Co-operative principles
● Not tested on animals	● Support for education
● Community involvement	● Participates in local business initiatives
● Cause related marketing	● Supports national business initiatives
● Charitable giving	● Commitment to reporting
● Religious foundation	● Employee schemes
● Support for social causes	● Refusal to trade in certain markets

Source: Howard and Willmott (2001)

Table 13.1 sets out the various, sometimes unconnected, issues placed under the umbrella of CSR. One strand concerns the environment (of which animal welfare can be considered a subset). Another focuses on labour rights and on the impact of businesses on communities where they operate – a focus of this chapter. In part, this confusion is due to the relative newness of the concept(s) but it is also arguably because CSR 'has many cultural variants as a result of divergent capitalisms' (McIntosh et al. 2003). Stakeholder societies like Germany and Japan have a tradition of accounting for employee concerns (and are unlikely to be familiar with the term 'CSR'). US firms have a strong tradition of philanthropic and charitable donation. The terminology in this area reflects its variety and is itself in a state of flux. Terms such as 'sustainable development',[2] 'sustainability', 'ethics', 'corporate citizenship'

---

[2] Arguably this is relatively well defined as 'development that meets the need of the present without compromising the ability of future generations to meet their own needs' (Brundtland 1987) but it too has been subject to significant scrutiny and amendment; according to Holmberg and Sandbrook (1992), 70 definitions are now current.

and 'corporate social responsibility' are used interchangeably and imprecisely, often as synonyms. In practice, the limits of the term 'ethical' are apparent from the example reported by Carmichael:

> 'The ethics officer of a major defence contractor was asked if staff ever raised concerns about the firm's involvement in the manufacture of weapons of mass destruction. He look puzzled, and replied "Our only client is the US government and the US government operates in the defence of freedom." End of discussion.' (2001: 134)

Most definitions of CSR, however, agree that responsible companies will act beyond their legal obligations to ensure that various commitments are met, such as obligations to employees, suppliers, customers, and the wider environment and local communities (Joseph and Parkinson 2002).[3]

CSR is controversial. Advocates of CSR argue that it has many benefits for employers. Some advocates emphasize the defensive aspects of CSR in protecting reputation, profits and share price. Others adopt a more ambitious, proactive stance, seeing a CSR role in redefining the corporate mission, protecting reputation, offering a distinctive positioning, building credibility and trust with employees and customers, assisting recruitment and retention and fostering dialogue with interest groups (CIPD 2002: 8). Some commentators see it as a corporate fig leaf to enhance reputations (Klein 2000; Christian Aid 2004), others as a wasteful distraction from the proper activities of firms (Henderson 2001; Wolf 2002); as Milton Friedman (1973) famously stated, 'there is one and only one social responsibility of business – to use its resources and engage in activities designed to increase its profits so long as it stays within the rules of the game ...'[4] Most businesses see CSR/ethics as a niche issue, but in some cases, for example the Co-op bank and retailer, ethical issues have become mainstream by being applied to existing product lines rather than niche alternatives (Buckley 2002). Some businesses appear to be hostile to the concept altogether; the chairman and chief executive of ExxonMobil, Lee Raymond, declared that 'we don't invest to make social statements at the expense of shareholder return' (cited in McNulty 2003).

HRM and corporate social responsibillity

Labour issues are frequently at the heart of 'ethical' disputes and these often fall under the remit of human resources (HR) departments. Issues of discrimination, working conditions, health and safety, harassment, pay, child labour, forced labour,

---

[3] A similar terminological confusion exists in the so-called 'anti-globalization' movement. Some of this group prefer the term 'alter globalization', others define them as 'new global movements' (Lloyd 2001b). These terminological differences reflect wider ideological differences between those who wish to reinforce the sovereignty of states against global and foreign capital and those striving for a 'non-national alternative to the present form of globalization that is equally global' (Hardt 2002).

[4] According to Friedman (1973), those who advocated the 'social responsibilities of business' were preaching 'pure and unadulterated socialism'.

'whistleblowing', freedom of association and collective bargaining – all employment relations matters – are prominent in debates around CSR. Thus Shell's CSR report (2001) devotes considerable attention to employee rights, health and safety, diversity, working hours and wages. From January 2007, the FTSE4Good index will require companies exposed to supply chain risks to demonstrate policies on labour standards such as non-discrimination, forced labour, child labour and worker representation. The International Labour Organization (ILO) is notable in these debates and international trade union confederations are active within them (Elliot and Freeman 2003). Human resource management (HRM) departments are often heavily involved or have lead responsibility in CSR issues; one survey found the HR department was second only to the legal department in devising a company code of ethics (cited in CIPD 2002). The Gap employs more than 80 people around the world whose sole responsibility is to ensure that factories comply with ethical sourcing criteria and Nike has quadrupled the number of employees dealing with labour practices (Murray 2002). Moreover, the employment practices of some leading transnationals, such as Nike (McCawley 2000; Klein 2000; Skapinker 2002) and McDonald's (Vidal 1997; Royle 2000; Schlosser 2001; Maitland 2002) have come under close scrutiny. Some commentators have emphasized the ethical dimension of HR issues such as recruitment (Spence 2000), flexible working (Stanworth 2000) and human resource development (Woodall and Douglas 2000). Other studies have included redeployment and redundancy strategies as CSR issues (Segal et al. 2003).

It is also argued that a poor public reputation impairs a company's recruitment and retention of staff. According to Heertz (2001), directors of both BP and Shell reported being overwhelmed by the large number of concerned e-mails they received from staff following adverse TV and press coverage of their operations in Colombia and Nigeria. This echoes the experience of Nike staff who, according to a Nike official, in the wake of various scandals surrounding the firm 'were going to barbecues and people would say: "How can you work for Nike?" … I don't know if we were losing employees but it sure as hell didn't help in attracting them' (Skapinker 2002). The CIPD survey of graduate workplace attitudes in 2001 (see CIPD 2002) found that for two-thirds of graduates, a company's ethical reputation would influence their decision on whether or not to apply for a specific job.

Some companies use their appraisal and pay systems to encourage responsible behaviour by their staff. Thus for the chief executive of Statoil, Norway's largest oil company, bonus payments are partly dependent on the outcomes of indicators on health and safety, the environment and employee satisfaction (Maitland 2003). The HR department of Adidas has made performance in human rights a factor in calculating annual bonuses for country managers (Crawford 2000). As the section on codes of conduct (below) makes clear, HR considerations are also central to most such codes. Labour regulation in international trade (discussed later in this chapter), is also important. It is certainly claimed that the good reputation of firms attracts 'top-class graduates', improves retention rates and morale and increases productivity (see, for example, PricewaterhouseCoopers in Save the Children 2000: 34). It has been argued that 'if employees don't see the point of CSR initiatives, or understand the message, initiatives are unlikely to be effective' (CIPD 2002: 7). Moreover, the CIPD sees CSR as being intrinsic to being a 'good' employer, the skills of HR being key to communicating and engaging employees for an effective implementation of a broader CSR strategy.

ARM Holdings: CSR in action

Formal statements relating to CSR are normally associated with large firms but they are also found in some small ones. With just 700 employees in the UK, Japan and the USA, computer chip designer ARM Holdings is one of the smallest companies on the FTSE 100. It found that increasing pressure from the financial community for ethical investments meant it had to seek formal recognition of its work in the field of CSR. This meant the introduction of formal policies and procedures, as the lack of these meant that the company was not meeting the ethical criteria of investment funds. The company signed up as a member of the Institute of Business Ethics (IBE), which seeks to encourage high standards of behaviour from companies. ARM became the pilot organization for the IBE's 'Good Corporation' charter. This provided the company with external, independent recognition of its record on CSR as well as meeting the criteria of financial investors.

The 'Good Corporation' charter checks adherence to 21 principles, covering good practice towards employees, customers, suppliers, the community, the environment and shareholders. The various ARM sites were visited by auditors to check adherence to the principles. To comply with the charter, ARM introduced policies in areas such as whistleblowing, equal opportunities and the employment of people with disabilities. The company also had to improve its employee consultation mechanisms. The organization envisages CSR being managed like a business project with advance planning, clear measures of performance and internal audits. The HR department is part of a wider team managing CSR issues, with key responsibility for employment issues. Reporting on CSR is undertaken through the firm's annual report.

Source: IRS (2001)

Case study question: *In firms like ARM, how can those in the HR function use CSR initiatives to their advantage?*

The rise of corporate social responsibility

Ethical pressures on businesses to behave responsibly have existed for centuries. The specific issues have shifted, but issues around the protection of workers, environmentalism and consumer protection are long-standing. A striking example is that of slavery: few considered this lucrative trade immoral until the second half of the eighteenth century, yet within 30 years the practice was outlawed in the UK. Quaker-led campaigns, beginning with the first important anti-slavery petitions to Parliament in 1783, eventually led to the abolition of the slave trade with the colonies in 1807. The end of slavery in the Caribbean plantations was achieved in 1834. The efforts of abolitionists to encourage the purchase of sugar from non-slave-owning countries strongly mirrors the activities of organizations like the Fairtrade Foundation today.

In the nineteenth century, industrialists like Hershey, Cadbury, Fry and Rowntree (Quakers all) sought to humanize capitalism by creating better living conditions for workers. Robert Owen had similarly attempted to use enlightened methods at his textile mill in New Lanark (Thompson 1968). The rise of trade unions in the nineteenth century was accompanied by a series of parliamentary measures to improve working conditions, notably that which restricted child labour and the long (and international) campaign for the ten-hour day. Factory Commission reports from the period quote one spinner as saying that but for the Factory Acts, the competition among mill owners was severe enough to force round-the-clock working with no breaks other than for meals (cited in Donkin 2001). Reformers like John Ruskin (1862) made a clear distinction between 'well-gotten and ill-gotten wealth'. More recently, issues like trade with apartheid South Africa, the former dictatorship of Chile and the sale of powdered milk by Nestlé in Africa have had considerable attention.

With the end of the cold war, a profound shift towards an aggressive capitalism was evident, unrestrained by an available alternative (Marquand 1997). This witnessed the faltering of traditional social democracy (Sassoon 1996), the retreat of the state (Kuttner 1997; Hutton 1995) and a new ascendancy of corporate power (Korten 1995; Luttwak 1996; Lloyd 2000; Klein 2000; Monbiot 2000). Capitalism was both resurgent and triumphant. A character in Don DeLillo's *Underworld* captures this well: 'Many things that were anchored to the balance of power and the balance of terror seem to be undone, unstuck. Things have no limits now. Money has no limits … Money is undone' (1998: 76).

However, it was this that led to particular concerns as to the nature of capitalism intensifying, especially as trade continues to liberalize under the auspices of the World Trade Organization (WTO) (House of Commons 1999). The triumph of capitalism and the creation of a civilization in which business values 'are seen as central has paradoxically generated a public which demands that business behaves better' (Hutton 2000: 13). It is argued that the new centrality of business in contemporary life means that business must acknowledge that it too has citizenship responsibilities; its ideological 'victory' means that paradoxically it has greater pressures upon it to act with integrity and accountability, paying attention to wider social purposes. As Sen argues: 'critiques of capitalism have, to a considerable extent, become more widely shared after their dissociation from the particular institutional remedies traditionally championed by socialists' (1996). Concerns as to the conduct of capitalism grew as its role became more prominent. This concern is echoed by the remarks of the World Bank's president James Wolfensohn in 1999 that 'at the level of people, the system isn't working' (cited in Faux and Mishel 2000).

Several concerns were evident; the particular model of globalization that was being promoted and the greater inequality that arose from it, and the role and (lack of) accountability of corporate power, including the employment practices of transnationals. The inequalities produced by the prevailing model of globalization have been widely noted. In a much publicized critique, the Nobel prize winner and former chief economist of the World Bank, Joseph Stiglitz (2002), argued that the prevailing form of globalization had a 'devastating effect … on developing countries and especially the poor within those countries'. In Russia the percentage of those living in poverty rose from 2 per cent in 1989 to 23.8 per cent in 1998; other 'post-communist countries have seen comparable, if not worse, increases in poverty' (Stiglitz 2002: 153). In 1996 the United Nations Development Programme reported that the assets of the world's 358 billionaires exceeded the combined incomes of 45 per cent of the world's population (cited in Faux and Mishel 2000). Michael Eisner, the head of Disney, earned $576 million in 1998, or roughly the GDP of the Seychelles (Heertz 2001).[5] CEO pay in the USA during the 1990s went from 85 times more than what average blue-collar employees received in 1990 to some 475 times what blue-collar workers received in 1999 (Frank 2002). At the same time, 40 million Americans have no health insurance and 20 per cent are 'functionally illiterate' (Lloyd 2001a: 22). The need for businesses to reassert their legitimacy in the wake of these trends is perceived to be a factor behind the rise of CSR.

The increased role and power of large corporations was another key concern (Klein 2000; Monbiot 2000; Heertz 2001). As the state began to withdraw from key economic activities, business was asked to fill the gaps, playing a substantially greater role in providing products and services that were once the domain of the state. The spread of globalization was said to have altered the position of multinationals in a fundamental manner. It is argued that it has weakened the political institutions of the nation state and elevated the role of multinationals (Korten 1995). The profits of the world's ten largest firms is equal to the GDP of 29 African countries (Elliot and Denny 2003). The 12 most important global industries, such as textiles and the media, are each more than 40 per cent controlled by five or fewer corporations (McIntosh et al. 1998). Industries such as the banana trade are said to be 'controlled by a small number of multinational corporations' (Fairtrade Foundation 2000: 6). Similarly, the coffee trade is said to be dominated by four transnationals that account for 40 per cent of worldwide retail sales (Fairtrade Foundation 2002). The ambition of some corporations was arguably well beyond that of increasing market share; Starbucks sought, according to its marketing director, to 'align ourselves with one of the greatest movements towards finding a connection with your soul' (cited in Klein 2000: 138). Through private finance initiatives (PFIs) and public-private partnerships, private firms have a growing (international) role in providing public services such as prisons, health and education (Sachdev 2001). The patenting of seeds, drugs and genes has been a major source of anxiety (Klein 2002). Concern about the role, power

---

[5] The protests of businesses at greater regulation often mirror that of the millers of Dickens's Coketown (1854, 1995): 'They were ruined, when they were required to send labouring children to school; they were ruined, when inspectors were appointed to look into their works; they were ruined, when such inspectors considered it doubtful whether they were quite justified in chopping people up with their machinery; they were utterly undone, when it was hinted that perhaps they need not always make quite so much smoke.'

and activities of such firms became the uniting theme for a wide array of groups: 'corporations are increasingly serving as the common thread by which labour, environmental and human rights violations can be stitched together into a single ideology' (Klein 2000: 266). These concerns have been given renewed impetus by a spate of board-level scandals in the USA, such as Enron, Tyco and WorldCom.

The most obvious manifestation of this concern is the emergence of the so-called 'anti-globalization movement'. The anti-globalization movement coheres around a shared disillusionment rather than specific concerns or proffered solutions. It is, in Lloyd's phrase, 'the critique without the antidote' (2001a: 25). Some within its ranks call for globalization to be reshaped, others for it to be resisted. More radical voices still question the entire basis of economic organization, predicting environmental disaster unless a profound shift in direction takes place; 'the profitable exchange of goods within the ship is a less urgent matter than how to keep the whole ship above water' (Midgley 2001: 97; Levett 2001). CSR is the means by which some businesses engage and connect with these movements and concerns.

Brands, boycotts and multinationals

For many multinationals, their key asset is the reputation of their brands; when Ford bought Jaguar, it was estimated that the physical assets were only 16 per cent of the value; when Vodafone bought Orange they were only 10 per cent (Bunting 2001). However, the icons of consumerism are also those that are most vulnerable to bad publicity. As Cowe and Williams argue, there 'appears to be a considerable latent interest across a broad swathe of the population, which can erupt against individual companies or on specific issues' (2000: 5). All companies trading with regimes incurring human rights abuses risk consumer boycott and opprobrium. As a consequence, *The Economist* argues, 'The more companies promote the value of their brands, the more they will need to be seen as ethically robust and environmentally pure' (2001a). For example, when Heineken pulled out of Burma in 1996, the CEO said: 'Public opinion and issues surrounding this market have changed to a degree that could have an adverse effect on our brand and corporate reputation' (cited in Klein 2000: 424).

The examples of companies affected by boycotts or threatened boycotts are many. Recently, PepsiCo, Phillips, C&A, Ralph Lauren, Motorola, Carlsberg and Kodak have been persuaded to sell their operations in Burma, fearing a damaging boycott if they did not do so; similarly, Kimberley Clark has been persuaded to sell off its tobacco operations (Heertz 2001). In Italy, Benetton was obliged to review its operations in Turkey following cases of child labour (Tsogas 2001). In the early 1990s, US citizens' groups organized a 'toycott' against Toys 'R' Us to protest against the use of child labour in China – the company has since endorsed a code prohibiting the use of child or slave labour by its contractors (Cavanaugh 1997). Starbucks announced a line of fair-trade certified coffee prior to a planned protest (Klein 2002). ExxonMobil has periodically been subject to international boycotts because of its policies and views on global warming.

Boycotts can extend beyond the products themselves. In 1998, Céline Dion's concert tour was picketed by human-rights activists in Boston, Philadelphia and Washington. Her sponsor, Ericsson, was among Burma's most important foreign investors, refusing to cease its dealings with the junta despite the campaign for an international boycott. According to Klein: 'when the brand-bashing moved beyond Ericsson proper and began to spill over onto Dion's diva image, it took only a week of protests to induce Ericsson to announce its withdrawal from Burma' (2000: 360). (It is noteworthy that the fair-trade movement itself uses forms of branding. Its logo signifies to the consumer that the product has met certain environmental and social standards.)

The Internet, part of the communications revolution aspect of globalization, has significantly amplified the speed and potential power of consumer protests. The 'internet nakedness', to use Carmichael's term (2001), of companies means that behaviour previously hidden in far-flung corners of the globe can now be used to confront Western consumers at their desks or in their homes. The rise of the Internet makes direct access to large international audiences possible at fairly low costs. The British 'McLibel' case, where McDonald's sued two unemployed environmental activists for a libellous leaflet, led to far greater (adverse) attention to McDonald's activities than if the company had decided not to sue. Before McDonald's decided to sue, only a few hundred copies of the leaflet involved in the dispute had been distributed. It has now been translated into 26 languages as well as being the subject of documentaries, books, websites and a mountain of journalism (Vidal 1997). Nike too has been affected by a (less dramatic) instance of negative publicity through the Internet. In 2001, Jonah Perretti, a student at the Massachusetts Institute of Technology, responded to Nike's offer to personalize customers' trainers by asking for the word 'sweatshop' to be printed on the side. When Nike refused, Mr Perretti e-mailed the company saying: 'Thank you for the time and energy you have spent on my request. Could you please send me a color snapshot of the 10 year old Vietnamese girl who makes my shoes?' His e-mail exchange with Nike was flashed around the world.

The limits to this form of pressure upon corporations are well known. As Klein notes 'the most significant limitation of brand-based campaigns [is that] they can be powerless in the face of corporations that opt out of the branding game' (2000: 424). Second, applying pressure through consumption skews power to wealthier consumers: 'Rather than empowering all, consumer and shareholder activism empowers those with greater purchasing power and those with an ability to change their patterns of consumption with relative ease. It is a form of protest that favours the middle class – an expression of the dissatisfactions of the bourgeoisie' (Heertz 2001).

The countervailing power of non-governmental organizations

Arguably, the rise in the power of corporations has been mirrored by the growth in the number and influence of NGOs, some of which are also global actors (notably the International Red Cross, Greenpeace International and Amnesty International) and which can apply pressure on businesses to make policies that are socially and environmentally responsible. The growth in the size, number and influence of NGOs is striking. The Fairtrade Foundation's logo was harmonized among 17 countries, so that by the end of 2003 all 'fair-trade' produce had the same logo. In 1975 there were 1,400 NGOs; by 1995 there were 28,900 (Hutton 2000). By 1990 more than a quarter of development aid was routed through NGOs. Greenpeace grew from having 800,000 members in 1985 to 2.5 million in 1990 (Lloyd 2001a). The WTO ministerial meeting attracted 100 NGOs in 1996; three years later in Seattle there were over 1,000. Surveys find that NGOs command far greater public trust in industrialized countries than do governments, companies and the media (Jonquieres 2000). It is argued that they have emerged as a result 'of the frustrations brought about by existing institutional structures' (McIntosh et al. 2003: 69).

NGOs themselves are characterized by high levels of diversity in size, aims and nature (as McIntosh et al. 2003 argue, the term embraces the Ku Klux Klan and Al Qaeda as well as Save the Children). They can persuade transnational corporations to become better global citizens – mobilizing consumers to act as a potentially powerful check upon the actions of transnationals 'shaping the rules and norms of business behaviour' (McIntosh et al. 2003). A key role that some NGOs are playing is in the development, administration and promotion of standards, codes and certifications. NGOs have played a major role in development and monitoring of many codes, including the influential SA8000 (discussed in the following section), the Apparel Industry Partnership and the Fair Labor Association in the USA and the Fairtrade Foundation and Ethical Trading Initiative in the UK (Tsogas 2001). Similarly, the code on child labour drafted by Unicef, the ILO and an association of Pakistani manufacturers was signed by all the major soccer-ball manufacturers; it provides for outside monitoring as well as education and rehabilitation for the child labourers (Klein 2000: 432). NGOs like Amnesty International have also been involved in the training of senior staff in multinationals (Finch 2002). Partnerships between NGOs and businesses have seen the New York based Rainforest Alliance (RA) provide CSR information for, and on, Chiquita Brands International, as well as verifying whether the latter's 115 farms meet RA standards (Silver 2004); interestingly, the cost of bringing the farms up to RA standards ($20 million) has already been more than repaid by cost savings on lower pesticide spending, recycling and a lower investment risk rating.

Codes of conduct: mandatory or voluntary?

One of the key developments of the burgeoning CSR debate is the growth of codes of conduct among companies. Generally developed in response to particular crises in supply chains, codes of conduct are written statements of principle or policy intended to serve as the expression of a commitment to particular business conduct. Most of the codes that have propelled the topic into the spotlight are operational codes – that is, codes that enterprises apply to themselves and their business partners to set out commitments to a specific conduct (Diller 1999). They can be distinguished from model codes that are generic statements issued by a body such as an international agency or NGO that forms the basis for firms to devise their own codes. By showing efforts to improve workplace conditions, businesses seek to pre-empt consumer boycotts as well as accusations of unacceptable or illegal business practices: 'Such efforts may also obviate the need for government regulation by demonstrating that industry best practice satisfies the public interest' (Diller 1999).

However, the content, distribution and purpose of these codes has been widely criticized. Hepple (2002) found: the choice of labour issues was highly selective; that codes were made unilaterally without the involvement of trade unions; implementation and monitoring were poor; and sanctions for non-compliance were weak. According to Klein:

'without exception, they were drafted by public relations departments in cities like New York and San Francisco in the immediate aftermath of an embarrassing media investigation ... Their original purpose was not reform but to "muzzle the offshore watchdog" groups, as Alan Rolnick, lawyer for the American Apparel Manufacturers Association, advised his clients.' (2000: 430)

Codes of conduct raise an array of issues including: availability and access; sufficient translation – Klein (2000) berates Shell for failing to translate its manifesto, 'Profits and Principles', into any language other than English and Dutch and attacks The Gap for having codes that, until 1998, were only available in English; the distribution of codes to the relevant workers; the (independent) monitoring of codes (often through all the layers of contracting and subcontracting); and enforcement and sanctions in the event of breaches of the code as workers may have no way of 'reporting non-compliance without risking disciplinary treatment or dismissal' (Diller 1999). The monitoring of codes by large accounting firms has been particularly controversial, especially after the Enron crisis, because of perceived conflict of interest problems; similar concerns are expressed on internal monitoring (Tsogas 2001; Klein 2002; Kolk and van Tulder 2002).

The content of codes also varies markedly. An ILO review of 215 codes, focusing on coverage of labour practices, found 'significant discrepancies' in content and operation between them. Occupational health and safety was the most cited labour issue, appearing in 75 per cent of the codes reviewed. Discrimination in hiring and terms and conditions were addressed in 66 per cent of the codes. The elimination of child labour (including refusing to use it or other companies that do use it) appeared in 45 per cent of the codes, the level of wages appeared in 40 per cent while prevention of using or refusal to use forced labour appeared in only 25 per cent of the codes. The principles of freedom of association and collective bargaining appeared in only 15 per cent (Diller 1999). According to Diller, 'the content of codes often appears to be largely decided in non-transparent and non-participatory processes, which may be conducted within executive boardrooms or through ad hoc negotiations between parties with varying degrees of access to information and bargaining power' (1999). Furthermore, most 'codes and labelling programmes tend to reflect their drafters' own definitions of what the desired improvements in labour practices should be'

(Diller 1999). Some codes, for example those of Caterpillar and Sara Lee Knit Products, favour the elimination of trade union activities.[6] Similarly, McDonald's corporate social responsibility report was, for example, not subject to independent verification and 'is short on numbers and contains almost no data that allows comparison with past performance' and makes no reference to trade unions and collective bargaining (Maitland 2002). In the UK the clothing retailer C&A left the Ethical Trading Initiative (ETI), 'finding the commitment to freedom of association and collective bargaining in contradiction with its own anti-union practice' (Tsogas 2001: 72). Few codes reiterated all internationally recognized grounds of discrimination and child labour.[7]

Poor monitoring of existing codes (and wider transparency) has been widely criticized (Elliot and Freeman 2003). Thus, in their examination of the sporting goods industry, Tulder and Kolk (2001) found underdeveloped compliance mechanisms among some major firms and the sanctions for non-observance of codes were generally not made clear.

The SA8000 code is an effort to introduce some consistency and rigour into codes. It was drafted by the Council on Economic Priorities Accreditation Agency (CEPAA), a consumer watchdog in New York, along with several large corporations, NGOs and trade unions. A private auditing company inspects factories for adherence to a set of standards covering key issues such as health, safety, overtime, child labour, and so on. Those factories that meet the code are certified as 'SA8000' (SA stands for social accountability). Under this model, brand-name multinationals like Avon and Toys 'R' Us, rather than trying to enforce their own codes around the world (these include core ILO codes and 'a living wage'), simply place their orders with factories that have been found to comply with the SA8000 code (Tsogas 2001).

The voluntary nature of codes of conduct is to many businesses a less threatening alternative to externally imposed regulation. According to the *Journal of Commerce*, 'the voluntary code helps diffuse a contentious issue in international trade negotiations: whether to make labour standards part of trade agreements. If ... the sweatshop problem is solved outside the trade context, labour standards will no longer be in the hands of protectionists' (cited in Klein 2000: 437). Although many businesses argue that the abundance of codes gives them the flexibility to ensure reporting is appropriate to each individual business, the proliferation of codes and wide variation in their content has come under growing criticism. One senior corporate executive stated that 'private fixing and imposition of standards can be haphazard and ultimately discriminatory' (cited in House of Commons 1999: 7). It also makes it 'virtually

---

[6] The code for Sara Lee Knit Products reads: 'The company believes in a union-free environment except where the laws and cultures require [it] to do otherwise ... [and] believes that employees themselves are best able to voice their concerns directly to management.'

[7] ILO Convention 138, ratified by 89 countries, sets the minimum age for work in developed countries at 15 for full-time employment, 13 for light work, and 14 and 12 as optional limits for some developing countries. It is one of the ILO's core conventions and widely used in codes of conduct to define child labour (Save the Children 2000).

impossible to compare and benchmark corporate social and environmental perform-ance' (Doane 2002). Furthermore, following a survey, the Institute of Business Ethics argues that such codes are not often 'active documents, but lie dormant in company filing cabinets' (cited in Heertz 2001).

These failings have in turn led to the call for more mandatory approaches (Christian Aid 2004). Some legislative provisions already exist. The USA has statutory provisions banning the import of goods manufactured by prison labour and by indentured (bonded) child labour (House of Commons 1999). The USA also has pro-cedures under its amended Section 301 of the 1974 Trade Act whereby it can impose import restrictions on countries failing to respect internationally recognized workers' rights (although its deployment has been used to further foreign policy aims, as against Nicaragua, rather than to enhance labour reforms). The governments of EU countries have a power of whole or partial withdrawal of trading, exercisable only in relation to forced or prison labour, and currently deployed against Myanmar (Burma) (House of Commons 1999).

Nike

Perhaps more than any other multinational, Nike has been the subject of enormous controversy surrounding its employment practices. Many observers have contrasted the firm's payments to stars who endorse the products with the wages earned by those engaged in producing them. For example, the basketball player Michael Jordan earned more ($20 million) in 1992 for endorsing Nike's running shoes than Nike's entire 30,000 strong Indonesian workforce for making them (Ross 1997). The company has also been severely embarrassed by the publication of images of such things as a young Pakistani boy sewing together a Nike football and of reports claiming that workers in one of its contracted factories in Vietnam were being exposed to toxic fumes at up to 177 times the Vietnamese legal limit (Wazir 2001).

Dogged by allegations of this sort, in May 1998 Nike's CEO, Phillip Knight, told an audience that 'Nike has become synonymous with slave wages, forced overtime and arbitrary abuse' (cited in McCawley 2000). Knight committed the company to act in a responsible manner and made a number of specific promises concerning the treatment of workers in the subcontracted production operations, mainly in South-East Asia. These commitments became part of the firm's Code of Conduct which states that:

'Nike is committed to being a responsible corporate citizen. We work strenuously to improve the lives and working conditions of all workers. We don't own these factories, but we take pride in our relationships with them.'

Among the specific promises that it makes are the following:

- The minimum age will be raised to 18 for workers in Nike shoe factories and 16 for those in clothing factories;
- The contractor will provide each employee with at least the minimum wage, or the prevailing industry wage, whichever is higher, and will not deduct from employee pay for disciplinary infractions;

● The contractor will comply with legally mandated work hours, provide for one day off in seven and require no more than 60 hours of work per week on a regularly scheduled basis (or comply with local limits if they are lower);

● Nike will include non-governmental organizations in factory monitoring, and the company will make inspection results public.

Some observers argue that the Nike Code of Conduct ensures that workers are not exploited, especially when one considers that many of those employed in 'sweatshops' have left even harder, lower-paying jobs in agriculture to move to garment factories. This argument is often used to make the case against boycotts of Nike and other MNCs; it is argued that such boycotts will only force the employees into less favourable forms of work, prostitution or poverty. The defenders of Nike also make the point that a consumer can have no idea about the conditions in the production of unbranded goods and thus the brand is a safeguard that can be used to check the company's actions. Others are less convinced of the impact of the firm's Code of Conduct in particular or the benefits it brings to local communities in general. For instance, a report entitled 'Still Waiting For Nike To Do It', published by the San Francisco-based Global Exchange, argues that the Code of Conduct has been of 'little benefit to Nike workers' or that its provisions 'have helped only a tiny minority, or else have no relevance to Nike factories at all' (quoted in Wazir 2001). The report also indicates that in many Nike factories the employees are still being coerced into working up to 70 hours per week and are being humiliated in front of other workers or threatened with dismissal if they refuse to do the extra work. 'During the last three years, Nike has continued to treat the sweatshop issue as a public relations inconvenience rather than as a serious human rights matter,' said Leila Salazar, corporate accountability director for Global Exchange (Wazir 2001).

Whether you think that Nike takes its responsibilities to those involved in the production process seriously enough or not, the organization's experience 'provides a vivid illustration of the perils facing companies that believe they can ignore the effects of campaigning organizations' (Skapinker 2002).

Case study question: *What is the potential for the HR function in organizations like Nike to play a part in the company's desire to be seen as a good corporate citizen?*

Labelling initiatives and socially responsible investment

Similar but less widespread than codes of conduct is the development of labelling programmes. These act as verification tools for CSR by using a highly visible means of communication – a physical label as to the social conditions surrounding the production of the good. Labels show symbols or logos that seek to differentiate the product. Some social label initiatives have high NGO involvement, notably that of the Fairtrade Foundation which was set up by CAFOD (Catholic Agency for Overseas Development), Christian Aid, Oxfam and Traidcraft. A similar selectivity in the areas covered by codes (though less stark) was also found in the labelling programmes examined by the ILO (Diller 1999). Labelling schemes 'remain rare, and are generally narrowly focused on selected products, countries and issues – particularly child labour. There are difficulties over the potential proliferation of labels, their genuineness and practicalities of conveying worthwhile information on a product such as a vest or a football' (House of Commons 1999: 12).

Socially responsible investment (SRI) has grown rapidly in many developed countries. SRI 'generally indicates investment-related decisions that seek social change while maintaining economic returns' (Diller 1999). SRI initiatives take two main forms: first, through investment fund screening (the inclusion or exclusion of a firm in investment portfolios based on 'ethical' criteria); or second, through shareholder initiatives where shareholders act to change corporate behaviour. Thus, for example, the Church of England sold its shares in GKN in 2000 on the grounds that the engineering company's sale of weapons to foreign regimes was unacceptable (Clark 2000).

The problems of corporate social responsibility: 'greenwash' and 'corporate gloss'

There has been widespread criticism of the actual practice of CSR as undertaken by some businesses. There is a real danger that 'socially responsible' policies could be a form of 'greenwashing' or 'corporate gloss' – where, hiding behind a superficially responsible screen, corporations can abuse their power. According to Hutton 'nearly every company pays lip service to this new cultural business exigency, but very few take it seriously, instead believing it can be discharged through better public relations or tokenistic nods towards what most directors see as little more than politically correct behaviour with little value' (2000: 1).

Some tentative, emerging empirical evidence seems to confirm Hutton's analysis. The contribution of the leading 400 UK companies of pre-tax profits to the (UK) community essentially remained the same between 1990 and 2001 – at a modest 0.42 per cent (Benjamin 2002). Recent research (cited in Doane 2002) found that while 79 of the FTSE100 published some social information on their website, only 16 companies used any qualitative performance data to support their policy assertions. The lack of hard data is prevalent even where it should be relatively easy to obtain. Thus 'only ten of the FTSE100 report data on the ethnic diversity of their workforce and none provide quantitative data on child labour in their supply chain or on workdays lost through stress' (Joseph 2002). Few reports – the accountants KPMG (in 1999) estimated that one in six – were checked by third parties for accuracy and 'where they are it tends to be the data collection processes rather than the end results that are audited' (Joseph 2002). According to Doane (2002) 'while some companies utilise the accounting sector to provide a statement of verification for the contents of a report, these loose statements do little to provide assurance that the report is accurate. For example, it is common practice for a verification statement to ignore what has not been included in the report.'[8] Moreover, a survey by PricewaterhouseCoopers found

---

[8] This in turn raises the wider issue of whether interested parties have a formal method of redress if they believe the published information to be a misrepresentation.

that nearly 30 per cent of chief executives tend to agree that CSR is mainly a public relations issue (cited in CIPD 2002).

There are also some striking examples of the lack of sufficient attention to CSR principles. Enron notoriously promoted its CSR credentials while internally betraying them. The DIY chain B&Q was accused of spending more on advertising a charity initiative than on the project itself (Pickard 2002). Perhaps the example provided by Klein is the most vivid:

'During the 1997–98 academic year, elementary school students in more than eight hundred classrooms across the US sat down at their desks to find that today's lesson was building a Nike sneaker, complete with a swoosh and an endorsement from an NBA star … the make-your-own Nike exercise purports to raise awareness about the company's environmentally sensitive production process. Nike's claim to greenness relies heavily on the fact that the company recycles old sneakers to recover community centre basketball courts, which … it then brands with the Nike swoosh.' (2000: 93)

More recently, the CSR debate has been complicated by concerns that while charitable donations have been increasing, firms are increasingly adept at exploiting loopholes to minimize their tax burden (Teather 2004; Cowe 2004b). Controversy has also arisen by the decision of major coffee producers, including Kraft Foods, Lavazza and Lyons, to shun the more demanding certification requirements of the world's leading certification body, the Fairtrade Foundation, in favour of the less stringent criteria of the New York based Rainforest Alliance (McAllister 2004). Doane argues 'the market does not provide sufficient incentives for companies to report on their social and environmental impacts on a voluntary basis' (2002) and calls, with others (for example, Henriques 1999; Christian Aid 2004), for a shift to a more mandatory basis to surmount the difficulties currently experienced. There is also, sometimes, an absence of measures that accurately capture performance and that can be applied across organizations (ideally across sectors and geographic boundaries) (Joseph 2002).

Labour regulation in a global economy

Opinion is sharply divided on the impact of multinationals in their use of labour. For example, many multinationals are accused of being anti-union. The relative absence of freedom of association and collective bargaining rights from codes of conduct has been noted (Diller 1999; Tsogas 2001). Starbucks has been accused of shutting down plants after they had unionized (Klein 2000). In 1995, The Gap's clothes were revealed to have been made in a factory in El Salvador where the manager responded to a union drive by firing 150 people and vowing that 'blood will flow' if organizing continued (Klein 2000: 327). McDonald's was revealed (in San Francisco 1974) to have used lie detectors to ask about employees' union sympathies (cited in Vidal 1997). McDonald's also employed (in the 1970s) John Cooke to keep trade unions out of the company. He stated, 'unions are inimical to what we stand for and how we operate'. The official history of McDonald's, 'Behind the Arches', states that of the 400 serious organization attempts in the early 1970s, none was successful. McDonald's set up a 'flying squad' of experienced managers who were dispatched to restaurants as soon as word was received of attempts to unionize (cited in Vidal 1997: 230). Royle cites a McDonald's (1985) memo for recruitment used in Germany. Managers were asked to ascertain whether the applicant had any membership or interest in a trade union. If so, the interviewing manager should: '...bring the interview to a close after a few additional questions and tell the applicant he will receive a reply in a few days ... of course the applicant should in no circumstances be employed' (2000: 97).

The treatment of employees more generally has also been a focus of concern. Significant levels of verbal abuse and sexual harassment were found in all nine of Nike's Indonesian factories (Skapinker 2002). Another sportswear maker, Reebok, also found poor working conditions in its Indonesians factories (Griffith 1999). The Gap has been criticized on health and safety standards, poor working conditions and low pay (Lawrence 2002). Serious sexual discrimination has been alleged; Klein cites General Motors which, in its Mexican operations, stated that it 'will not hire female job applicants found to be pregnant' in order to avoid 'substantial financial liabilities imposed by the Mexican social security system' (2000: 23).

Commentators like Legrain (2002) argue that the benefits of multinationals to developing economies (the transfer of technology and management skills in particular) are substantial and ignored by critics, that wage rates paid by firms like Nike are far higher than the legal minimum wage in foreign factories and that labour turnover can be low. According to *The Economist,* 'it is the branded multinationals that pay the best wages and have the best working conditions' (2001b). Similarly, Wolf maintains that 'TNCs pay higher wages and offer better training than domestic companies' (2003). But even these perspectives concede that working conditions have improved since they 'became the target of activists campaigns' and that prior to these, in Nike plants for example, 'workers were forced to jog round the factory and lick the floor, and were hit with shoe parts' (Legrain 2002: 59). It is questionable whether Nike and other multinationals would have embarked on improving and monitoring the working conditions of their contractors were it not for the activities of trade unions and NGOs in highlighting these issues.

Countries like the USA do have trade policies that set standards in the areas of animals, ivory and prison labour (Ross 1997). In June 1999 President Clinton ordered that in future federal contractors would be obliged to certify that neither forced nor indentured child labour is used to produce the goods they vend (Save the Children 2000). The Fairtrade movement explicitly links labour standards and trade. However, the broader issue of linking trade to labour standards is highly controversial. Organizations such as the WTO contend that such regulation would impair markedly the attractiveness of developing countries to inward investment. In some areas, notably child labour, some international norms have secured widespread international acceptance, such as the ILO conventions on child labour (Save the Children 2000). It is thus possible that more piecemeal international labour regulation could secure legitimacy; indeed the case for such standards is gathering sophistication (Elliot and Freeman 2003; Palley 2004; CAFOD 2004).

Conclusion

CSR is a nascent, evolving, disputed but influential concept. Although a definitive definition remains elusive, a common element is an awareness that business operates in a wider community and that its future interests are bound up with that community. It is also a concept that has rapidly acquired a high public profile, partly in the wake of trends such as globalization, greater corporate power (and the issues this raises) and diminishing government intervention. In a wider climate of corporate distrust, CSR is a useful tool in engaging with the concerns of employees, customers and interest groups. This is especially important for 'brands' whose reputation can be tarnished by consumer boycotts or NGO campaigns. HRM plays a key, sometimes central, role in issues raised by CSR, as many CSR issues having a strong labour/employment relations aspect. Labour issues are important to most codes of conduct. HRM skills can also be crucial to the implementation of CSR strategies, and thus to wider corporate legitimacy and accountability.

The actual practice of CSR is distinctly uneven. Criticisms of 'corporate gloss' or public relations are often well founded. In part, this may be because CSR is still in its infancy. Although codes of conduct and other forms of voluntary regulation have proliferated, the limits and weaknesses of such regulation have led in turn to calls for an extension of mandatory regulation. However, while it seems unlikely that such calls will have anything more than a piecemeal international impact, within specific countries and/or regions the potential of such measures is much more significant.

Review questions

1 What are the main areas of a firm's business that 'CSR' can cover?

2 How can the HR function use the interest on the part of senior management in CSR to its advantage?

3 What is distinctive about the international dimension to CSR initiatives?

4 On balance, what does the experience of companies that have engaged with CSR tell us about how much difference it makes to the behaviour of firms?

Further reading

Christian Aid (2004) 'Behind the Mask: The Real Face of Corporate Social Responsibility', accessible at http://www.christian-aid.org.uk/news/media

> This provides a vigorous critique of the actual practice of CSR. Several case studies are used to argue that the claims made by some firms mask inaction or limited action. It attacks the voluntary approach, calling for mandatory regulation of transnationals.

CIPD (Chartered Institute of Personnel and Development) (2002) *Corporate Social Responsibility*, Autumn, London: CIPD.

> This provides an overview of the issue, with particular attention to the implications of CSR for HR staff and departments.

Elliot, A.K. and Freeman, R.B. (2003) *Can Labor Standards Improve Under Globalisation?* Washington, DC: Institute for International Economics.

> This is a broad examination of a range of issues around labour standards, including the role of codes of conduct and the ILO. Detailed case studies are examined.

Kolk, A. and van Tulder, R. (2002) 'The Effectiveness of Self-regulation: Corporate Codes of Conduct and Child Labour', *European Management Journal*, 20(3), 260–71.

> This article is a case study examining how some leading multinationals deal with the complex and emotive issue of child labour through codes of conduct and the issues raised by their approaches.

References

Benjamin, A. (2002) 'Still Less Than Half Per Cent' in *The Giving List*, *Guardian* supplement, 25 November.

Brundtland, G. (1987) *Our Common Future*, Oxford: Oxford University Press.

Buckley, S. (2002) 'All Sweetness and Light at the Co-op', *Financial Times*, 26 November.

Bunting, M. (2001) 'The New Gods', *Guardian*, 9 July.

CAFOD (Catholic Agency for Overseas Development) (2004) 'The Rough Guide to Labour Standards', accessible at http://www.cafod.org.uk

Carmichael, S. (2001) 'Accounting for Ethical Business' in T. Bentley and D. Stedman Jones (eds) *The Moral Universe*, Winter, London: Demos.

Cavanaugh, J. (1997) 'The Global Resistance to Sweatshops' in A. Ross (ed.) *No Sweat: Fashion, Free Trade and the Rights of Garment Workers*, London: Verso.

Christian Aid (2004) 'Behind the Mask: The Real Face of Corporate Social Responsibility', accessible at http://www.christian-aid.org.uk/news/media

Cicutti, N. (2002) 'Pension Funds Fail to Invest Ethically', *Financial Times*, 15 July.

CIPD (Chartered Institute of Personnel and Development) (2002) *Corporate Social Responsibility*, Autumn, London: CIPD.

Clark, A. (2000) 'Church is Dumping GKN', *Guardian*, 21 November.

Cowe, R. (2000) 'Ford Puts Clean-Cut Image Into Reverse', *Guardian*, 25 November.

Cowe, R. (2004a) 'Transparency Issue Can Be Easily Clouded', *Financial Times*, 29 November.

Cowe, R. (2004b) 'Tax Avoidance Is Rising Up the Ethical Agenda', *Financial Times*, 29 November.

Cowe, R. and Williams, S. (2000) *Who Are the Ethical Consumers?* London: Co-operative Bank.

Crawford, R. (2000) 'Adidas's Human Rights Policy Back on Track', *Financial Times*, 21 December

DeLillo, D. (1998) *Underworld*, London: Picador.

Denny, C. (2002a) 'Nestlé Claims £3.7m From Famine-Hit Ethiopia', *Guardian*, 19 December.

Denny, C. (2002b) 'Nestlé to Plough Debt Back into Ethiopia', *Guardian*, 23 December.

Denny, C. (2003) 'Nestlé U-Turn on Ethiopia Debt', *Guardian*, 24 January.

Dickens, C. (1854, 1995) *Hard Times*, London: Penguin Books.

Diller, J. (1999) 'A Social Conscience in the Global Marketplace? Labour Dimensions of Codes of Conduct, Social Labelling and Investor Initiatives', *International Labour Review*, 138(2).

Doane, D. (2001) *Taking Flight: The Rapid Growth of Ethical Consumerism*, London: New Economics Foundation.

Doane, D. (2002) *Market Failure: The Case For Mandatory Social and Environmental Reporting*, London: Institute for Public Policy Research (IPPR).

Donkin, R. (2001) *Blood, Sweat and Tears*, London: Texere Publishing.

Eaglesham, J. (2002) 'Green Groups Say Ministers Bow to Industry Demands', *Financial Times*, 26 November.

Economist (2001a) 'The Case For Brands', 8 September.

Economist (2001b) 'Who's Wearing the Trousers?', 8 September.

Elliot, A.K. and Freeman, R.B. (2003) *Can Labor Standards Improve Under Globalisation?* Washington, DC: Institute for International Economics.

Elliot, L. and Denny, C. (2003) 'New Issues', *Guardian*, 8 September.

Fairtrade Foundation (2000) *Unpeeling the Banana Trade*, London at http://www.fairtrade.org.uk

Fairtrade Foundation (2002) *Spilling the Beans on the Coffee Trade*, London at http://www.fairtrade.org.uk

Faux, J. and Mishel, L. (2000) 'Inequality and the Global Economy' in W. Hutton and A. Giddens (eds) *On The Edge*, London: Jonathan Cape.

Finch, J. (2002) 'Norsk Hydro Makes Rights Its Business', *Guardian*, 20 March.

Frank, T. (2002) *One Market under God*, London: Vintage.

Friedman, J. (1999) 'Why Companies Should Care About Conflict' in M. McIntosh (ed.) *Visions of Ethical Business*, London: Financial Times Prentice Hall.

Friedman, M. (1973) 'The Social Responsibility of Business Is To Increase Its Profits', in G.D. Chryssides and J.H. Kaler (eds) (1993) *An Introduction to Business Ethics*, London: Thomson Business Press.

Griffith, V. (1999) 'US Students To Campaign Over Sweatshops', *Financial Times*, 19 October.

Hardt, M. (2002) 'Today's Bandung?', *New Left Review*, March–April.

Heertz, N. (2001) *The Silent Takeover*, London: Heinemann.

Henderson, D. (2001) *Misguided Virtue, False Notions of Corporate Social Responsibility*, London: Institute of Economic Affairs.

Henriques, A. (1999) 'Opening Up For Business: The Logic of Legislation' in M. McIntosh (ed.), *Visions of Ethical Business*, London: Financial Times Prentice Hall.

Hepple, B. (ed.) (2002) 'Enforcement: The Law and Politics of Cooperation and Compliance', in *Social and Labour Rights in a Global Context*, Cambridge: Cambridge University Press.

Holmberg, J. and Sandbrook, R. (1992) 'Sustainable Development: What Is To Be Done?' in J. Holmberg (ed.) *Policies for a Small Planet*, London: Earthscan.

House of Commons, Trade and Industry Select Committee (1999) *Ethical Trading*, Sixth report, London: The Stationery Office (TSO).

Howard, M. and Willmot, M. (2001) 'Ethical Consumption in the Twenty-first Century', in T. Bentley and D. Stedman Jones (eds) *The Moral Universe*, London: Demos.

Hutton, W. (1995) *The State We're In*, London: Jonathan Cape.

Hutton, W. (2000) *Society Bites Back: The Good Enterprise, the Purposeful Consumer and the Just Workplace*, London: The Industrial Society.

IRS (2001) *Businesses Behaving Responsibly*, Employment Review, London: IRS, No. 739, 6–11.

Jonquieres, G. (2000) 'NGOs In Winning Battle To Sway Opinion', *Financial Times*, 6 December.

Joseph, E. (2001) 'Corporate Social Responsibility – Delivering the New Agenda', *New Economy*, 8(2), 121–23.

Joseph, E. (2002) 'Promoting Corporate Social Responsibility', *New Economy*, 9(2), 96–101.

Joseph, E. and Parkinson, J. (2002) 'Confronting the critics', paper for the Institute of Public Policy Research (IPPR) debate, London, 18 January.

Klein, N. (2000) *No Logo*, London: Flamingo.

Klein, N. (2002) *Fence and Windows*, London: Flamingo.

Kolk, A. and van Tulder, R. (2002) 'The Effectiveness of Self-regulation: Corporate Codes of Conduct and Child Labour', *European Management Journal*, 20(3), 260–71.

Korten, D.C. (1995) *When Corporations Rule the World*, London: Earthscan.

Kuttner, R. (1997) *Everything for Sale*, New York: Alfred A. Knopf.

Lawrence, F. (2002) 'Sweatshop Campaigners Demand Gap Boycott', *Guardian*, 22 November.

Legrain, P. (2002) *Open World: The Truth About Globalisation*, London: Abacus.

Levett, R. (2001) 'Sustainable Development and Capitalism', *Renewal*, 9(2/3), 59–72.

Lloyd, J. (2000) 'Cultivating the World', *Financial Times*, 20 September.

Lloyd, J. (2001a) *The Protest Ethic*, London: Demos.

Lloyd, J. (2001b) 'The New Deal', *Prospect*, December.

Luttwak, E. (1996) *Turbo Capitalism: Winners and Losers in the Global Economy*, Austin, TX: Texere Publishing.

Maitland, A. (2002) 'McDonald's Responds To Anti-Capitalist Calling', *Financial Times*, 15 April.

Maitland, A. (2003) 'Tools To Build a Reputation', *Financial Times*, 20 January.

Maitland, A. (2004) 'Problem That Is Gaining Higher Political Profile', *Financial Times*, 29 November.

Marquand, D. (1997) *The New Reckoning; Capitalism, States and Citizens*, Oxford: Polity Press.

McAllister, S. (2004) 'Who Is The Fairest Of Them All?' *Guardian*, 24 November.

McCawley, T. (2000) 'Racing To Improve Its Reputation', *Financial Times*, 21 December.

McIntosh, M., Leipzieger, D., Jones, J. and Coleman, G. (1998) *Corporate Citizenship*, Harlow: Financial Times Pitman Publishing.

McIntosh, M., Thomas, R., Leipzieger, D. and Coleman, G. (2003) *Living Corporate Citizenship*, Harlow: Financial Times Prentice Hall.

McNulty, S. (2003) 'The Oil Company the Greens Love To Hate', *Financial Times*, 11 June.

Midgley, M. (2001) 'Individualism and the Concept of Gaia' in T. Bentley and D. Stedman Jones (eds) *The Moral Universe*, Winter, London: Demos.

Monbiot, G. (2000) *Captive State: The Corporate Takeover of Britain*, London: Macmillan.

Murray, S. (2002) 'The Rapid Rise of a New Responsibility', *Financial Times*, 11 June.

Palley, T.I. (2004) 'The Economic Case for International Labour Standards', *Cambridge Journal of Economics*, 28(1), January, 21–36.

Pickard, J. (2002) 'B&Q Attacked Over Charity Project Adverts', *Financial Times*, 9 March.

Ross, A. (1997) 'Introduction' in A. Ross (ed.) *No Sweat: Fashion, Free Trade and the Rights of Garment Workers*, London: Verso.

Royle, T. (2000) *Working for McDonald's in Europe*, London: Routledge.

Ruskin, J. (1862, 2000) *Unto This Last*, Nelson: Hendon Publishing Co.

Sachdev, S. (2001) *Contracting Culture: from CCT to PPPs*, London: Unison.

Sassoon, D. (1996) *One Hundred Years of Socialism*, London: I.B. Tauris.

Save the Children (2000) *Big Business, Small Hands*, London: Save the Children.

Schlosser, E. (2001) *Fast Food Nation*, London: Allen Lane.

Segal, J.P, Sobczak, A. and Triomphe, C.E. (2003) *Corporate Social Responsibility and Working Conditions*, Dublin: European Foundation for the Improvement of Living and Working Conditions.

Sen, A. (1996) 'Social Commitment and Democracy: The Demands of Equity and Financial Conservatism' in P. Barker (ed.) *Living as Equals*, Oxford: Oxford University Press.

Shell (2001) *People, Planets and Projects*, London: Shell.

Sikka, P. (2004) 'Revelation, Chapter One', *The Giving List*, *Guardian* Supplement, 8 November.

Silver, S. (2004) 'How To Grow a Good Name In Green Bananas', *Financial Times*, 26 November.

Skapinker, M. (2002) 'Why Nike Has Broken Into a Sweat', *Financial Times*, 7 March.

Spence, L. (2000) 'What Ethics In The Employment Interview?' in D. Winstanley and J. Woodall (eds) *Ethical Issues in Contemporary Human Resource Management*, London: Macmillan.

Stanworth, C. (2000) 'Flexible Working Patterns' in D. Winstanley and J. Woodall (eds) *Ethical Issues in Contemporary Human Resource Management*, London: Macmillan.

Stiglitz, J. (2002) *Globalization and its Discontents*, London: Allen Lane.

Teather, D. (2004) 'Gap Year', *The Giving List*, *Guardian* Supplement, 8 November.

Thompson, E.P. (1968) *The Making of the English Working Class*, London: Pelican.

Tsogas, G. (2001) *Labor Regulation in a Global Economy*, New York: M.E. Sharpe.

Tulder, R. and Kolk, A. (2001) 'Multinationality and Corporate Ethics: Codes of Conduct in the Sporting Goods Industry', *Journal of International Business Studies*, 32(2): 267–283.

Vidal, J. (1997) *McLibel: Burger Culture on Trial*, London: Pan.

Vidal, J. (2003) 'Fair Trade', *Guardian*, 8 September.

Wazir, B. (2001) 'Nike Accused of Tolerating Sweatshops', *Observer*, 20 May.

Wolf, M. (2002) 'Response to Confronting the Critics', paper for the Institute of Public Policy Research (IPPR) debate, London, 18 January.

Wolf, M. (2003) 'An Unfinished Revolution', *Financial Times World 2003* supplement, 23 January.

Woodall, J. and Douglas, D. (2000) 'Winning Hearts and Minds: Ethical Issues in Human Resource Development' in D. Winstanley and J. Woodall (eds) *Ethical Issues in Contemporary Human Resource Management*, London: Macmillan.

Part Four

The future

Chapter 14

Conclusions and looking ahead

Tony Edwards and Chris Rees

Introduction

This book has covered a number of aspects of the field of international human resource management (IHRM) with the primary focus being on the challenges facing multinational companies (MNCs) in managing an international workforce. In this concluding chapter we do not provide a summary of each of the chapters in turn, but rather pull together some of the key themes. We identify five of these and focus in particular on the final one, change, as it has relevance for future developments in the field.

Globalization

Globalization has become one of the most hotly debated topics of our time. Much of the controversy around globalization relates to whether its effects are positive or negative. For optimistic observers, globalization must bring net benefits to national economies since it allows countries to specialize in areas of relative strength and it entails spreading technologies and practices that have the potential to bring efficiency gains; if it did not bring such gains then governments, firms and individuals simply would not engage with it. For more pessimistic observers, globalization is not simply about free choices but rather it is about the strong exploiting the weak; global capital is becoming increasingly 'footloose' and is unconstrained in its ability to exploit unprotected and vulnerable workforces and communities.

Yet this debate about globalization's effects presupposes that it is a novel phenomenon. Thus a separate debate has centred on whether it is really occurring or not. There are certainly some indications that the international economy has become highly globalized: patterns of trade and foreign direct investment (FDI) have grown steadily over the last 60 years, both in value terms and as a proportion of gross domestic product (GDP); huge sums of money can be transferred instantly at very low cost from one side of the world to the other; travel and communication across countries have been revolutionized by technological developments; and international institutions, such as the World Trade Organization (WTO) and International Monetary Fund (IMF), have not only grown in influence but have also provided a firm underpinning to international economic activity that was lacking in previous periods. The result, from this perspective, is an unprecedented degree of globalization that has revolutionized our lives.

A counter-view plays down the extent to which contemporary developments are unprecedented. The sceptics of globalization argue that when judged in a long-term, historical context, the recent increases in FDI and trade are not that remarkable. Indeed, some aspects of internationalization indicate that previous periods were characterized by stronger linkages between countries, of which the higher levels of migration in the late nineteenth century compared with the late twentieth century is a prime example. In some ways, then, as Hirst and Thompson (1999) point out, the economy has become less globalized than it was in previous periods. Even in relation to those aspects of internationalization that have unquestionably grown in recent years, there is some dispute about whether the flows across countries warrant the term global. For example, many observers argue that international economic activity is concentrated within, and between, three areas of the world – North America, Europe and South-East Asia – and that regionalization is a more appropriate term to capture this development.

This debate has tended to become polarized with each side highlighting particular developments or phenomena that support their argument. We have tried to steer a 'middle course' that has adopted a balanced view of the evidence. In short, we have argued that cross-border flows of economic activity have become more important and that MNCs are increasingly adopting integrated modes of production or service provision. This theme was developed explicitly in Chapter 1 where we discussed the concept of globalization. It was then picked up in subsequent chapters: in Chapter 3, where we examined the motivation for the internationalization of the firm and debates about the extent to which MNCs have become globally oriented; in Chapter 4, where we investigated the structures and strategies that firms can pursue at the international level; in Chapter 5, which considered the increasingly important issue of the transfer of human resource (HR) practices across borders; and in Chapter 6, where we examined the issue of cross-border mergers and acquisitions.

Competitive challenges

If we accept the term globalization as shorthand for the growing linkages across borders, and especially the deepening of these linkages, then it follows that globalization is associated with a number of challenges. Some of these challenges relate to governments and their ability to control and regulate their national economy. There are certainly some signs of the state being more constrained in its ability to regulate in distinctive ways, such as the control of financial systems. In relation to the labour market, there are some indications of a move towards governments deregulating labour markets as a response to the concern of multinational capital moving to other countries. This is perhaps most notable in Germany where the government is push-ing ahead with a series of deregulatory measures.

However, the way in which globalization constrains the role of the state is often exaggerated. For instance, while financial flows across borders have become so large that governments' reserves of foreign currency look puny in comparison, national regulatory authorities still possess the ability to regulate the banking system in ways that differ markedly from their counterparts in other countries. Similarly, in the sphere of labour markets, laws and institutions at national level governing such issues as redundancy, employee representation and discrimination continue to vary in significant ways. Indeed, governments can collaborate to combat the pressures of globalization through constructing international institutions, something that we studied in depth in Chapter 12 on international employee representation.

The challenges of globalization are also felt at the level of the firm, of course. Included in these challenges are the opportunities that have resulted from dramatic changes to the economic and social systems in many countries over the last 20 years. The countries that were part of the former Soviet Union and those in central and east-ern Europe that were strongly influenced by it are no longer an isolated block of the world and are rapidly becoming integrated into the global economy. Similarly, China has undertaken a dramatic shift from being an isolated, state-controlled communist system to becoming an open, market-based system. For MNCs, there is obviously no obligation to operate in these countries but the attractions of cheap labour and poten-tially large consumer markets are inducing growing numbers to do so. As we saw in the case of China in Chapter 7, establishing sites in a rapidly evolving economy and inte-grating these into a firm's global operations brings with it a number of difficulties that are particularly acute in the field of human resource management (HRM).

The challenges to firms have come not only in the form of increasing their geo-graphic reach but also in the way that many MNCs have sought to achieve a higher degree of integration. This has implications for how firms: transfer knowledge across national borders, the topic of Chapter 8; develop international managers capable of managing integrated operations, something that was discussed in Chapter 9; and recruit and select international managers, an issue we considered in Chapter 10. In addition, much attention in this regard has focused on the structures and strategies that MNCs adopt to facilitate this integration. As we saw in Chapter 4, authors such as Bartlett and Ghoshal argue that the 'transnational' network-based form provides the 'solution' to the challenges of managing across borders. We also argued that this vision of how firms organize themselves plays down the political aspects of organizations and also pays insufficient attention to the way that MNCs are embedded in their country of origin.

Embeddedness

It is this notion of 'embeddedness' that is the third theme of the book that we wish to highlight. Despite the process of globalization, we know that economic activity is embedded in distinct settings. Throughout the book we have used the concept of a 'national business system' to understand the way that the contexts in which firms operate continue to differ, and we have highlighted the interaction between institutions in different spheres of the economy. The persistence of contrasting national business systems means that the contexts in which firms manage their workforces differ markedly. This was developed in some depth in Chapter 2.

The way that MNCs are embedded in the national business system of their country of origin is central to understanding how they manage their workforces across borders. Given that the vast majority of MNCs retain strong links with their country of origin, this embeddedness informs their management style in a range of ways, something that was developed explicitly in Chapters 3, 4, 5 and 6. The evidence relating to US MNCs, some of which we have reviewed in this book, demonstrates that there is a strong 'country of origin effect' in areas such as performance management, diversity and the handling of collective relations.

As the geographic spread of MNCs increases, the embeddedness in their original business system declines. As this tendency progresses, MNCs have more scope to tap into the distinctive expertise that is present in business systems besides their original one. Thus through the process of 'reverse diffusion' MNCs can draw on practices that are in place in their foreign subsidiaries and spread these around their international operations. More generally, a high geographic spread increases the range of expertise within the organization, creating strong incentives for knowledge to be transferred across borders. The process of transferring HR practices specifically and knowledge more generally is rarely straightforward, however, since it is heavily shaped and constrained by embeddedness, as we saw in Chapters 5 and 8.

One implication of the way that MNCs are embedded in distinct national contexts is that practices that are transferred across their sites will be amended as they are implemented in a new setting. This might be because of a conscious decision by management that for a practice to operate effectively it must be adapted to fit the distinctive context into which it is being transferred, or it might be that a practice is ostensibly the same as that in the unit in which it originated but in practice it operates significantly differently. We saw an illustration of this in the discussion of the performance management system in AutoPower in China in Chapter 7, and this was also a theme of Chapter 11 on international pay and reward. This process of 'hybridization' is evidence of the contested nature of transfer within MNCs.

Contestation

The transfer of HR practices within MNCs is far from being the only aspect of globalization that is contested. As we have already noted, the impact of globalization has been one of the most controversial social and political issues of our time. There are many groups that have gained materially from globalization – bureaucrats and politicians associated with international institutions, brokers and bankers involved with the international financial system, and the managers and executives of MNCs – and that are thus firm proponents of the benefits it brings. On the other hand, the so-called 'anti-globalization' protest groups that have organized rallies to coincide with

meetings of world leaders at various locations during the last few years are one manifestation of the opposition to this process, as are the boycotts and campaigns
organized against particular companies, such as Exxon and Nike, that have been
accused of harming their environment or exploiting their workforces. The response
of many companies has been to stress their socially responsible nature through
formal codes of conduct, a phenomenon we investigated in Chapter 13.

Most of our focus on the contested nature of globalization has been on the relationships between different groups within MNCs. All organizations are characterized
by political struggles, of course, but this is a particularly important aspect of MNCs.
Groups of organizational actors in different units of a multinational can derive some
influence within the wider company from the way that they control resources on
which other groups depend. Where these resources are something that is specific to a
national business system, the influence of the group in question is enhanced. At a
number of points in the book we have seen the importance of the politics of multinationals: in Chapter 4 we charted the way in which some groups may be reluctant to
engage in the collaborative networking that is envisaged in the 'transnational' organizational form; in Chapter 5 we examined the way in which the transfer of practices
may be resisted where it is perceived to challenge the interests of a particular group;
and in Chapter 6 we stressed the highly political nature of cross-border mergers and
acquisitions given the way that a lot of key issues are 'up for grabs' during and immediately after a merger.

In this vein, some writers have argued that multinationals should be characterized
as a 'transnational social space' (Morgan et al. 2003). That is, the fact that a multinational crosses 'institutional divides' means that the way in which it functions – its
structure and the norms and values that predominate – is more varied and contested
than in firms based only in one country. Managing these tensions, or instilling 'order'
as Morgan and his colleagues put it, is thus a key part of the business of management
in MNCs. At the political level there is also an evident struggle to establish a degree of
order to an international economic and social space that is under-institutionalized
compared with national business systems. Some attempts to fill this space are emerging, principally at the regional level through the actions of regional institutions, one
illustration of which is the moves towards international employee representation that
we studied in Chapter 12.

Change

While globalization has certainly not erased national distinctiveness, some argue that
it is gradually driving a process of convergence. One strand of this argument is that
many countries such as China are adopting some of the key features of advanced capitalist societies as they open up to the international economy. One illustration of this
in the field of HRM has been the erosion of the principle of the 'iron rice bowl' in
which employees were guaranteed a certain level of income and a high level of job
security, with this being gradually replaced with greater emphasis on 'flexibility' in
employment. Among the developed countries, many national models of HRM are

apparently under pressure to change. As we mentioned earlier in this chapter, one example of this is the recent reforms of the German labour market and the more general 'erosion' of the German model of employment relations (Hassel 1999, 2002), while another example is France where significant changes in patterns of corporate ownership have created pressures on large firms to deliver more 'shareholder value' along Anglo-Saxon lines (Morin 2000). Evidence of convergence across countries is perhaps most evident in relation to MNCs. The internationalization of German, French and Swedish firms has coincided with them adopting many of the structures and practices that have been common among UK and US MNCs, such as devolved business units and performance-related pay (Ferner and Quintanilla 1998).

Arguments concerned with convergence have come under intense criticism, however. One line of criticism has been that a close inspection of the data reveals that marked differences between countries remain intact. For instance, in Chapter 2 we examined the issue of the level of collective bargaining and reviewed Thelen's (2001) argument that in some countries, such as Germany, Sweden and Italy, there continues to be a willingness on the part of employers to engage in multi-employer bargaining while in other countries this tendency has been eroded, as in the UK, or was never very strong, as in the USA. Thus no neat process of convergence towards decentralized forms of bargaining is evident. Another point that is made to combat the convergence thesis is that employment regulations continue to differ markedly across countries. One of the most obvious of these differences concerns regulations governing lay-offs: while the principle of 'employment at will' is well embedded in the USA, meaning that employers face few constraints in making redundancies, most European countries have worker protection laws that stipulate the grounds that firms have for making redundancies and that govern the process of staff being laid off. More generally, what is considered normal or acceptable practice in HRM continues to vary across countries. One illustration of this is the way that attitudes to systems of performance appraisal make explicit categorizations of employees, with open distinctions between employees being quite routine in countries such as the USA but meeting suspicion and resistance in other countries such as China.

How can we make sense of these apparently conflicting sources of evidence? One assessment is that while globalization is causing great changes both in national models of HRM and in firm-level structures and practices, these changes are not all occurring at the same pace, nor are they all in the same direction. The different pace and direction of change can be explained in part by the exposure of countries to globalization, but also through the notion of 'institutional complementarities' within business systems. That is, the nature of institutions in one sphere of an economy has knock-on effects in other spheres. Thus where two countries are characterized by similar institutions in one area and these undergo an ostensibly similar change, the impact on the wider business systems in question can be quite different. In the HRM field, one illustration concerns practices in the area of diversity. Where two units of a multinational in different countries both implement a practice designed to increase the proportion of the workforce that is from ethnic minorities, the impact of this practice will be heavily dependent on such factors as the pre-existing ethnic composition of the workforce, prevailing patterns of job segregation by ethnicity, the legal regulation of discrimination and prevailing norms concerning the legitimacy of 'affirmative action'. Thus the way in which the practice operates and the impact it has will vary according to the national context, causing change in both settings but not necessarily of the same sort.

An additional way of resolving the conundrum of convergence and divergence *between* national systems is to examine the growing diversity *within* national models of HRM. There have been a number of sources of this growing diversity, many of which are related to globalization. For instance, the degree to which production or service provision is subject to international competition varies markedly by sector: those such as electronics, automotive and investment banking are organized along similar lines across countries and are dominated by multinational firms; in contrast, those such as security and catering are more subject to distinctive national factors with small firms predominating. Thus the pressures of globalization are not felt evenly across sectors within countries, with some firms playing to global 'rules of the game' and others playing to local ones. A related factor is the growth of FDI. Where FDI is significant this has meant that production and service provision are conducted by a range of firms with differing backgrounds and preferences, resulting in a greater diversity of practices in place within a sector. Evidently, these developments are leading to greater heterogeneity within countries. Thus Katz and Darbishire (2000) argue that growing diversity within countries is a common development, something that they term 'converging divergences'.

All in all, our assessment is that there are lots of signs of change, many of which are driven by the process of globalization. There is, however, no neat process of convergence. Thus the field of IHRM is likely to remain focused on the nature and importance of differences in the way that people are managed. As we have argued, however, these differences are evolving. HRM may come in different national styles, but none of these styles is free from pressures to change.

References

Ferner, A. and Quintanilla, J. (1998) 'Multinationals, National Business Systems and HRM: The Enduring Influence of National Identity or a Process of "Anglo-Saxonisation"', *International Journal of Human Resource Management*, 9(4), 710–31.

Hassel, A. (1999) 'The Erosion of the German System of Industrial Relations', *British Journal of Industrial Relations*, 37(3), 483–505.

Hassel, A. (2002) 'The Erosion Continues: Reply', *British Journal of Industrial Relations*, 40(2), 309–17.

Hirst, P. and Thompson, P. (1999) *Globalization in Question*, Cambridge: Polity Press.

Katz, H. and Darbishire, O. (2000) *Converging Divergences: Worldwide Changes in Employment Systems*, Ithaca, NY: Cornell University Press.

Morgan, G., Kelly, B., Sharpe, D. and Whitley, R. (2003) 'Global Managers in Japanese Multinationals: Internationalization and Management in Japanese Financial Institutions', *International Journal of Human Resource Management*, 14(3), 389–407.

Morin, F. (2000) 'A Transformation in the French Model of Shareholding and Management', *Economy and Society*, 29(1), 36–53.

Thelen, K. (2001) 'Varieties of Labor Politics in the Developed Democracies' in P. Hall and D. Soskice (eds) *Varieties of Capitalism: The Institutional Foundations of Comparative Advantage*, Oxford: Oxford University Press.

Index

Note: page numbers in **bold** indicate chapters. Organizations, countries, firms, and most authors mentioned only once are omitted.